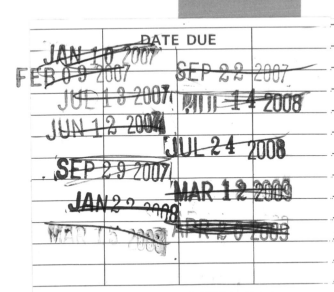

"Watase has a gift for involving characterization. Though she sometimes uses Miaka for laughs, she also lets us see her heroine's compassion and courage. The Emperor Hotohori is not quite as noble as he seems, nor is the wily Tamahome as self-centered as he would have others believe him to be. Even treacherous empress-candidate Nuriko has many levels. Watase's storytelling is an engaging one. She paces her story well and knows when to pump up the energy."

—Tony Isabella

"One of the best manga ever, it can be enjoyed by female and male readers alike."

—Protoculture Addicts

"There are two points in Fushigi Yugi's favor. The first is Watase herself, who has written margin notes for the compilation. Unlike many creators who rabbit on about trivia, she wants to talk about her craft, and has interesting points to make about research and the creative process. The second is that the strip succeeds in being quite charming; in spite of its derivative storyline—at one point a character admits the similarities to an RPG! But any comic that leaves me wanting to know what happens next definitely delivers value for money."

—Manga Max

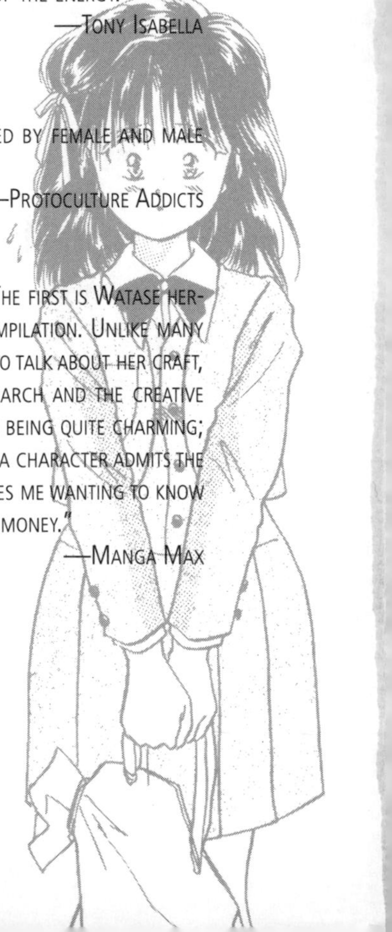

ANIMERICA EXTRA GRAPHIC NOVEL

fushigi yûgi™

The Mysterious Play
VOL. 5: RIVAL

This volume contains the FUSHIGI YÛGI installments from ANIMERICA EXTRA
Vol. 3, No. 11 through Vol. 4, No. 5 in their entirety.

STORY & ART BY YÛ WATASE

English Adaptation/Yuji Oniki
Touch-Up Art & Lettering/Bill Spicer
Cover Design/Hidemi Sahara
Layout & Graphics/Carolina Ugalde
Editor/William Flanagan

Managing Editor/Annette Roman
V.P. of Editorial/Hyoe Narita
Publisher/Seiji Horibuchi
V.P. of Sales & Marketing/Rick Bauer

Printed in Canada

Published by Viz Communications, Inc.
P.O. Box 77010, San Francisco, CA 94107

10 9 8 7 6 5 4 3 2
First printing, September 2001
Second printing, October 2002

ANIMERICA EXTRA GRAPHIC NOVEL

fushigi yûgi™

The Mysterious Play
VOL. 5: RIVAL

Story & Art By
YÛ WATASE

CONTENTS

STORY THUS FAR

Chipper junior-high-school girl Miaka and her best friend Yui are physically drawn into the world of a strange book—*The Universe of the Four Gods*. Miaka is offered the role of the lead character, the Priestess of the god Suzaku, and is charged with gathering the seven Celestial Warriors of Suzaku who will help her complete a quest to save the nation of Hong-Nan, and in the process grant her any wish she wants. She has already found six warriors: Tamahome, Hotohori, Nuriko, Chichiri, Tasuki, and Mitsukake.

Yui's fate is much crueler than Miaka's. Upon entering the book, Yui suffers rape and manipulation which drives her to attempt suicide. Now, Yui has become the Priestess of the god Seiryu, the enemy of Suzaku and Miaka.

Miaka's true love, Tamahome, goes willingly to become Yui's prisoner to avert a war between Qu-Dong and the less powerful Hong-Nan. In the meantime, Miaka goes on a journey with Hotohori and Nuriko to find the other Celestial Warriors, and now, only one warrior, Chiriko, remains to be found before they can go retrieve Tamahome. But even if they find the warrior, will vengeful Yui let Tamahome go?

THE UNIVERSE OF THE FOUR GODS *is based on ancient China, but Japanese pronunciation of Chinese names differs slightly from their Chinese equivalents. Here is a short glossary of the Japanese pronunciation of the Chinese names in this graphic novel:*

CHINESE	JAPANESE	PERSON OR PLACE	MEANING
Hong-Nan	Konan	Southern Kingdom	Crimson South
Qu-Dong	Kutô	Eastern Kingdom	Gathered East
Changhung	Chôkô	A Northern Town	Expansive Place
Zhong-Rong	Chûei	Second Son	Loyalty & Honor
Chun-Jing	Shunkei	Third Son	Spring & Respect
Yu-Lun	Gyokuran	Eldest Daughter	Jewel & Orchid
Jie-Lian	Yuiren	Youngest Daughter	Connection & Lotus
Diedu	Kodoku	A Potion	Seduction Poison

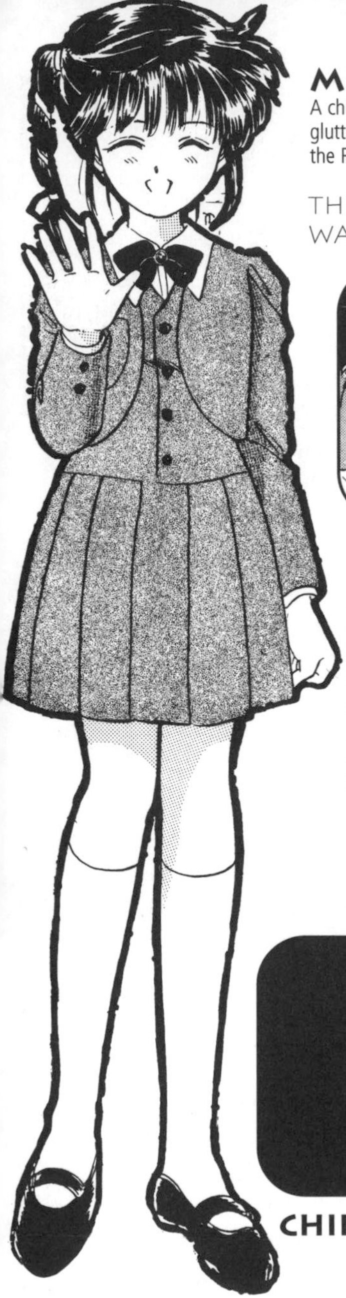

MIAKA
A chipper junior-high-school glutton who has become the Priestess of Suzaku.

THE CELESTIAL WARRIORS OF SUZAKU

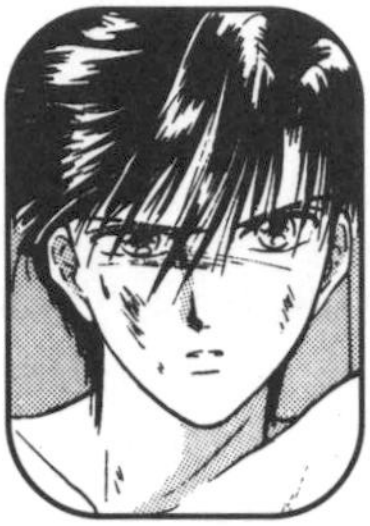

TAMAHOME
A dashing miser.

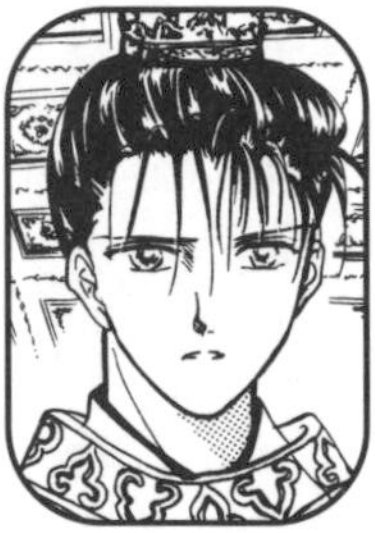

HOTOHORI
The beautiful emperor of Hong-Nan.

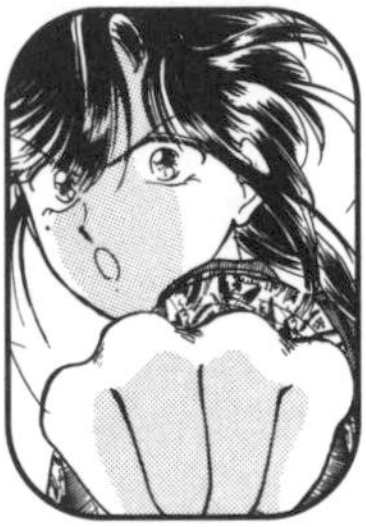

NURIKO
An amazingly strong cross-dresser.

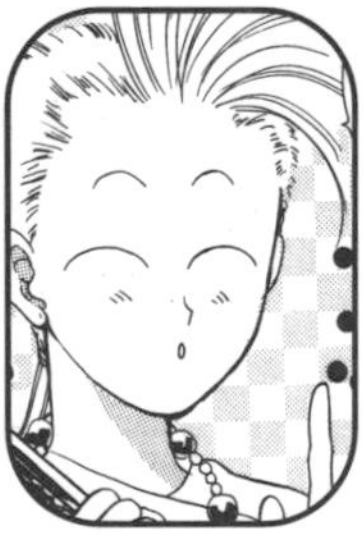

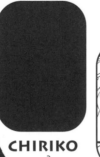

CHICHIRI
Former disciple of the oracle.

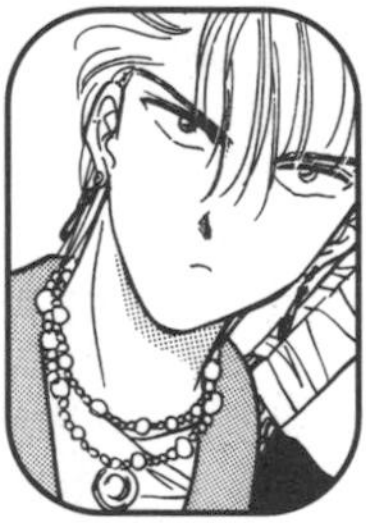

TASUKI
An ornery ex-bandit.

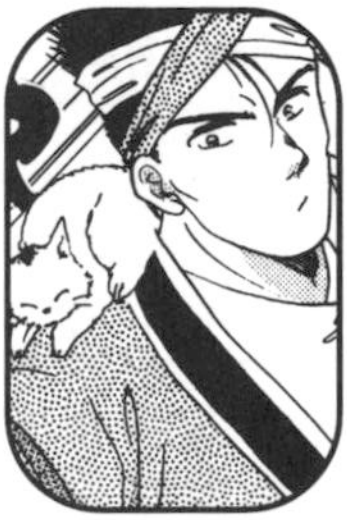

MITSUKAKE
A silent healer.

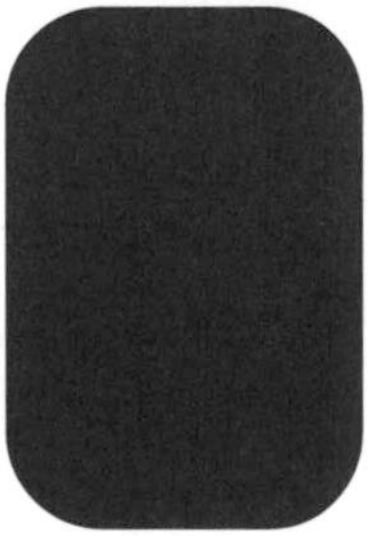

CHIRIKO
?

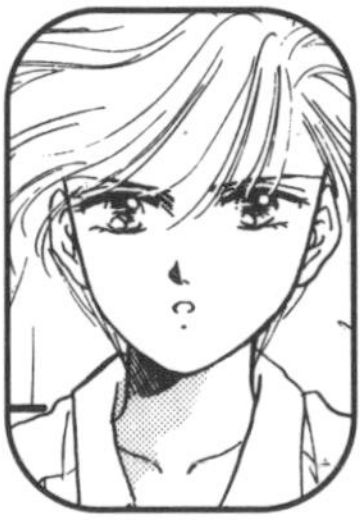

YUI
Miaka's former best friend, but now her enemy and the Priestess of Seiryu.

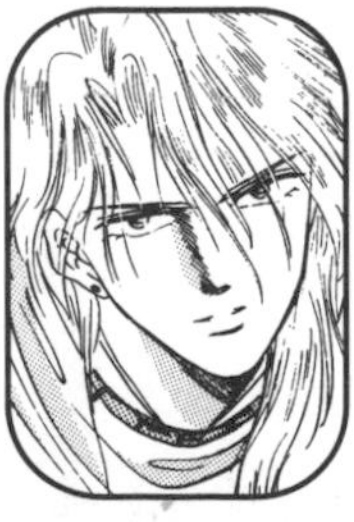

NAKAGO
A general of Qu-Dong and a Celestial Warrior of Seiryu.

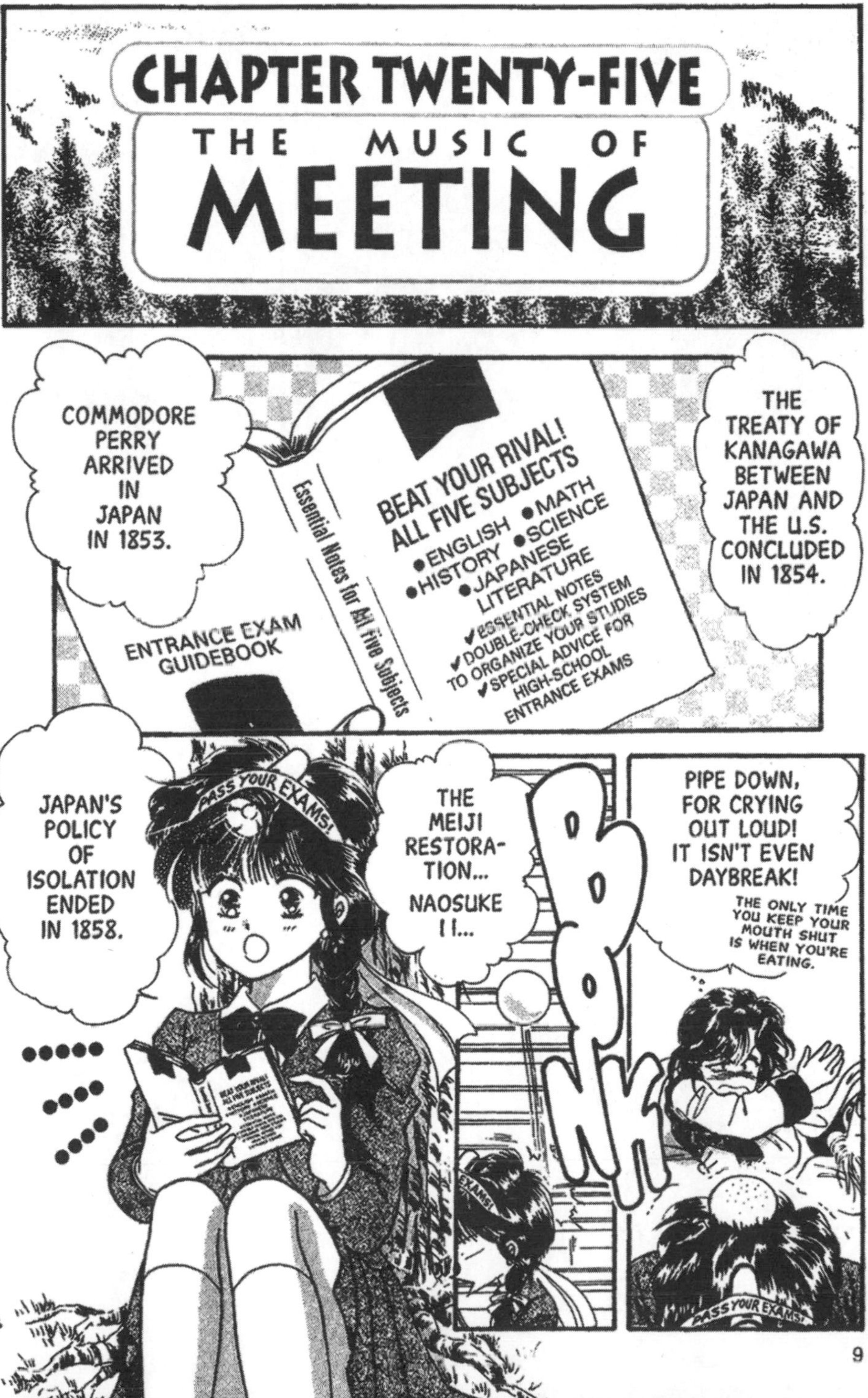

CHAPTER TWENTY-FIVE
THE MUSIC OF MEETING
COMMODORE PERRY ARRIVED IN JAPAN IN 1853.
ENTRANCE EXAM GUIDEBOOK
Essential Notes for All Five Subjects
BEAT YOUR RIVAL! ALL FIVE SUBJECTS
●ENGLISH ●MATH ●HISTORY ●SCIENCE ●JAPANESE LITERATURE
✔ESSENTIAL NOTES
✔DOUBLE-CHECK SYSTEM TO ORGANIZE YOUR STUDIES
✔SPECIAL ADVICE FOR HIGH-SCHOOL ENTRANCE EXAMS
THE TREATY OF KANAGAWA BETWEEN JAPAN AND THE U.S. CONCLUDED IN 1854.
PASS YOUR EXAMS!
JAPAN'S POLICY OF ISOLATION ENDED IN 1858.
THE MEIJI RESTORATION... NAOSUKE II...
●●●●● ●●●● ●●●●
PIPE DOWN, FOR CRYING OUT LOUD! IT ISN'T EVEN DAYBREAK!
THE ONLY TIME YOU KEEP YOUR MOUTH SHUT IS WHEN YOU'RE EATING.
PASS YOUR EXAMS!

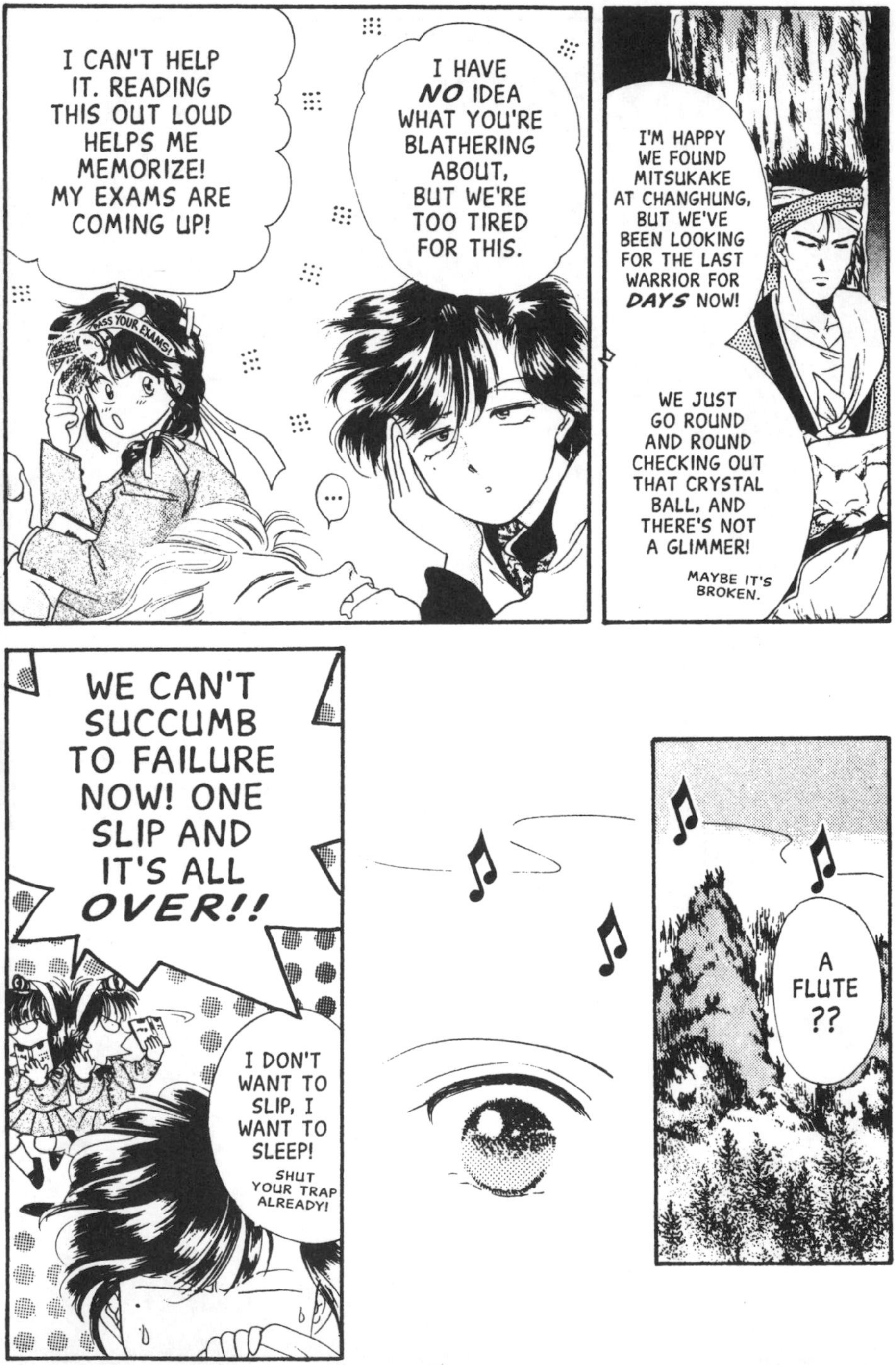
I CAN'T HELP IT. READING THIS OUT LOUD HELPS ME MEMORIZE! MY EXAMS ARE COMING UP!
PASS YOUR EXAMS!
I HAVE **NO** IDEA WHAT YOU'RE BLATHERING ABOUT, BUT WE'RE TOO TIRED FOR THIS.
...
I'M HAPPY WE FOUND MITSUKAKE AT CHANGHUNG, BUT WE'VE BEEN LOOKING FOR THE LAST WARRIOR FOR **DAYS** NOW!
WE JUST GO ROUND AND ROUND CHECKING OUT THAT CRYSTAL BALL, AND THERE'S NOT A GLIMMER!
MAYBE IT'S BROKEN.
WE CAN'T SUCCUMB TO FAILURE NOW! ONE SLIP AND IT'S ALL **OVER!!**
I DON'T WANT TO SLIP, I WANT TO SLEEP!
SHUT YOUR TRAP ALREADY!
A FLUTE ??

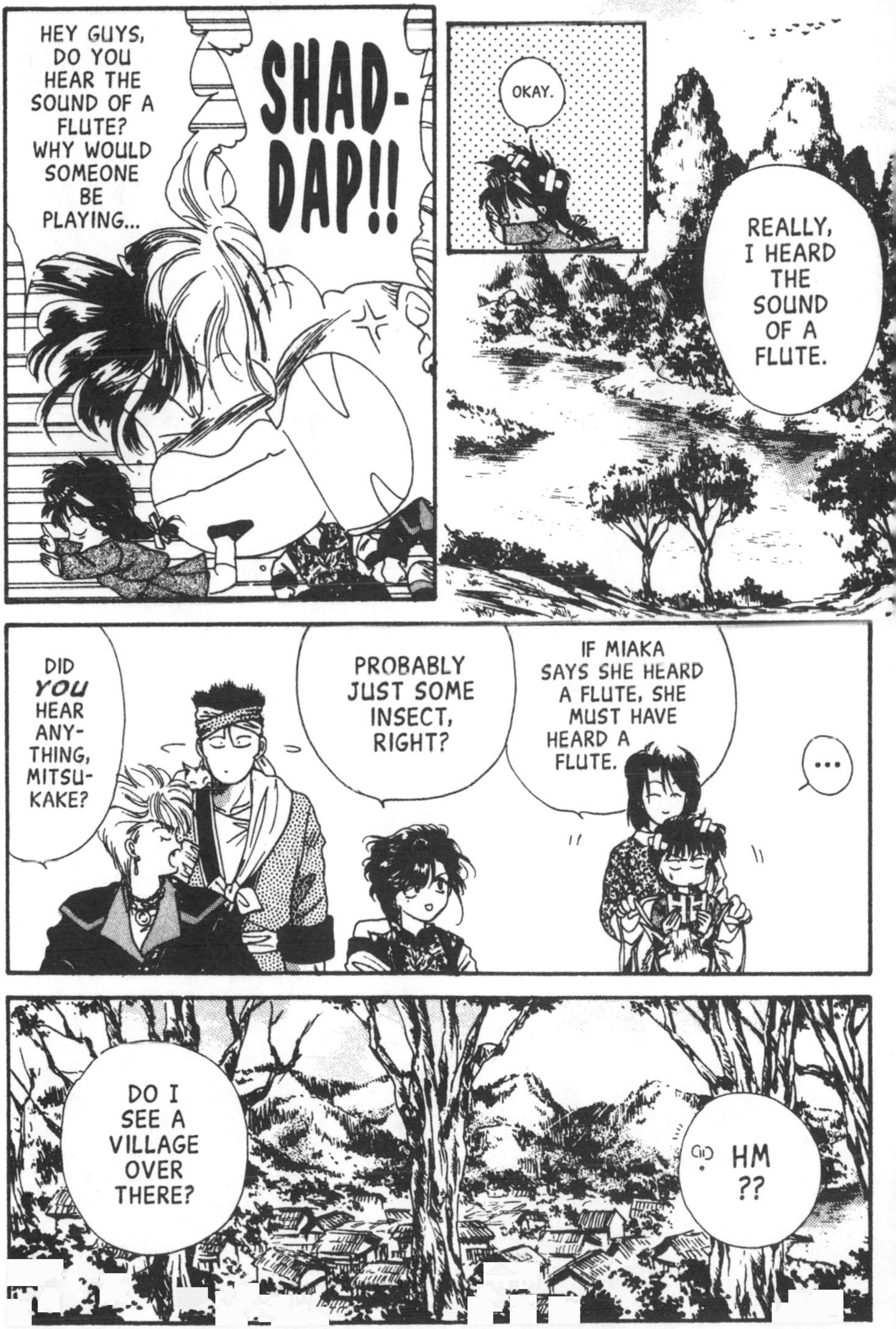
HEY GUYS, DO YOU HEAR THE SOUND OF A FLUTE? WHY WOULD SOMEONE BE PLAYING...
SHAD-DAP!!
OKAY.
REALLY, I HEARD THE SOUND OF A FLUTE.
DID *YOU* HEAR ANYTHING, MITSUKAKE?
PROBABLY JUST SOME INSECT, RIGHT?
IF MIAKA SAYS SHE HEARD A FLUTE, SHE MUST HAVE HEARD A FLUTE.
...
DO I SEE A VILLAGE OVER THERE?
HM ??

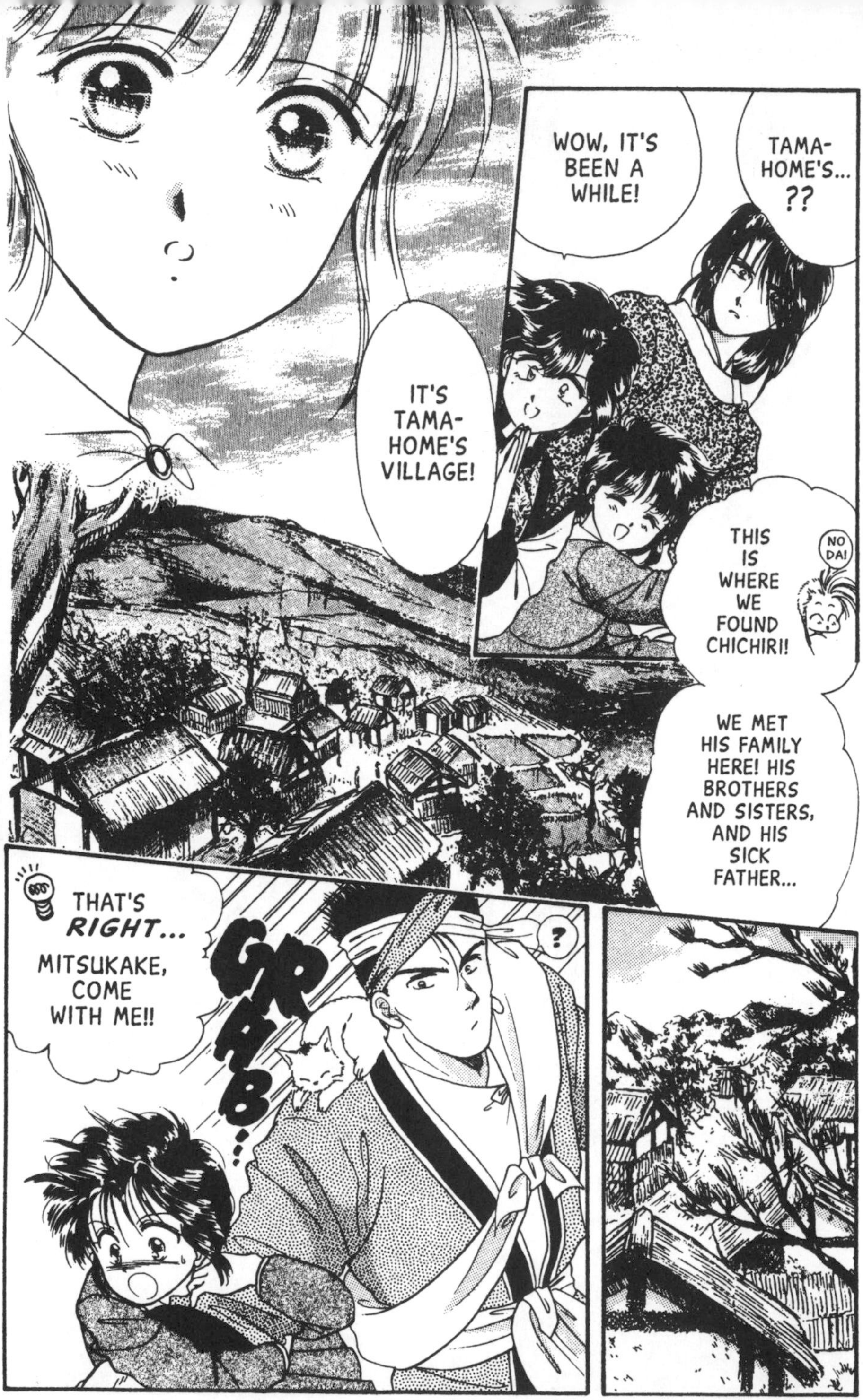

IT'S TAMA-HOME'S VILLAGE!
WOW, IT'S BEEN A WHILE!
TAMA-HOME'S... ??
THIS IS WHERE WE FOUND CHICHIRI!
NO DA!
WE MET HIS FAMILY HERE! HIS BROTHERS AND SISTERS, AND HIS SICK FATHER...
THAT'S *RIGHT*... MITSUKAKE, COME WITH ME!!
GRAB...
?

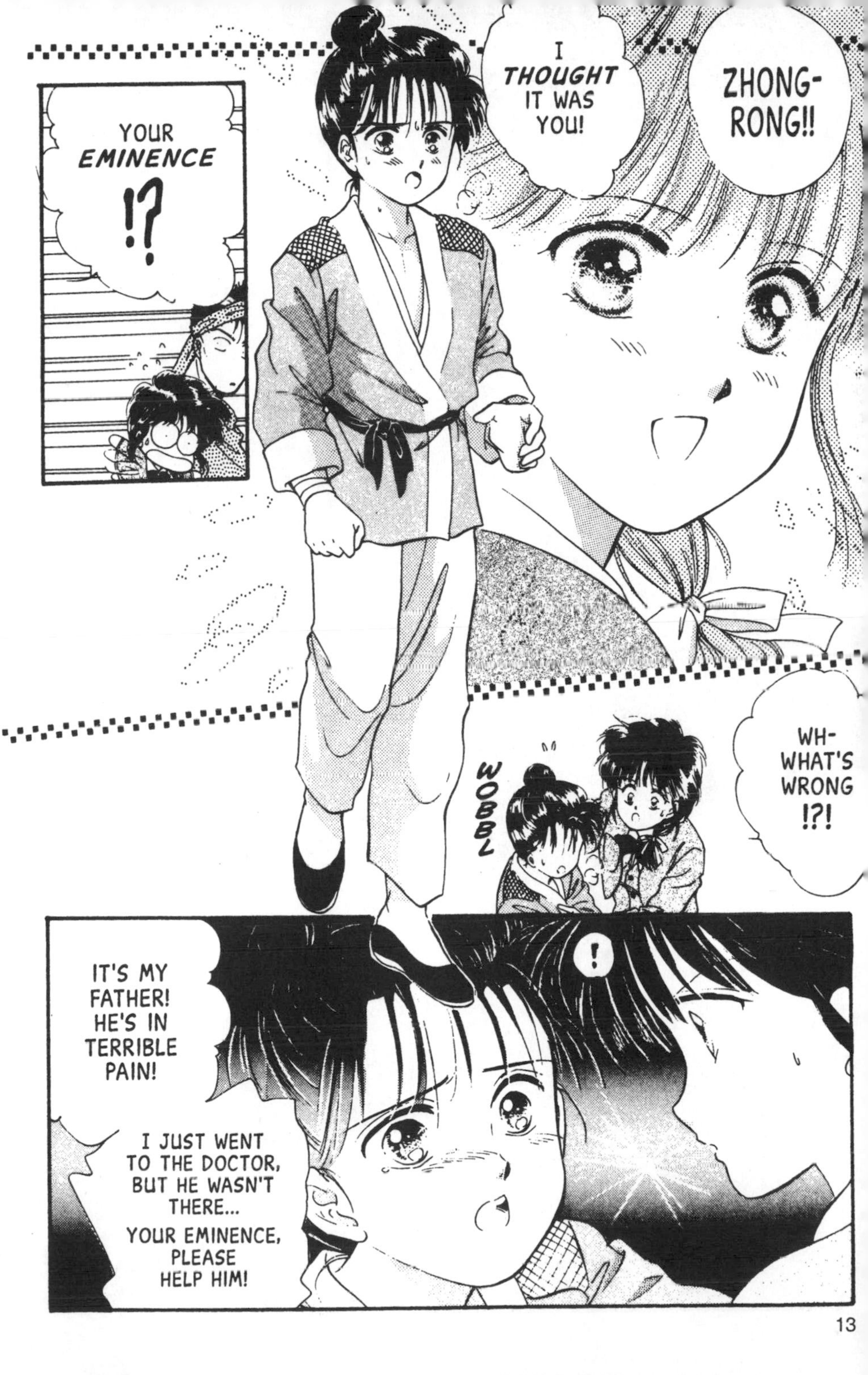
YOUR *EMINENCE* !?
I *THOUGHT* IT WAS YOU!
ZHONG-RONG!!
WOBBL
WH-WHAT'S WRONG !?!
IT'S MY FATHER! HE'S IN TERRIBLE PAIN!
I JUST WENT TO THE DOCTOR, BUT HE WASN'T THERE...
YOUR EMINENCE, PLEASE HELP HIM!
!

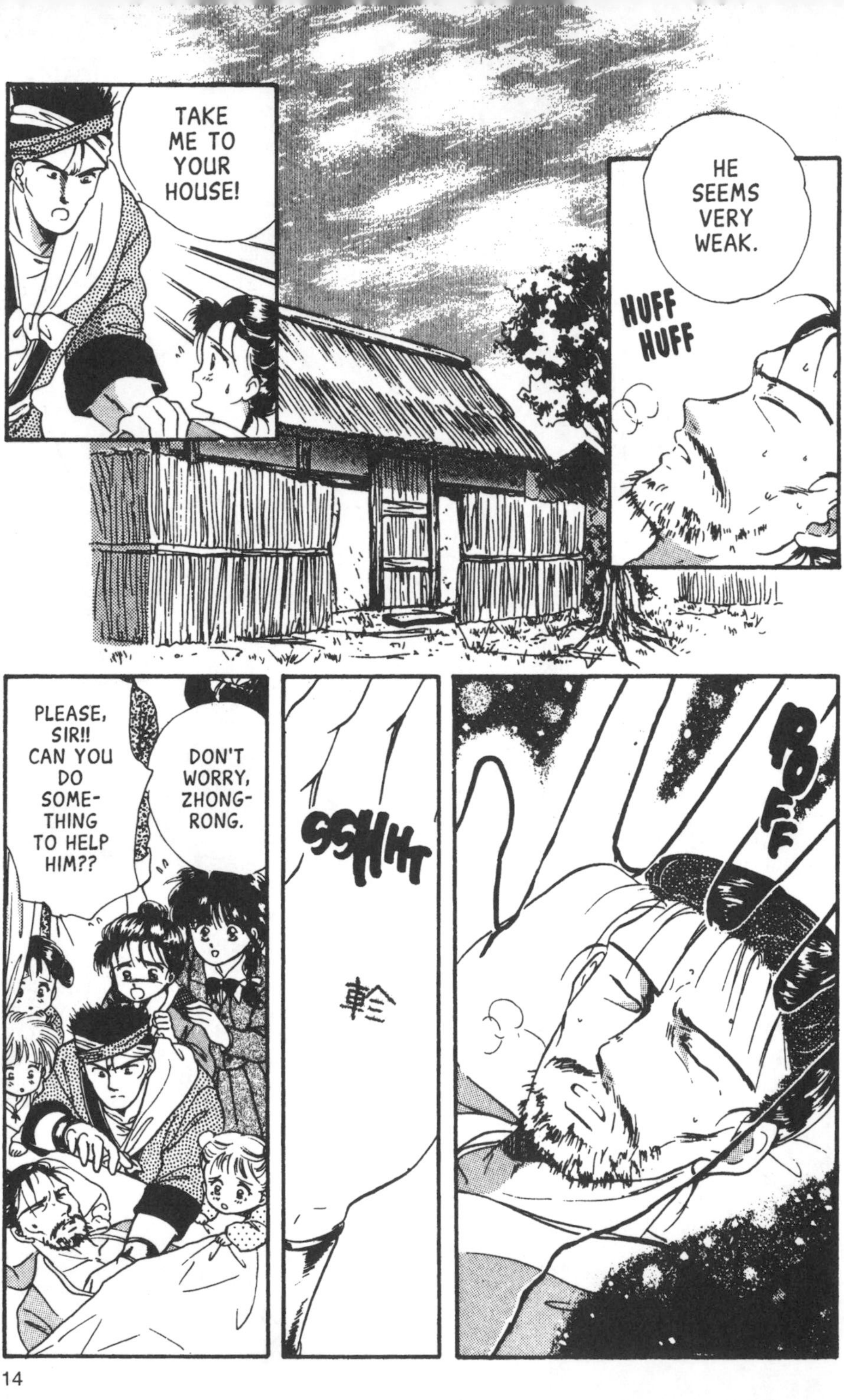
TAKE ME TO YOUR HOUSE!
HE SEEMS VERY WEAK.
HUFF HUFF
PLEASE, SIR!! CAN YOU DO SOME-THING TO HELP HIM??
DON'T WORRY, ZHONG-RONG.
SSHHT
ROFF

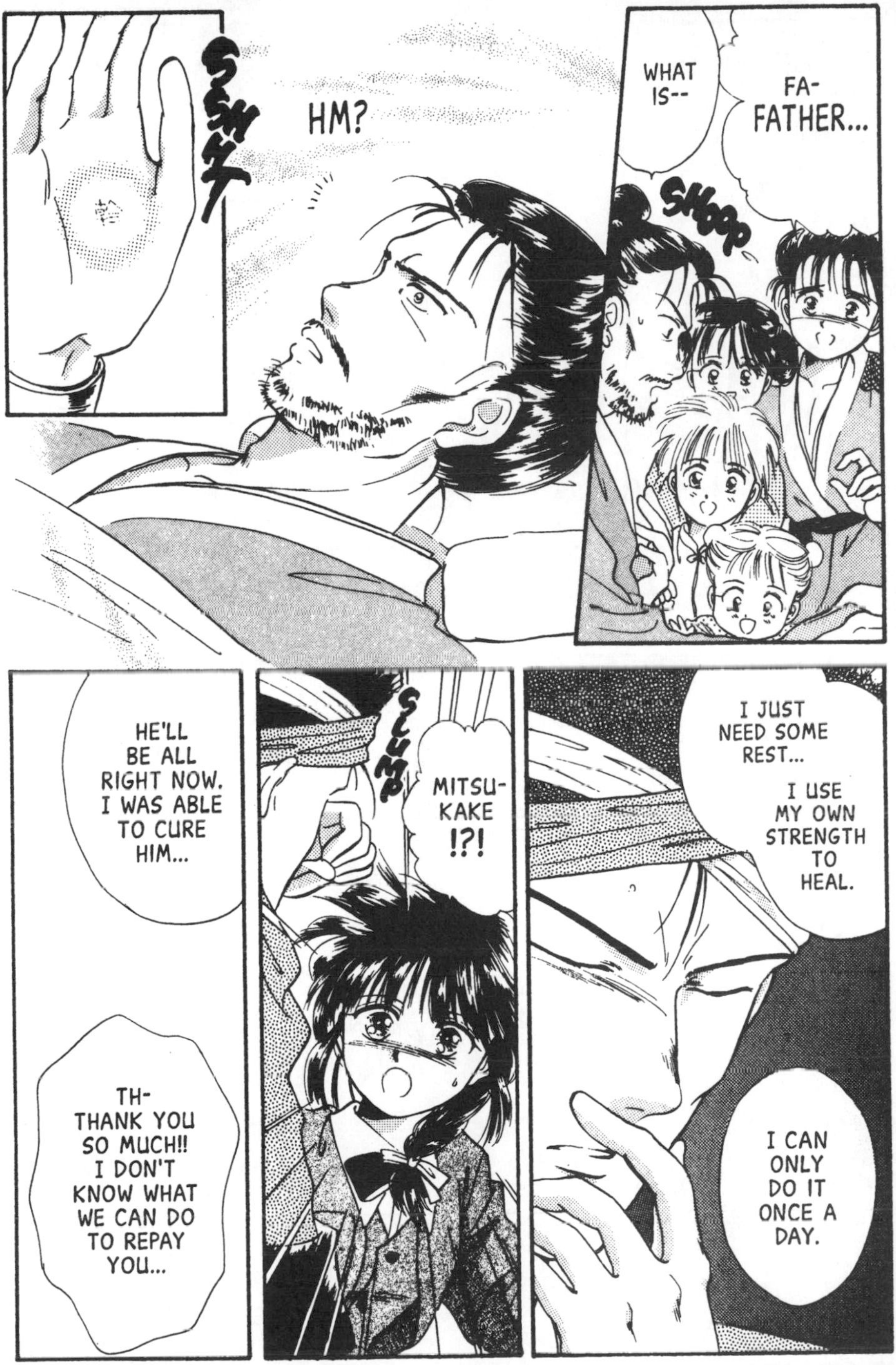
HM?
WHAT IS--
FA- FATHER...
SHOOP
HE'LL BE ALL RIGHT NOW. I WAS ABLE TO CURE HIM...
TH- THANK YOU SO MUCH!! I DON'T KNOW WHAT WE CAN DO TO REPAY YOU...
SLUMP
MITSU- KAKE !?!
I JUST NEED SOME REST...
I USE MY OWN STRENGTH TO HEAL.
I CAN ONLY DO IT ONCE A DAY.

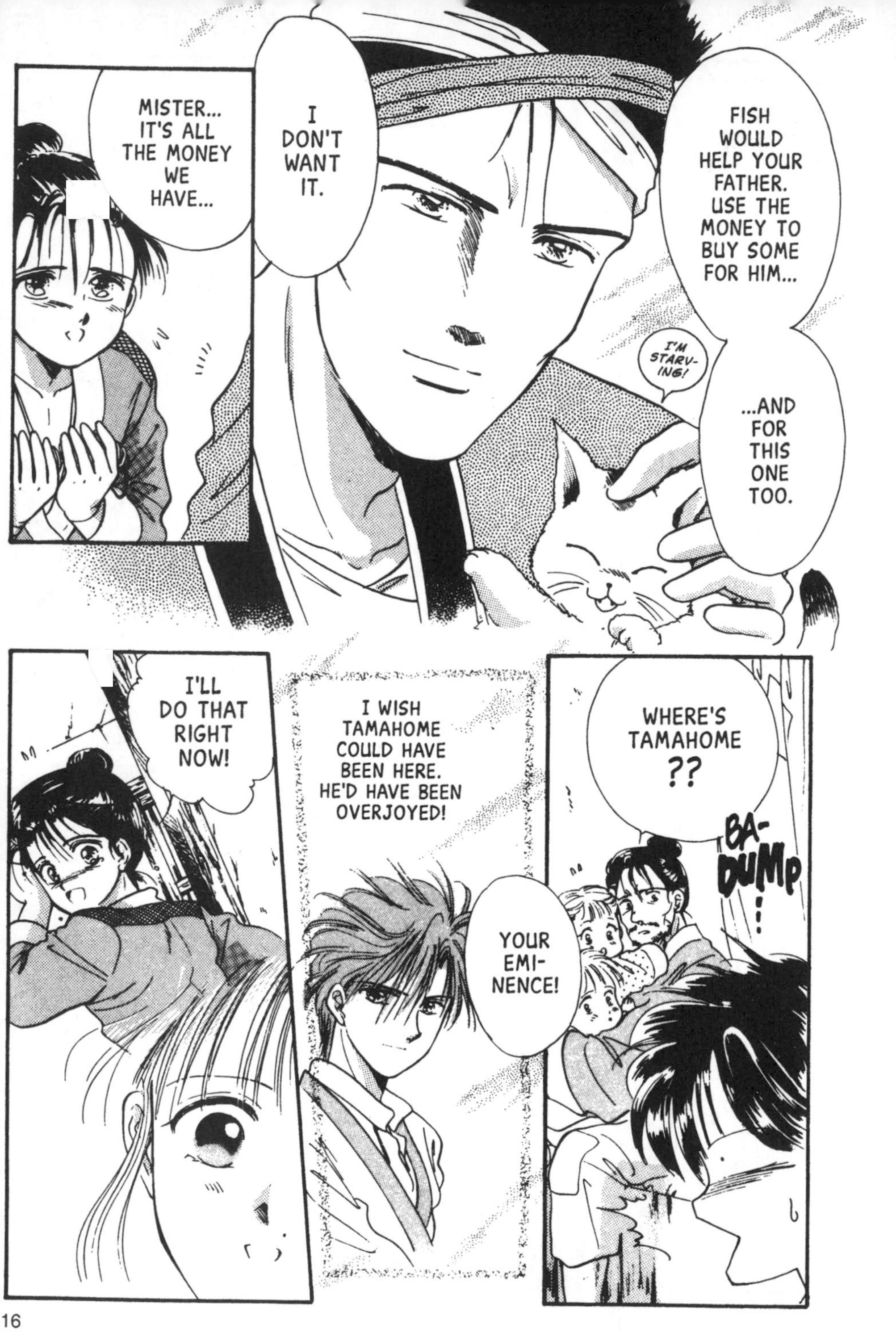
MISTER... IT'S ALL THE MONEY WE HAVE...
I DON'T WANT IT.
FISH WOULD HELP YOUR FATHER. USE THE MONEY TO BUY SOME FOR HIM...
I'M STARV-ING!
...AND FOR THIS ONE TOO.
I'LL DO THAT RIGHT NOW!
I WISH TAMAHOME COULD HAVE BEEN HERE. HE'D HAVE BEEN OVERJOYED!
YOUR EMI-NENCE!
WHERE'S TAMAHOME ??
BA-DUMP !

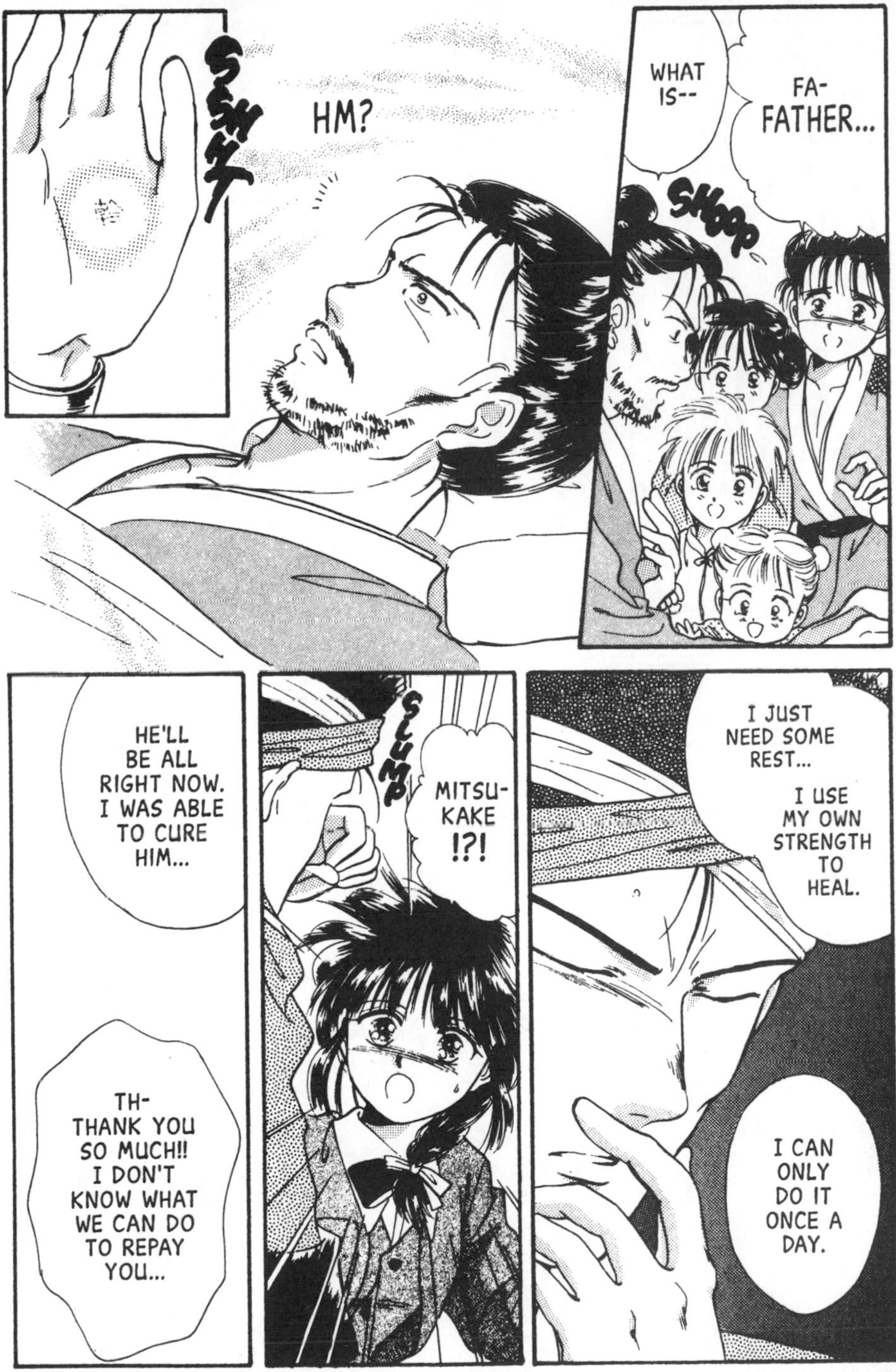
SSHK
HM?
WHAT IS--
FA-FATHER...
SHOOP
HE'LL BE ALL RIGHT NOW. I WAS ABLE TO CURE HIM...
TH-THANK YOU SO MUCH!! I DON'T KNOW WHAT WE CAN DO TO REPAY YOU...
SLUMP
MITSUKAKE !?!
I JUST NEED SOME REST...
I USE MY OWN STRENGTH TO HEAL.
I CAN ONLY DO IT ONCE A DAY.

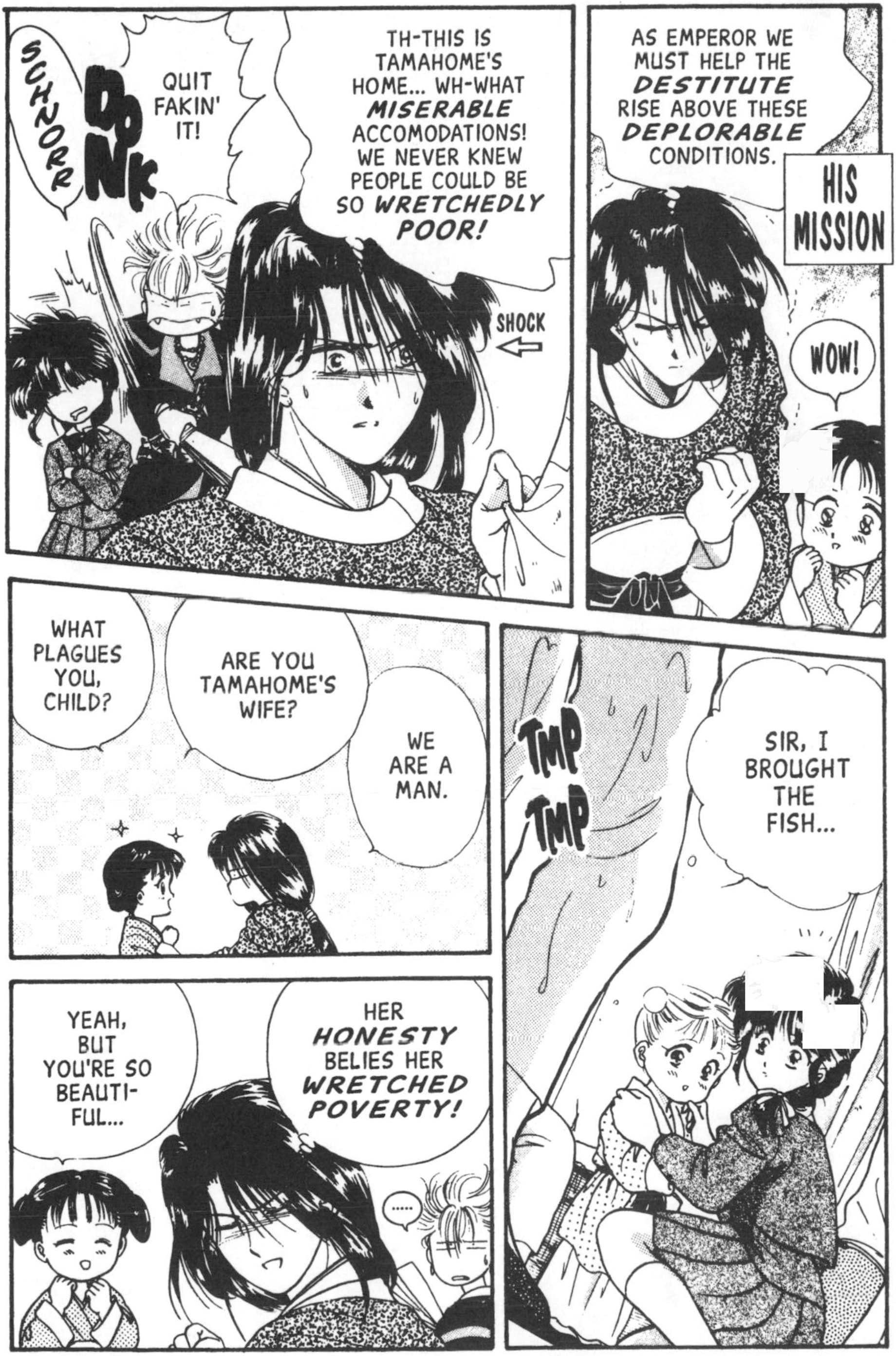
SCHNORR
DONK
QUIT FAKIN' IT!
TH-THIS IS TAMAHOME'S HOME... WH-WHAT MISERABLE ACCOMODATIONS! WE NEVER KNEW PEOPLE COULD BE SO WRETCHEDLY POOR!
SHOCK
AS EMPEROR WE MUST HELP THE DESTITUTE RISE ABOVE THESE DEPLORABLE CONDITIONS.
HIS MISSION
WOW!
WHAT PLAGUES YOU, CHILD?
ARE YOU TAMAHOME'S WIFE?
WE ARE A MAN.
YEAH, BUT YOU'RE SO BEAUTI-FUL...
HER HONESTY BELIES HER WRETCHED POVERTY!
......
TMP
TMP
SIR, I BROUGHT THE FISH...

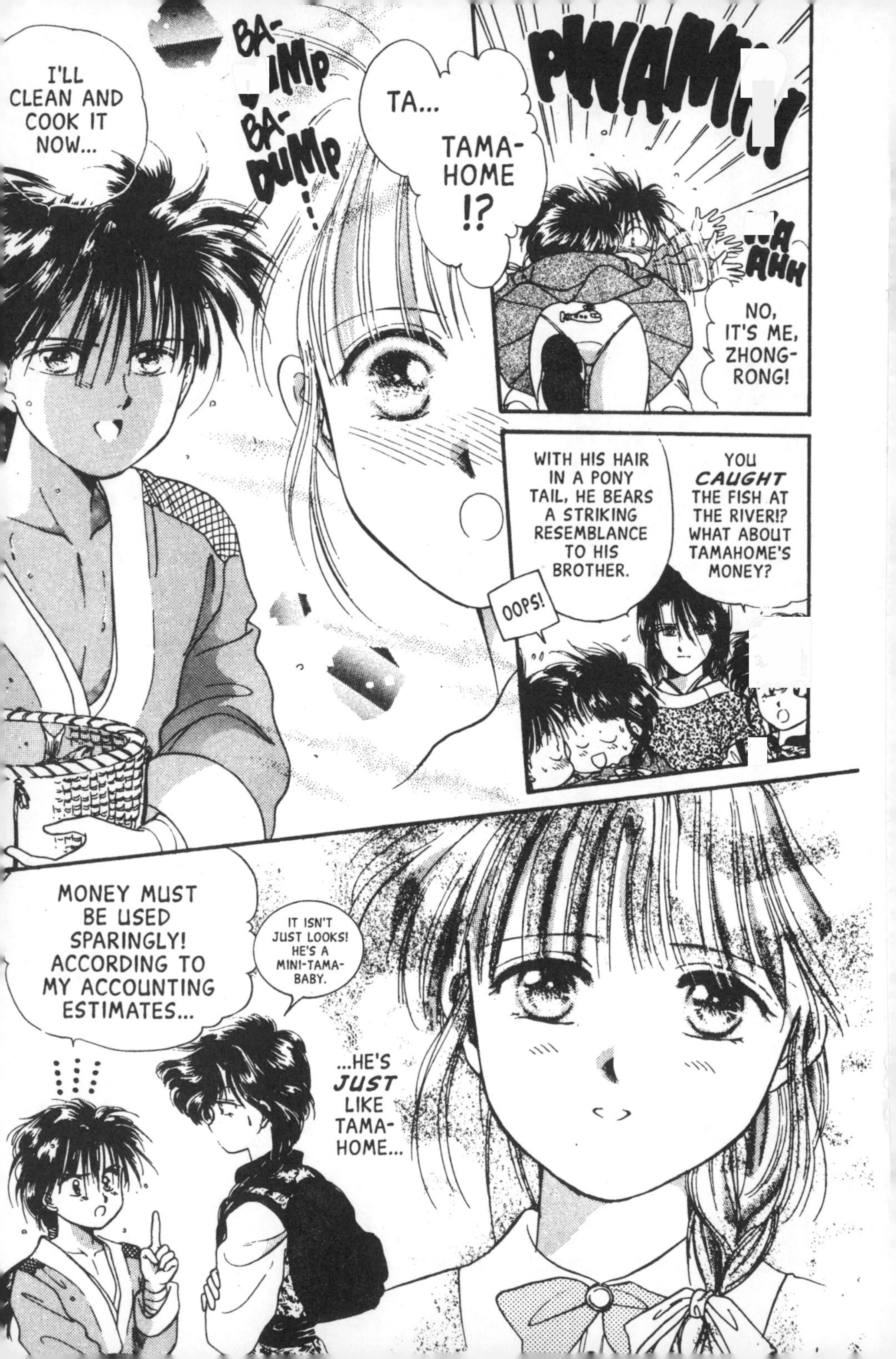
I'LL CLEAN AND COOK IT NOW...
BA-DUMP
TA... TAMA-HOME !?
NO, IT'S ME, ZHONG-RONG!
WITH HIS HAIR IN A PONY TAIL, HE BEARS A STRIKING RESEMBLANCE TO HIS BROTHER.
YOU *CAUGHT* THE FISH AT THE RIVER!? WHAT ABOUT TAMAHOME'S MONEY?
OOPS!
MONEY MUST BE USED SPARINGLY! ACCORDING TO MY ACCOUNTING ESTIMATES...
IT ISN'T JUST LOOKS! HE'S A MINI-TAMA-BABY.
...HE'S *JUST* LIKE TAMA-HOME...

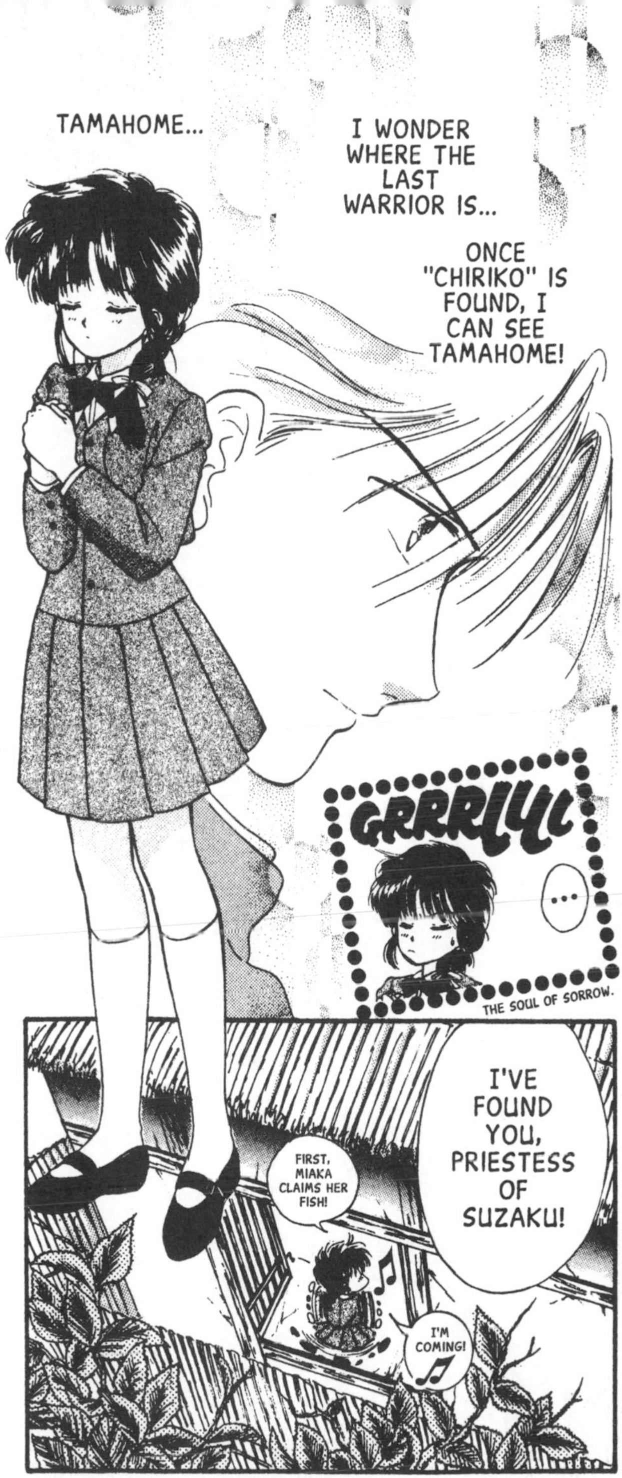
TAMAHOME...
I WONDER WHERE THE LAST WARRIOR IS...
ONCE "CHIRIKO" IS FOUND, I CAN SEE TAMAHOME!
GRRRLLL
...
THE SOUL OF SORROW.
FIRST, MIAKA CLAIMS HER FISH!
I'VE FOUND YOU, PRIESTESS OF SUZAKU!
I'M COMING!

Hi, it's me Yū. I'm watching "The Game City" on TV right now. In other words, it's one in the morning. I love this show because they introduce a lot of games! I want to play Street Fighter II Turbo. During my visit back home last year for New Year's, I went to the game center and completely revived my enthusiasm for games!! So I bought a Super Famicom unit (a little late I know), and borrowed Street Fighter II from my cousin (♂) and totally got into it. But the Street Fighter II at the game center is Turbo and has more moves, so it's more fun. By the way, the only character I can play is Chun Li. sob sob

I'm sure that anyone not familiar with the game doesn't have a clue as to what I'm talking about. So for your sake, I'll just talk about my visit back home. *I think.*

But you know, I love having a game console. "The Game City" was still broadcasting the commercial for Street Fighter II (that I mentioned in one of my earlier chat sections) so I just had to tape it. (They're not showing it anymore though). I didn't know that the person playing Chun Li in that commercial was the "Kiss Me" Miki Nagano. She did a total image overhaul!

Now then-- In December 1992, I went back home. There I met up with several friends, but I took my work with me, so I wasn't able to relax at all.

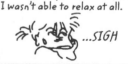

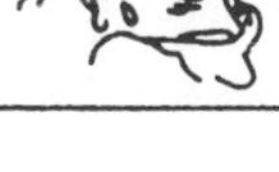
...SIGH

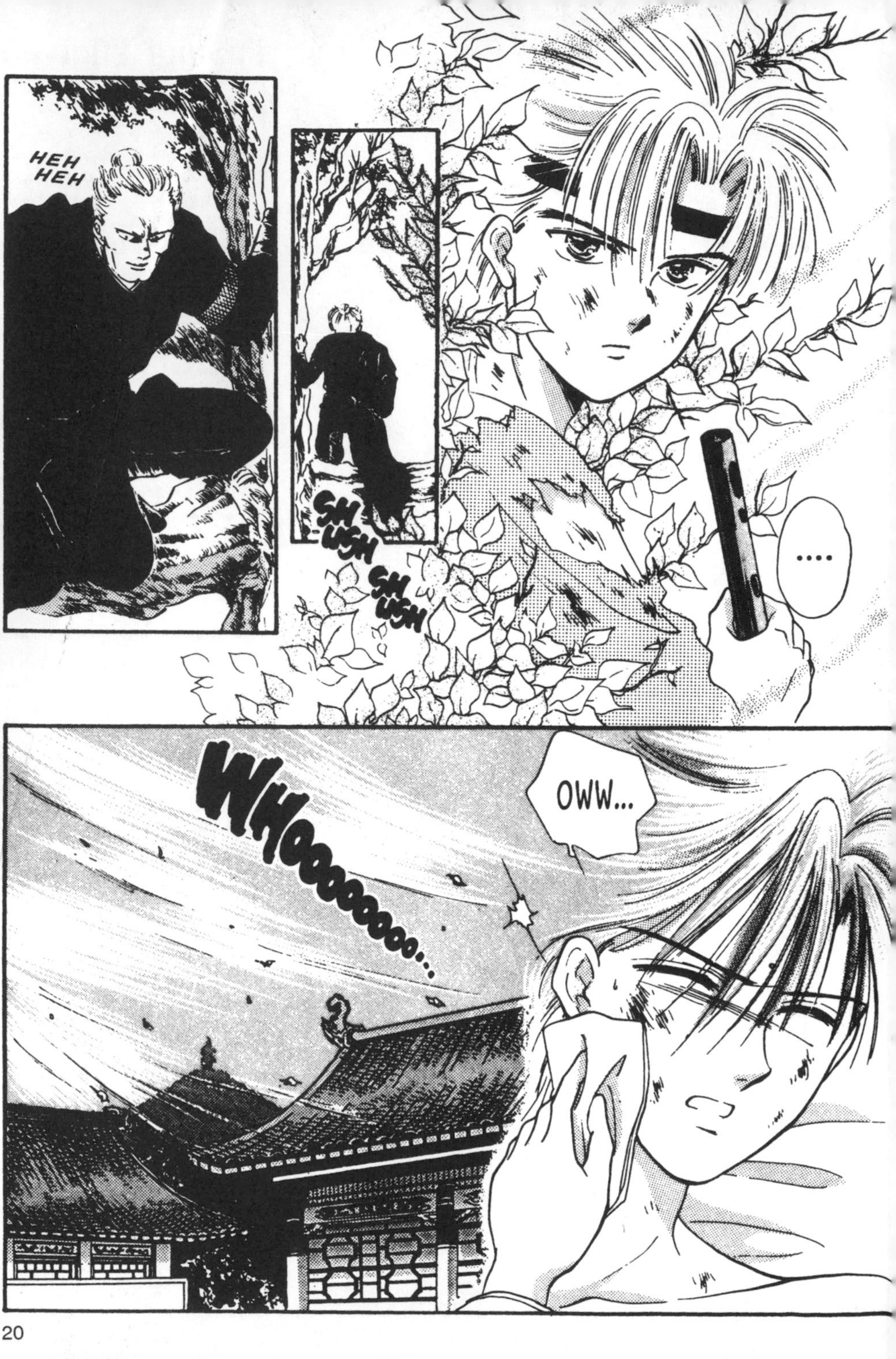
HEH HEH
SHUSH
SHUSH
....
WHOOOOOOOOO...
OWW...

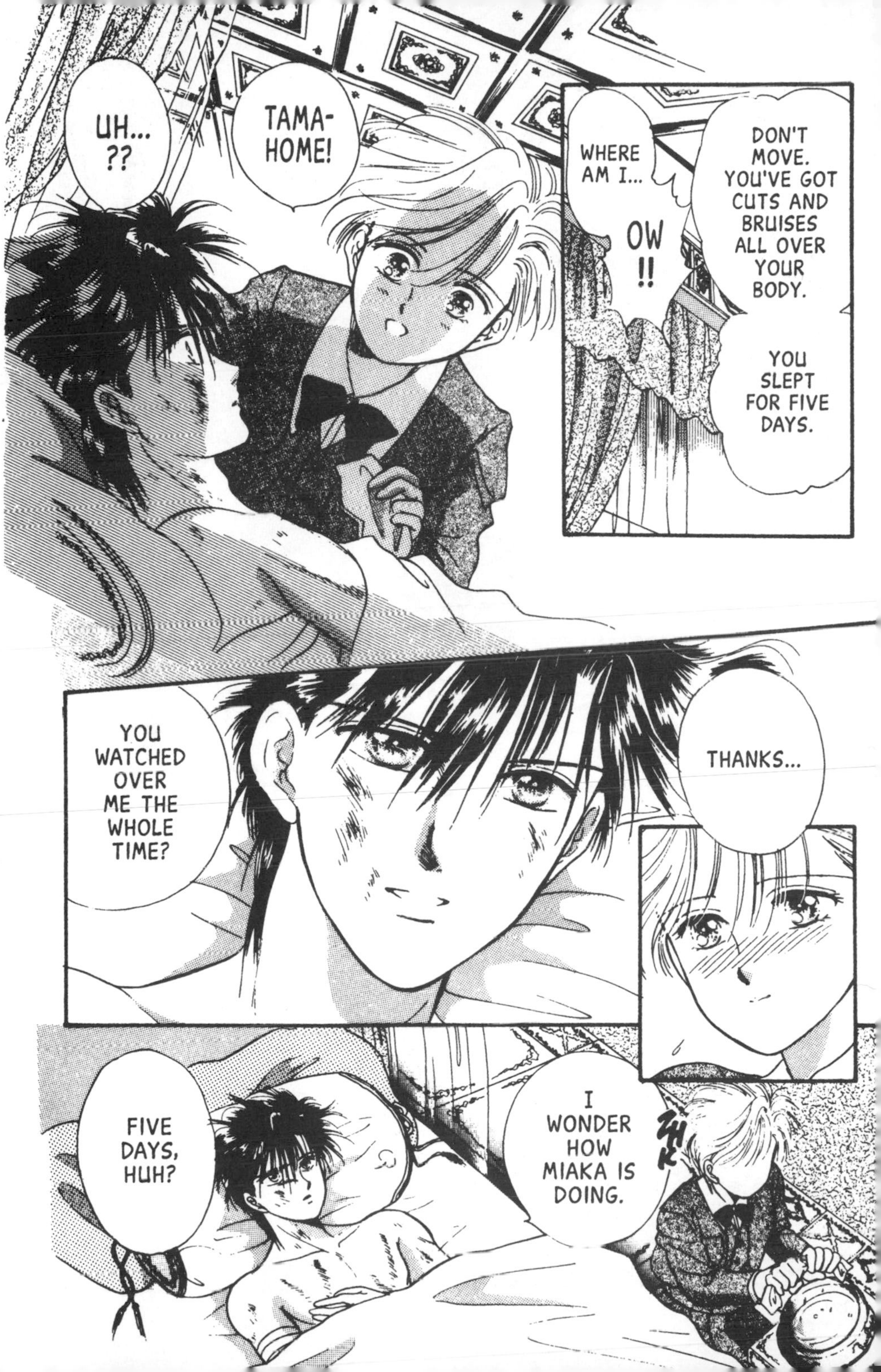
UH... ??
TAMA-HOME!
WHERE AM I...
OW !!
DON'T MOVE. YOU'VE GOT CUTS AND BRUISES ALL OVER YOUR BODY.
YOU SLEPT FOR FIVE DAYS.
YOU WATCHED OVER ME THE WHOLE TIME?
THANKS...
FIVE DAYS, HUH?
I WONDER HOW MIAKA IS DOING.
ZHK

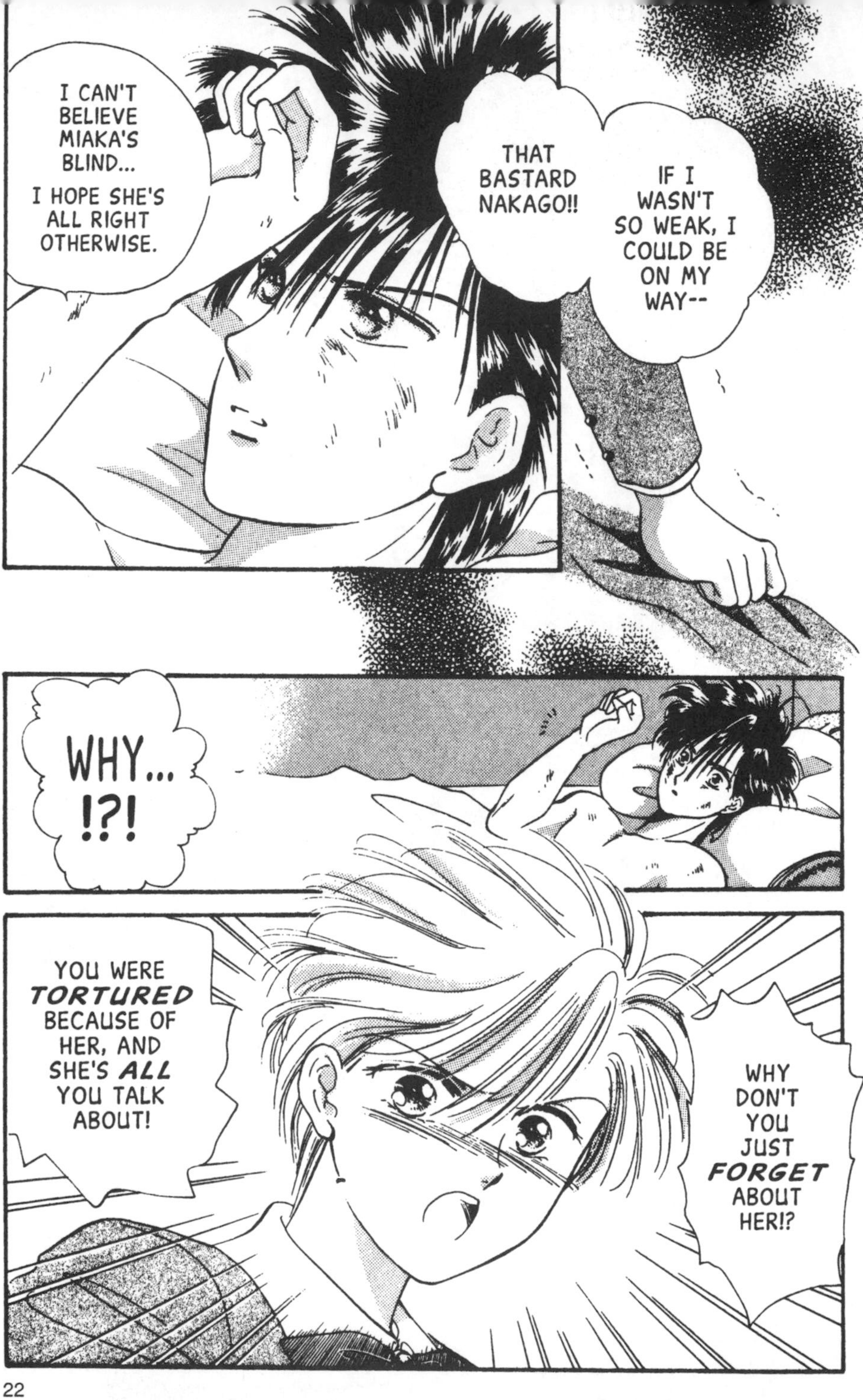
I CAN'T BELIEVE MIAKA'S BLIND... I HOPE SHE'S ALL RIGHT OTHERWISE.
THAT BASTARD NAKAGO!!
IF I WASN'T SO WEAK, I COULD BE ON MY WAY--
WHY... !?!
YOU WERE TORTURED BECAUSE OF HER, AND SHE'S ALL YOU TALK ABOUT!
WHY DON'T YOU JUST FORGET ABOUT HER!?

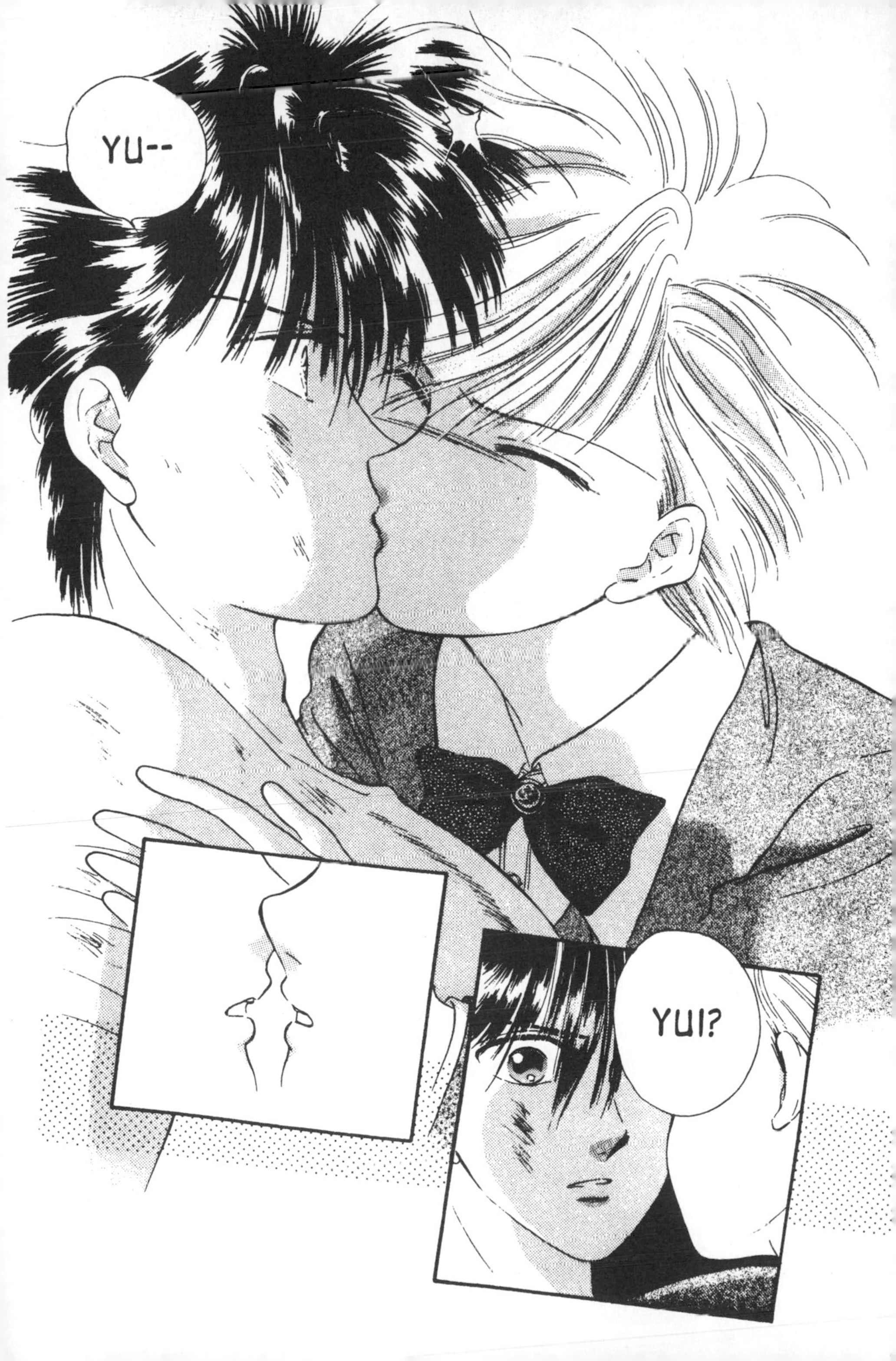
YU--
YUI?

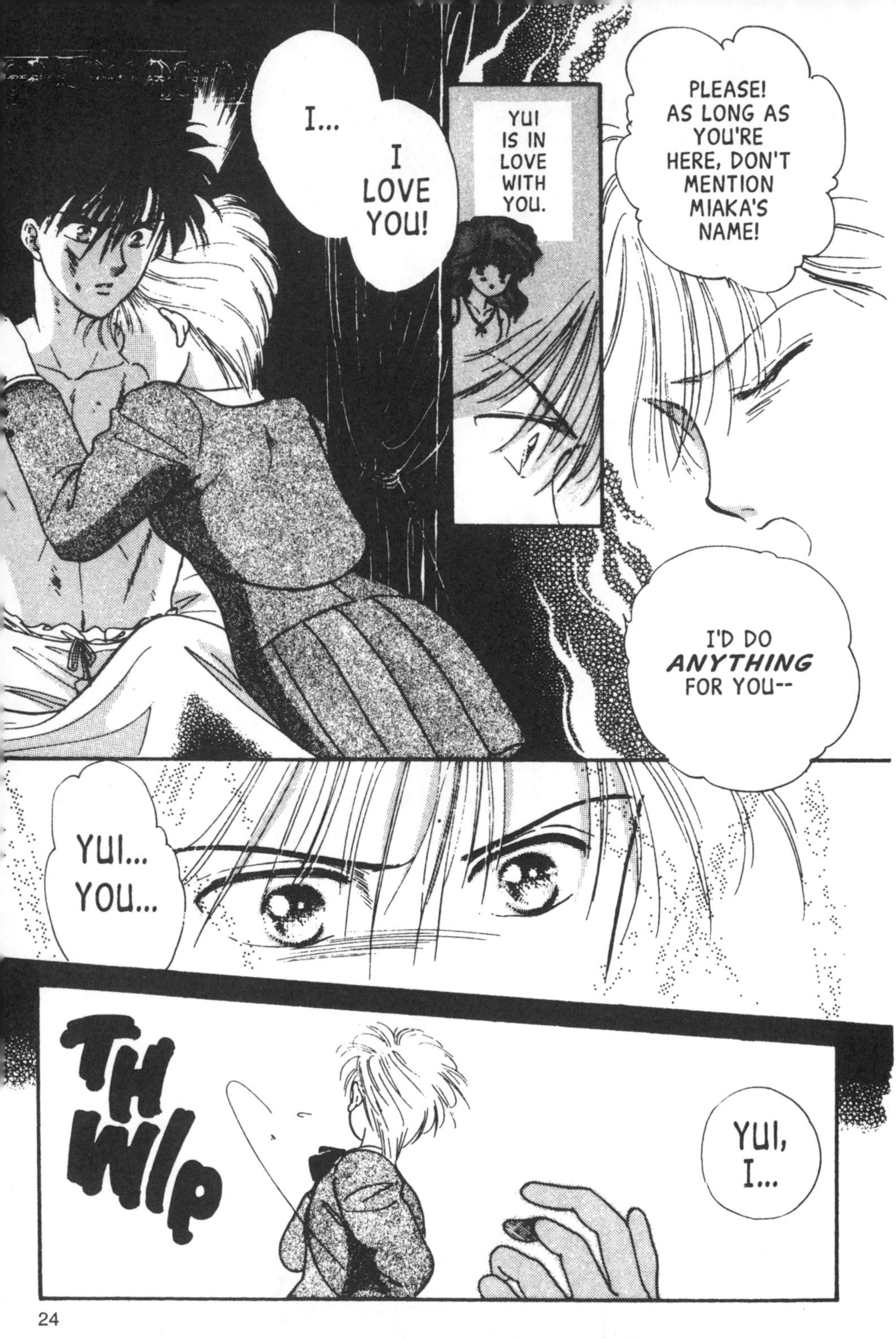
I...
I LOVE YOU!
YUI IS IN LOVE WITH YOU.
PLEASE! AS LONG AS YOU'RE HERE, DON'T MENTION MIAKA'S NAME!
I'D DO *ANYTHING* FOR YOU--
YUI... YOU...
THWIP
YUI, I...

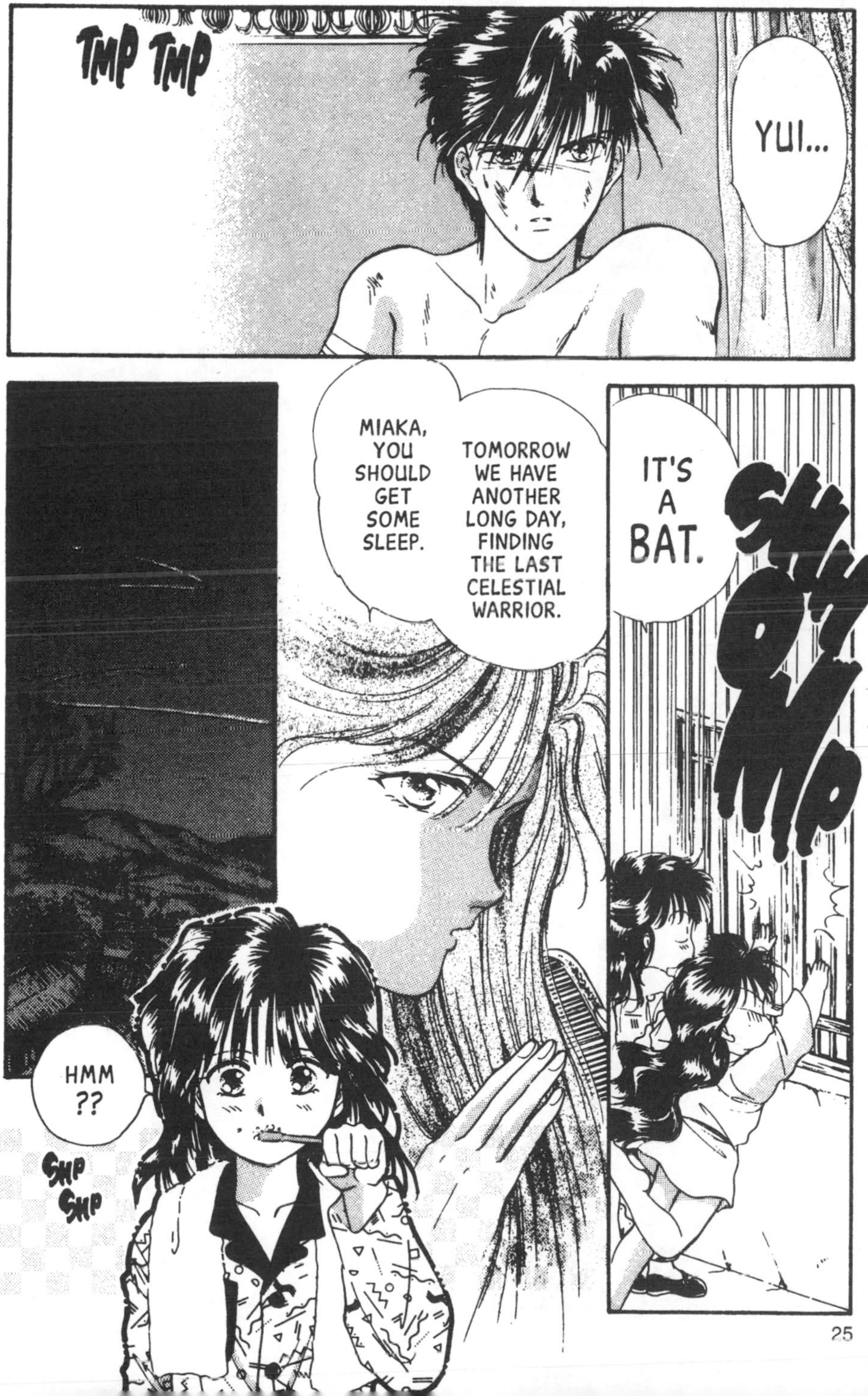
TMP TMP
YUI...
MIAKA, YOU SHOULD GET SOME SLEEP.
TOMORROW WE HAVE ANOTHER LONG DAY, FINDING THE LAST CELESTIAL WARRIOR.
IT'S A BAT.
HMM ??
SHP SHP

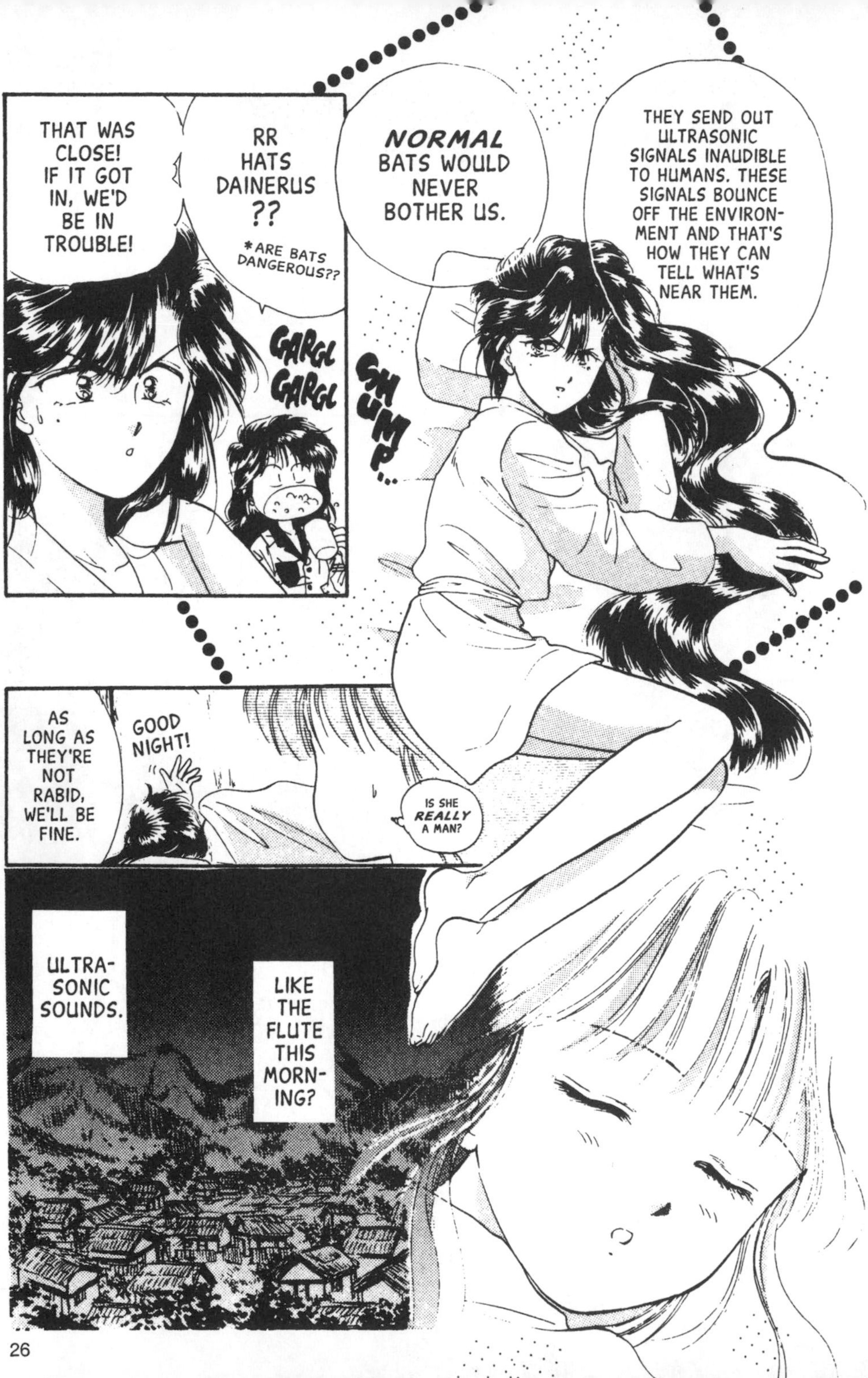
THAT WAS CLOSE! IF IT GOT IN, WE'D BE IN TROUBLE!
RR HATS DAINERUS ??
*ARE BATS DANGEROUS??
GARGL GARGL
NORMAL BATS WOULD NEVER BOTHER US.
THEY SEND OUT ULTRASONIC SIGNALS INAUDIBLE TO HUMANS. THESE SIGNALS BOUNCE OFF THE ENVIRON-MENT AND THAT'S HOW THEY CAN TELL WHAT'S NEAR THEM.
SHUMP...
AS LONG AS THEY'RE NOT RABID, WE'LL BE FINE.
GOOD NIGHT!
IS SHE REALLY A MAN?
ULTRA-SONIC SOUNDS.
LIKE THE FLUTE THIS MORN-ING?

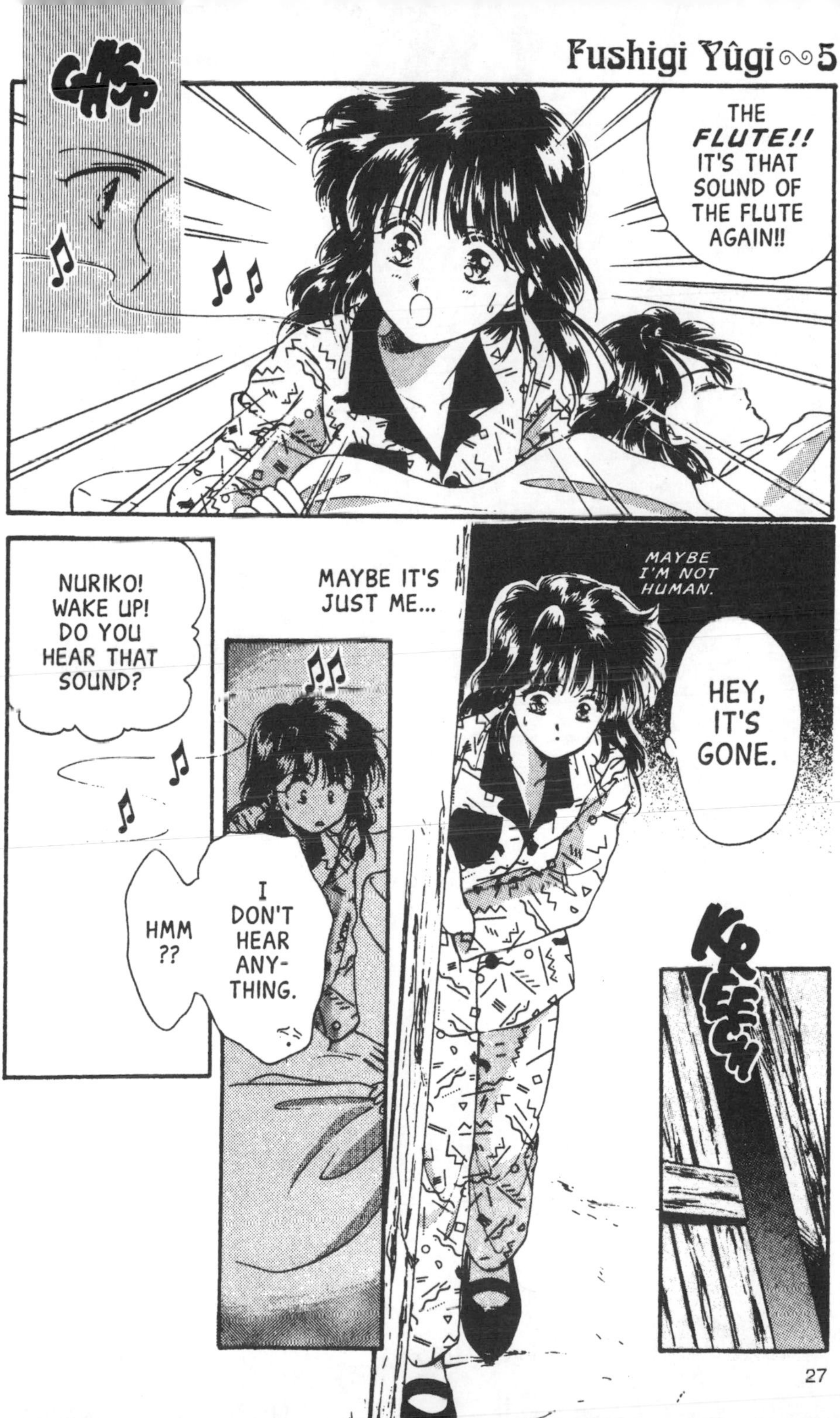
GASP
THE FLUTE!! IT'S THAT SOUND OF THE FLUTE AGAIN!!
NURIKO! WAKE UP! DO YOU HEAR THAT SOUND?
MAYBE IT'S JUST ME...
HMM ??
I DON'T HEAR ANY-THING.
MAYBE I'M NOT HUMAN.
HEY, IT'S GONE.
KREECH

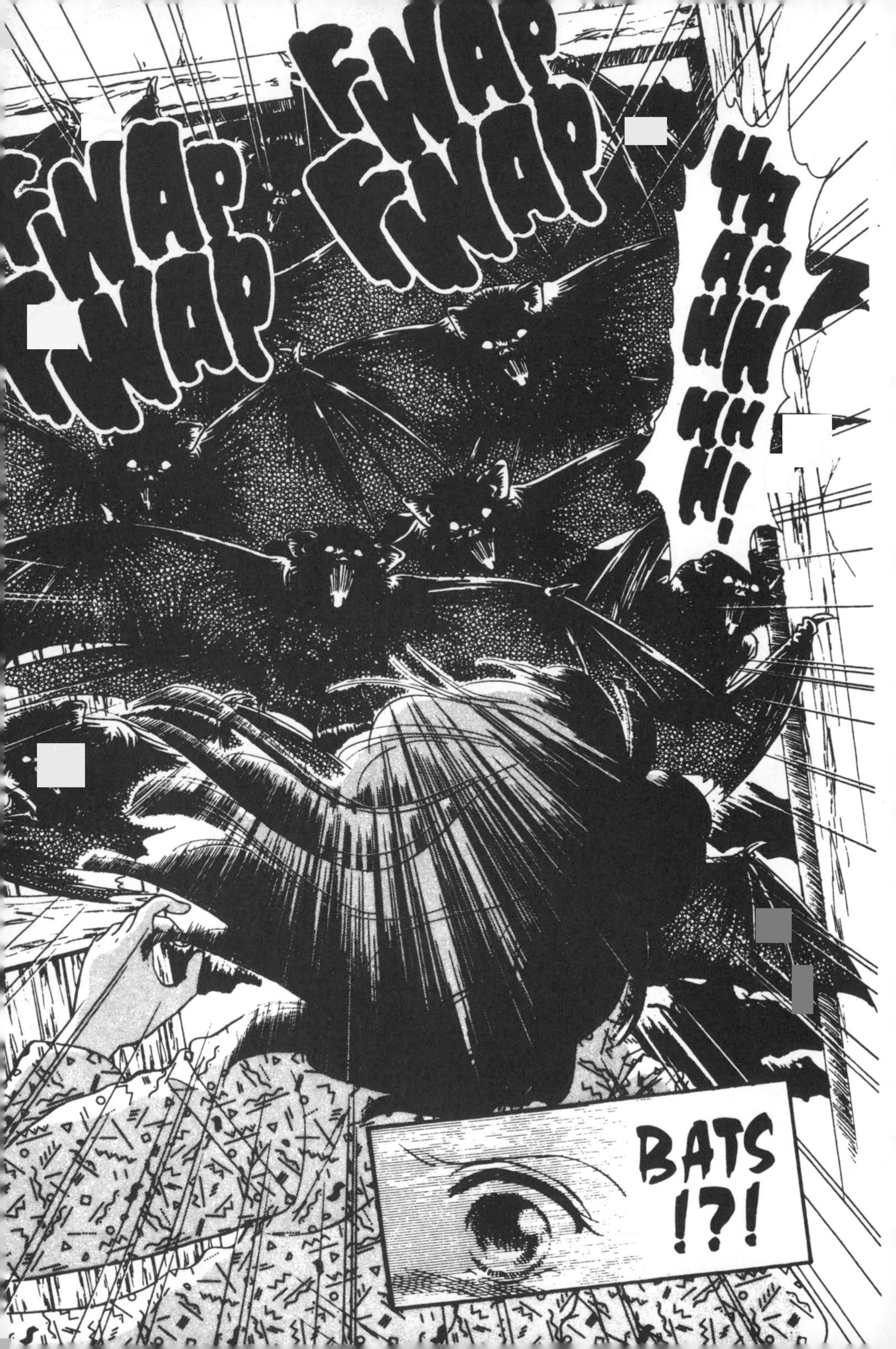
FWAP FWAP
FWAP FWAP
YAAAHHHHH!
BATS !?!

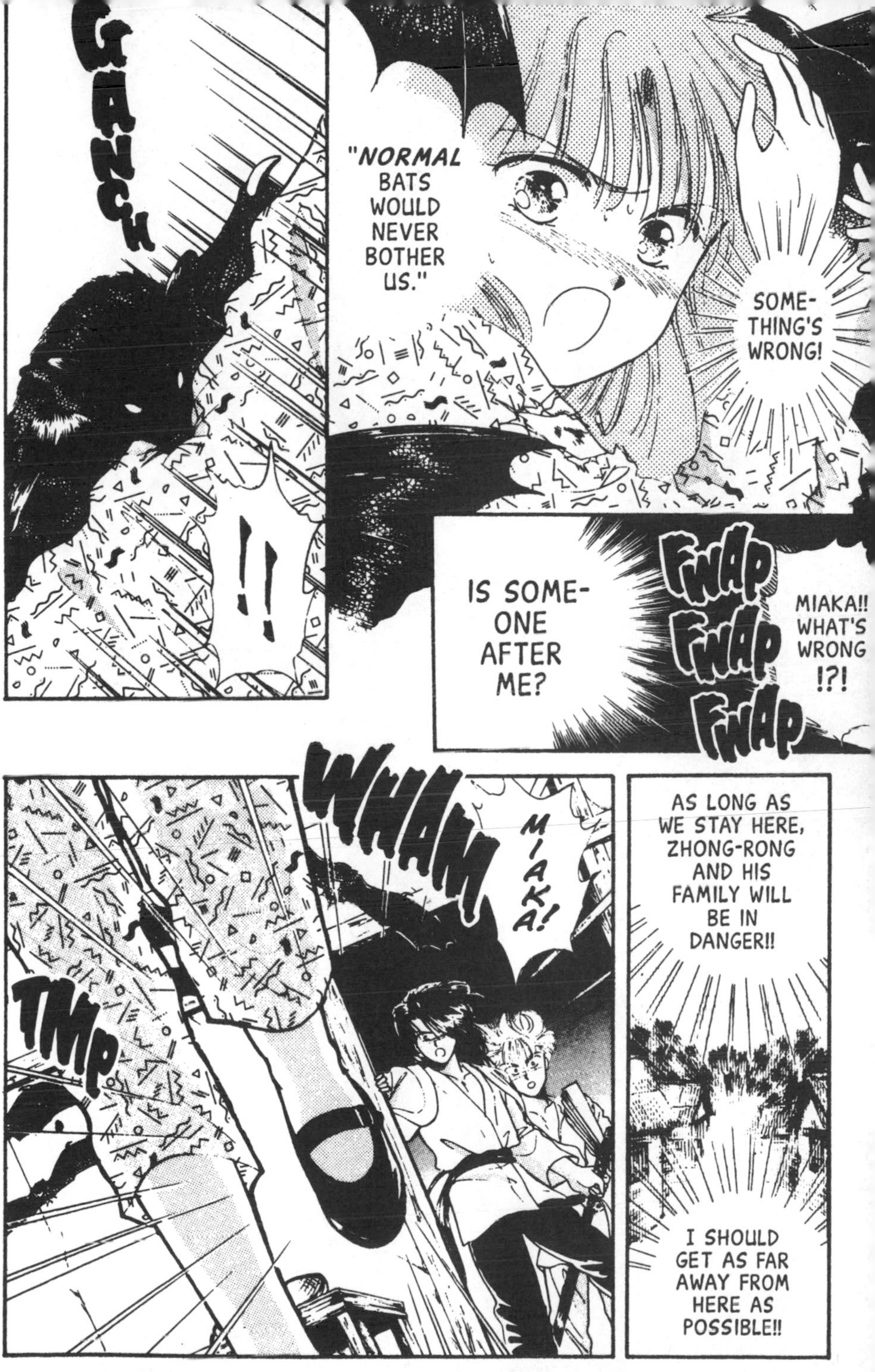
GANCH
!!
"NORMAL BATS WOULD NEVER BOTHER US."
SOME-THING'S WRONG!
IS SOME-ONE AFTER ME?
FWAP FWAP FWAP
MIAKA!! WHAT'S WRONG !?!
WHAM
MIAKA!
TMP
AS LONG AS WE STAY HERE, ZHONG-RONG AND HIS FAMILY WILL BE IN DANGER!!
I SHOULD GET AS FAR AWAY FROM HERE AS POSSIBLE!!

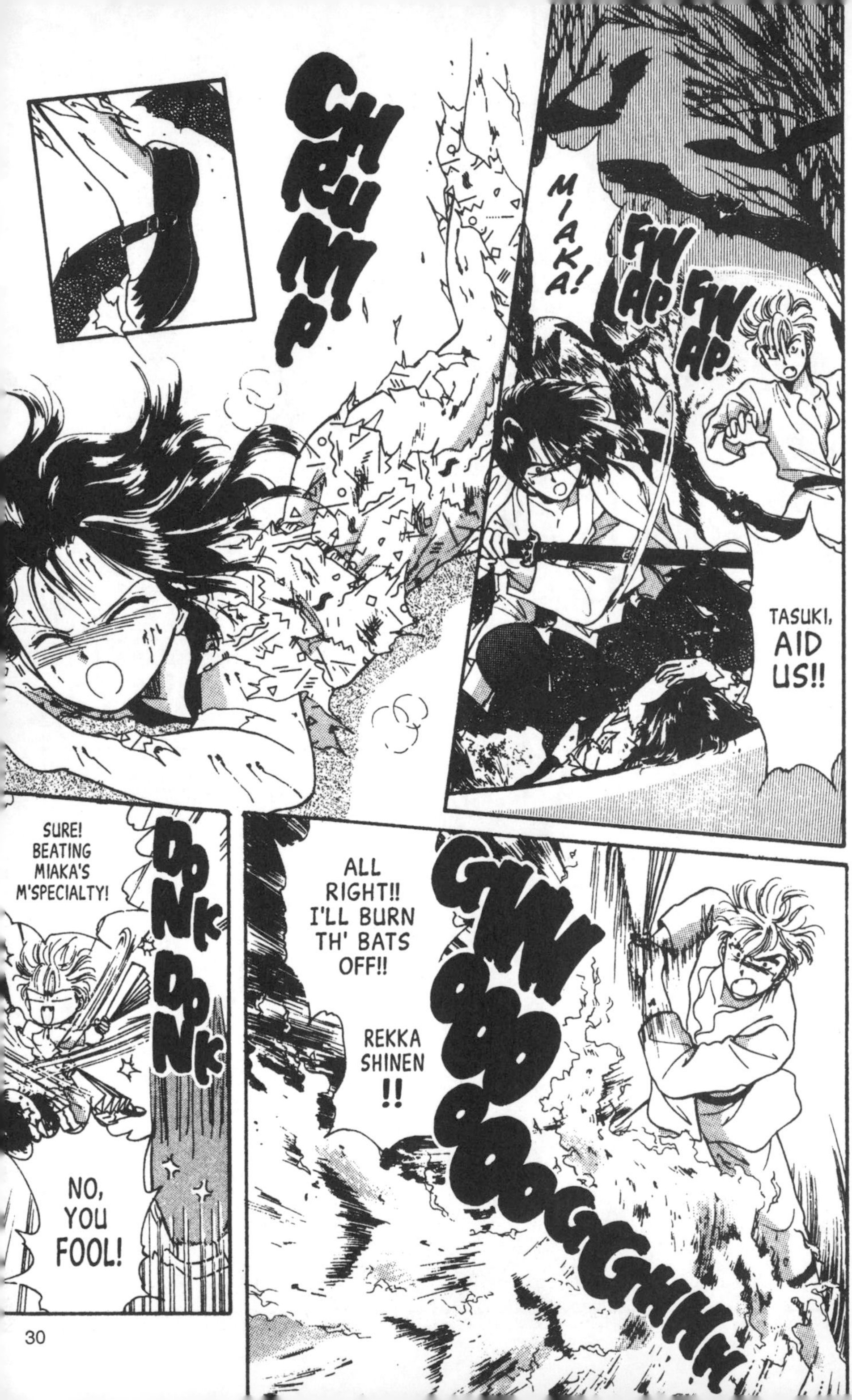
CHRUMP
MIAKA!
FWAP
FWAP
TASUKI, AID US!!
SURE! BEATING MIAKA'S M'SPECIALTY!
DONK
DONK
NO, YOU FOOL!
ALL RIGHT!! I'LL BURN TH' BATS OFF!!
REKKA SHINEN !!
GWOOOOOOGGHHH

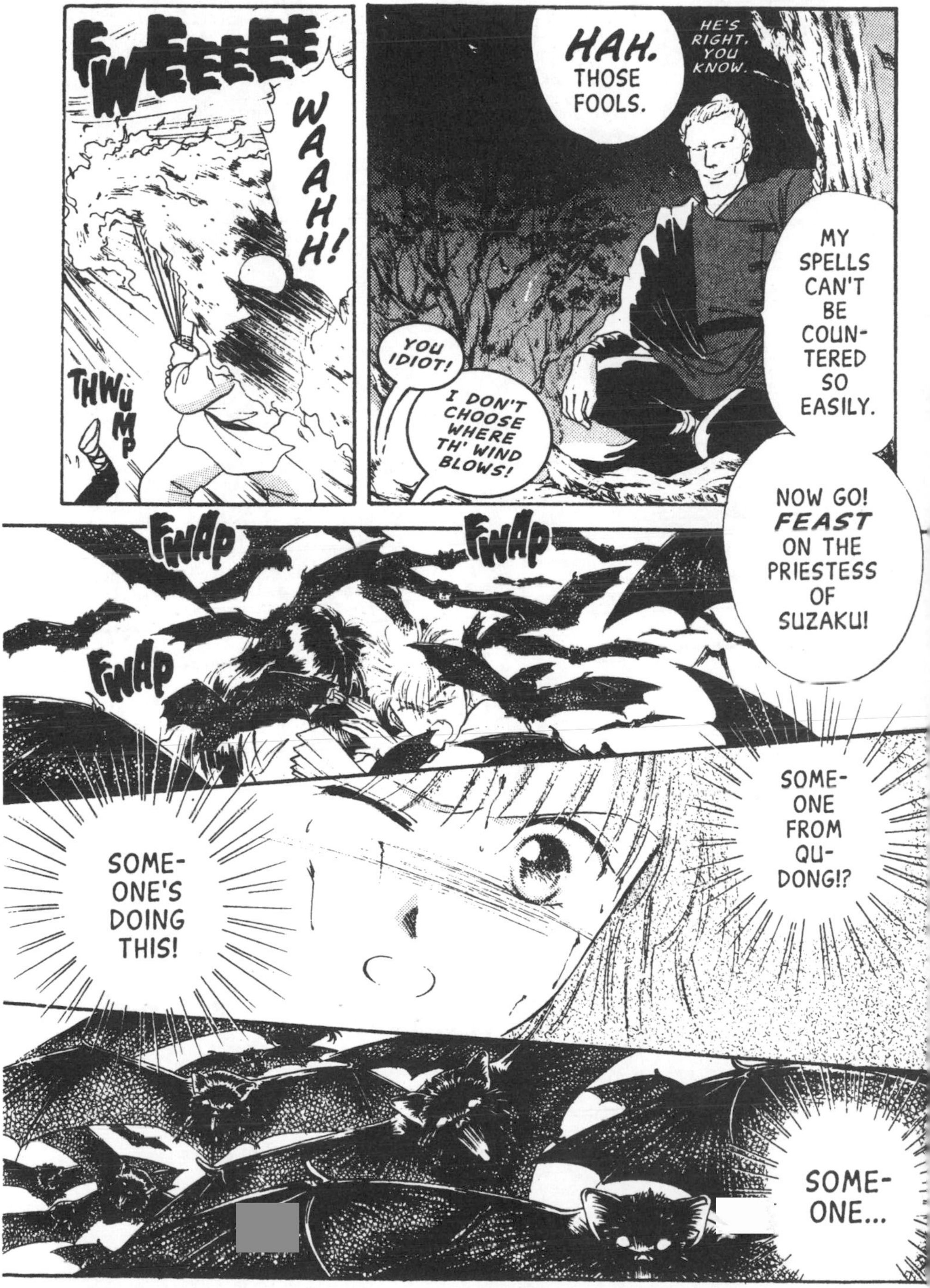
FWEEEEEE
WAAAHH!
THWUMP
HAH. THOSE FOOLS.
HE'S RIGHT, YOU KNOW.
YOU IDIOT!
I DON'T CHOOSE WHERE TH' WIND BLOWS!
MY SPELLS CAN'T BE COUNTERED SO EASILY.
NOW GO! FEAST ON THE PRIESTESS OF SUZAKU!
FWAP
FWAP
FWAP
SOMEONE'S DOING THIS!
SOMEONE FROM QU-DONG!?
SOMEONE...

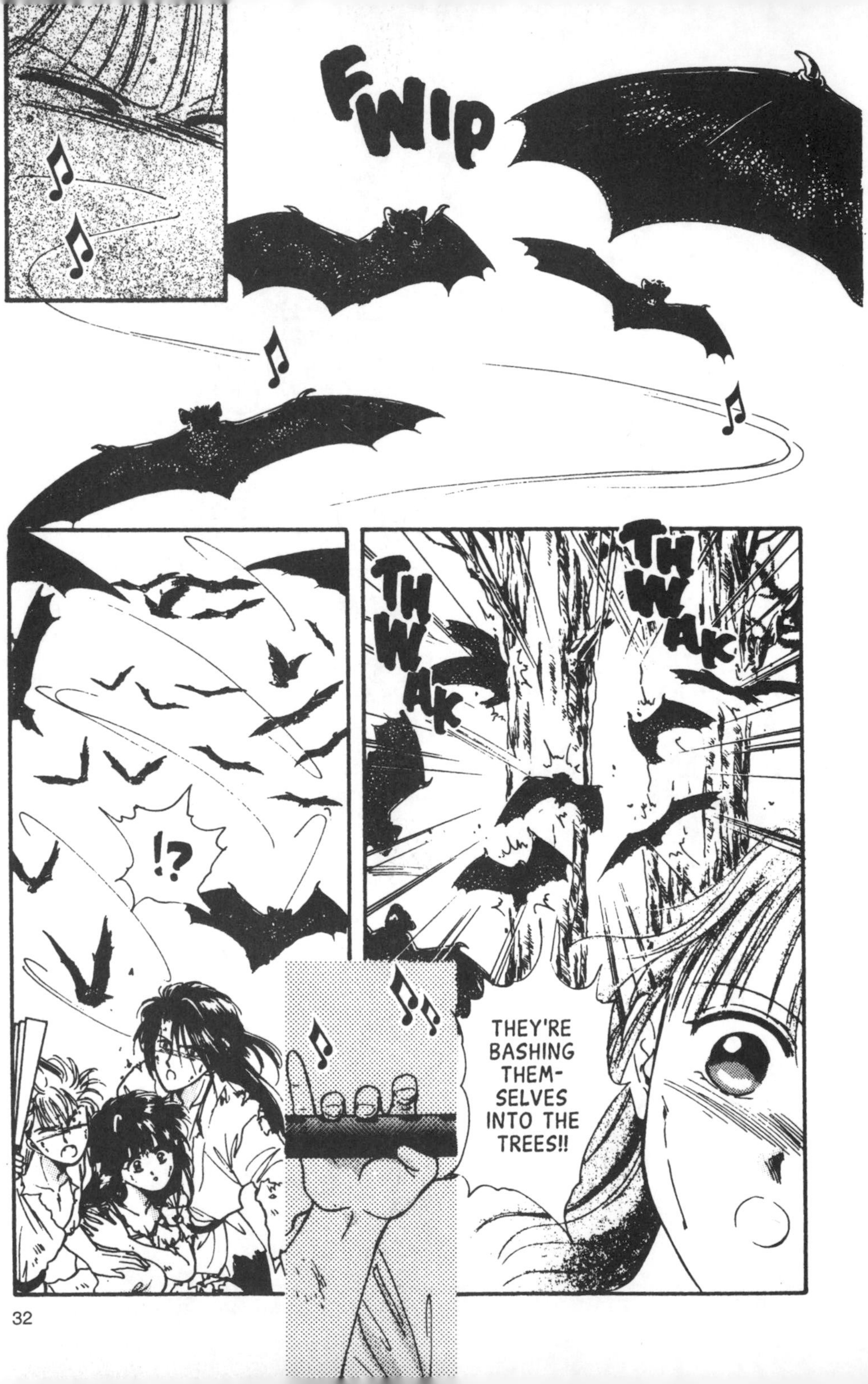
FWIP
!?
THWAK
THWAK
THEY'RE BASHING THEM-SELVES INTO THE TREES!!

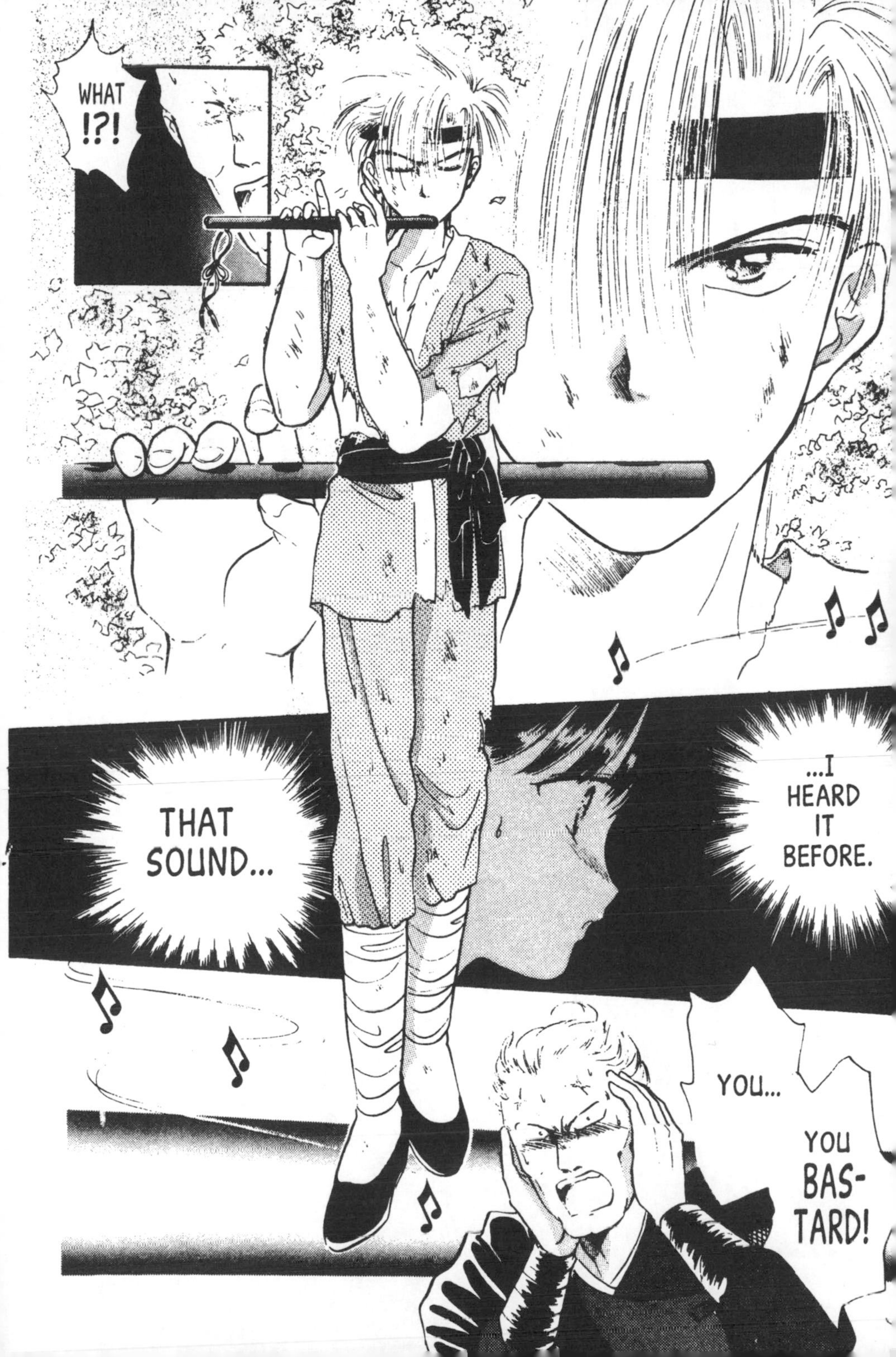
WHAT !?!
THAT SOUND...
...I HEARD IT BEFORE.
YOU...
YOU BAS-TARD!

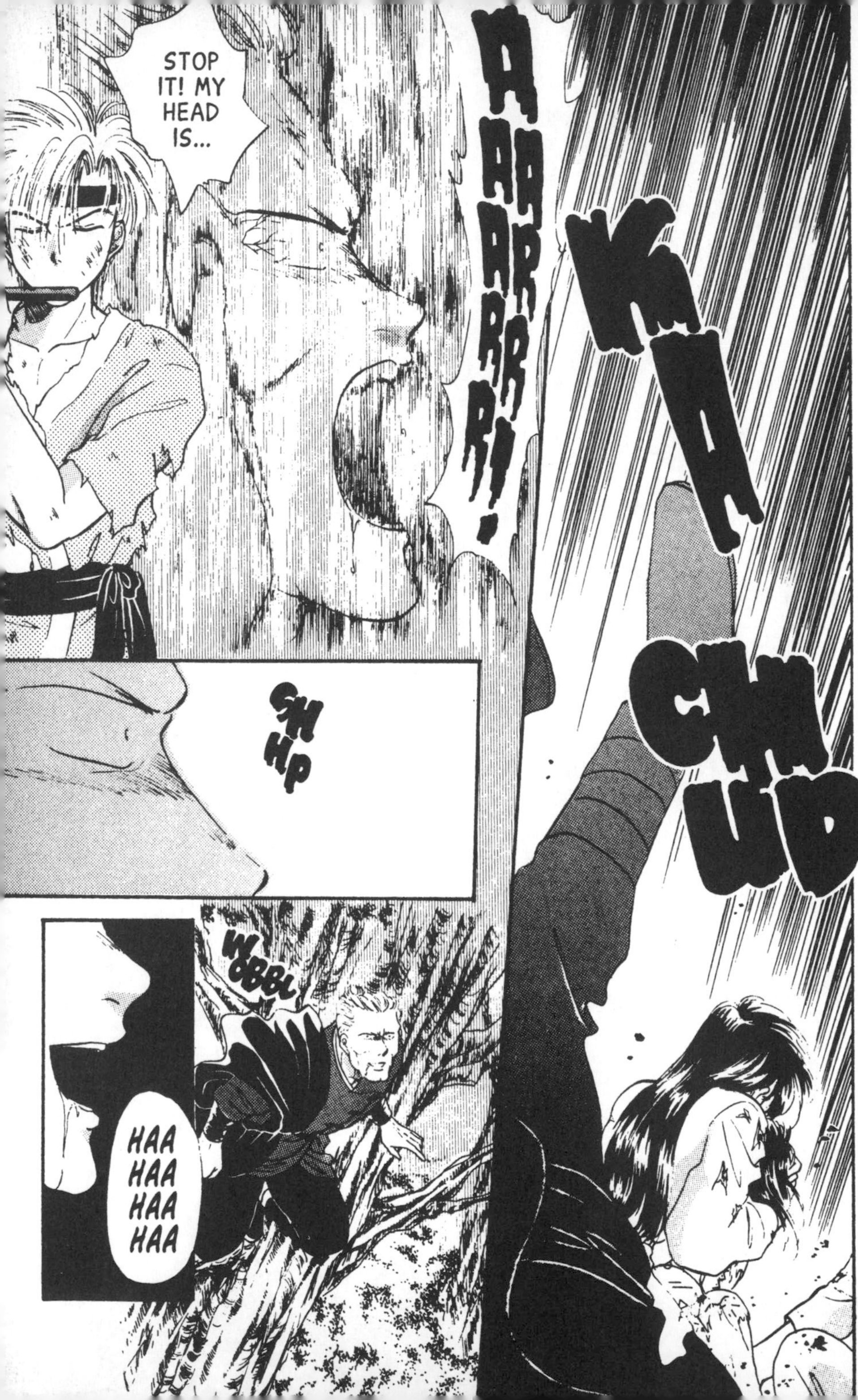

STOP IT! MY HEAD IS...
AAARRRRR!!
SHHP
WOBBL
HAA HAA HAA HAA HAA
KWAA
CHUD

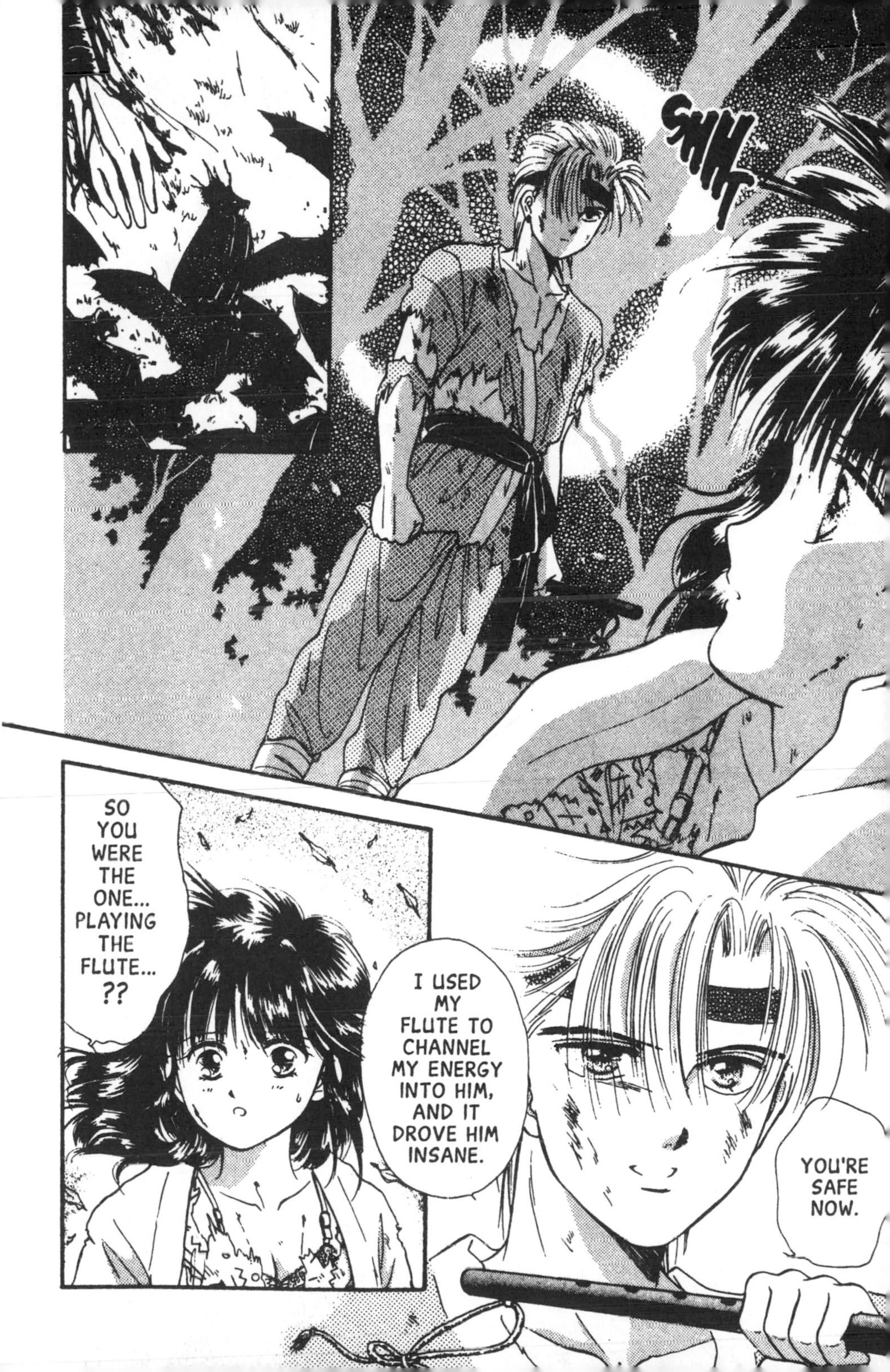
SHH
SO YOU WERE THE ONE... PLAYING THE FLUTE... ??
I USED MY FLUTE TO CHANNEL MY ENERGY INTO HIM, AND IT DROVE HIM INSANE.
YOU'RE SAFE NOW.

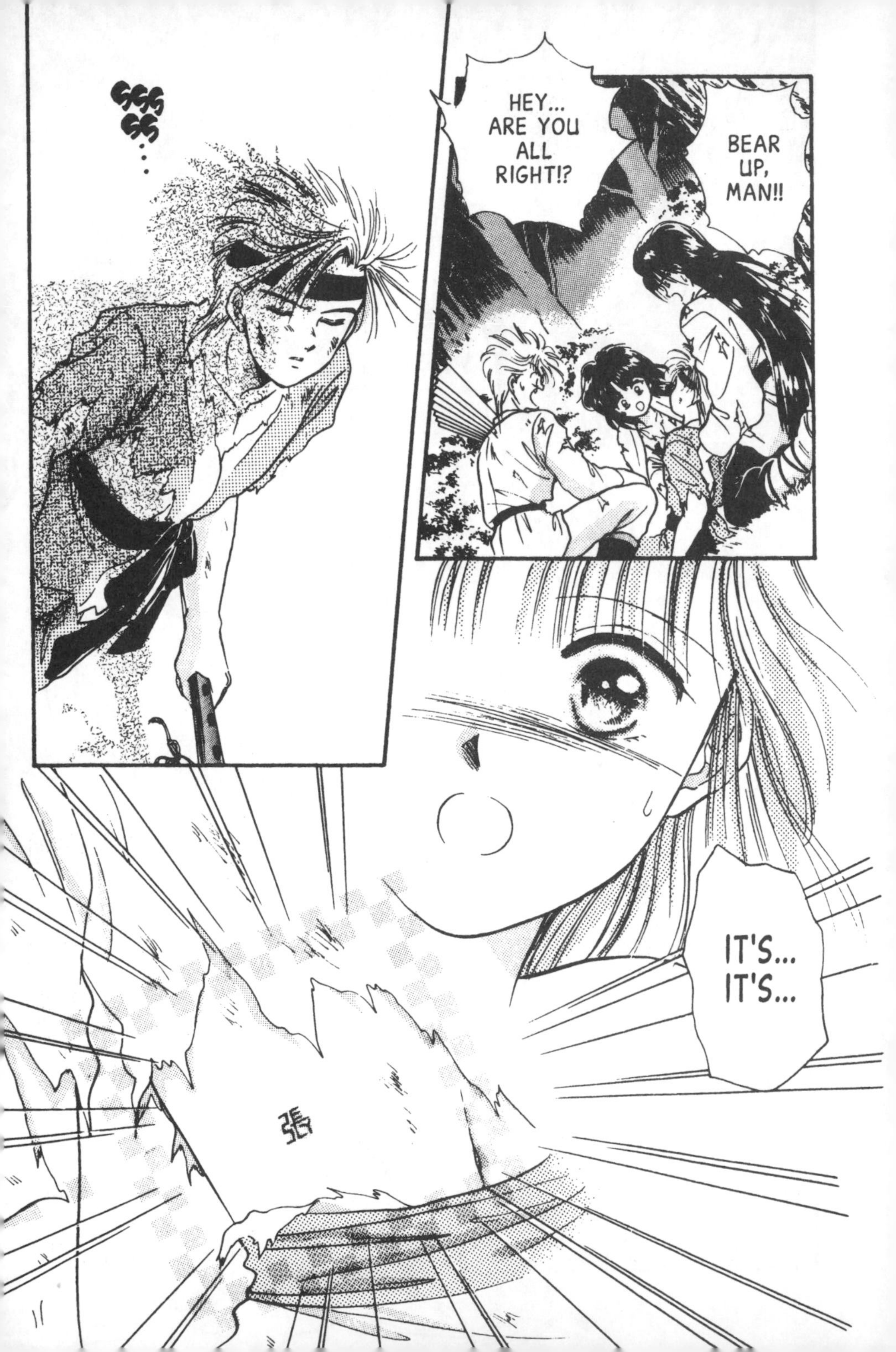
SSS SS...
HEY... ARE YOU ALL RIGHT!?
BEAR UP, MAN!!
IT'S... IT'S...
張

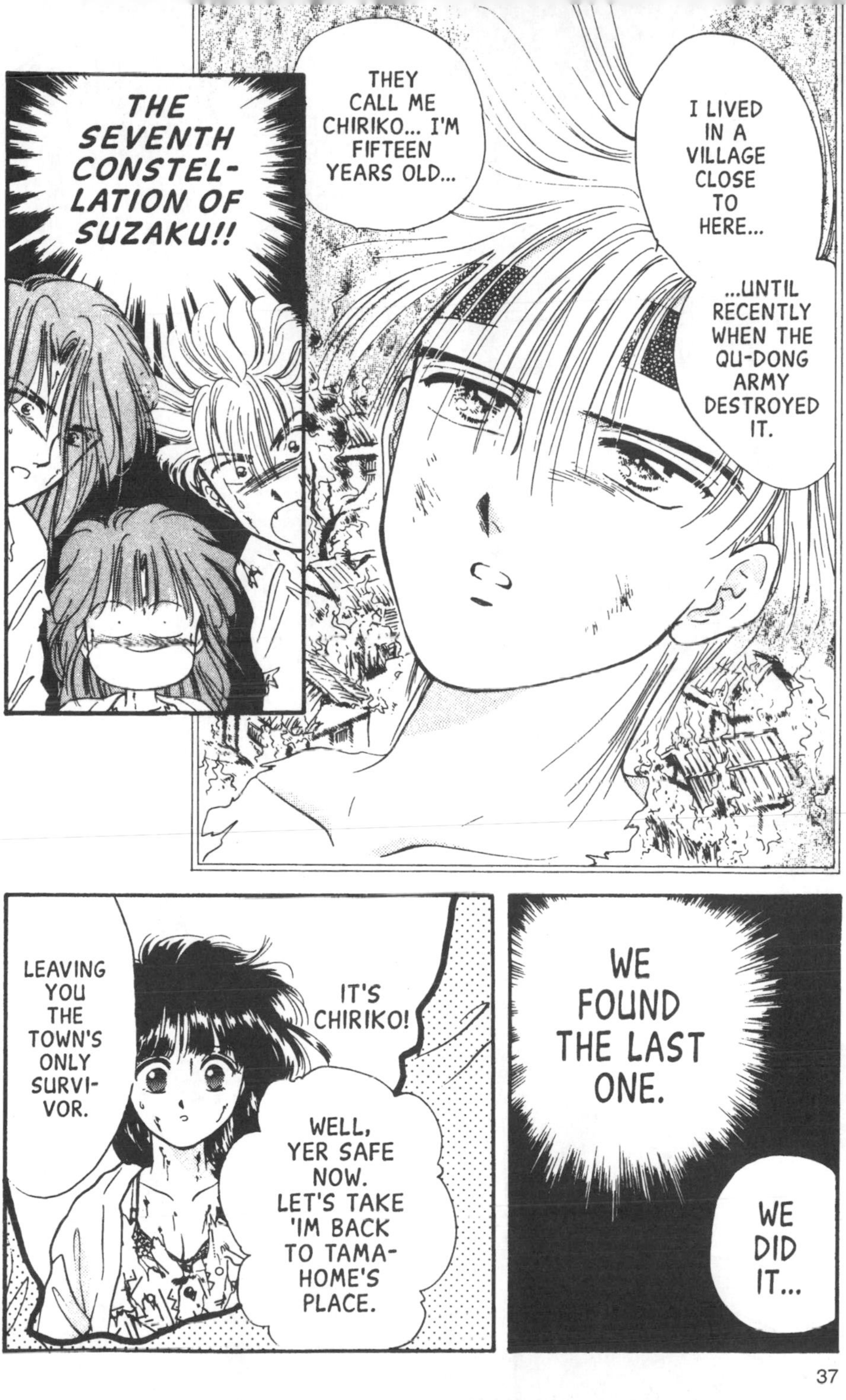
THE SEVENTH CONSTEL-LATION OF SUZAKU!!
THEY CALL ME CHIRIKO... I'M FIFTEEN YEARS OLD...
I LIVED IN A VILLAGE CLOSE TO HERE...
...UNTIL RECENTLY WHEN THE QU-DONG ARMY DESTROYED IT.
LEAVING YOU THE TOWN'S ONLY SURVI-VOR.
IT'S CHIRIKO!
WELL, YER SAFE NOW. LET'S TAKE 'IM BACK TO TAMA-HOME'S PLACE.
WE FOUND THE LAST ONE.
WE DID IT...

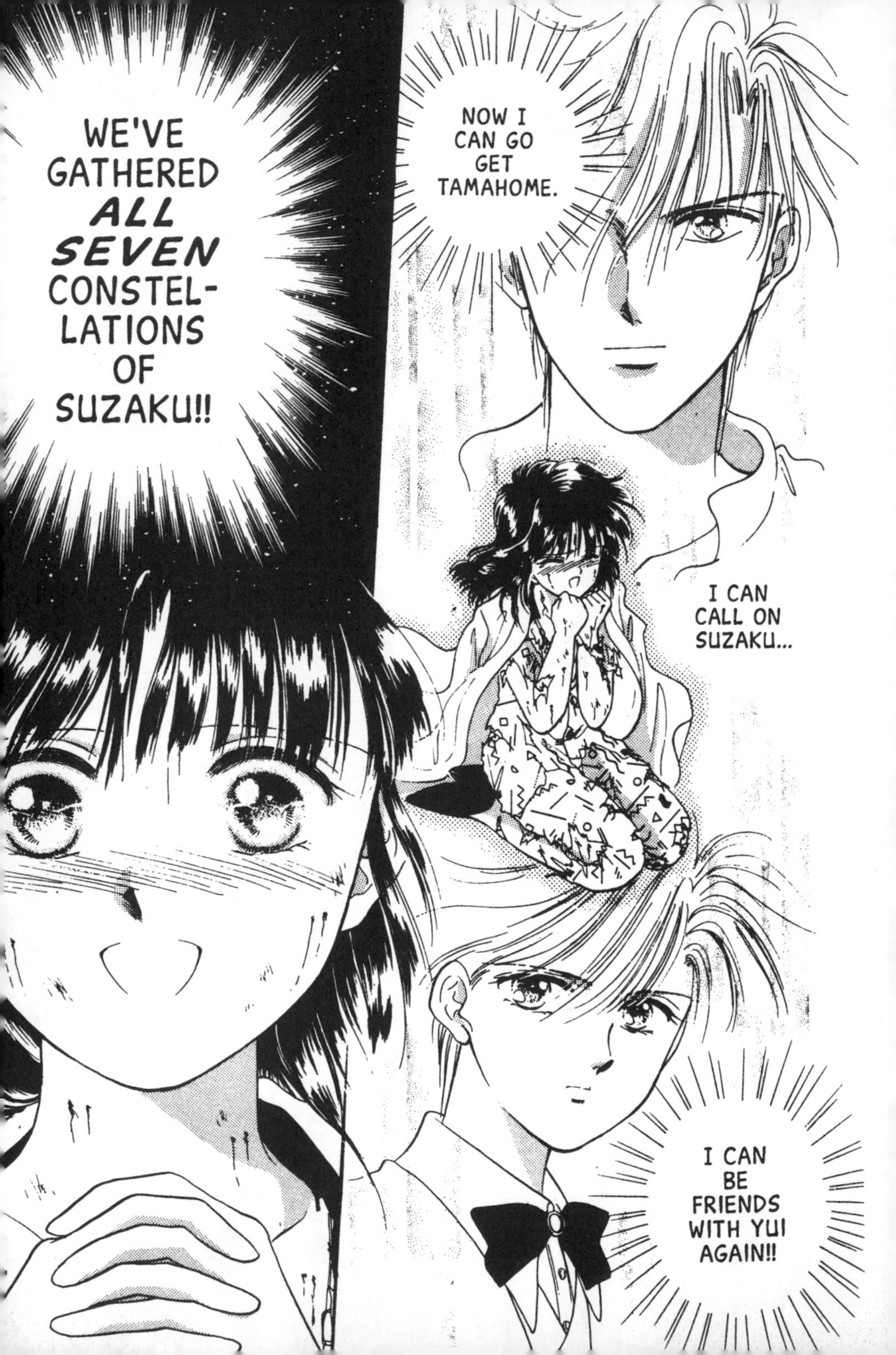
WE'VE GATHERED ***ALL SEVEN*** CONSTEL-LATIONS OF SUZAKU!!
NOW I CAN GO GET TAMAHOME.
I CAN CALL ON SUZAKU...
I CAN BE FRIENDS WITH YUI AGAIN!!

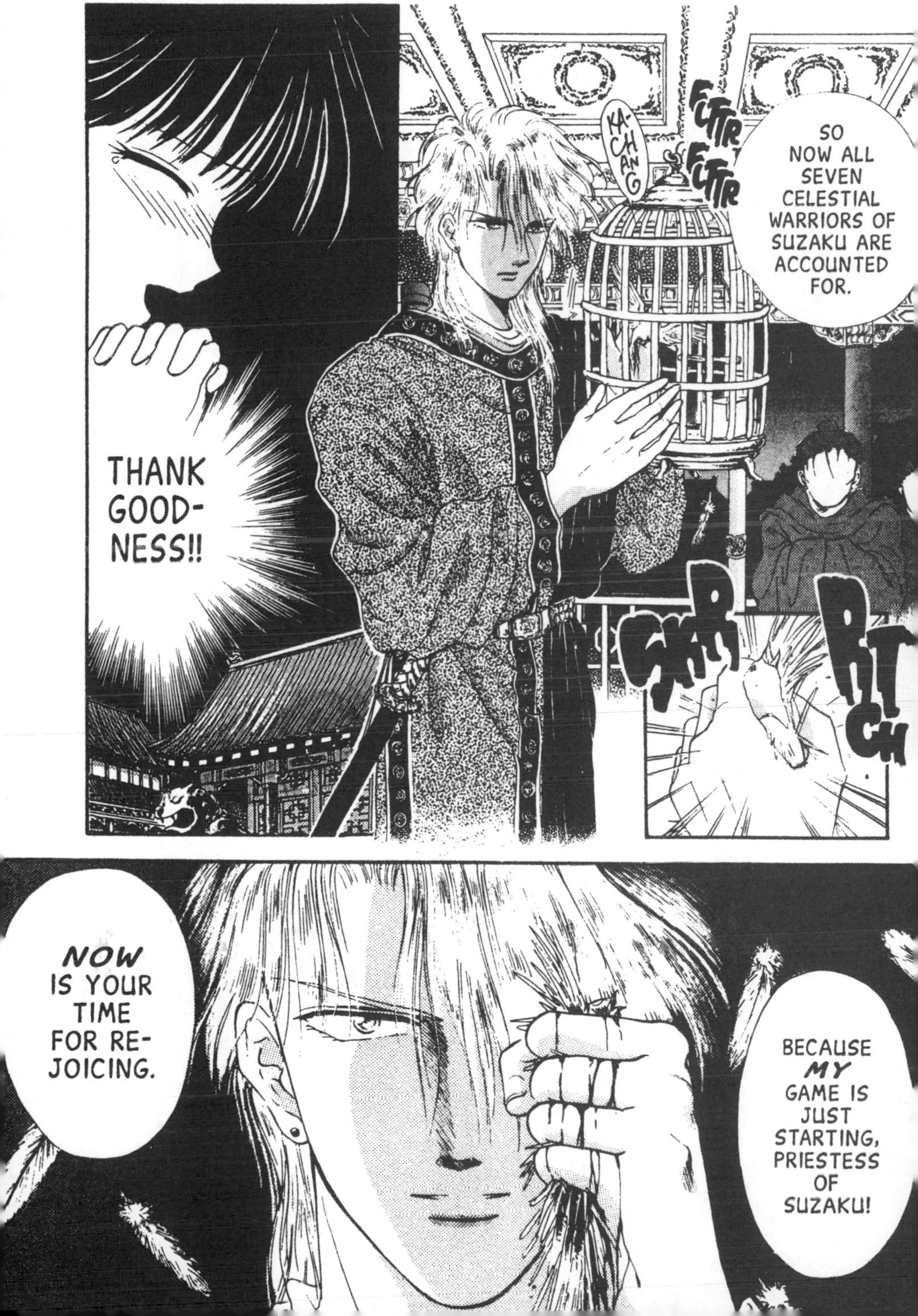
THANK GOODNESS!!
KA-CHANG
FLTTR
FLTTR
SO NOW ALL SEVEN CELESTIAL WARRIORS OF SUZAKU ARE ACCOUNTED FOR.
GKRR
RITCH
NOW IS YOUR TIME FOR REJOICING.
BECAUSE MY GAME IS JUST STARTING, PRIESTESS OF SUZAKU!

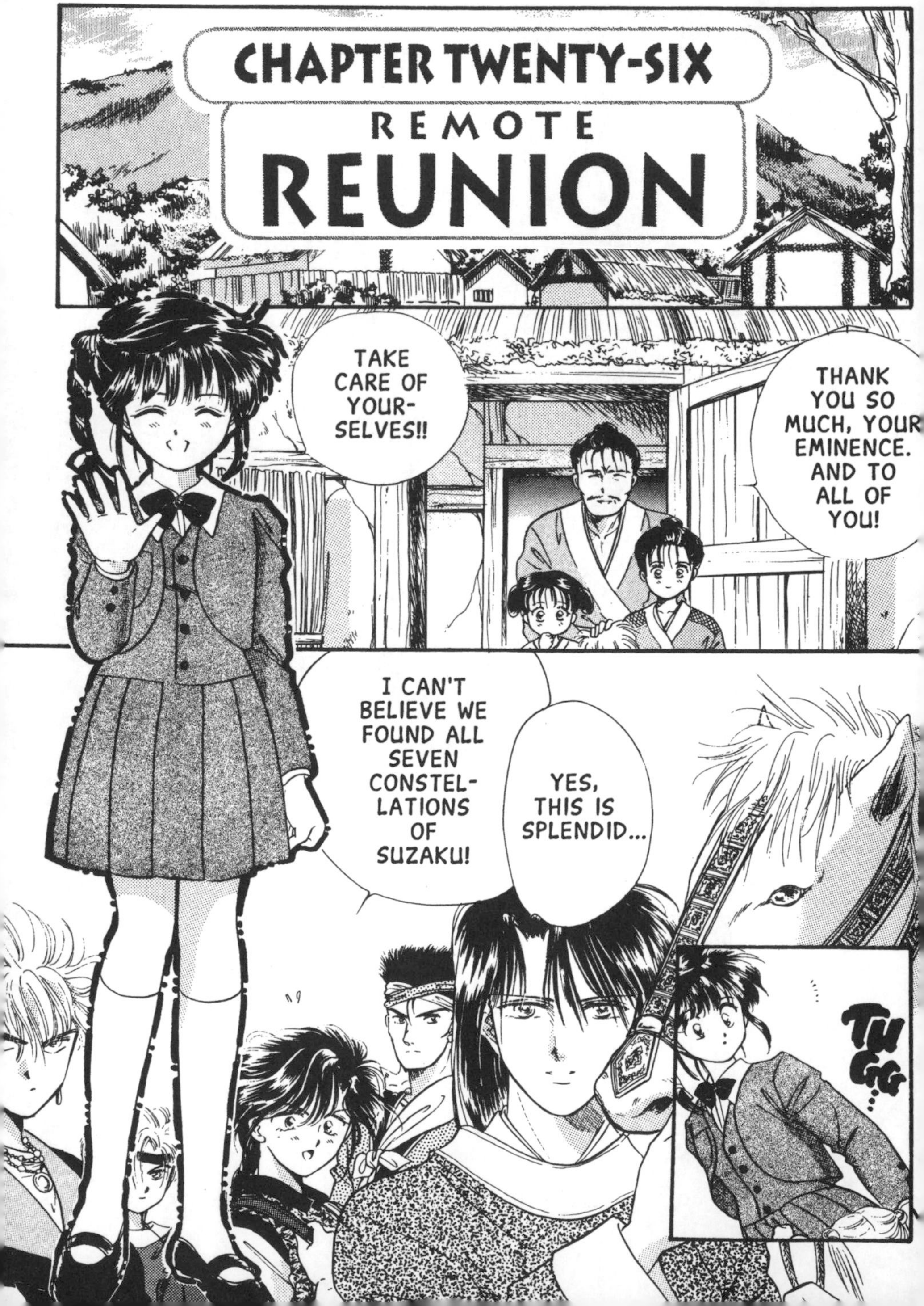
CHAPTER TWENTY-SIX
REMOTE REUNION
TAKE CARE OF YOURSELVES!!
THANK YOU SO MUCH, YOUR EMINENCE. AND TO ALL OF YOU!
I CAN'T BELIEVE WE FOUND ALL SEVEN CONSTELLATIONS OF SUZAKU!
YES, THIS IS SPLENDID...
TUGG...

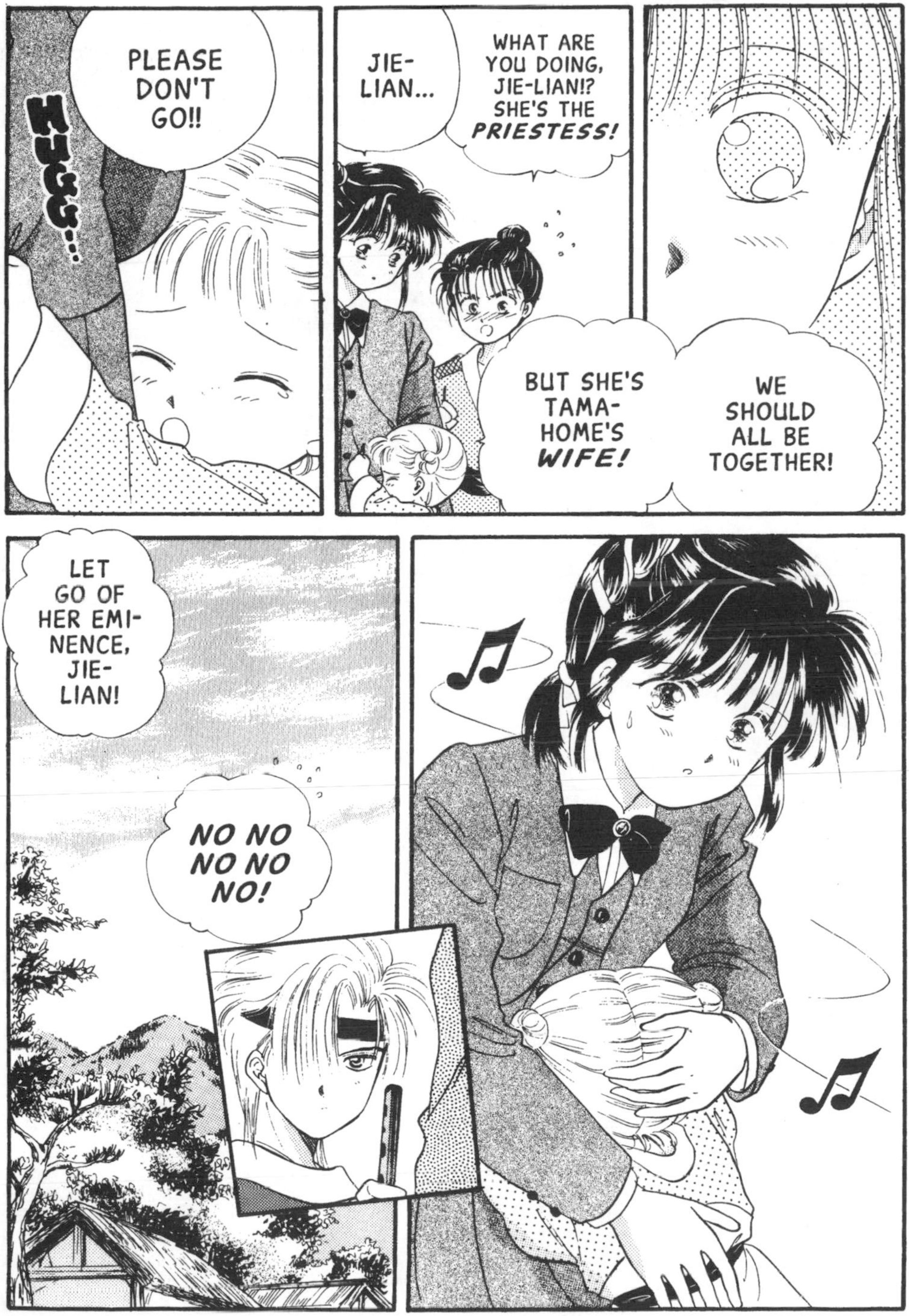
PLEASE DON'T GO!!
HUGG...
JIE-LIAN...
WHAT ARE YOU DOING, JIE-LIAN!? SHE'S THE *PRIESTESS!*
BUT SHE'S TAMA-HOME'S *WIFE!*
WE SHOULD ALL BE TOGETHER!
LET GO OF HER EMI-NENCE, JIE-LIAN!
NO NO NO NO NO!

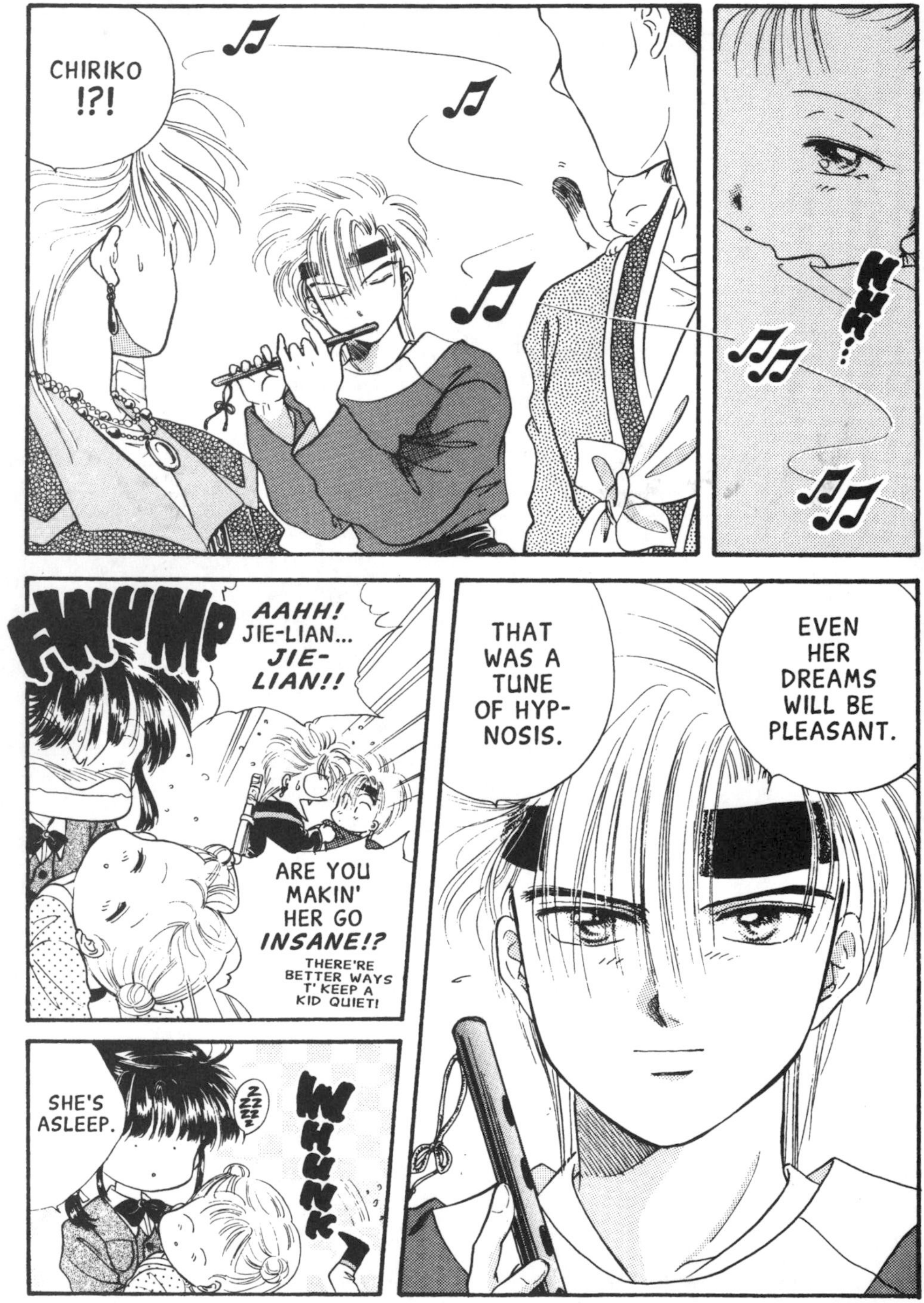
CHIRIKO !?!
HUH...
FWUMP
AAHH! JIE-LIAN... JIE-LIAN!!
ARE YOU MAKIN' HER GO INSANE!?
THERE'RE BETTER WAYS T' KEEP A KID QUIET!
THAT WAS A TUNE OF HYP-NOSIS.
EVEN HER DREAMS WILL BE PLEASANT.
SHE'S ASLEEP.
ZZZZ
WHUNK

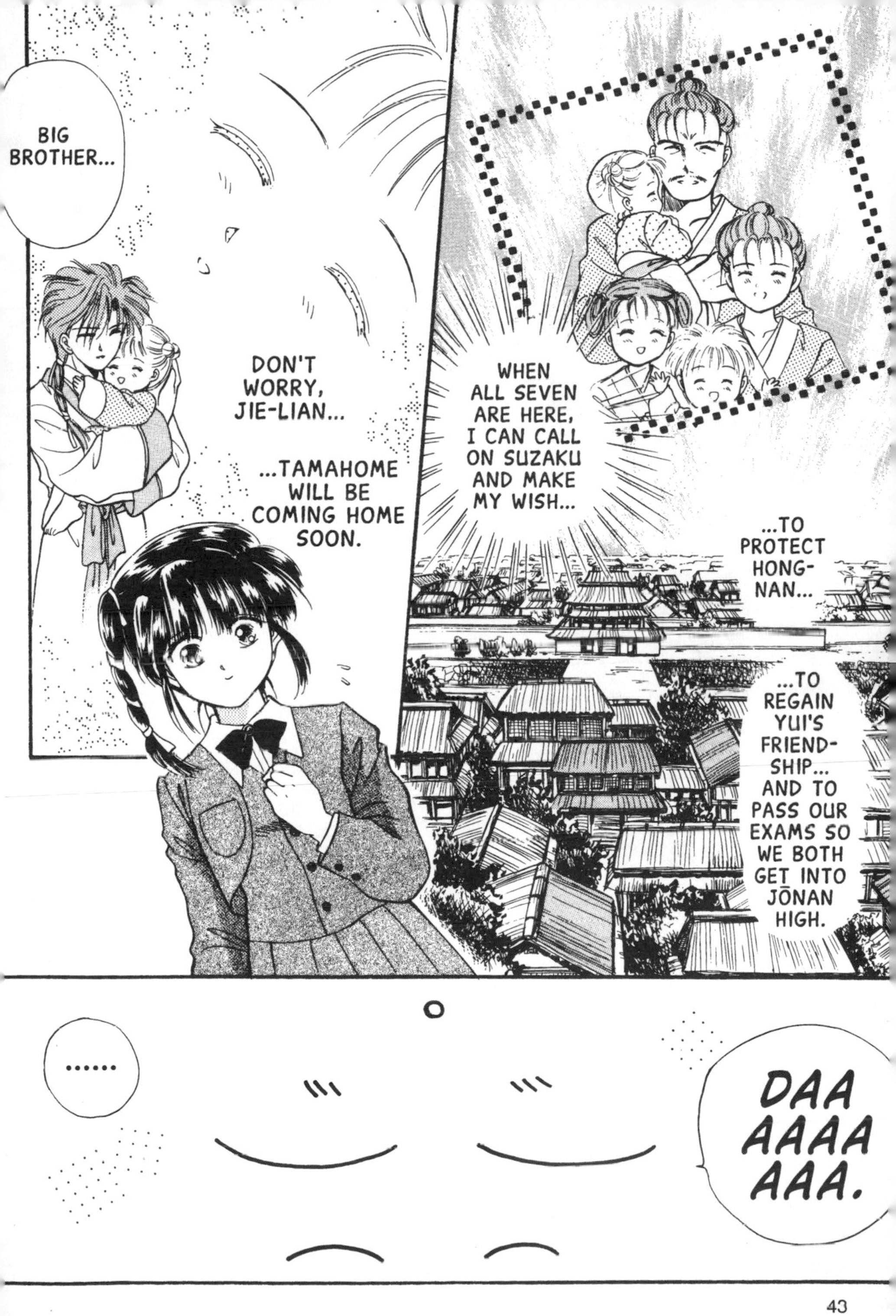
BIG BROTHER...
DON'T WORRY, JIE-LIAN...
...TAMAHOME WILL BE COMING HOME SOON.
WHEN ALL SEVEN ARE HERE, I CAN CALL ON SUZAKU AND MAKE MY WISH...
...TO PROTECT HONG-NAN...
...TO REGAIN YUI'S FRIEND-SHIP... AND TO PASS OUR EXAMS SO WE BOTH GET INTO JŌNAN HIGH.
......
DAA AAAA AAA.

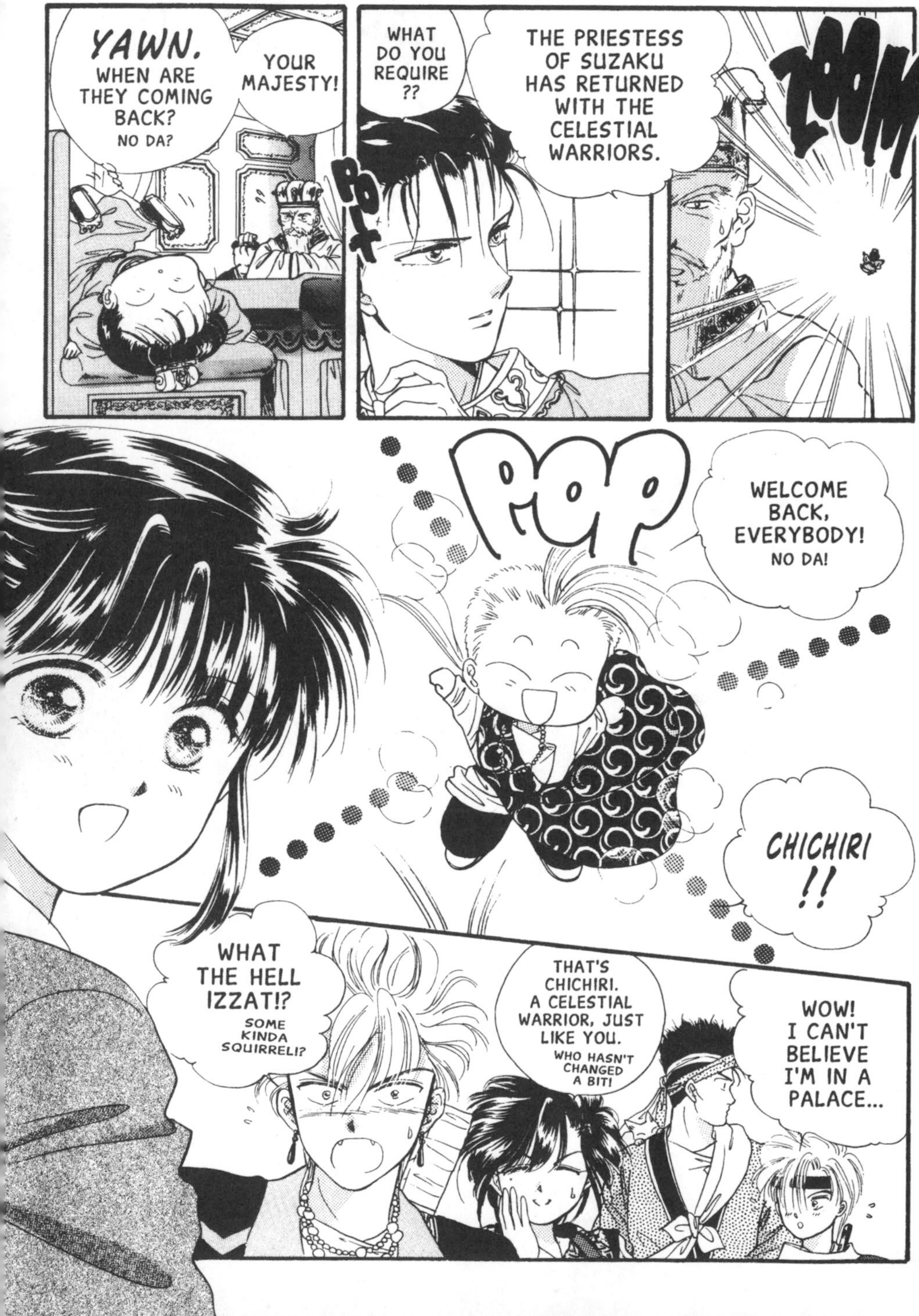
YAWN. WHEN ARE THEY COMING BACK? NO DA?
YOUR MAJESTY!
WHAT DO YOU REQUIRE ??
THE PRIESTESS OF SUZAKU HAS RETURNED WITH THE CELESTIAL WARRIORS.
ZOOM
POP
WELCOME BACK, EVERYBODY! NO DA!
CHICHIRI !!
WHAT THE HELL IZZAT!? SOME KINDA SQUIRREL!?
THAT'S CHICHIRI. A CELESTIAL WARRIOR, JUST LIKE YOU. WHO HASN'T CHANGED A BIT!
WOW! I CAN'T BELIEVE I'M IN A PALACE...

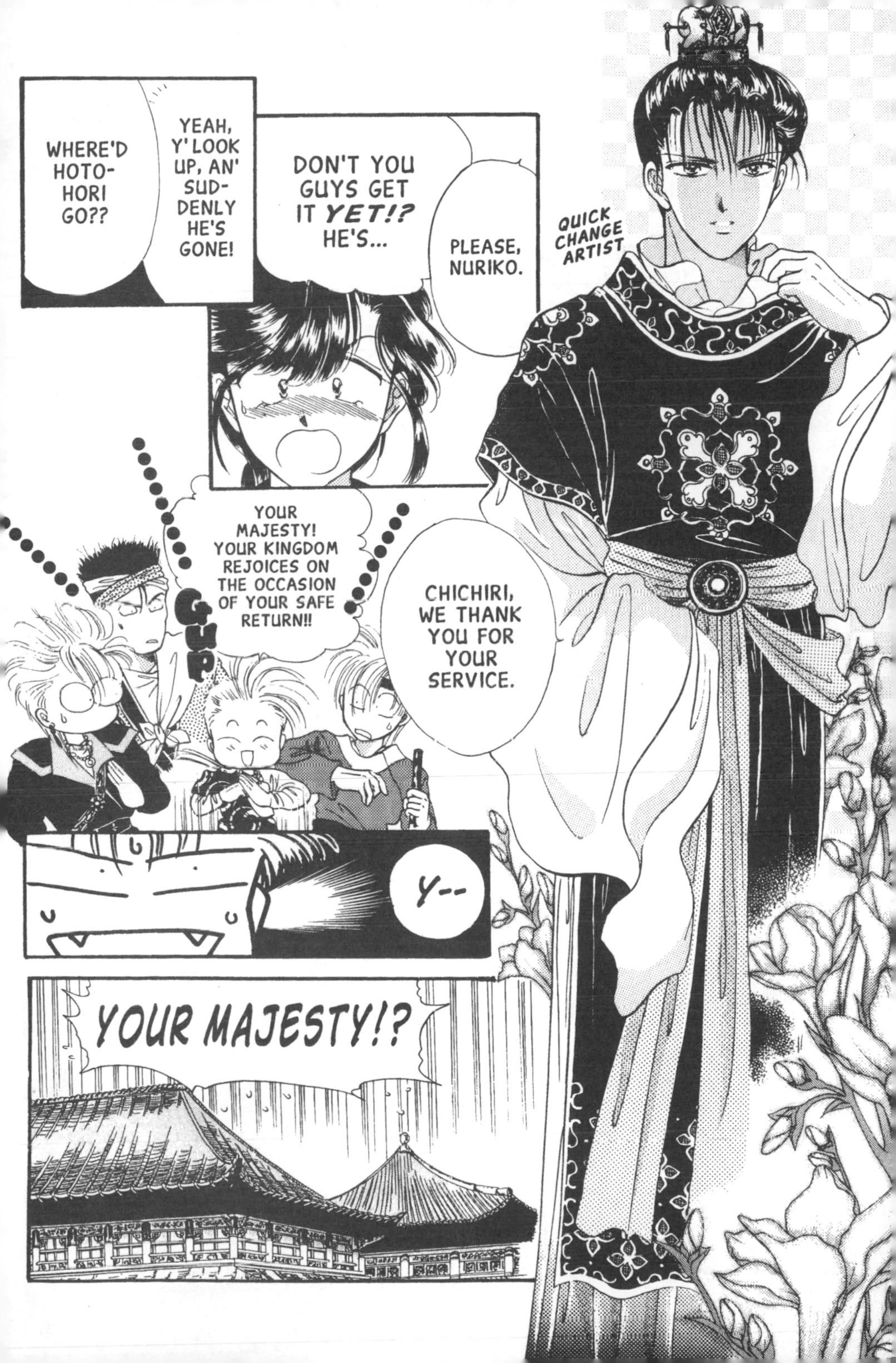
WHERE'D HOTO-HORI GO??
YEAH, Y' LOOK UP, AN' SUD-DENLY HE'S GONE!
DON'T YOU GUYS GET IT *YET!?* HE'S...
PLEASE, NURIKO.
YOUR MAJESTY! YOUR KINGDOM REJOICES ON THE OCCASION OF YOUR SAFE RETURN!!
GUP
Y--
YOUR MAJESTY!?
QUICK CHANGE ARTIST
CHICHIRI, WE THANK YOU FOR YOUR SERVICE.

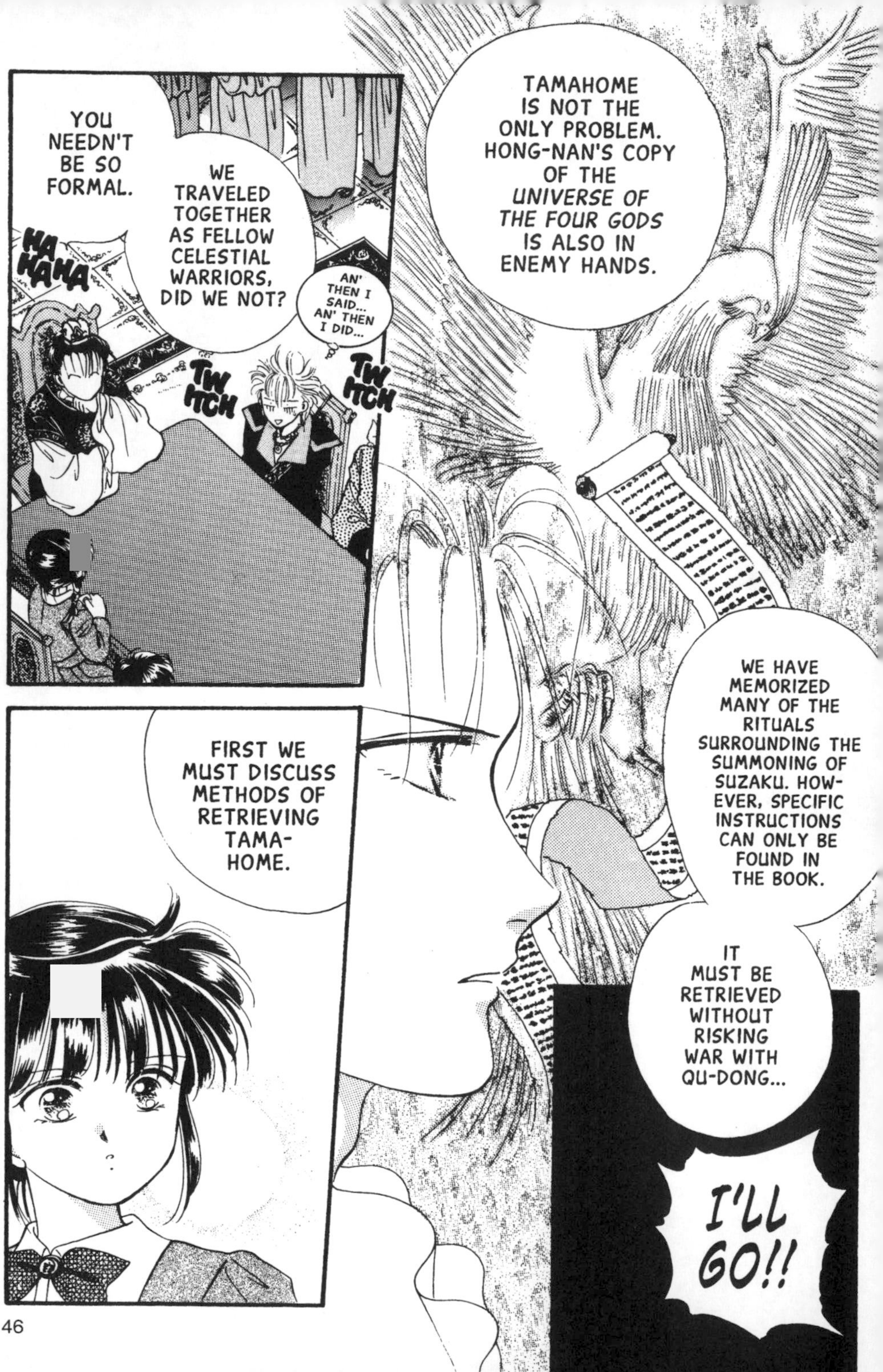

YOU NEEDN'T BE SO FORMAL.
WE TRAVELED TOGETHER AS FELLOW CELESTIAL WARRIORS, DID WE NOT?
HA HA HA
AN' THEN I SAID... AN' THEN I DID...
TWITCH
TWITCH
FIRST WE MUST DISCUSS METHODS OF RETRIEVING TAMA-HOME.
TAMAHOME IS NOT THE ONLY PROBLEM. HONG-NAN'S COPY OF THE *UNIVERSE OF THE FOUR GODS* IS ALSO IN ENEMY HANDS.
WE HAVE MEMORIZED MANY OF THE RITUALS SURROUNDING THE SUMMONING OF SUZAKU. HOW-EVER, SPECIFIC INSTRUCTIONS CAN ONLY BE FOUND IN THE BOOK.
IT MUST BE RETRIEVED WITHOUT RISKING WAR WITH QU-DONG...
I'LL GO!!

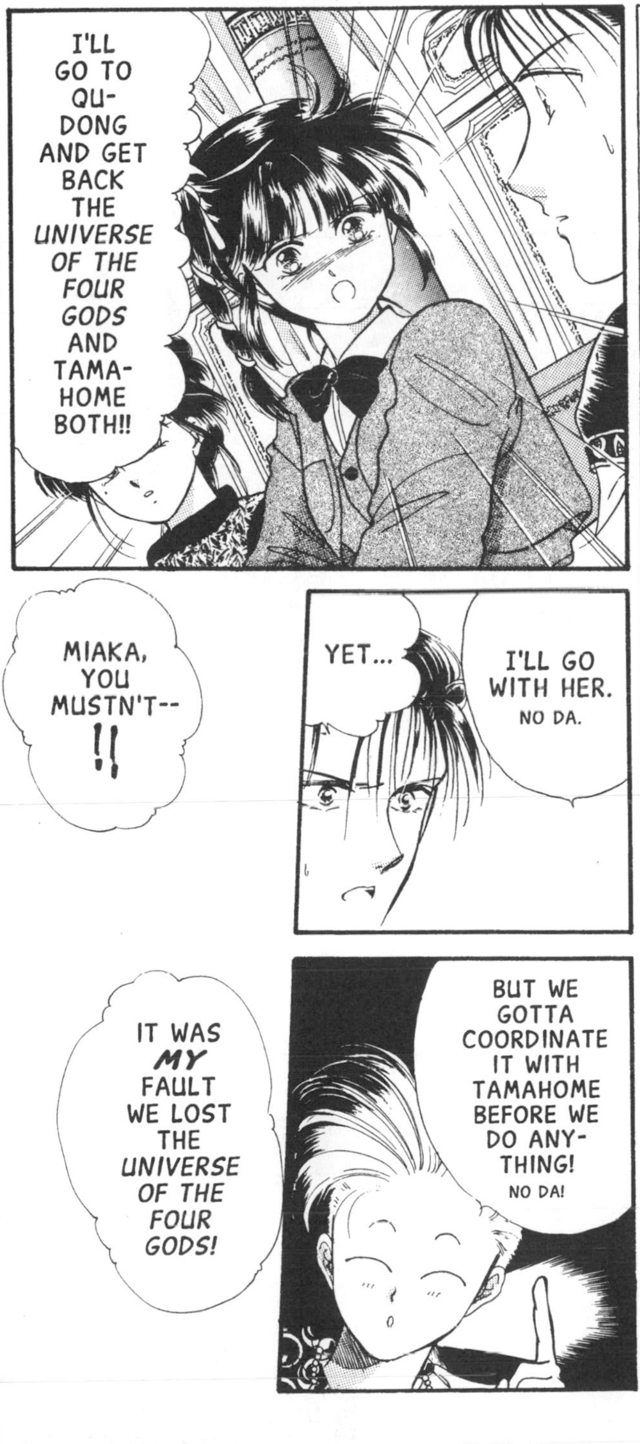
I'LL GO TO QU-DONG AND GET BACK THE *UNIVERSE OF THE FOUR GODS* AND TAMAHOME BOTH!!
MIAKA, YOU MUSTN'T-- !!
YET...
I'LL GO WITH HER. NO DA.
IT WAS *MY* FAULT WE LOST THE *UNIVERSE OF THE FOUR GODS*!
BUT WE GOTTA COORDINATE IT WITH TAMAHOME BEFORE WE DO ANYTHING! NO DA!

Since last year, I've been keeping an eye on Ugo Ugo Rūga (a live-action variety show) which is now becoming very popular. But in the Kansai region, it isn't catching on at all. That's right! The power of manga and anime in Kansai is outrageous!! I get dizzy over the onslaught of reruns! Modern kids have never seen this kind of great old anime!! *I'm in tears!!* Kansai rules. They've got Anime Daisuki! ("We love Anime!") on TV. They play OAVs on TV! All my anime on video were dubbed from these programs.
The commercials are different too. They don't run commercials like the ramen commercial "Suki ya nen!" ("I love it!" in Kansai dialect) in Tokyo! It's been two and a half years since I moved. Just when I thought I was getting settled in, I'm realizing how great Osaka is. There are all my friends who I haven't seen in such a long time! (I saw some on my last visit, but I'm remembering all the ones I didn't have time to see!) At the time, I got together with Y (a young gentleman) and K (a young lady--I wonder if they're reading this), and we went to go see Death Becomes Her, which was fun. The problem was when we went to the video arcade to kill some time. Y walked right up to Street Fighter II and using Ryu, cleared each stage all the way to the end!! That was the first time I saw Street Fighter II all the way through, but I soon wished I hadn't.
Later, I watched K play Terminator II, and it was fun, but Street Fighter II was still playing around in my head. But even worse than that...

TO BE CONTINUED...

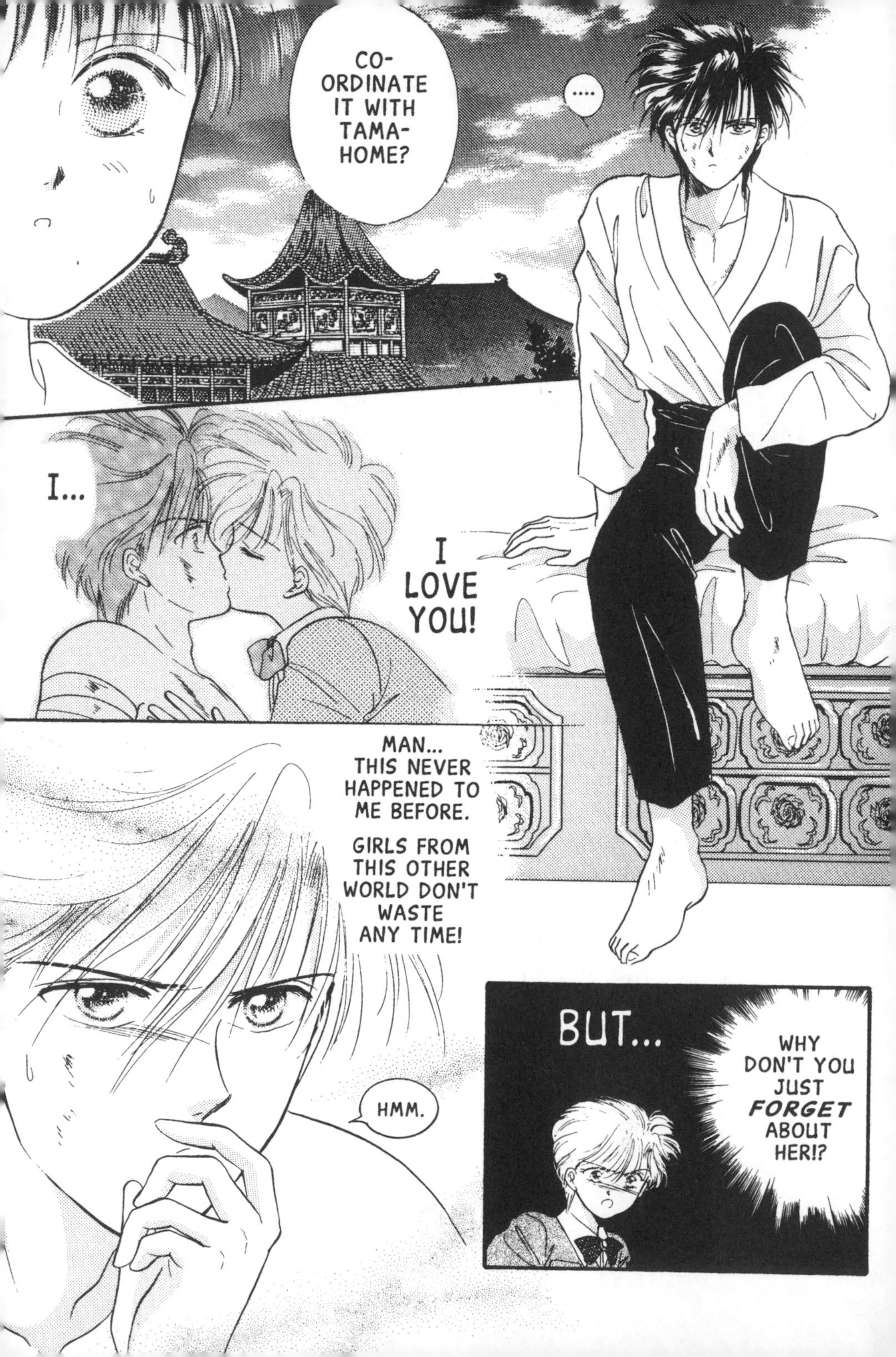
CO-ORDINATE IT WITH TAMA-HOME?
I...
I LOVE YOU!
MAN... THIS NEVER HAPPENED TO ME BEFORE.
GIRLS FROM THIS OTHER WORLD DON'T WASTE ANY TIME!
HMM.
....
BUT...
WHY DON'T YOU JUST *FORGET* ABOUT HER!?

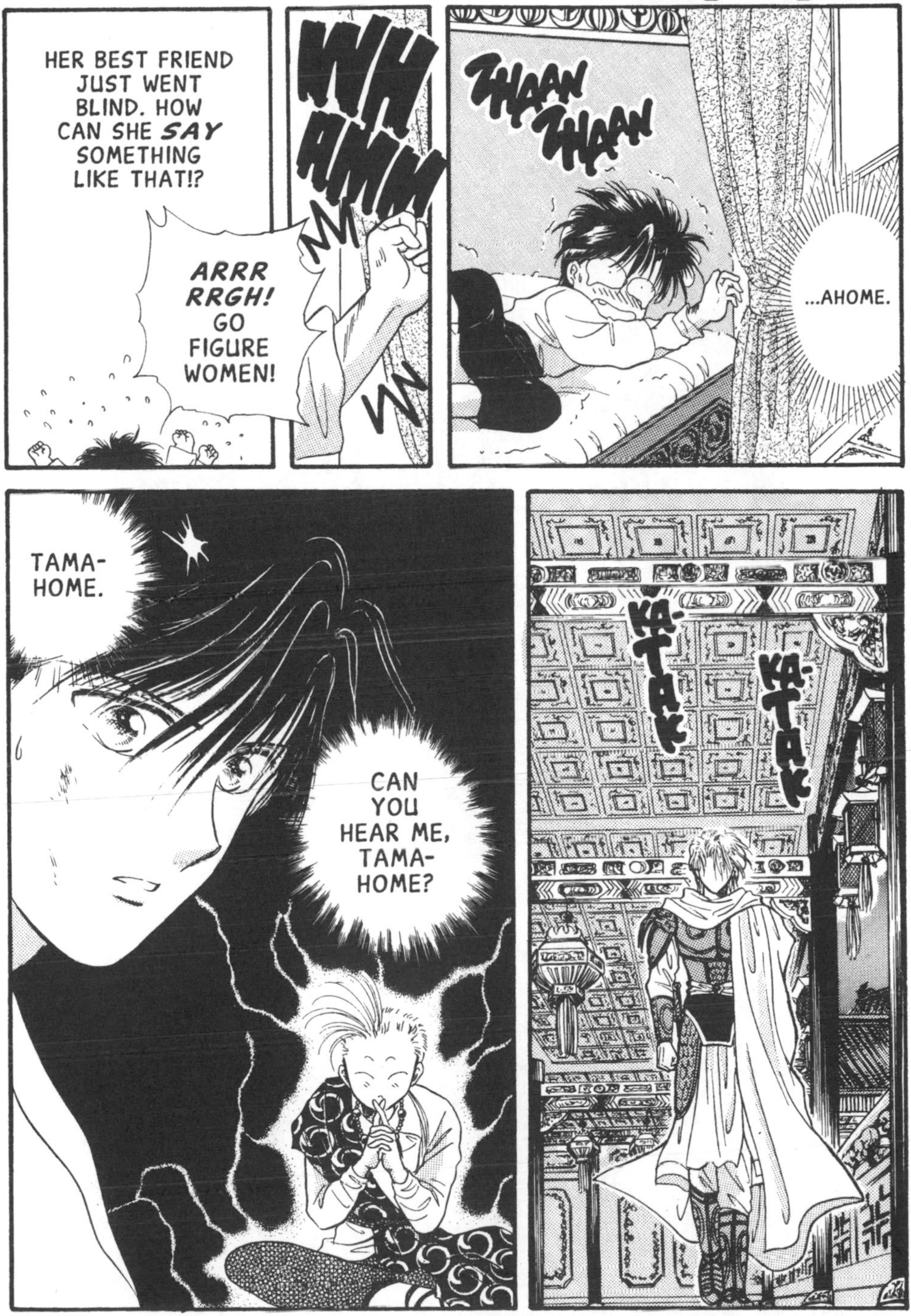
HER BEST FRIEND JUST WENT BLIND. HOW CAN SHE SAY SOMETHING LIKE THAT!?
ARRR RRGH! GO FIGURE WOMEN!
WHHAMM
WAAAN WAAAN
...AHOME.
TAMA-HOME.
CAN YOU HEAR ME, TAMA-HOME?
KA-TAK
KA-TAK

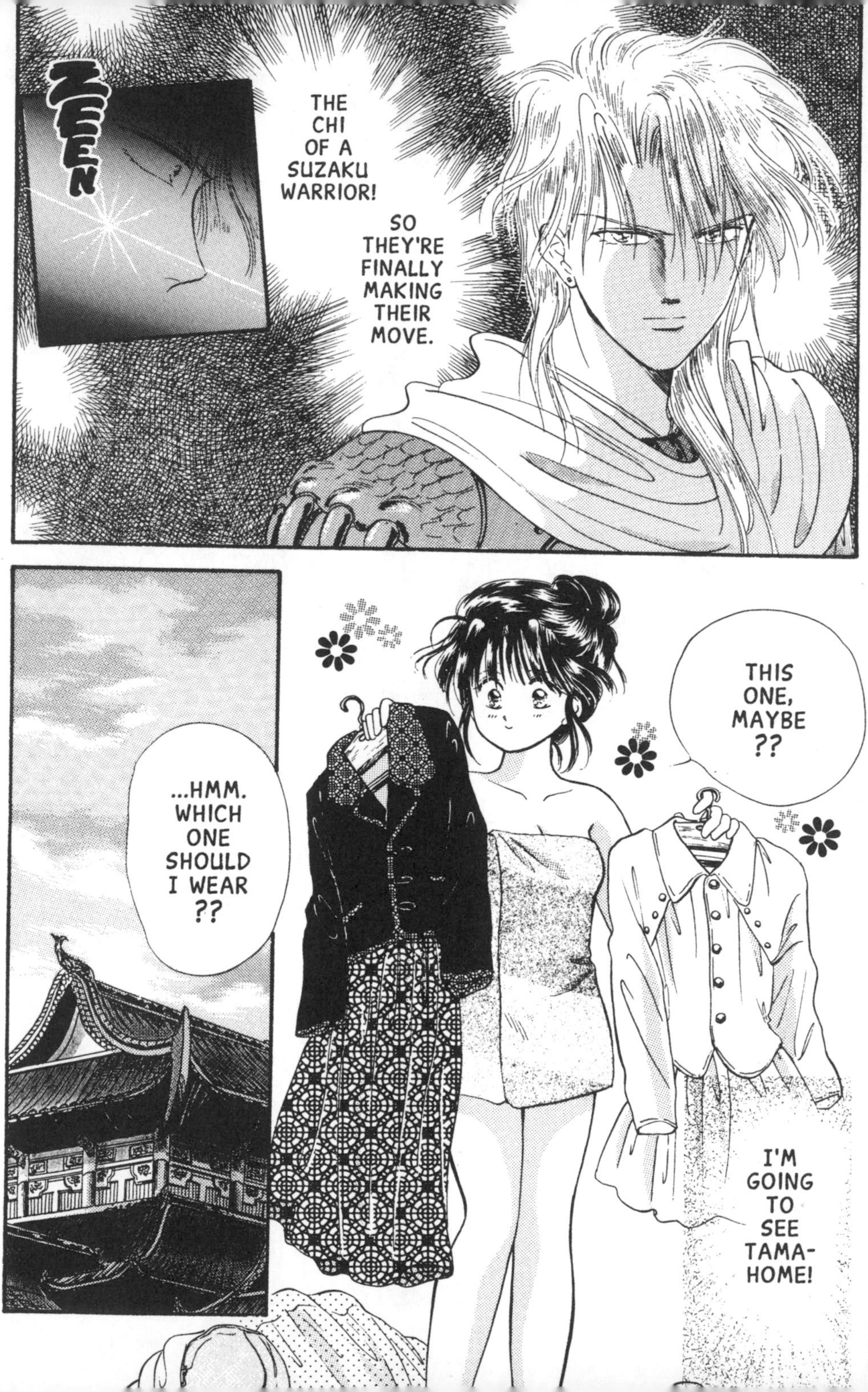
ZEEN
THE CHI OF A SUZAKU WARRIOR!
SO THEY'RE FINALLY MAKING THEIR MOVE.
...HMM. WHICH ONE SHOULD I WEAR??
THIS ONE, MAYBE??
I'M GOING TO SEE TAMA-HOME!

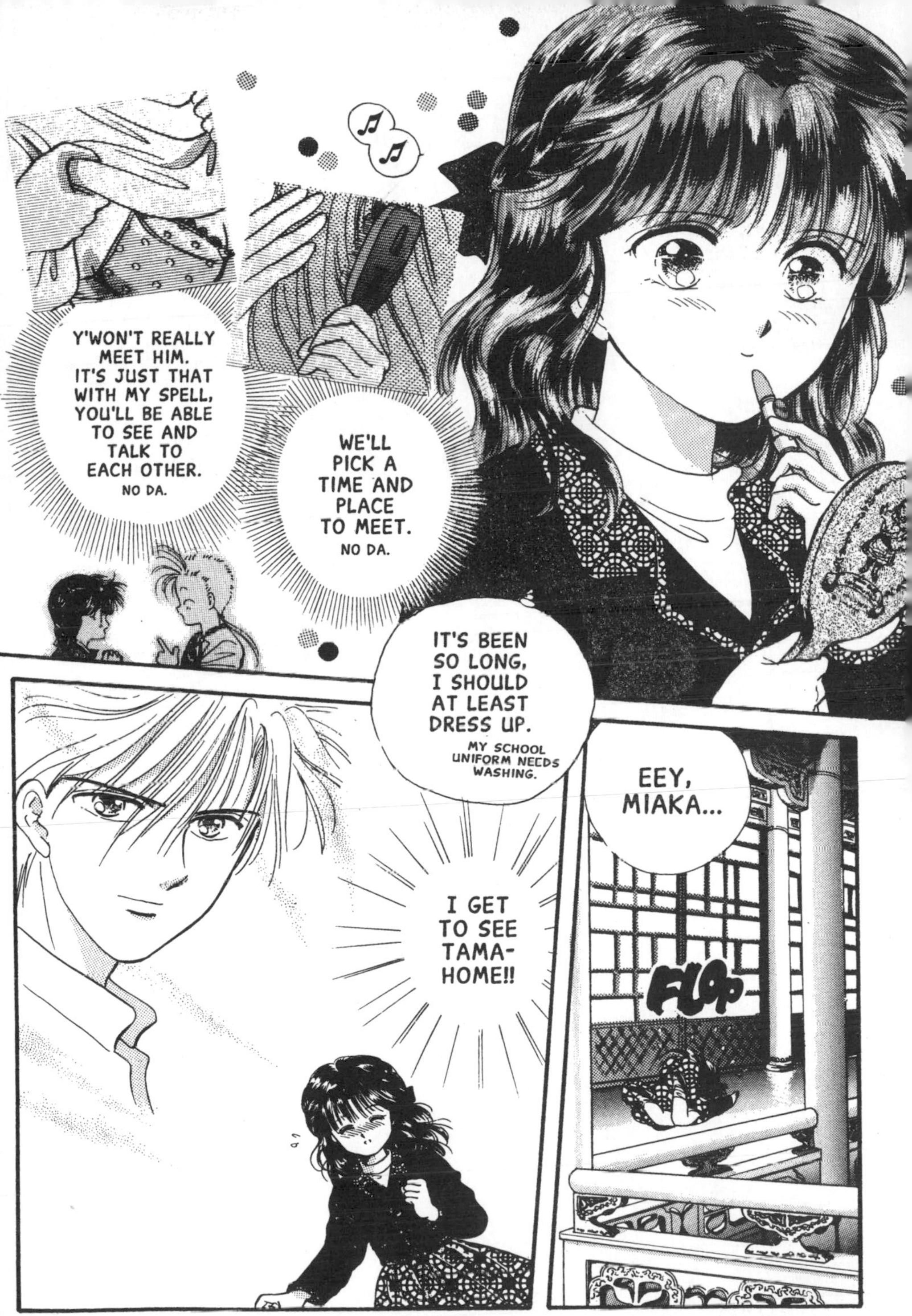
Y'WON'T REALLY MEET HIM. IT'S JUST THAT WITH MY SPELL, YOU'LL BE ABLE TO SEE AND TALK TO EACH OTHER. NO DA.
WE'LL PICK A TIME AND PLACE TO MEET. NO DA.
IT'S BEEN SO LONG, I SHOULD AT LEAST DRESS UP.
MY SCHOOL UNIFORM NEEDS WASHING.
I GET TO SEE TAMA-HOME!!
EEY, MIAKA...
FLOP

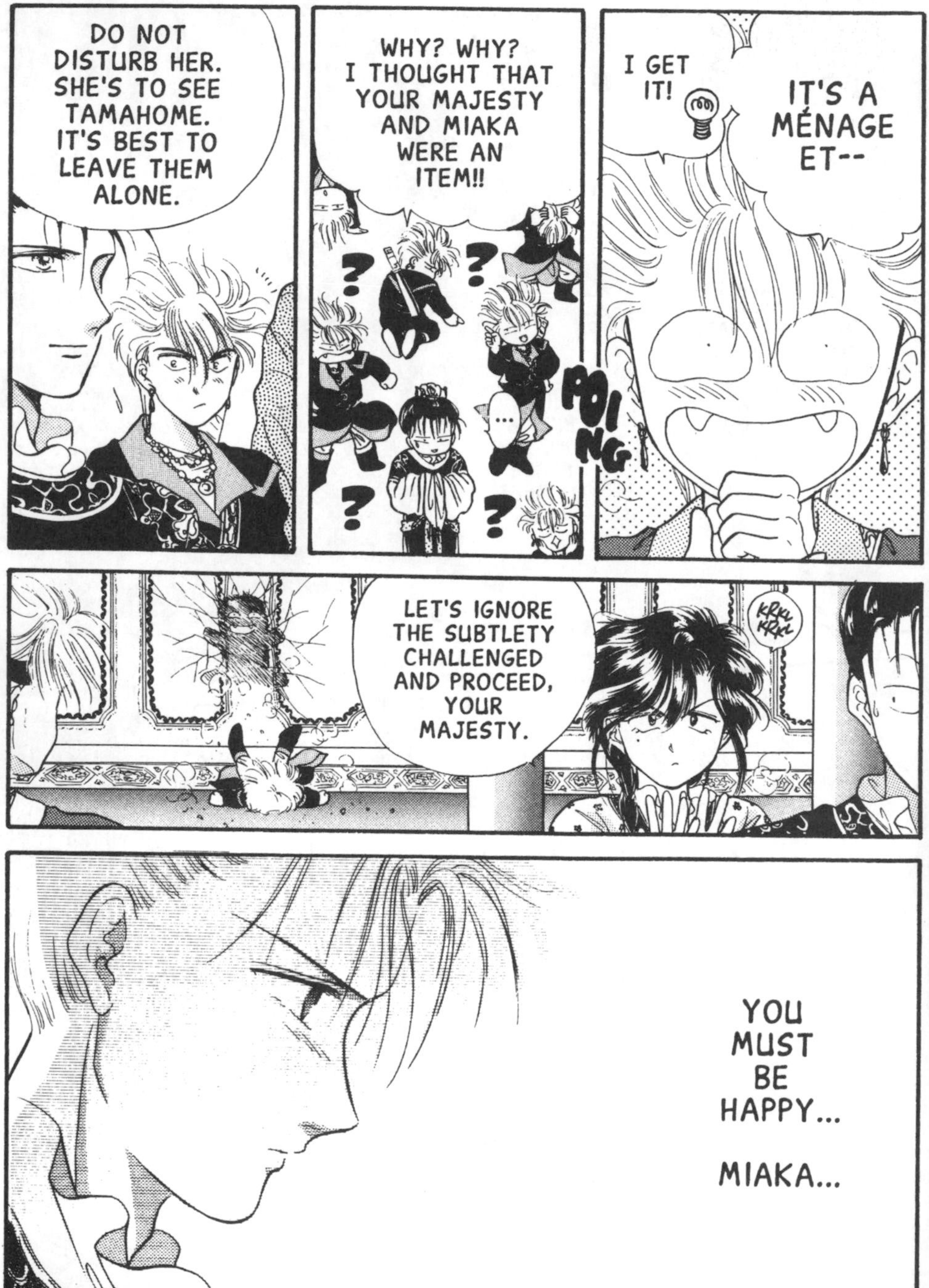
DO NOT DISTURB HER. SHE'S TO SEE TAMAHOME. IT'S BEST TO LEAVE THEM ALONE.
WHY? WHY? I THOUGHT THAT YOUR MAJESTY AND MIAKA WERE AN ITEM!!
...
POING
I GET IT!
IT'S A MÉNAGE ET--
LET'S IGNORE THE SUBTLETY CHALLENGED AND PROCEED, YOUR MAJESTY.
KRKL KRKL
YOU MUST BE HAPPY...
MIAKA...

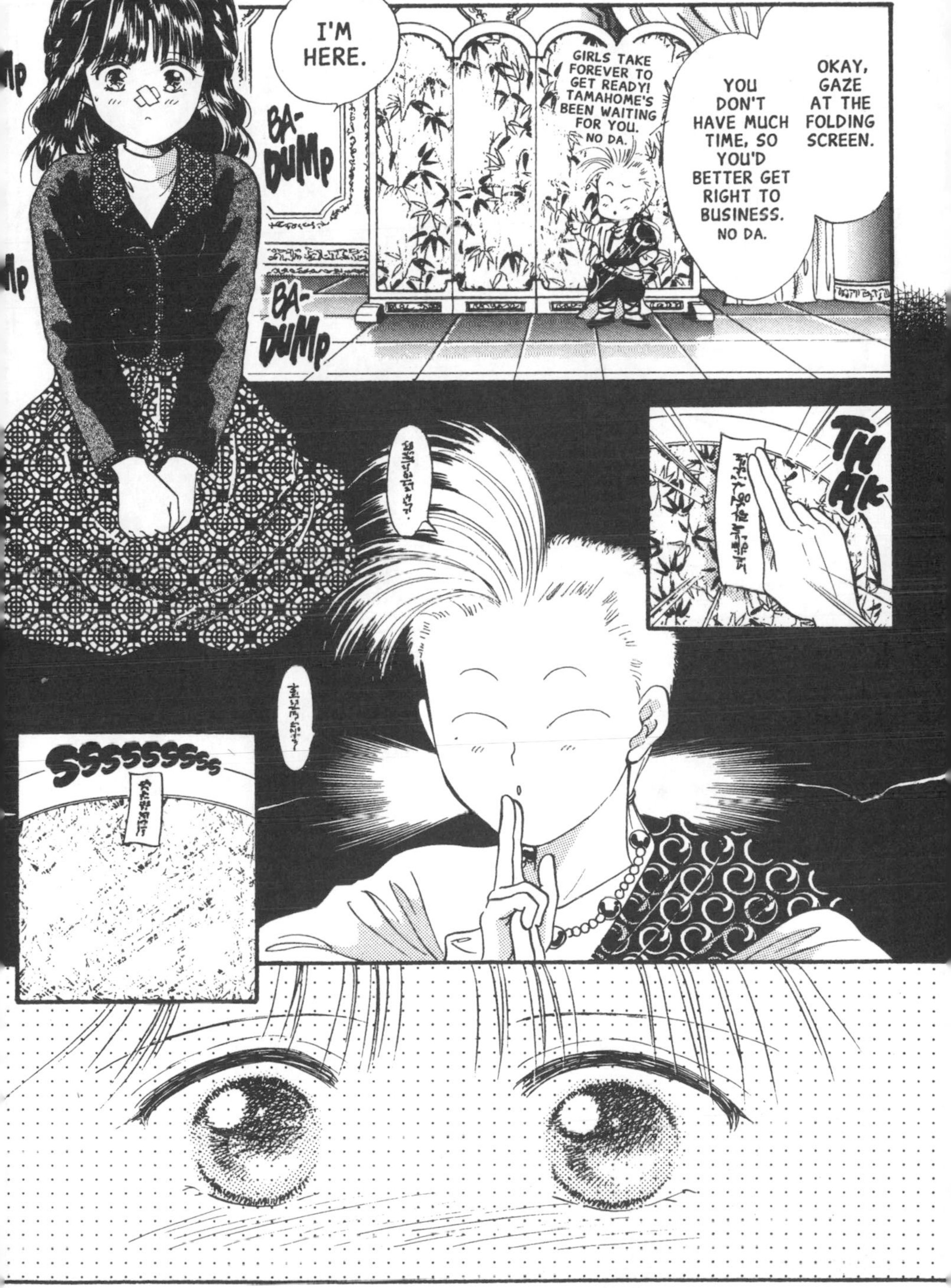
I'M HERE.
BA-DUMP
BA-DUMP
GIRLS TAKE FOREVER TO GET READY! TAMAHOME'S BEEN WAITING FOR YOU. NO DA.
YOU DON'T HAVE MUCH TIME, SO YOU'D BETTER GET RIGHT TO BUSINESS. NO DA.
OKAY, GAZE AT THE FOLDING SCREEN.
THAK
SSSSSSSSS

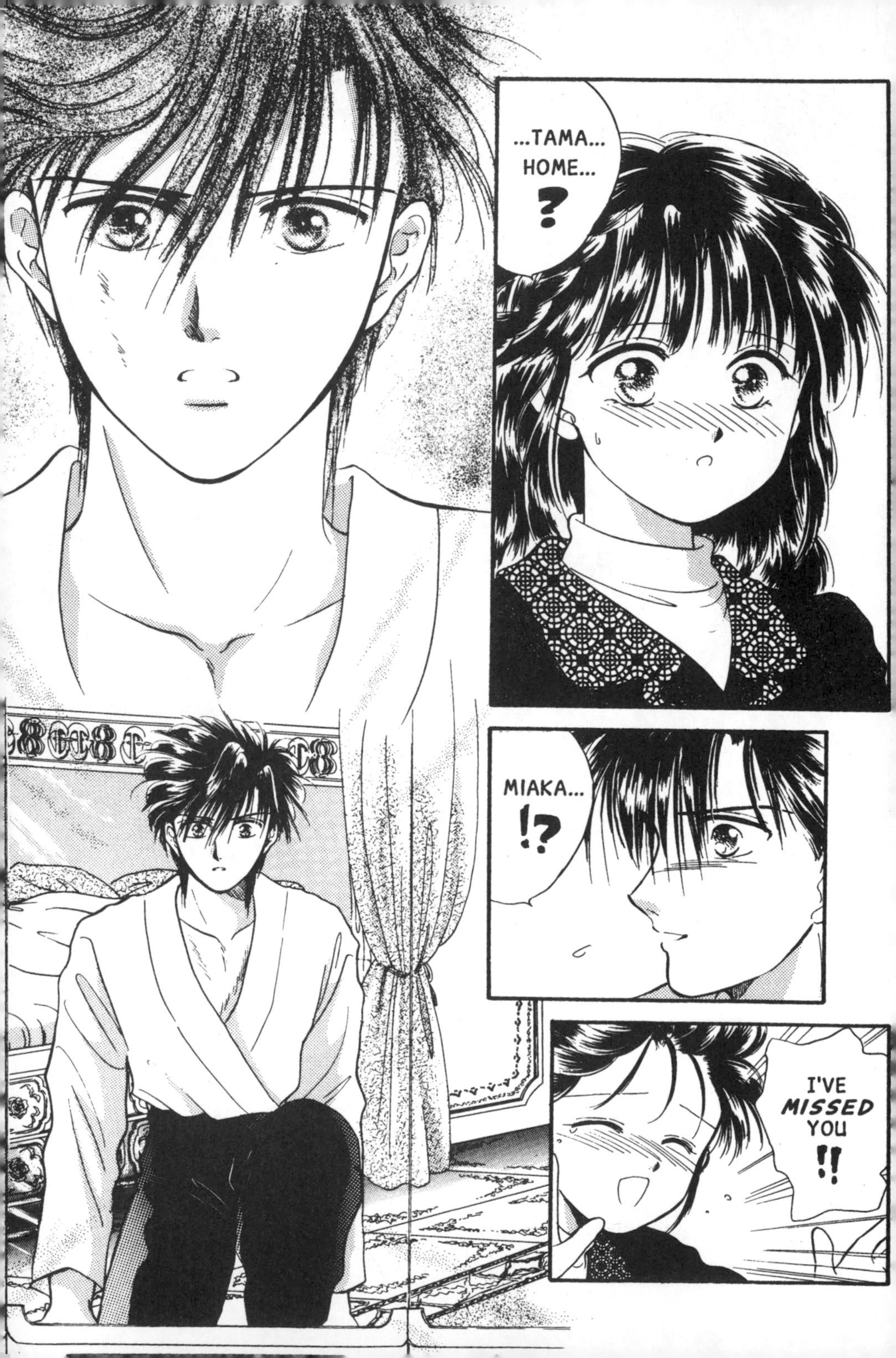
...TAMA... HOME... ?
MIAKA... !?
I'VE *MISSED* YOU !!

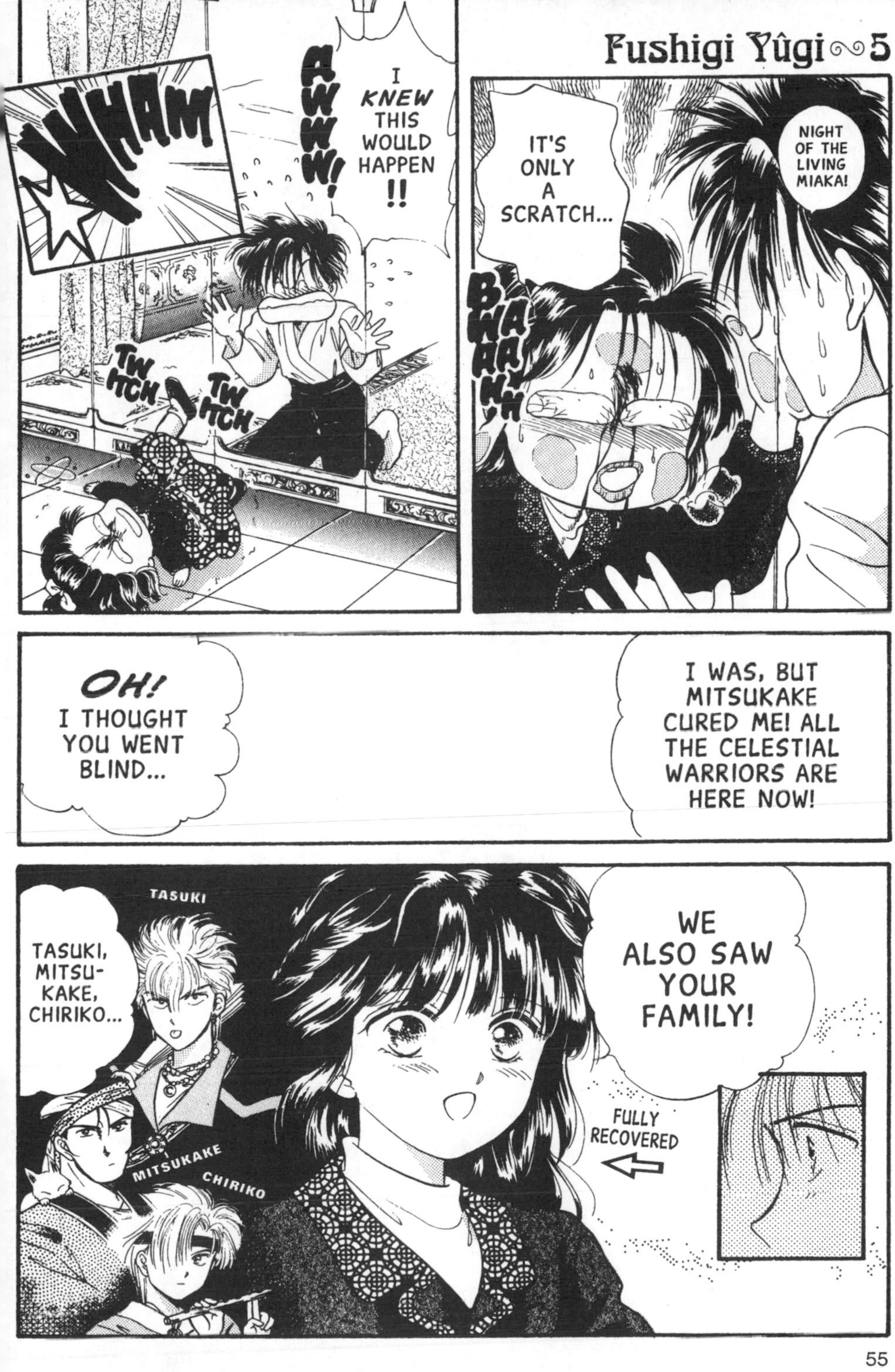
WHAM
AWWWW!
I KNEW THIS WOULD HAPPEN!!
TWITCH
TWITCH
IT'S ONLY A SCRATCH...
NIGHT OF THE LIVING MIAKA!
OH! I THOUGHT YOU WENT BLIND...
I WAS, BUT MITSUKAKE CURED ME! ALL THE CELESTIAL WARRIORS ARE HERE NOW!
TASUKI, MITSUKAKE, CHIRIKO...
TASUKI
MITSUKAKE
CHIRIKO
WE ALSO SAW YOUR FAMILY!
FULLY RECOVERED

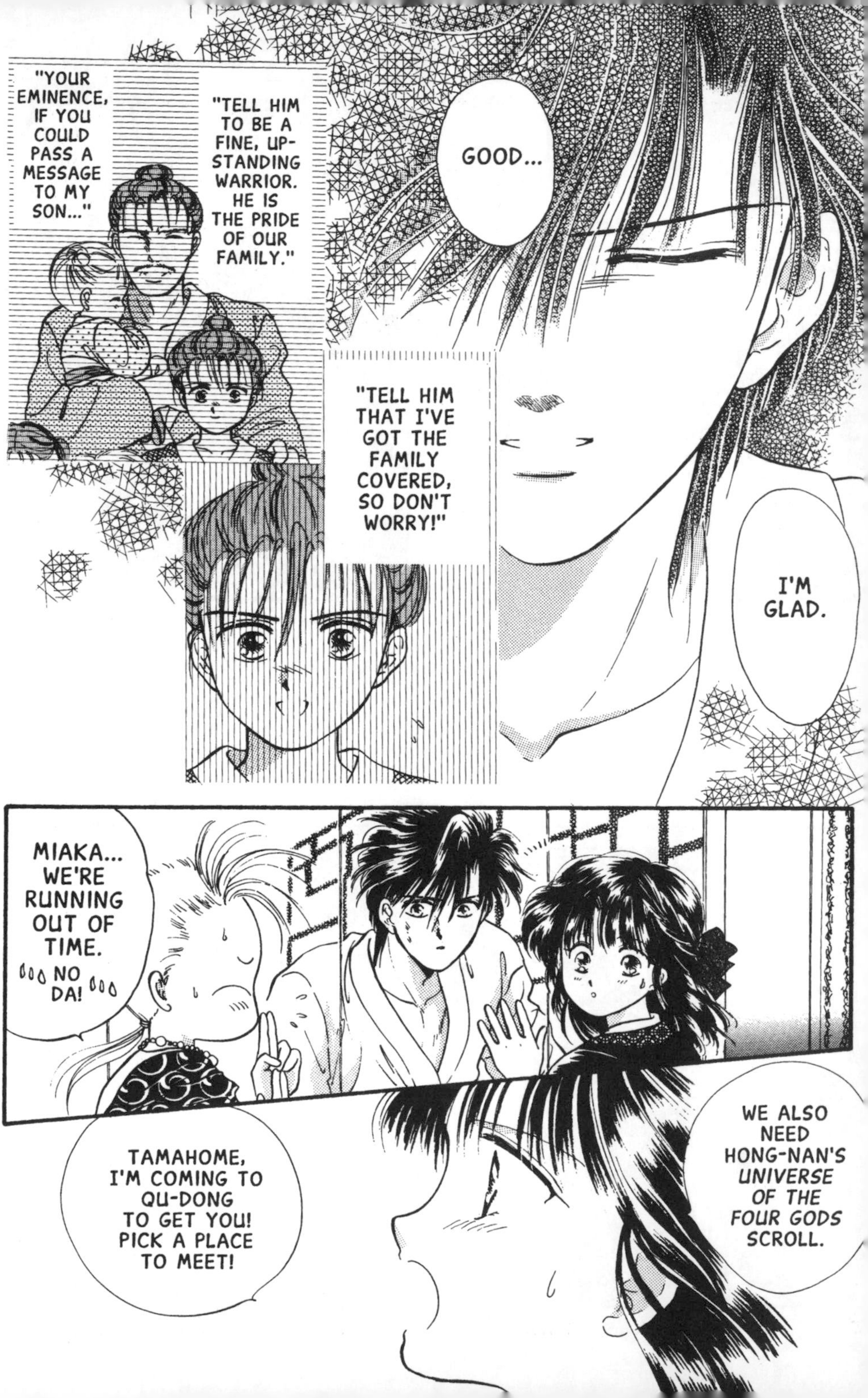
"YOUR EMINENCE, IF YOU COULD PASS A MESSAGE TO MY SON..."
"TELL HIM TO BE A FINE, UP-STANDING WARRIOR. HE IS THE PRIDE OF OUR FAMILY."
GOOD...
"TELL HIM THAT I'VE GOT THE FAMILY COVERED, SO DON'T WORRY!"
I'M GLAD.
MIAKA... WE'RE RUNNING OUT OF TIME. NO DA!
TAMAHOME, I'M COMING TO QU-DONG TO GET YOU! PICK A PLACE TO MEET!
WE ALSO NEED HONG-NAN'S UNIVERSE OF THE FOUR GODS SCROLL.

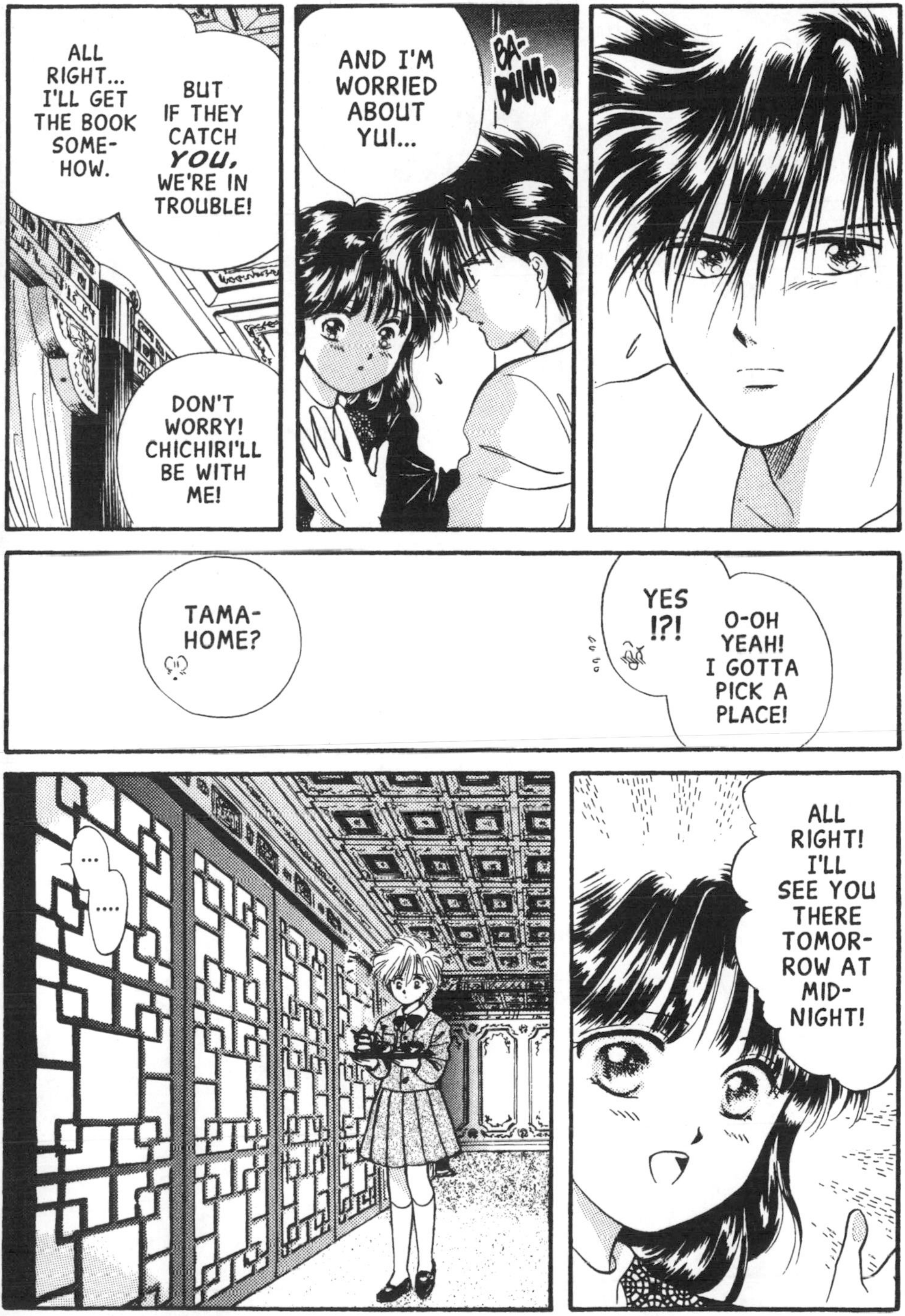
ALL RIGHT... I'LL GET THE BOOK SOME-HOW.
BUT IF THEY CATCH YOU, WE'RE IN TROUBLE!
DON'T WORRY! CHICHIRI'LL BE WITH ME!
AND I'M WORRIED ABOUT YUI...
BA-DUMP
TAMA-HOME?
YES !?!
O-OH YEAH! I GOTTA PICK A PLACE!
...
.....
ALL RIGHT! I'LL SEE YOU THERE TOMOR-ROW AT MID-NIGHT!

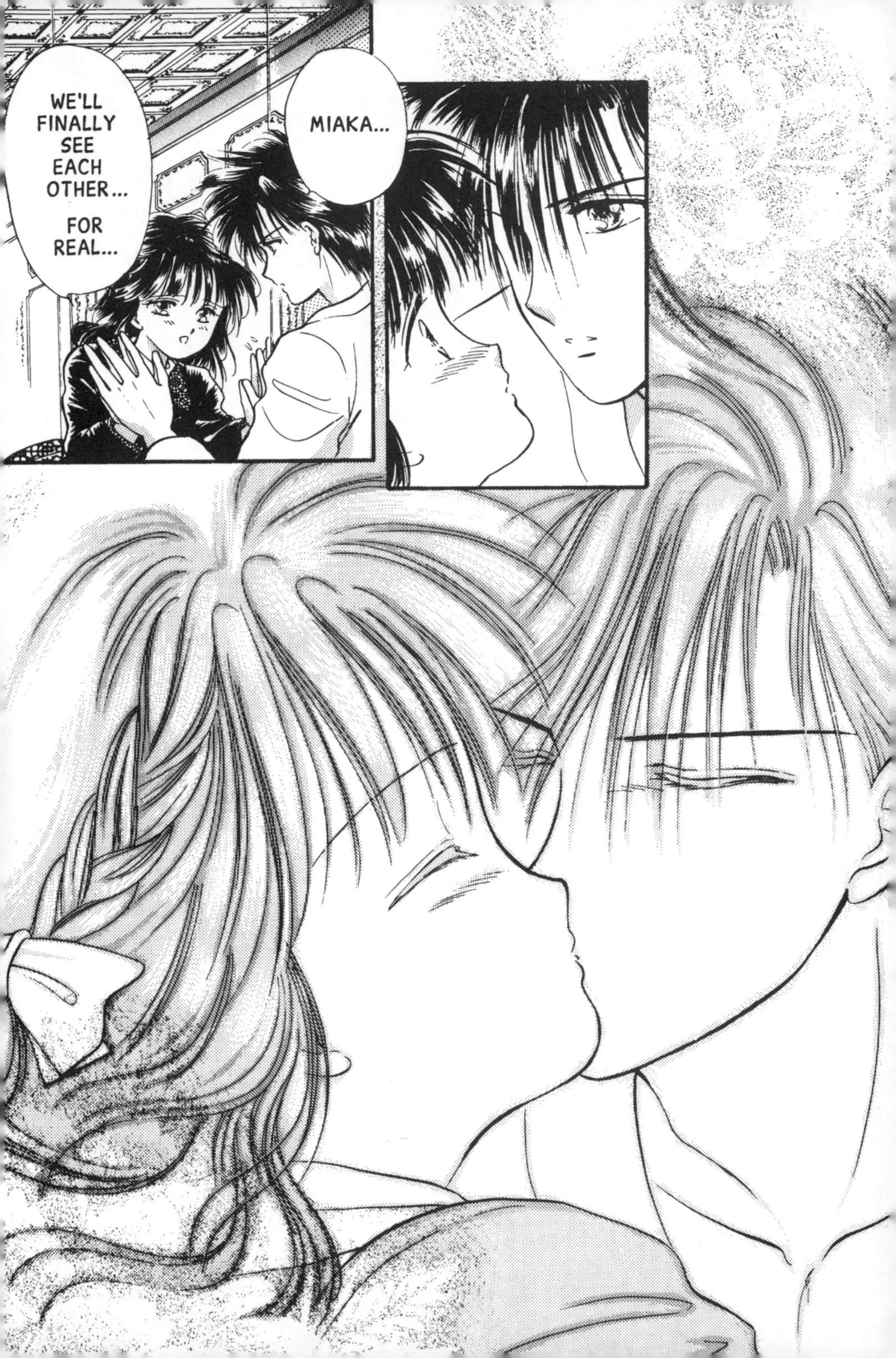
WE'LL FINALLY SEE EACH OTHER... FOR REAL...
MIAKA...

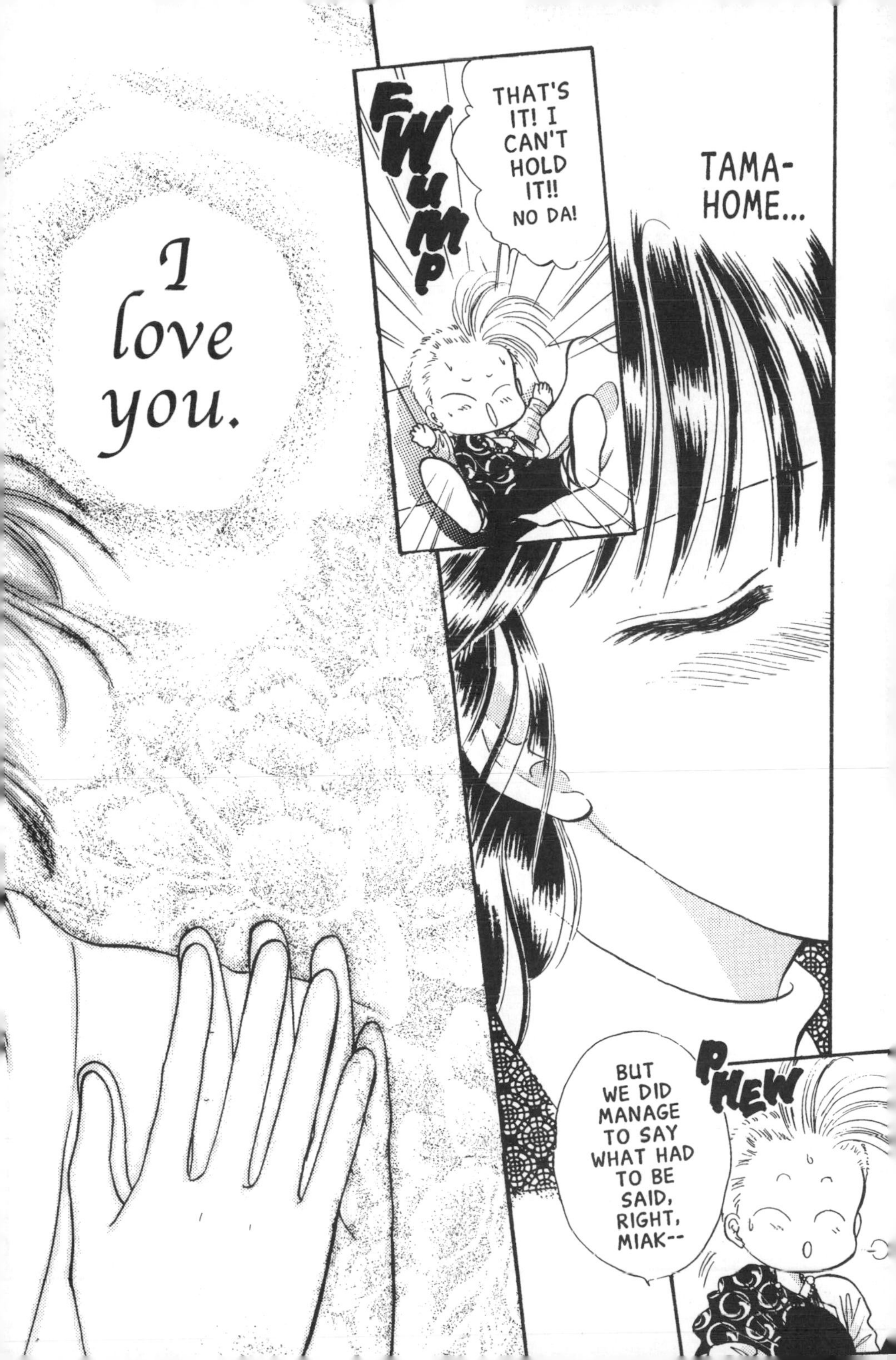
I love you.
FWUMP
THAT'S IT! I CAN'T HOLD IT!! NO DA!
TAMA-HOME...
PHEW
BUT WE DID MANAGE TO SAY WHAT HAD TO BE SAID, RIGHT, MIAK--

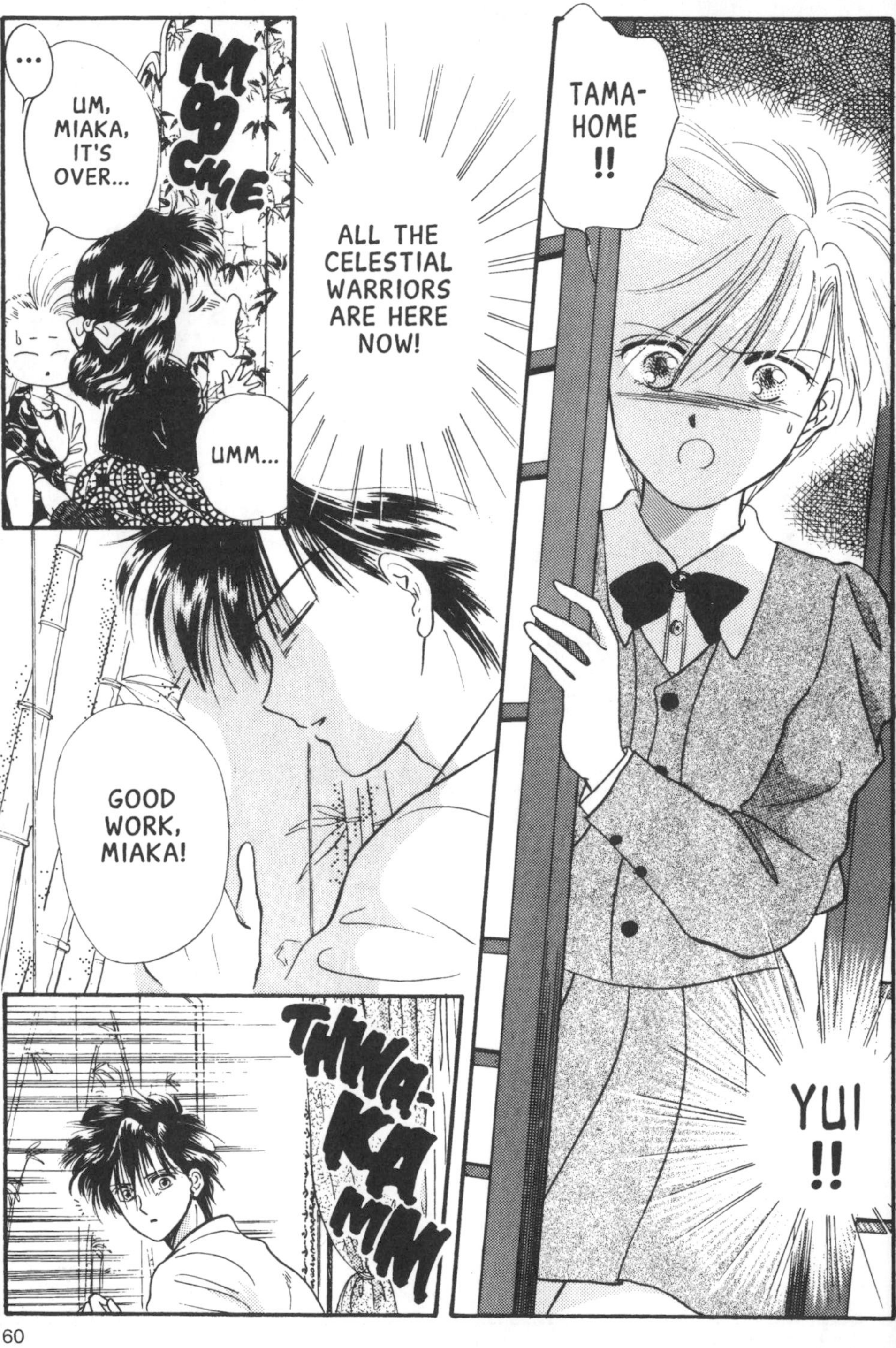

...
UM, MIAKA, IT'S OVER...
MOGGCHIE
UMM...
ALL THE CELESTIAL WARRIORS ARE HERE NOW!
GOOD WORK, MIAKA!
THWA-KA-MM
TAMA-HOME !!
YUI !!

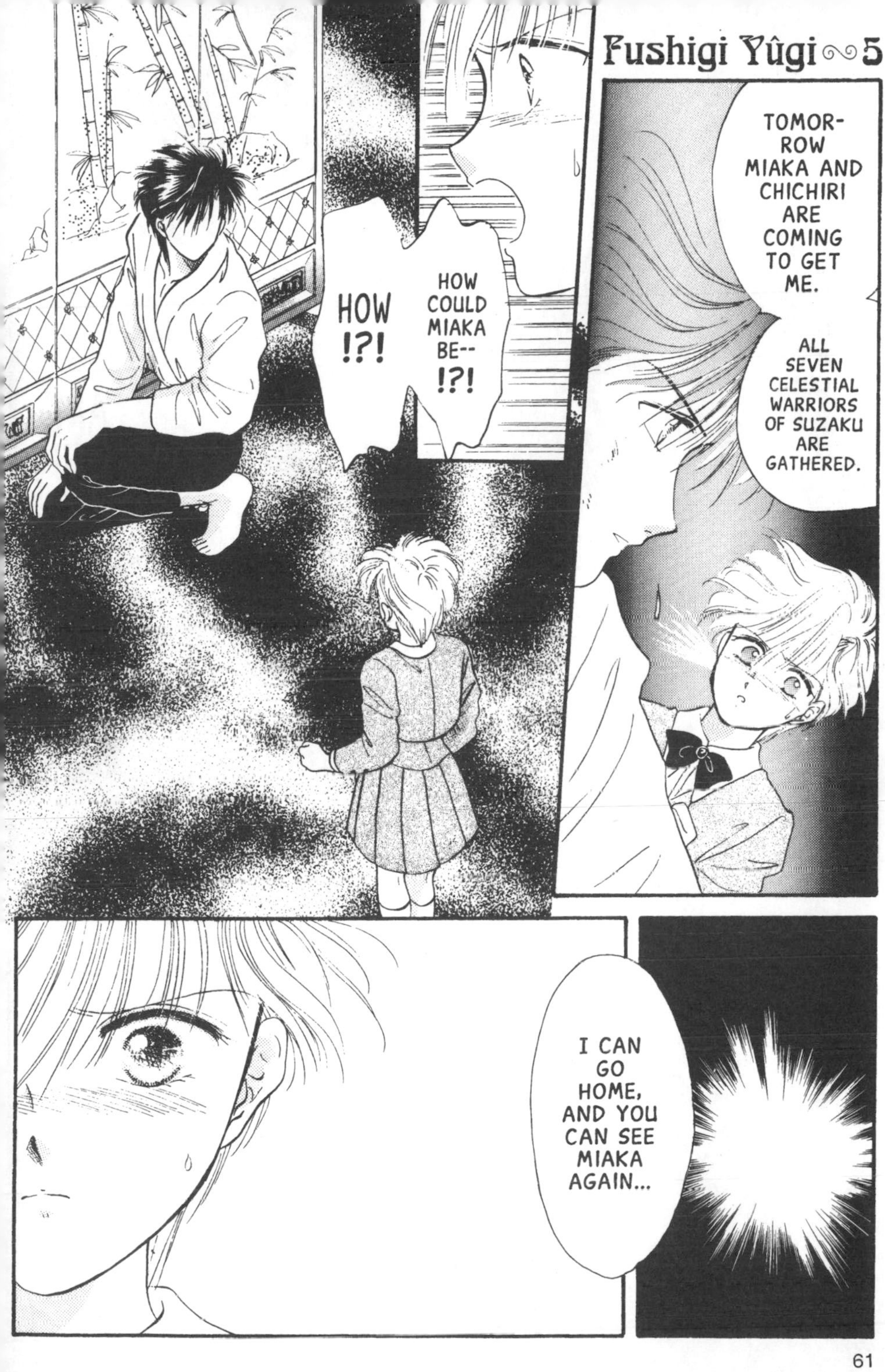
HOW !?!
HOW COULD MIAKA BE-- !?!
TOMORROW MIAKA AND CHICHIRI ARE COMING TO GET ME.
ALL SEVEN CELESTIAL WARRIORS OF SUZAKU ARE GATHERED.
I CAN GO HOME, AND YOU CAN SEE MIAKA AGAIN...

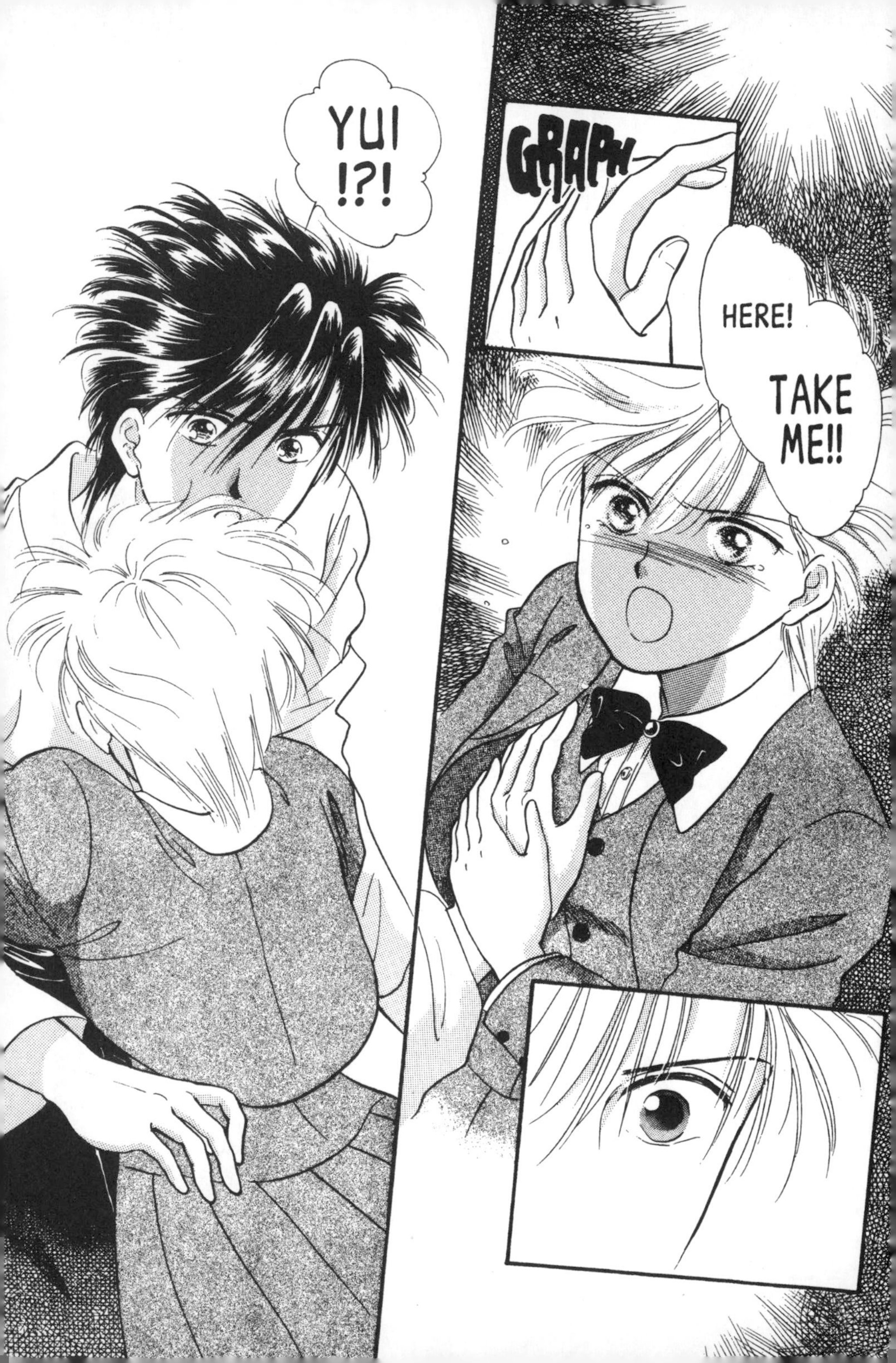
YUI !?!
GRAPH
HERE!
TAKE ME!!

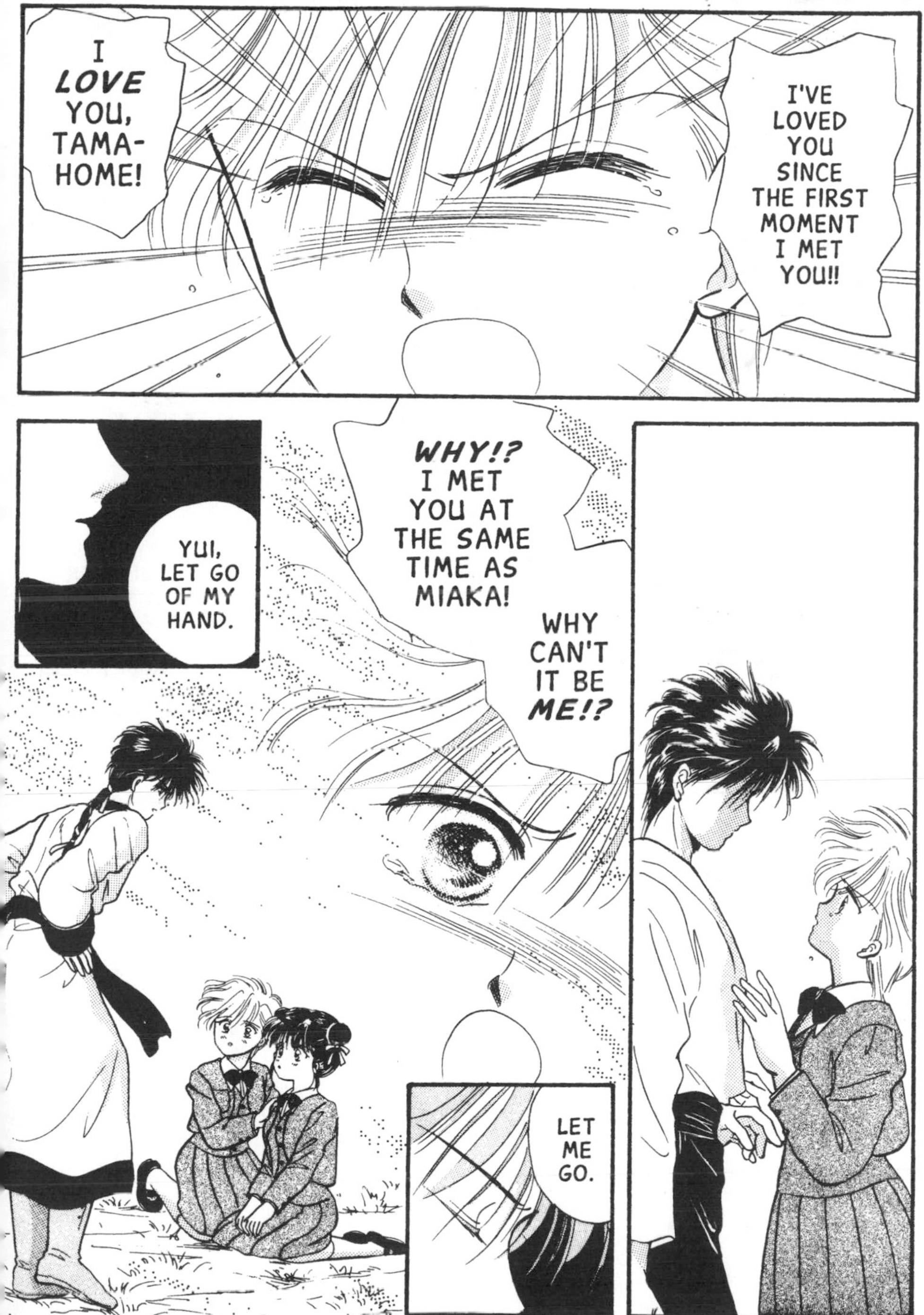
I LOVE YOU, TAMAHOME!
I'VE LOVED YOU SINCE THE FIRST MOMENT I MET YOU!!
YUI, LET GO OF MY HAND.
WHY!? I MET YOU AT THE SAME TIME AS MIAKA!
WHY CAN'T IT BE ME!?
LET ME GO.

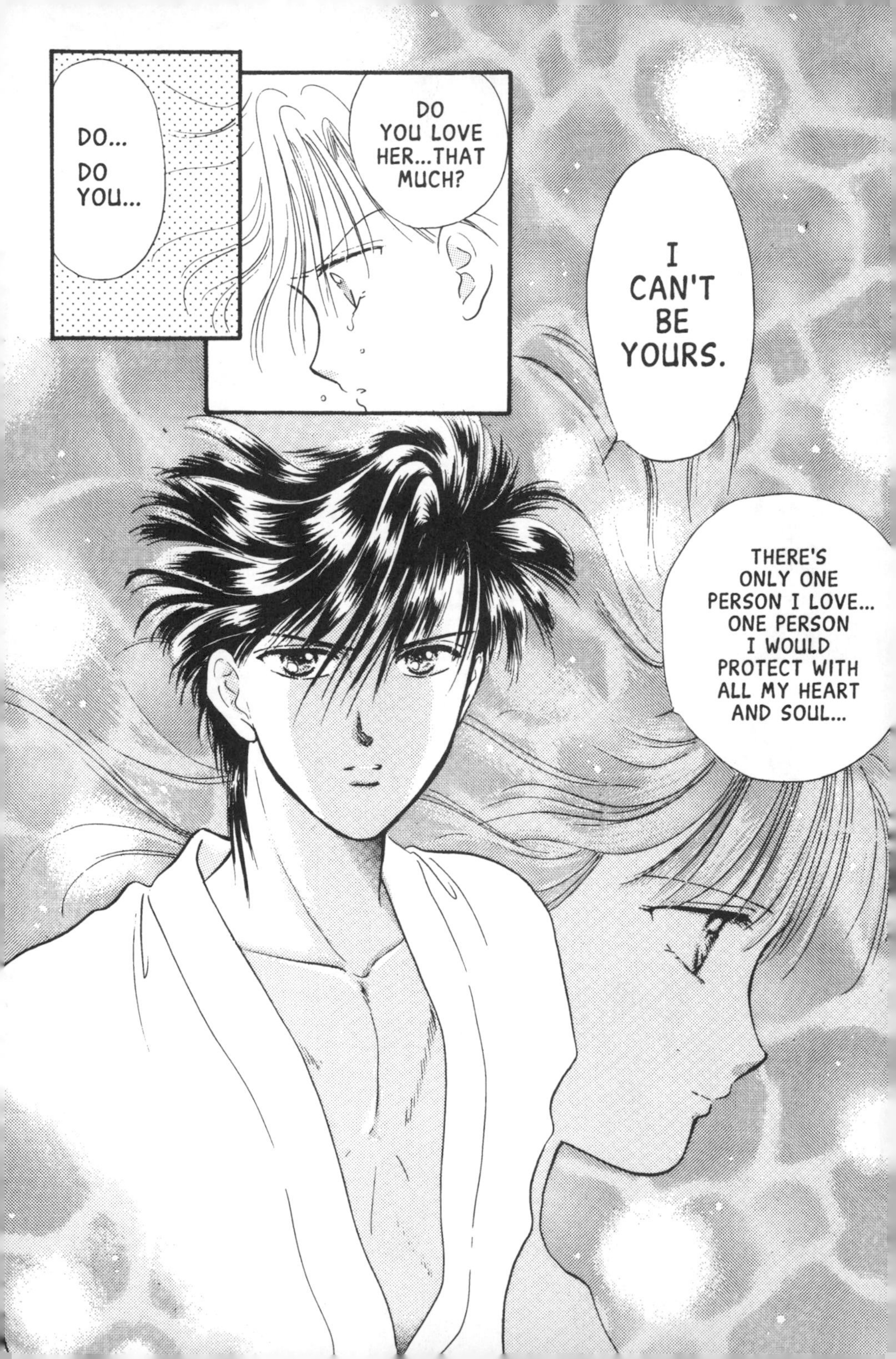
DO... DO YOU...
DO YOU LOVE HER...THAT MUCH?
I CAN'T BE YOURS.
THERE'S ONLY ONE PERSON I LOVE... ONE PERSON I WOULD PROTECT WITH ALL MY HEART AND SOUL...

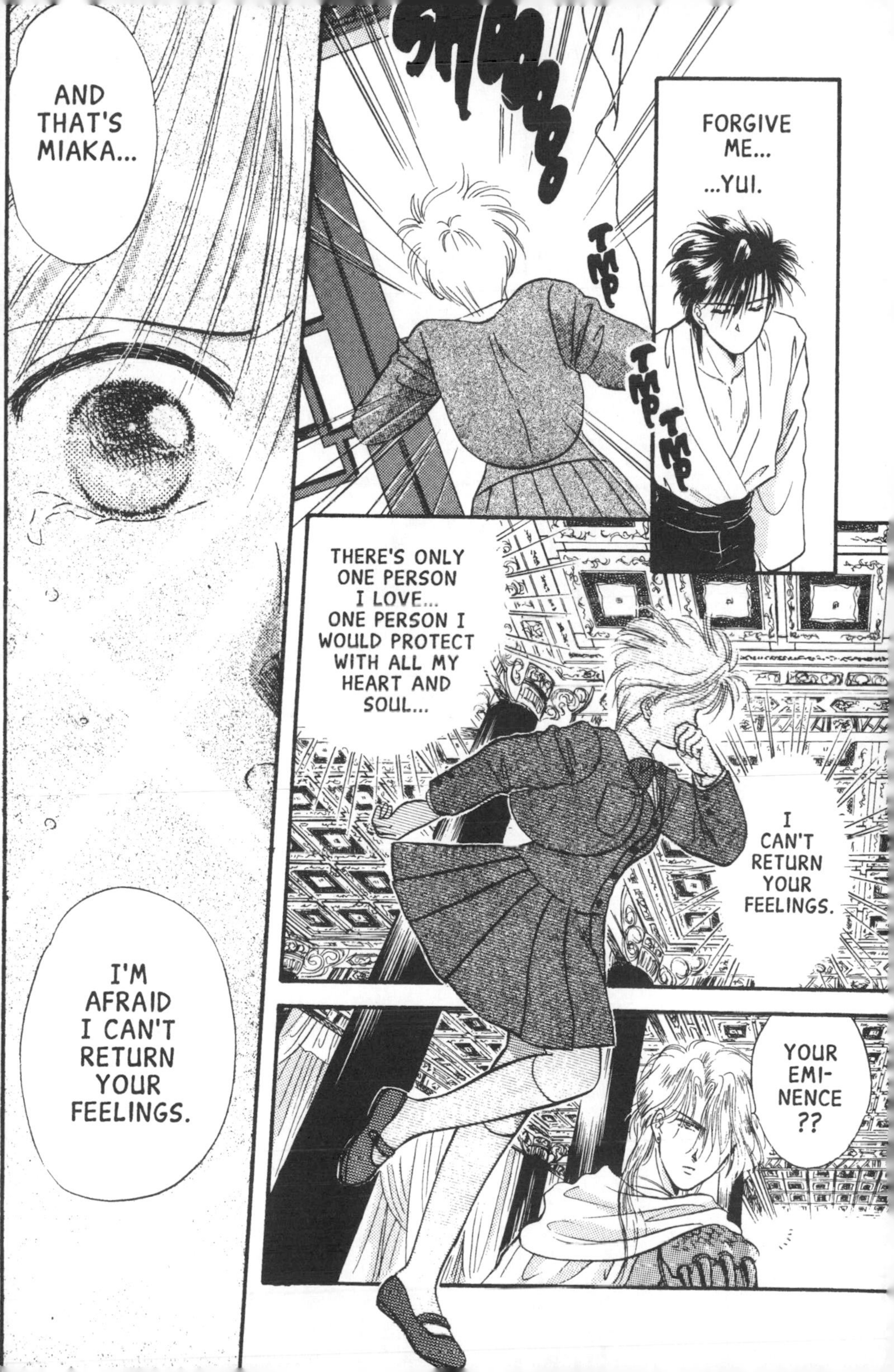
AND THAT'S MIAKA...
I'M AFRAID I CAN'T RETURN YOUR FEELINGS.
FORGIVE ME... ...YUI.
TMP
TMP
TMP
TMP
THERE'S ONLY ONE PERSON I LOVE... ONE PERSON I WOULD PROTECT WITH ALL MY HEART AND SOUL...
I CAN'T RETURN YOUR FEELINGS.
YOUR EMI-NENCE ??

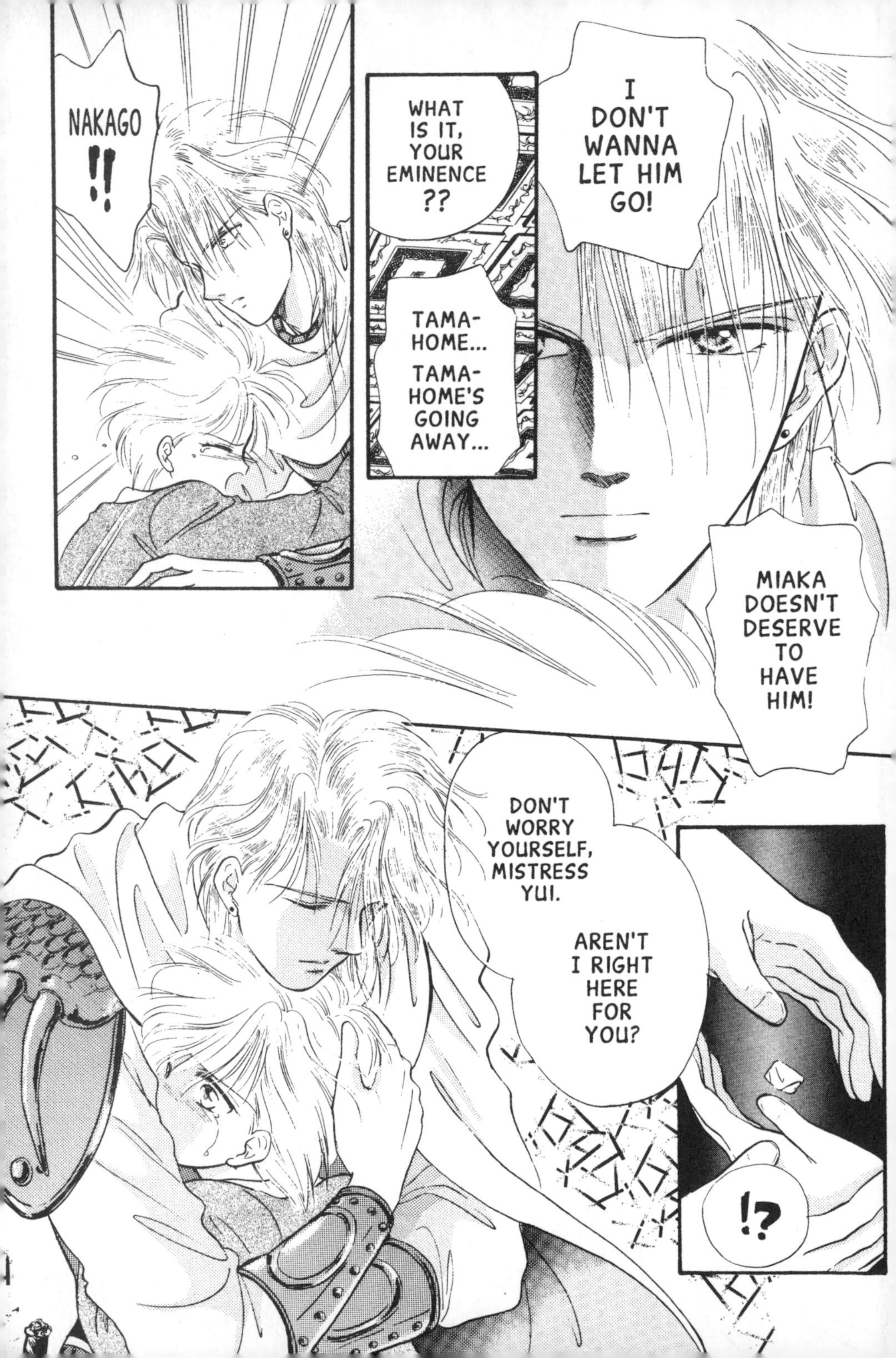
NAKAGO !!
WHAT IS IT, YOUR EMINENCE ??
TAMA-HOME... TAMA-HOME'S GOING AWAY...
I DON'T WANNA LET HIM GO!
MIAKA DOESN'T DESERVE TO HAVE HIM!
DON'T WORRY YOURSELF, MISTRESS YUI.
AREN'T I RIGHT HERE FOR YOU?
!?

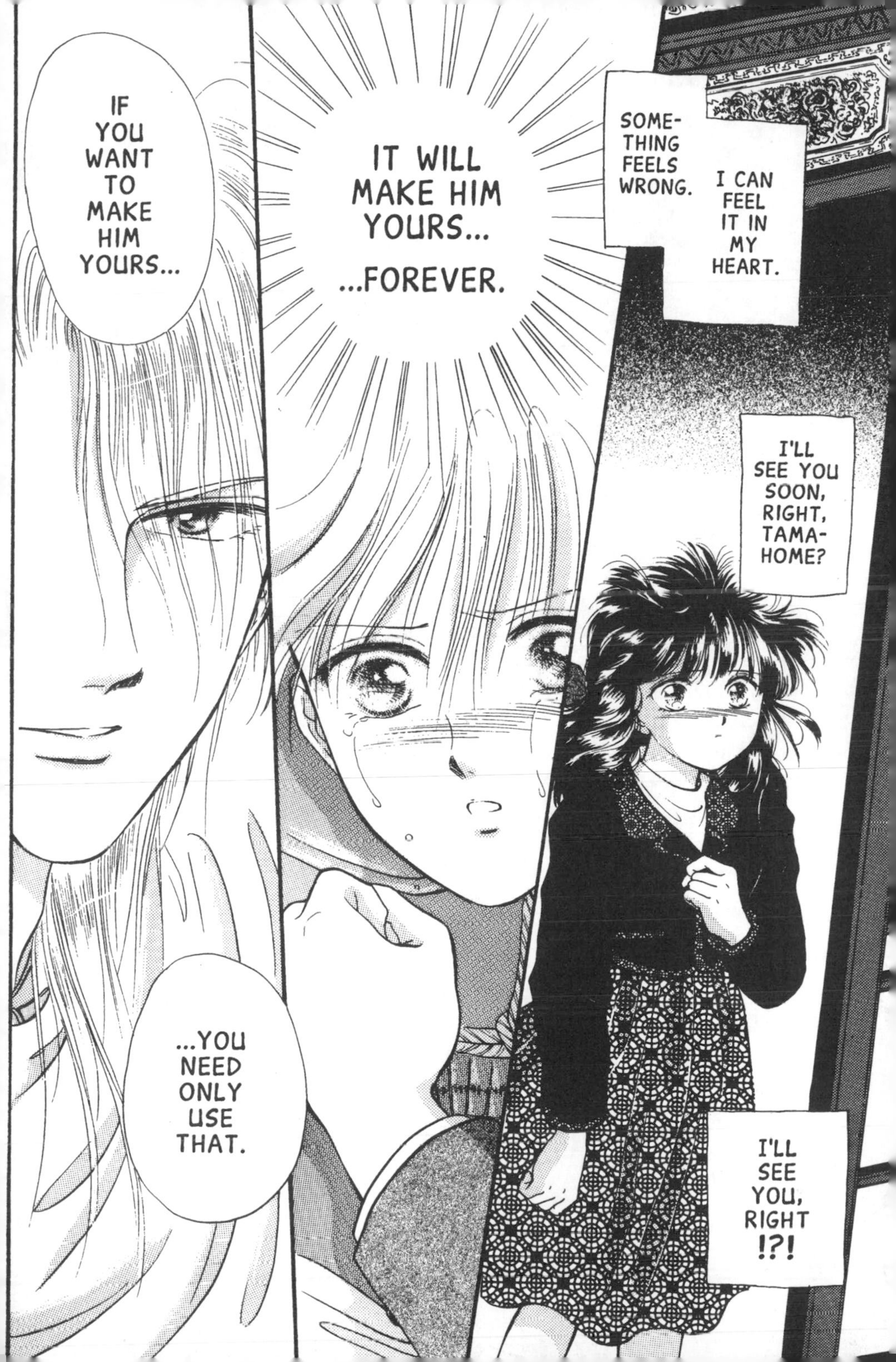
IF YOU WANT TO MAKE HIM YOURS...
...YOU NEED ONLY USE THAT.
IT WILL MAKE HIM YOURS...
...FOREVER.
SOME-THING FEELS WRONG.
I CAN FEEL IT IN MY HEART.
I'LL SEE YOU SOON, RIGHT, TAMA-HOME?
I'LL SEE YOU, RIGHT !?!

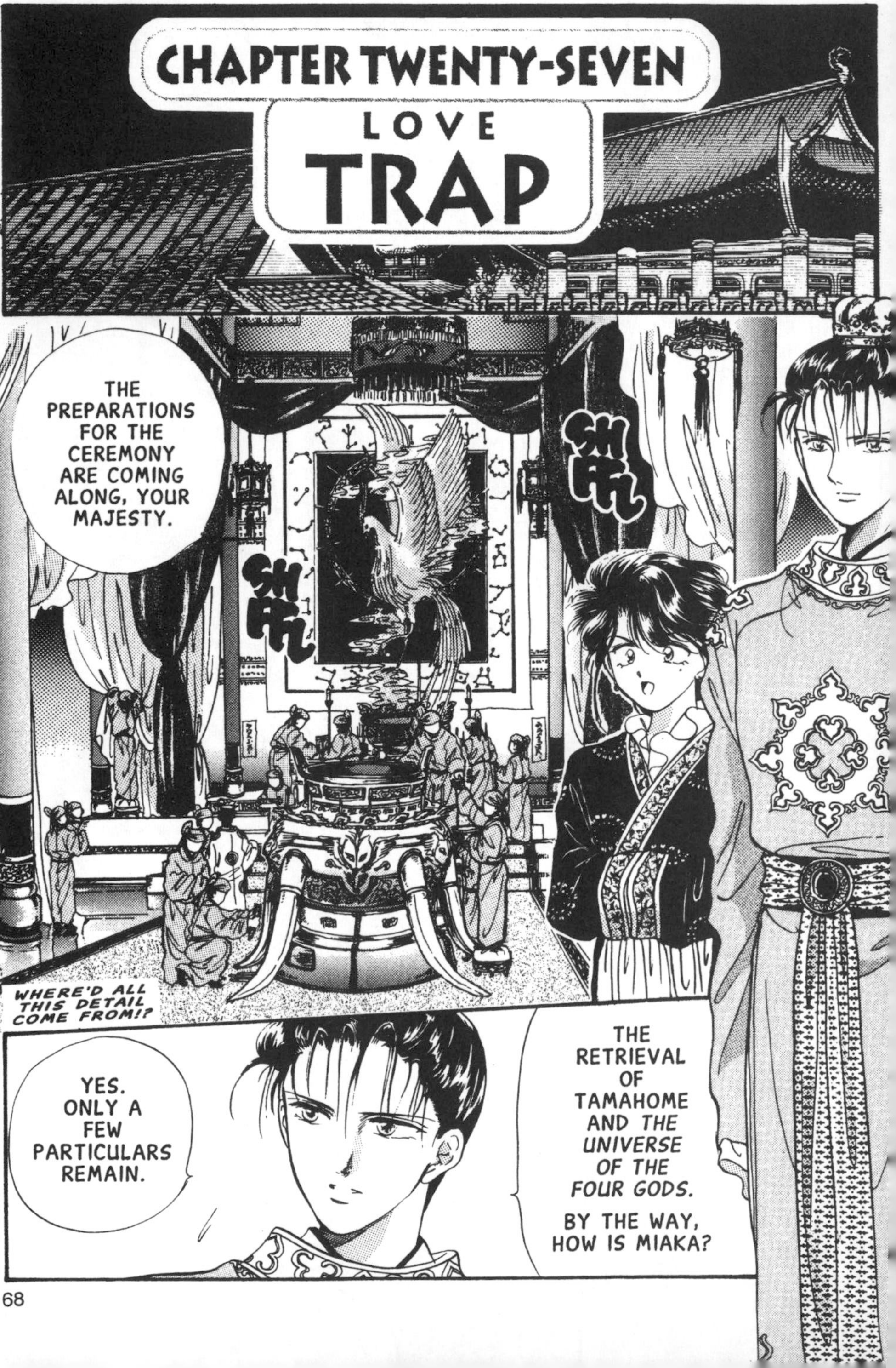
CHAPTER TWENTY-SEVEN
LOVE TRAP
THE PREPARATIONS FOR THE CEREMONY ARE COMING ALONG, YOUR MAJESTY.
SHFFL
SHFFL
WHERE'D ALL THIS DETAIL COME FROM!?
YES. ONLY A FEW PARTICULARS REMAIN.
THE RETRIEVAL OF TAMAHOME AND *THE UNIVERSE OF THE FOUR GODS.*
BY THE WAY, HOW IS MIAKA?

SKR CH SKR CH

PYTHAGOREAN THEOREM

1. The square of the hypotenuse, c, of a right triangle is equal to the sum of the squares of the adjacent sides, a and b.

2. CALCULATING THE HYPOTENUSE OF A RIGHT TRIANGLE. ← MEMORIZE!

The lengths of a right triangle.

b =

B

"GIVEN A RIGHT TRIANGLE WITH SIDES OF 4 CM, 5 CM, AND 6 CM, IF THE 6 CM SIDE IS THE BASE, CALCULATE THE HEIGHT OF THE TRIANGLE?" HUH??

SO I CAN ENTER ENEMY TERRITORY, BUT I CAN'T EVEN SOLVE THE PYTHAGOREAN THEOREM!?

$= \frac{5}{4}\sqrt{7}$ (cm)

$AH = h$
$BH = x$

$x^2 + h^2 = 4^2 \cdots ①$
$(6-x)^2 + h^2 = 5^2 \cdots ②$

$① - ② \quad -6^2 + 12x = 4^2 - 5^2$
$\therefore x = \frac{9}{4}$

$① \cdots h = \sqrt{4^2 - \left(\frac{9}{4}\right)^2}$

$\frac{5}{4}\sqrt{7}$

NOW IF "AH" EQUALS "H," THEN...

X2 PLUS H2 EQUALS...

GASP

WOW! MY ANSWER'S *COR-RECT!!*

I DIDN'T EVEN KNOW WHAT I WAS DOING!!

MAYBE I'M A GENIUS!!

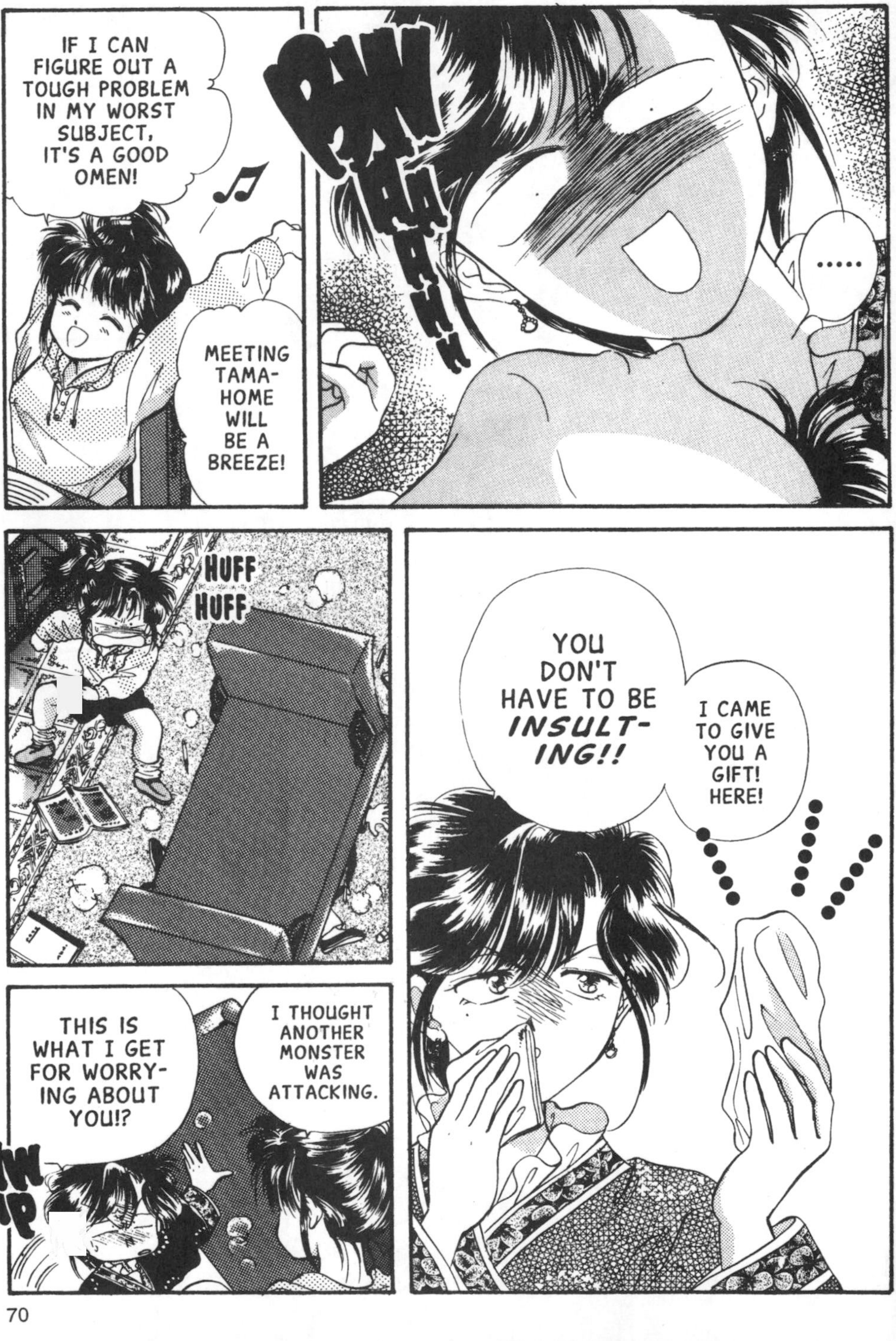
IF I CAN FIGURE OUT A TOUGH PROBLEM IN MY WORST SUBJECT, IT'S A GOOD OMEN!
♫
MEETING TAMA-HOME WILL BE A BREEZE!
.....
HUFF HUFF
THIS IS WHAT I GET FOR WORRY-ING ABOUT YOU!?
I THOUGHT ANOTHER MONSTER WAS ATTACKING.
WHIP
YOU DON'T HAVE TO BE *INSULT-ING!!*
I CAME TO GIVE YOU A GIFT! HERE!

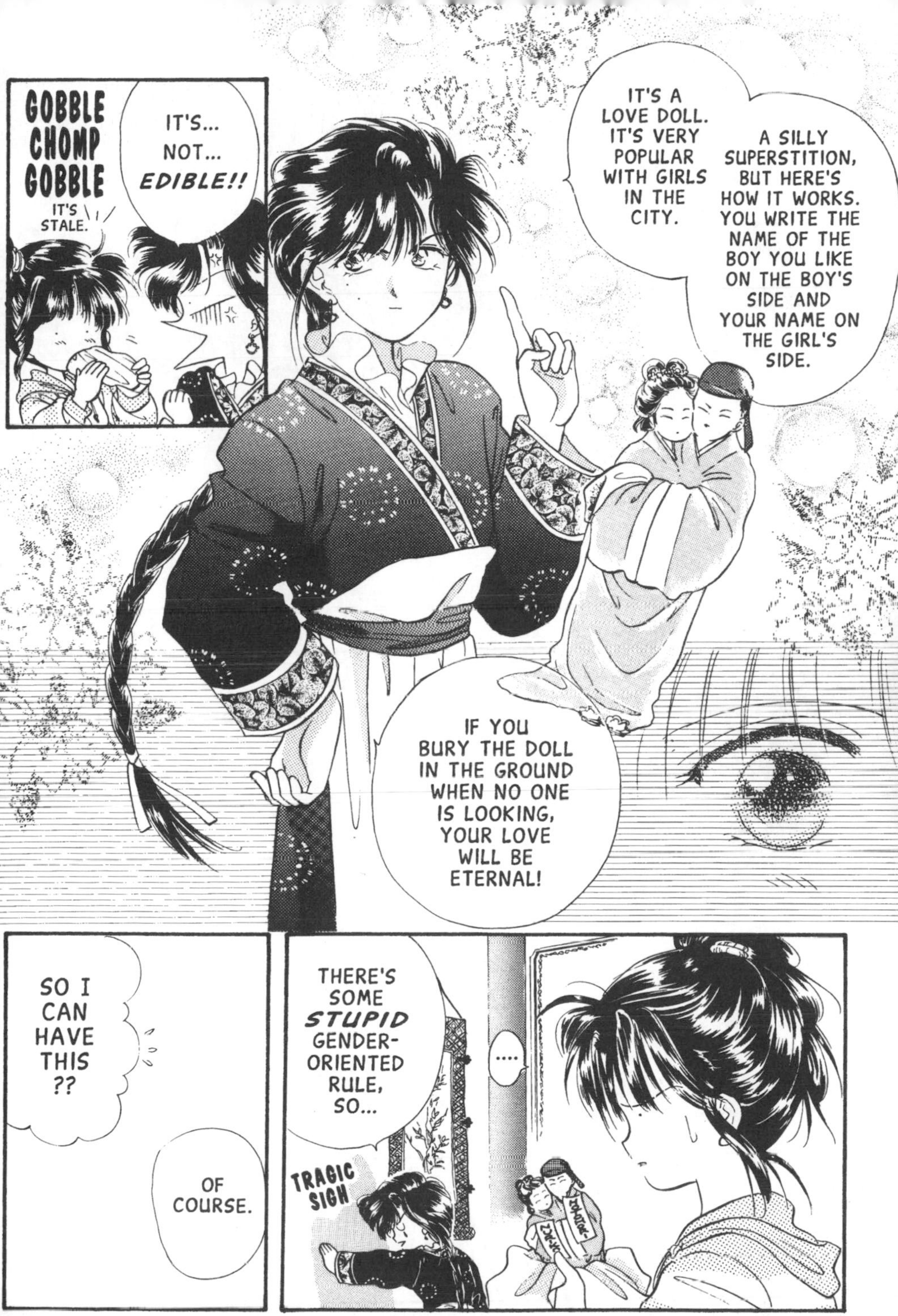
GOBBLE CHOMP GOBBLE
IT'S... NOT... EDIBLE!!
IT'S STALE.
IT'S A LOVE DOLL. IT'S VERY POPULAR WITH GIRLS IN THE CITY.
A SILLY SUPERSTITION, BUT HERE'S HOW IT WORKS. YOU WRITE THE NAME OF THE BOY YOU LIKE ON THE BOY'S SIDE AND YOUR NAME ON THE GIRL'S SIDE.
IF YOU BURY THE DOLL IN THE GROUND WHEN NO ONE IS LOOKING, YOUR LOVE WILL BE ETERNAL!
SO I CAN HAVE THIS??
OF COURSE.
THERE'S SOME STUPID GENDER-ORIENTED RULE, SO...
TRAGIC SIGH
....

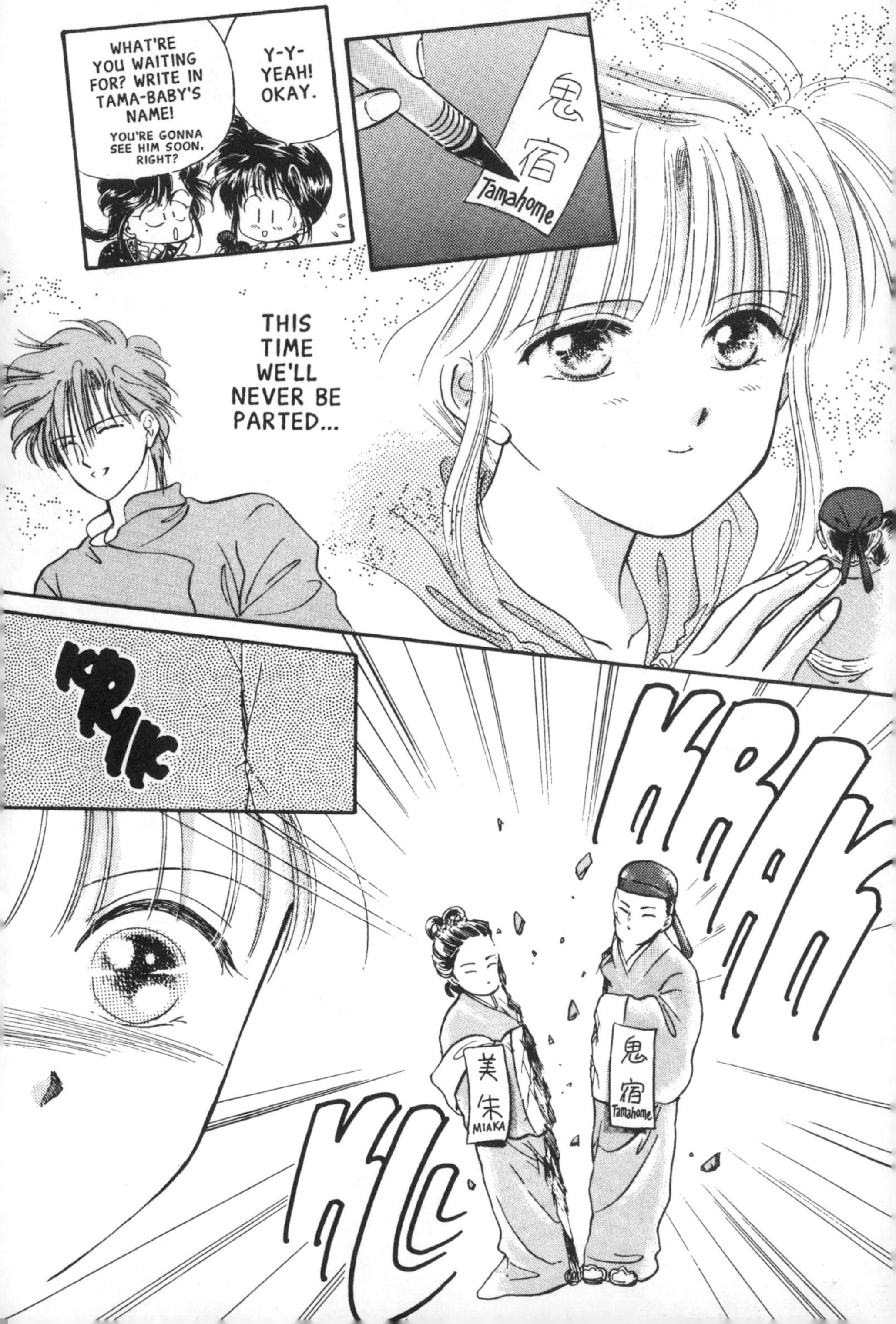
WHAT'RE YOU WAITING FOR? WRITE IN TAMA-BABY'S NAME!
YOU'RE GONNA SEE HIM SOON, RIGHT?
Y-Y-YEAH! OKAY.
鬼宿
Tamahome
THIS TIME WE'LL NEVER BE PARTED...
KRIK
美朱
MIAKA
鬼宿
Tamahome

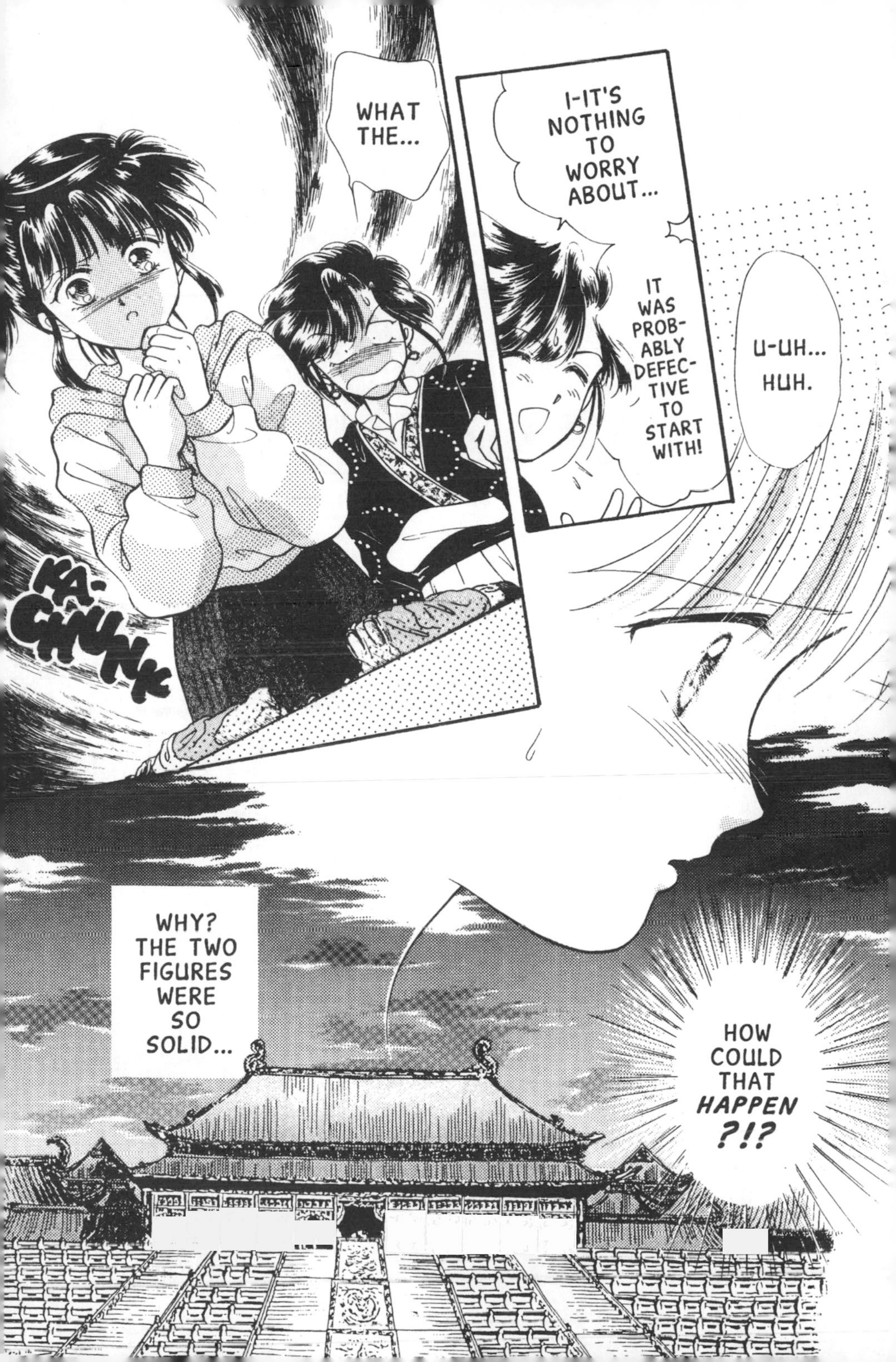
WHAT THE...
KA-CHUNK
I-IT'S NOTHING TO WORRY ABOUT...
IT WAS PROBABLY DEFECTIVE TO START WITH!
U-UH... HUH.
WHY? THE TWO FIGURES WERE SO SOLID...
HOW COULD THAT *HAPPEN* ?!?

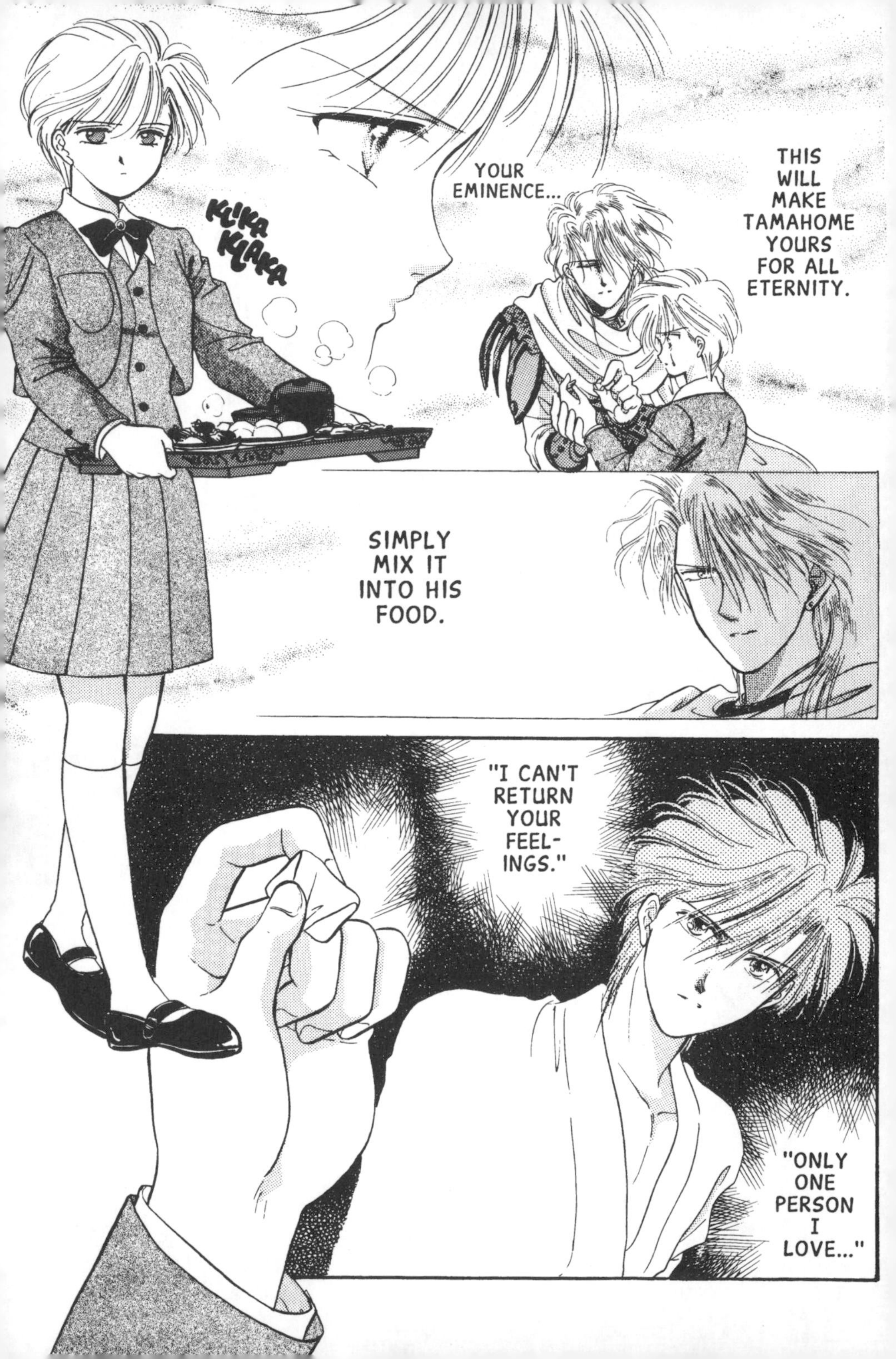
KLIKA KLAKA
YOUR EMINENCE...
THIS WILL MAKE TAMAHOME YOURS FOR ALL ETERNITY.
SIMPLY MIX IT INTO HIS FOOD.
"I CAN'T RETURN YOUR FEEL-INGS."
"ONLY ONE PERSON I LOVE..."

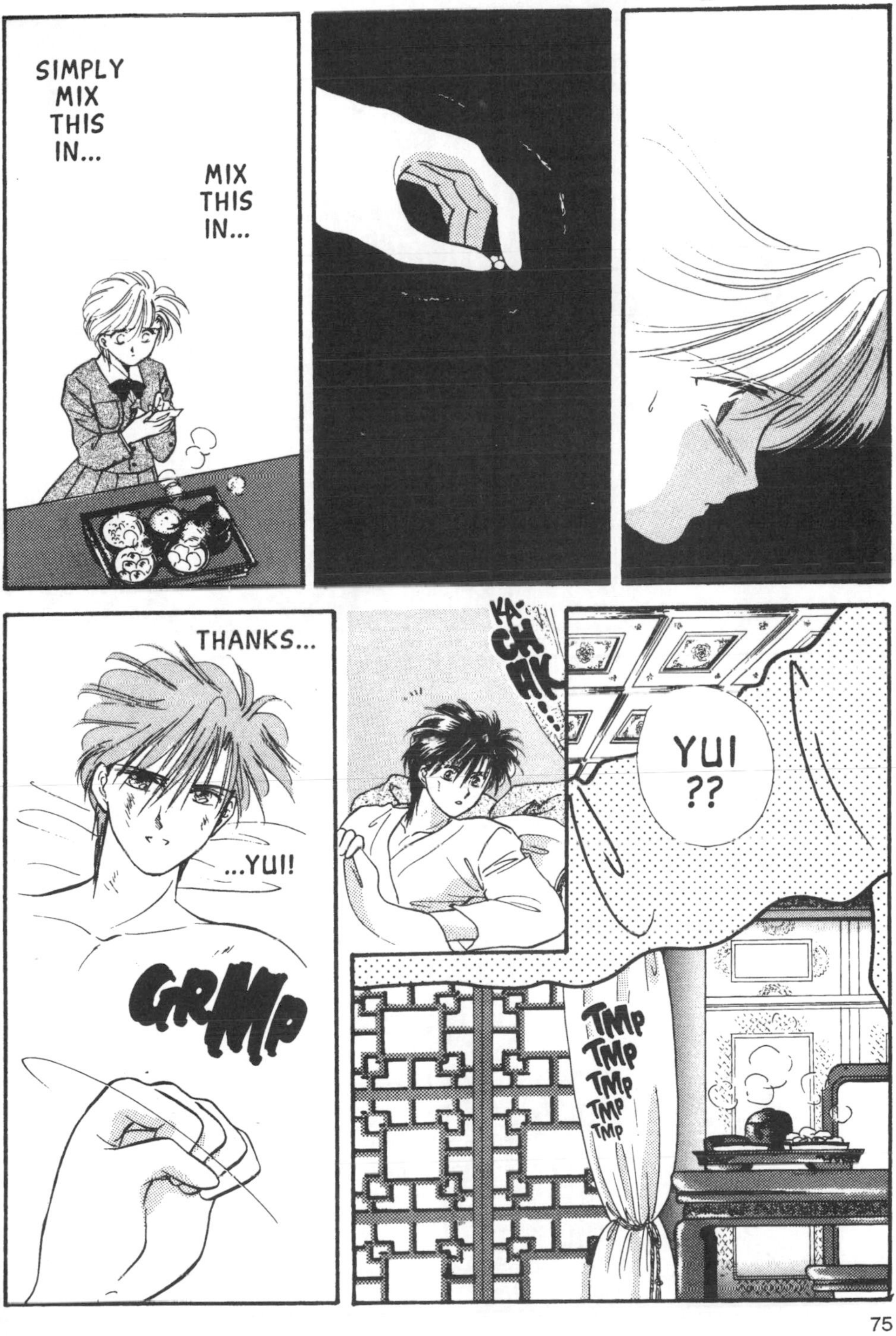
SIMPLY MIX THIS IN...
MIX THIS IN...
THANKS...
...YUI!
GRMP
KA-CHAK...
YUI ??
TMP TMP TMP TMP TMP

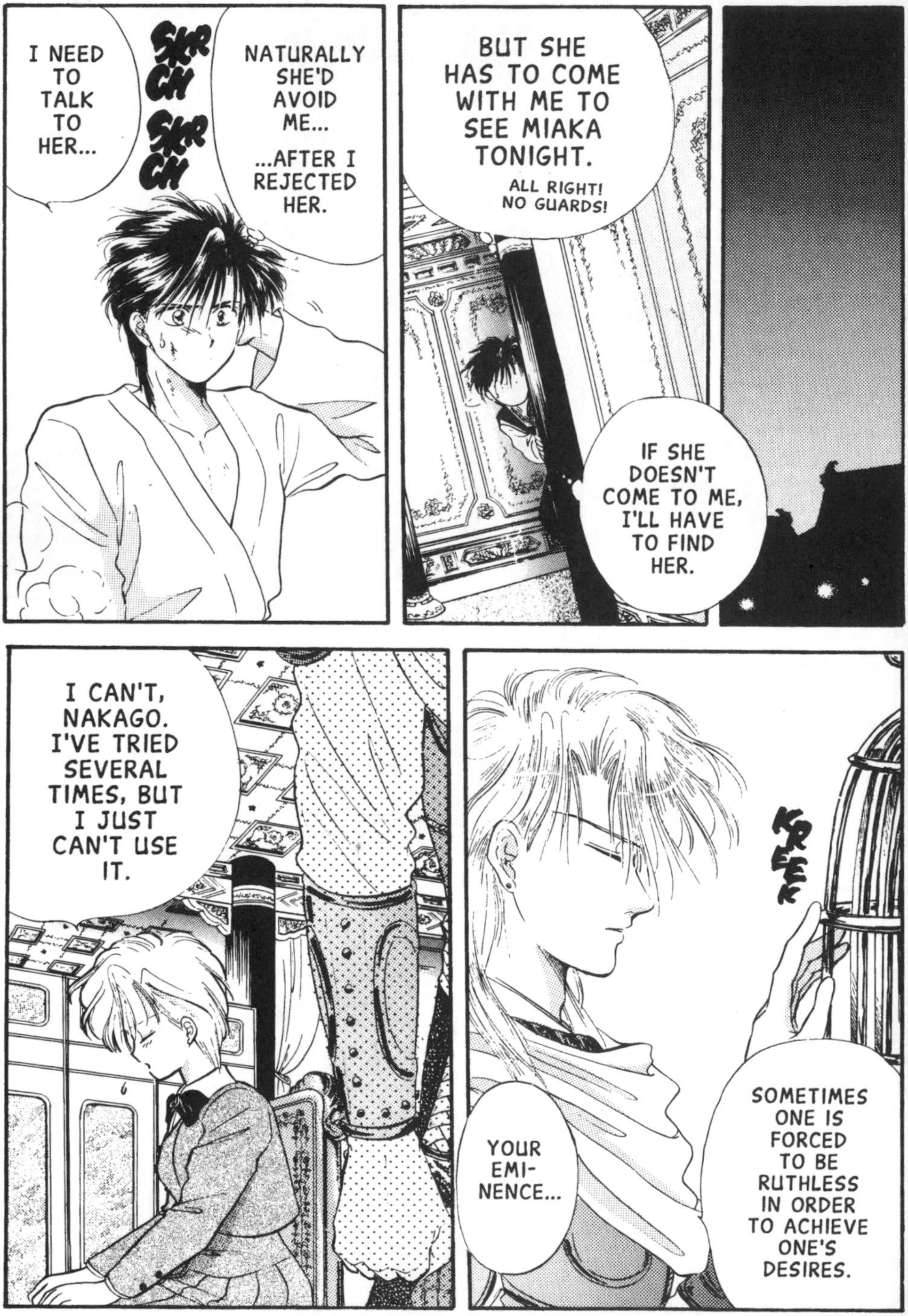
I NEED TO TALK TO HER...
SKRCH SKRCH
NATURALLY SHE'D AVOID ME...
...AFTER I REJECTED HER.
BUT SHE HAS TO COME WITH ME TO SEE MIAKA TONIGHT.
ALL RIGHT! NO GUARDS!
IF SHE DOESN'T COME TO ME, I'LL HAVE TO FIND HER.
I CAN'T, NAKAGO. I'VE TRIED SEVERAL TIMES, BUT I JUST CAN'T USE IT.
YOUR EMI-NENCE...
KREEK
SOMETIMES ONE IS FORCED TO BE RUTHLESS IN ORDER TO ACHIEVE ONE'S DESIRES.

WHEN *AREN'T* YOU

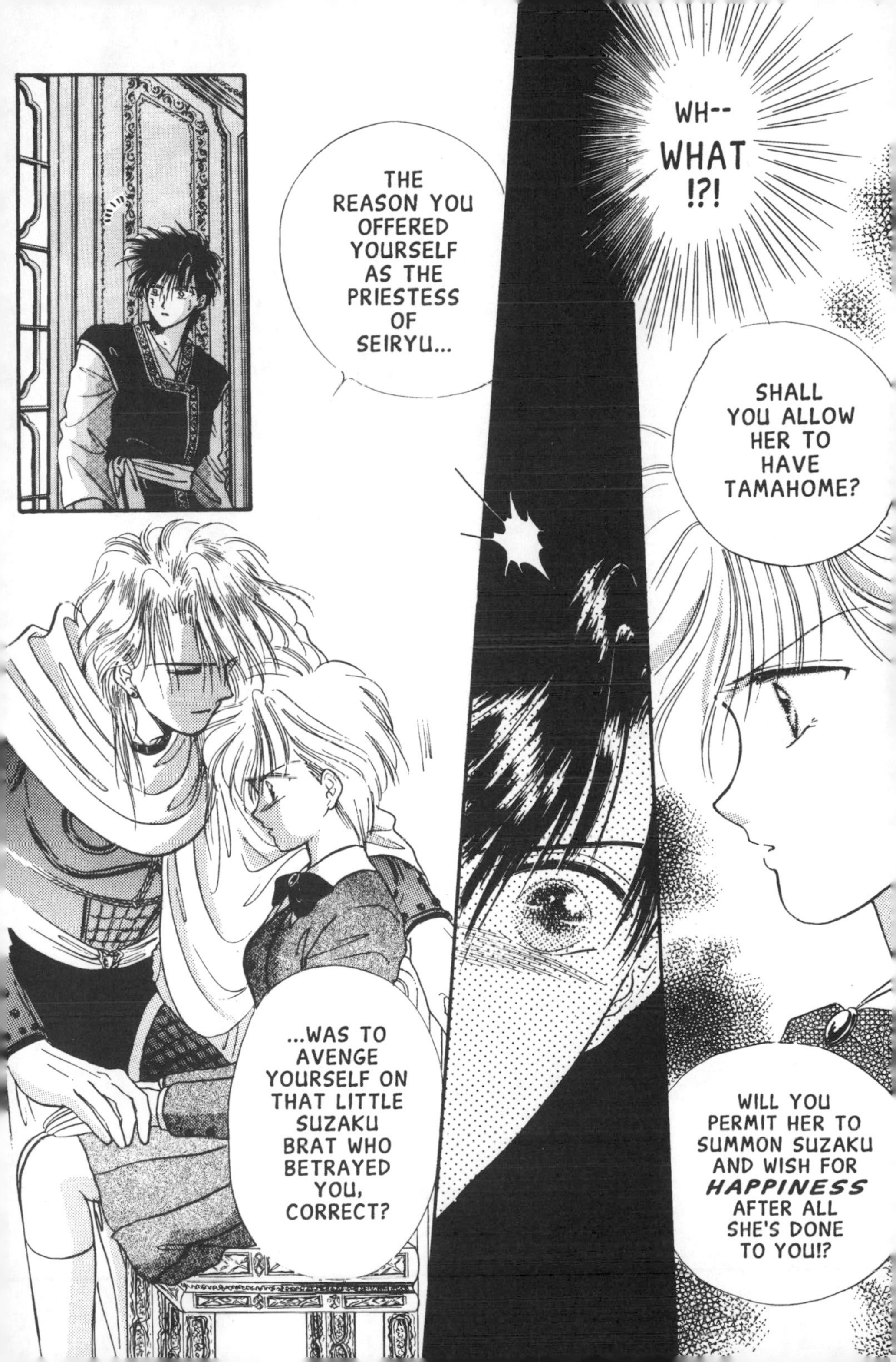
THE REASON YOU OFFERED YOURSELF AS THE PRIESTESS OF SEIRYU...
...WAS TO AVENGE YOURSELF ON THAT LITTLE SUZAKU BRAT WHO BETRAYED YOU, CORRECT?
WH-- WHAT !?!
SHALL YOU ALLOW HER TO HAVE TAMAHOME?
WILL YOU PERMIT HER TO SUMMON SUZAKU AND WISH FOR *HAPPINESS* AFTER ALL SHE'S DONE TO YOU!?

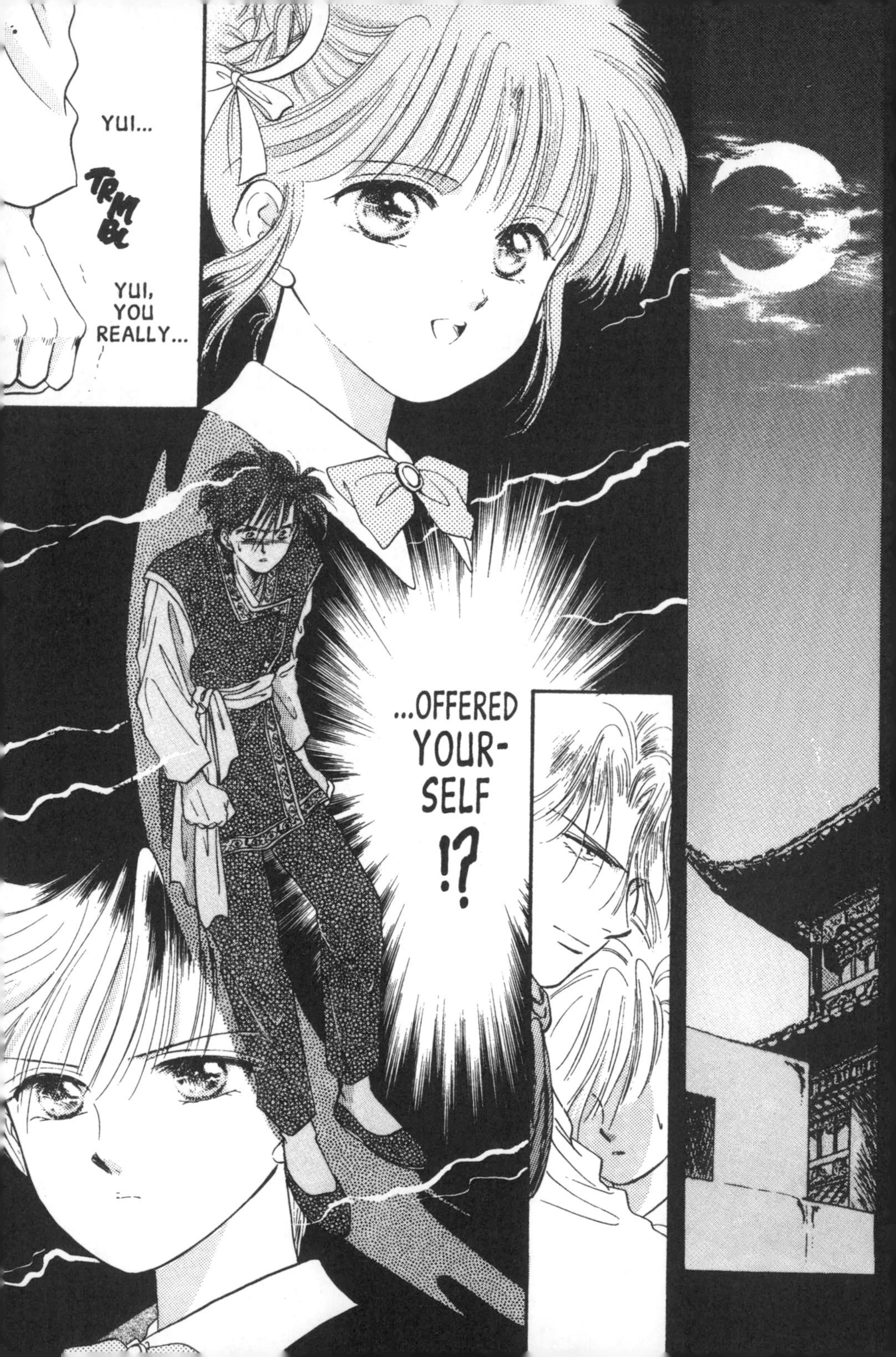
YUI...
TRMBL
YUI, YOU REALLY...
...OFFERED YOUR-SELF !?

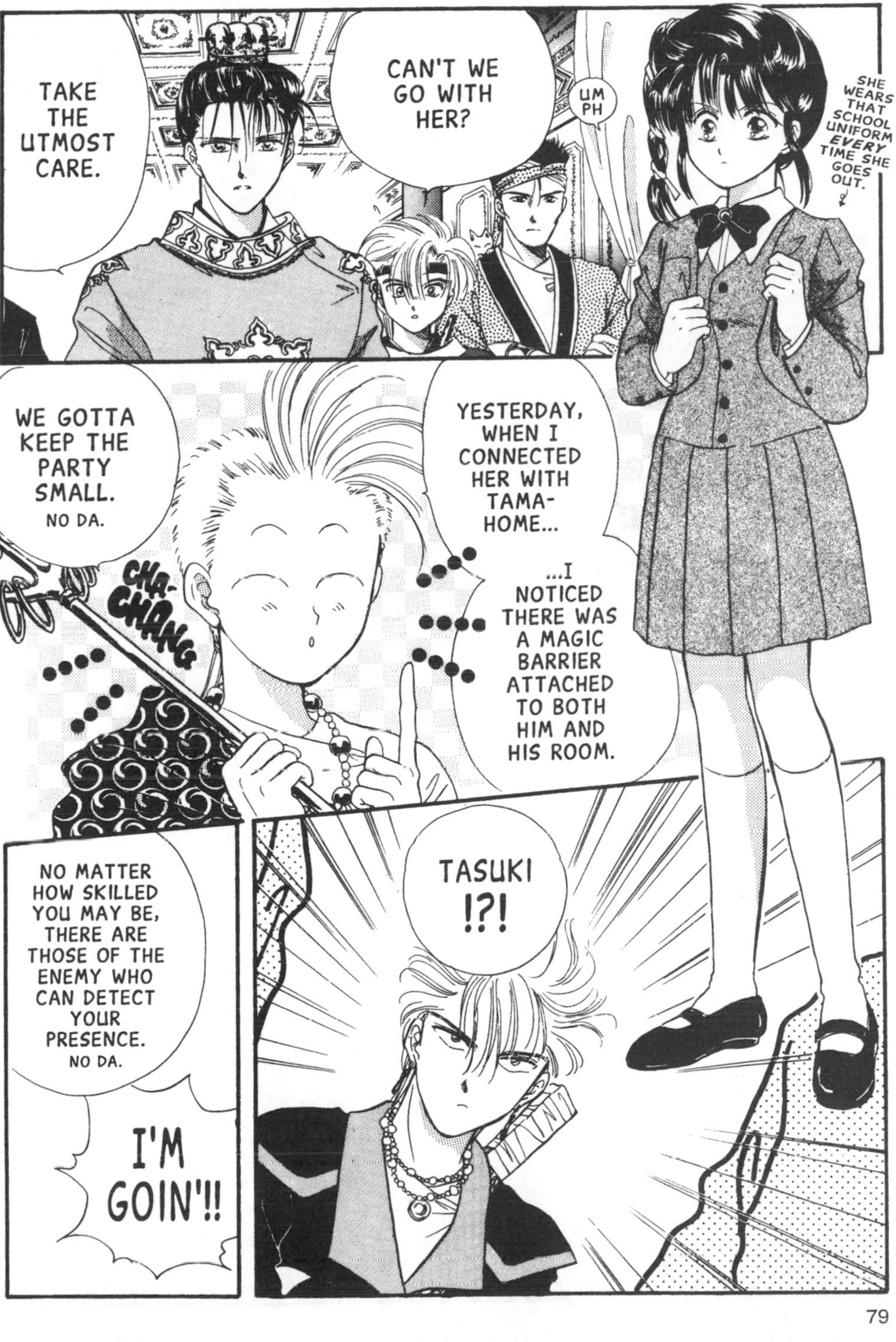

TAKE THE UTMOST CARE.
CAN'T WE GO WITH HER?
UMPH
WE GOTTA KEEP THE PARTY SMALL. NO DA.
CHA-CHANG
....
YESTERDAY, WHEN I CONNECTED HER WITH TAMA-HOME...
...I NOTICED THERE WAS A MAGIC BARRIER ATTACHED TO BOTH HIM AND HIS ROOM.
NO MATTER HOW SKILLED YOU MAY BE, THERE ARE THOSE OF THE ENEMY WHO CAN DETECT YOUR PRESENCE. NO DA.
I'M GOIN'!!
TASUKI !?!
SHE WEARS THAT SCHOOL UNIFORM EVERY TIME SHE GOES OUT.

NOBODY'D PICK UP ON ME!

I BEEN HEARIN' ALL ABOUT THIS TAMAHOME GUY.

I FIGGER IT'S ABOUT TIME T' MEET 'IM.

DIDN'T YOU HEAR WHAT CHICHIRI JUST SAID?

I HEARD, BUT IF I WAS GOIN' ALONG...

...I'D FIX YA UP WITH TH' MOST YUMMY YUMMY DUMPLINGS Y' EVER GOBBLED!!

BUT IT AIN'T GONNA HAPPEN, HUH?

SIGH

WE *HAVE* TO LET THE *POOR GUY* COME ALONG!!

····

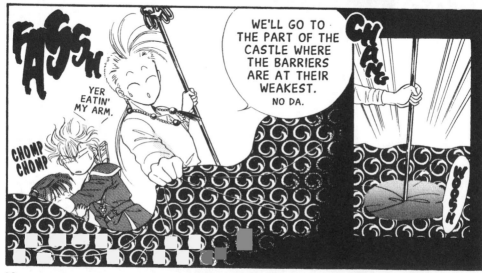

FASSH

YER EATIN' MY ARM.

CHOMP CHOMP

WE'LL GO TO THE PART OF THE CASTLE WHERE THE BARRIERS ARE AT THEIR WEAKEST. NO DA.

CHAK

ZOOOM

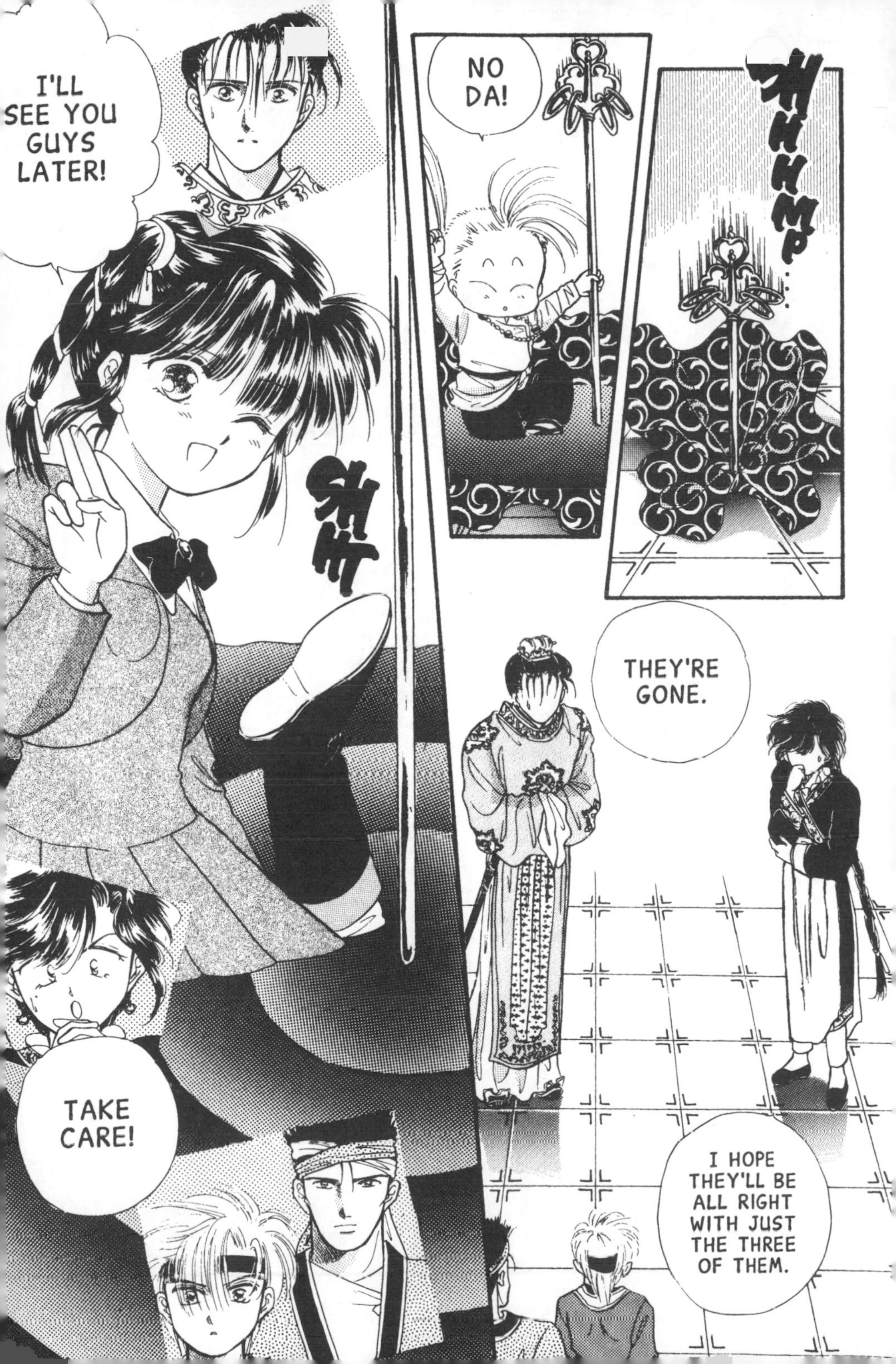
I'LL SEE YOU GUYS LATER!
TAKE CARE!
NO DA!
THEY'RE GONE.
I HOPE THEY'LL BE ALL RIGHT WITH JUST THE THREE OF THEM.

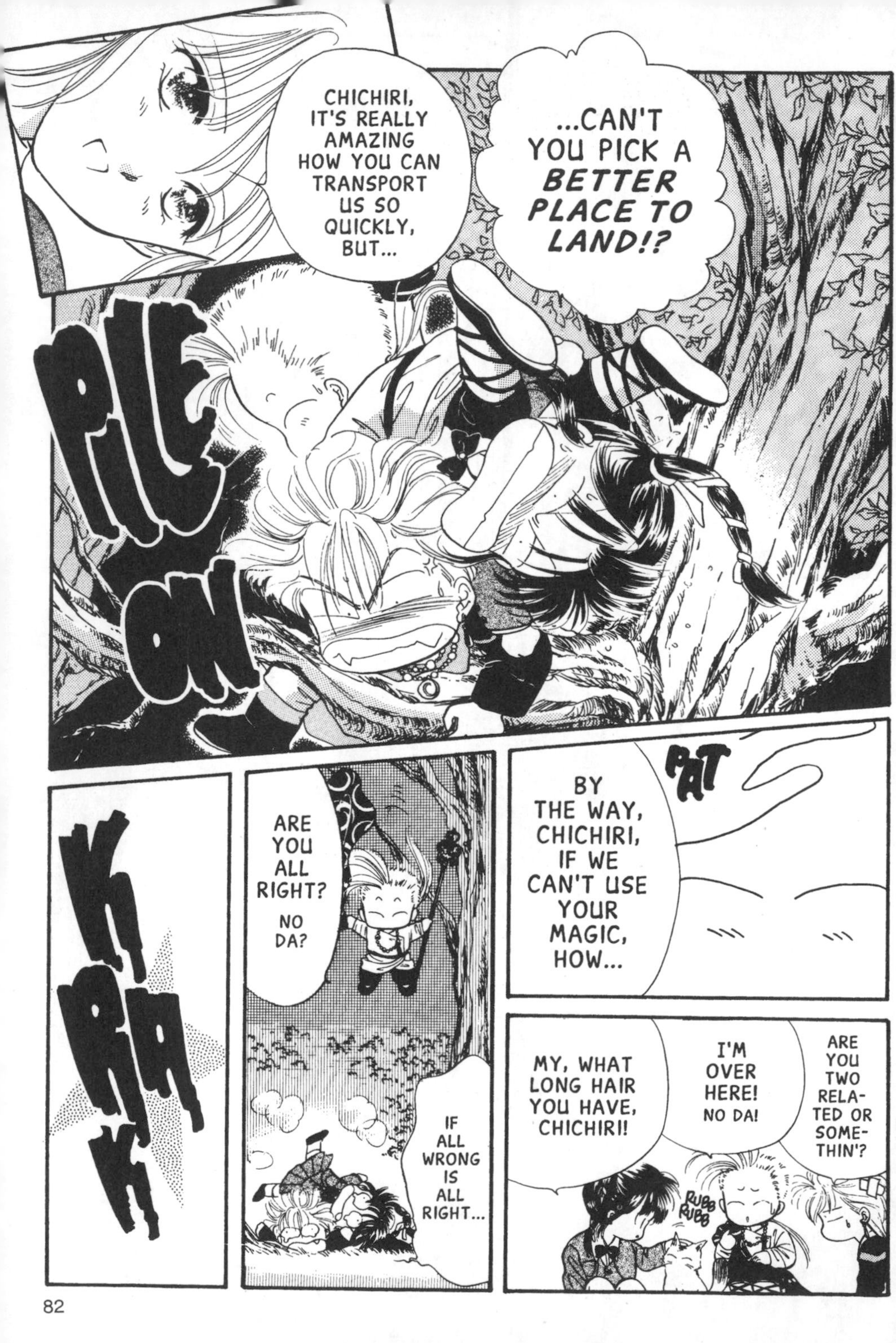
CHICHIRI, IT'S REALLY AMAZING HOW YOU CAN TRANSPORT US SO QUICKLY, BUT...
...CAN'T YOU PICK A *BETTER PLACE TO LAND!?*
PILE ON
ARE YOU ALL RIGHT? NO DA?
IF ALL WRONG IS ALL RIGHT...
PAT
BY THE WAY, CHICHIRI, IF WE CAN'T USE YOUR MAGIC, HOW...
MY, WHAT LONG HAIR YOU HAVE, CHICHIRI!
I'M OVER HERE! NO DA!
RUBB RUBB
ARE YOU TWO RELA-TED OR SOME-THIN'?

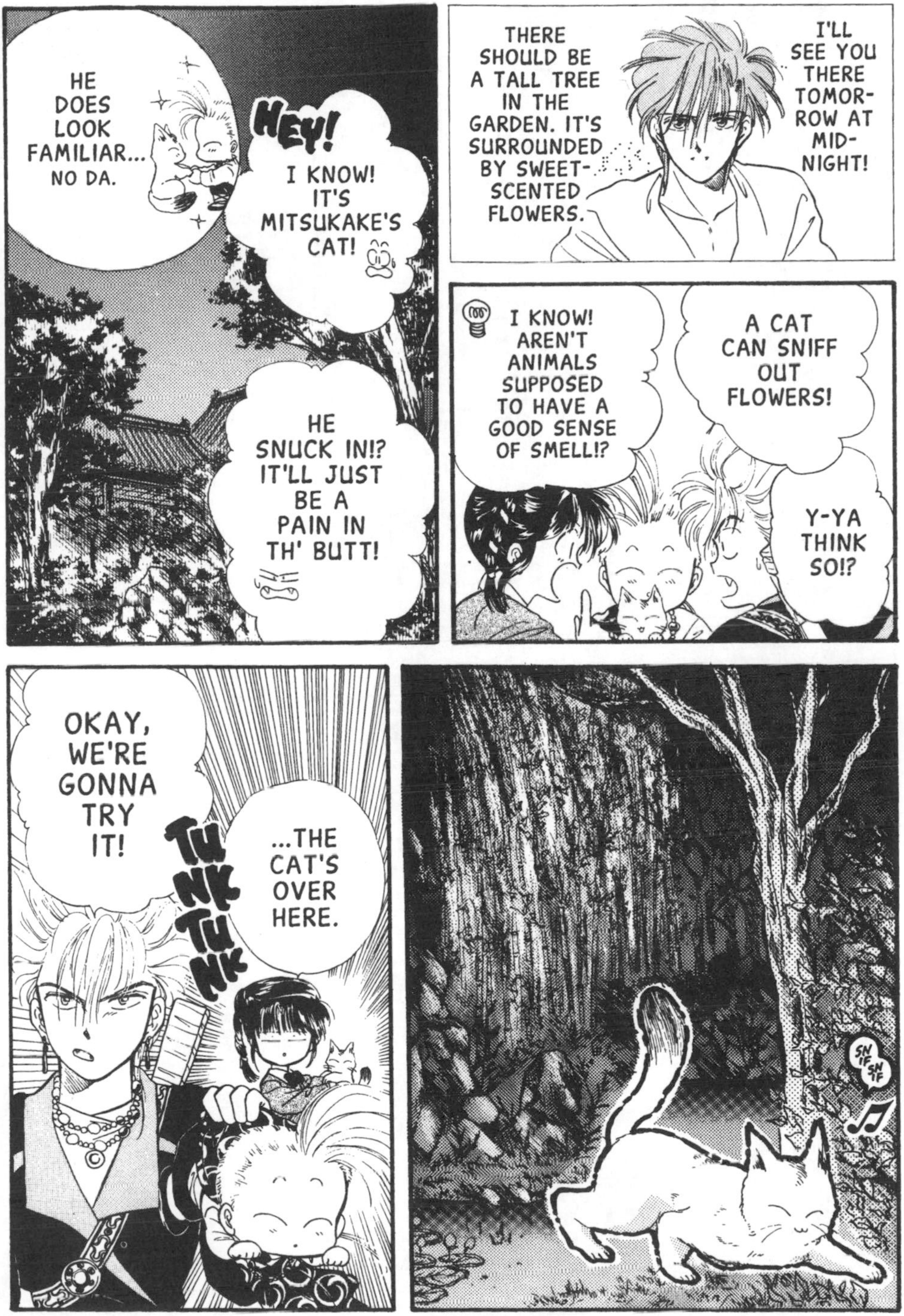
HE DOES LOOK FAMILIAR... NO DA.
HEY!
I KNOW! IT'S MITSUKAKE'S CAT!
HE SNUCK IN!? IT'LL JUST BE A PAIN IN TH' BUTT!
THERE SHOULD BE A TALL TREE IN THE GARDEN. IT'S SURROUNDED BY SWEET-SCENTED FLOWERS.
I'LL SEE YOU THERE TOMORROW AT MID-NIGHT!
I KNOW! AREN'T ANIMALS SUPPOSED TO HAVE A GOOD SENSE OF SMELL!?
A CAT CAN SNIFF OUT FLOWERS!
Y-YA THINK SO!?
OKAY, WE'RE GONNA TRY IT!
TUNK TUNK TUNK
...THE CAT'S OVER HERE.
SNIF SNIF

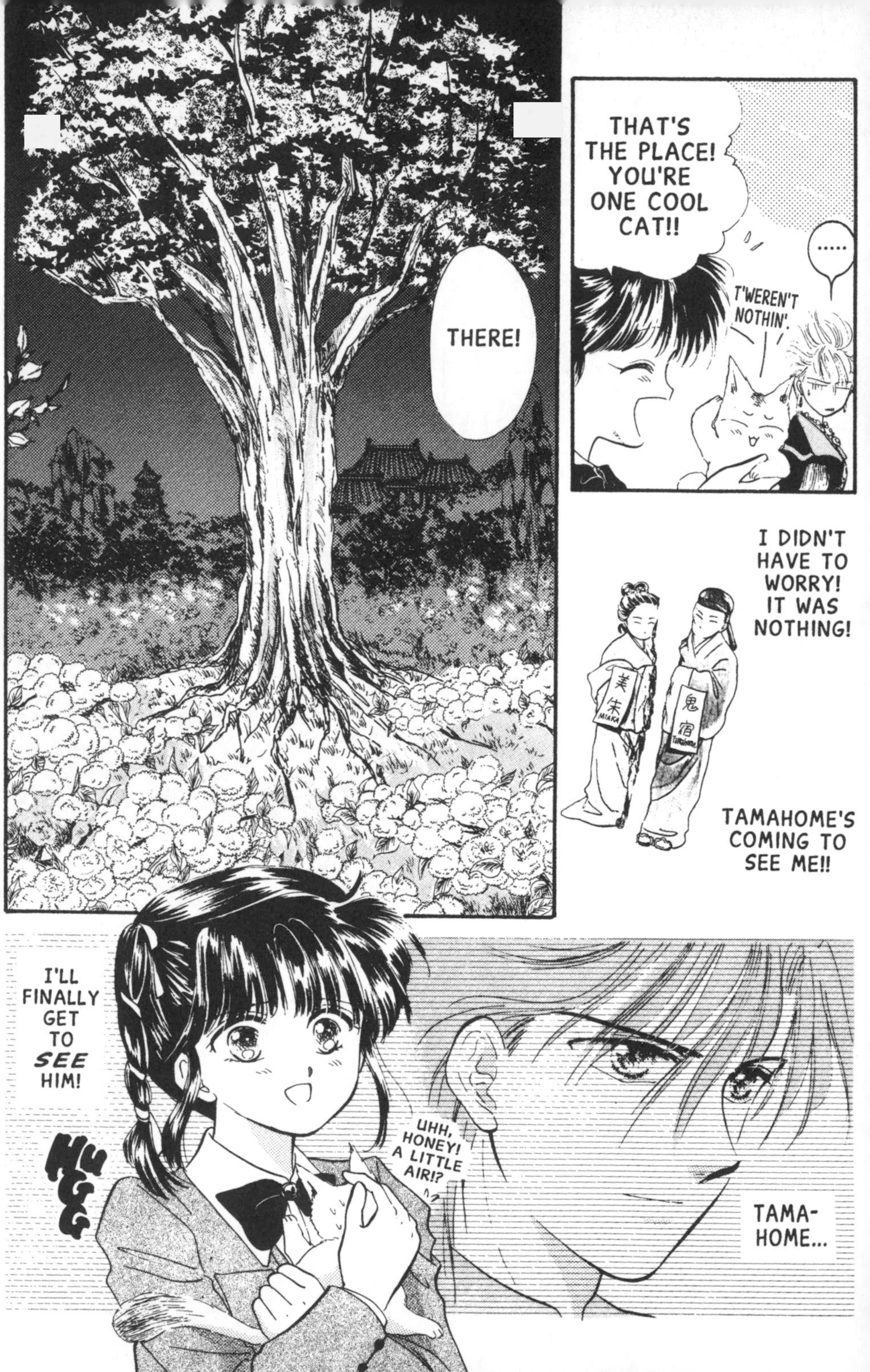
THERE!
THAT'S THE PLACE! YOU'RE ONE COOL CAT!!
T'WEREN'T NOTHIN'.
.....
I DIDN'T HAVE TO WORRY! IT WAS NOTHING!
美朱
MIAKA
鬼宿
TAMAHOME
TAMAHOME'S COMING TO SEE ME!!
I'LL FINALLY GET TO *SEE* HIM!
HUGG
UHH, HONEY! A LITTLE AIR!?
TAMA-HOME...

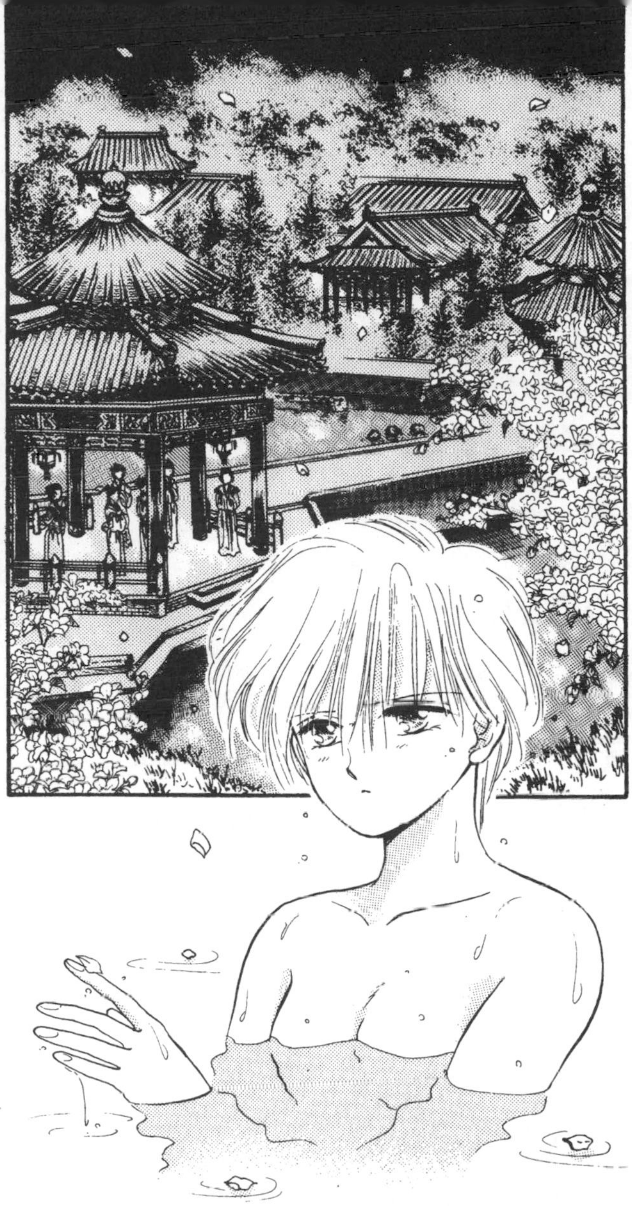

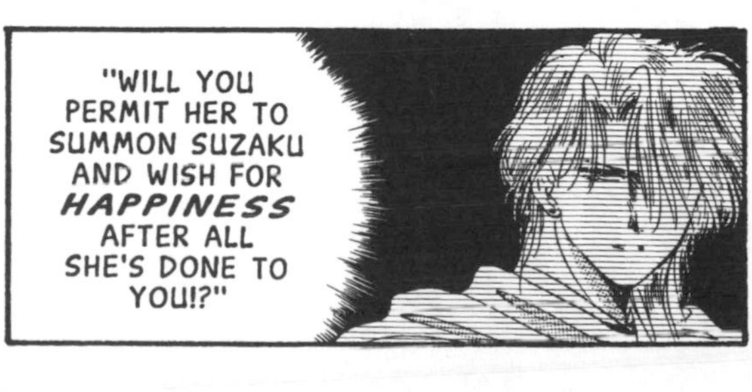
"WILL YOU PERMIT HER TO SUMMON SUZAKU AND WISH FOR HAPPINESS AFTER ALL SHE'S DONE TO YOU!?"

Rival

A couple of days later, I met my friends from my tech-school years. We didn't have anything better to do, so we sat around in cafes and looked for the local game centers. While one of my friends was snatching up dolls on the UFO catcher, Ms. A. and I played Street Fighter II on the super-size screen. I liked watching Ms. A. play almost more than watching the screen!
I played the tough guy saying, "What the hell're you doin'!? You bastard--you kicked me!!" And she would say, "Oh, how awful! Stop it, please!" or "Gosh, you shouldn't give in to your violent urges like that!" Eventually we got tired of the game center, so went to Karaoke, even though one of our friends was pregnant. I lost my voice from all the yelling at the game center so I just sat and listened to everyone else sing. *(What an idiot!) But actually, I had a cold!* Despite all the loud noises in the room, the five-month old fetus in my friend's tummy didn't wake up once!
I had a great time tapping out the time on her stomach (but that's just me). I'm really looking forward to when the baby is born. I was thinking about how this newborn child would eventually read my manga, and I can brainwash it into being my mind-slave. (Those're the kind of stupid thoughts I have.) I was so happy to be back in Osaka. I ate at my favorite okonomiyaki place six times!! Yet I didn't eat any takoyaki! I don't know why. It'll have to be a mystery.
The okonomiyaki shop "Ikkyu" is so good, your jaw drops, and your taste buds do a quintuple flip earning a perfect 10 from the judges! The key to okonomiyaki is pork! You hear me? Pork! I don't like meat, but the pork flavor is crucial. Trust me on this.

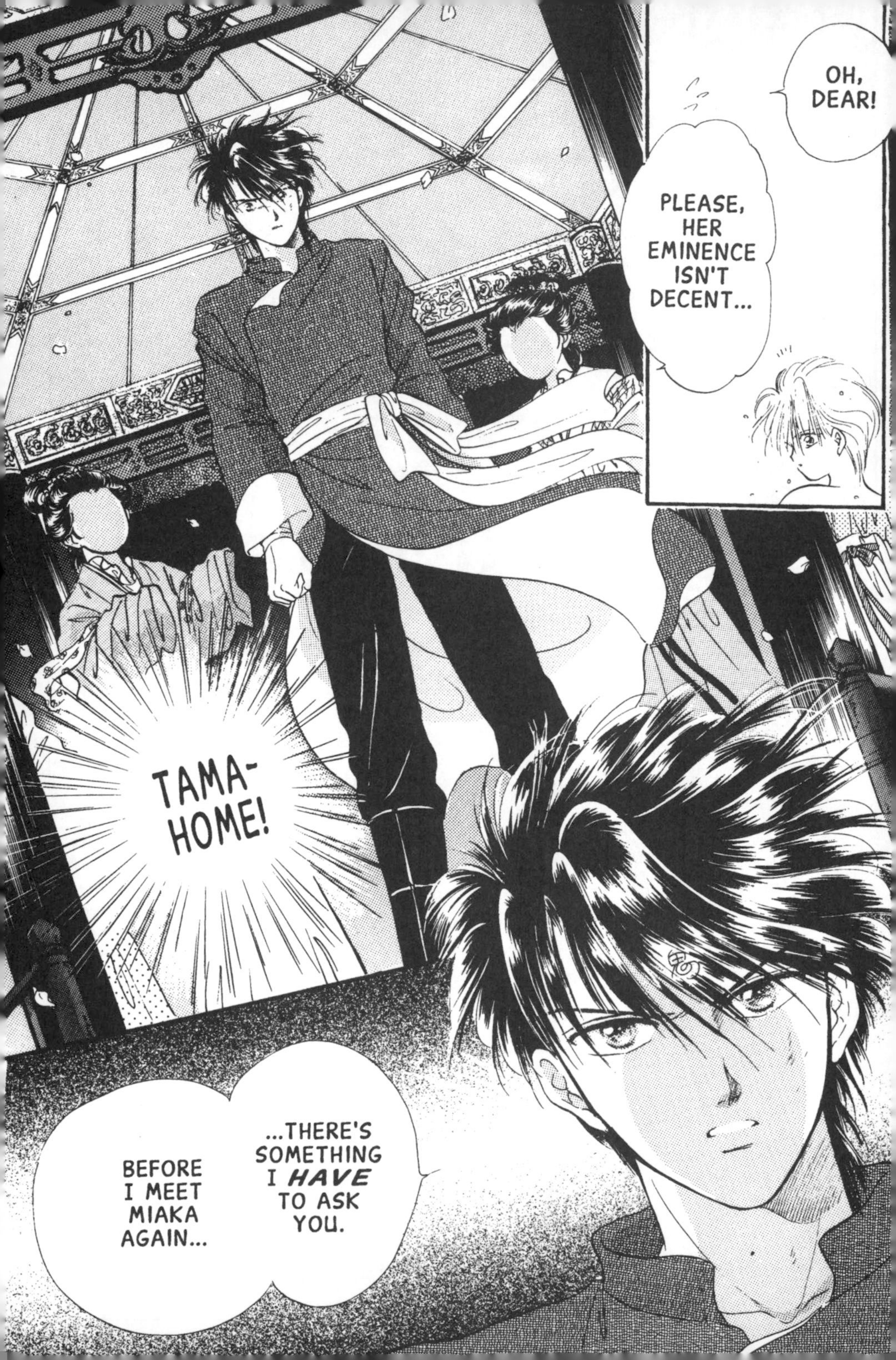
TAMA-HOME!
OH, DEAR!
PLEASE, HER EMINENCE ISN'T DECENT...
BEFORE I MEET MIAKA AGAIN...
...THERE'S SOMETHING I *HAVE* TO ASK YOU.

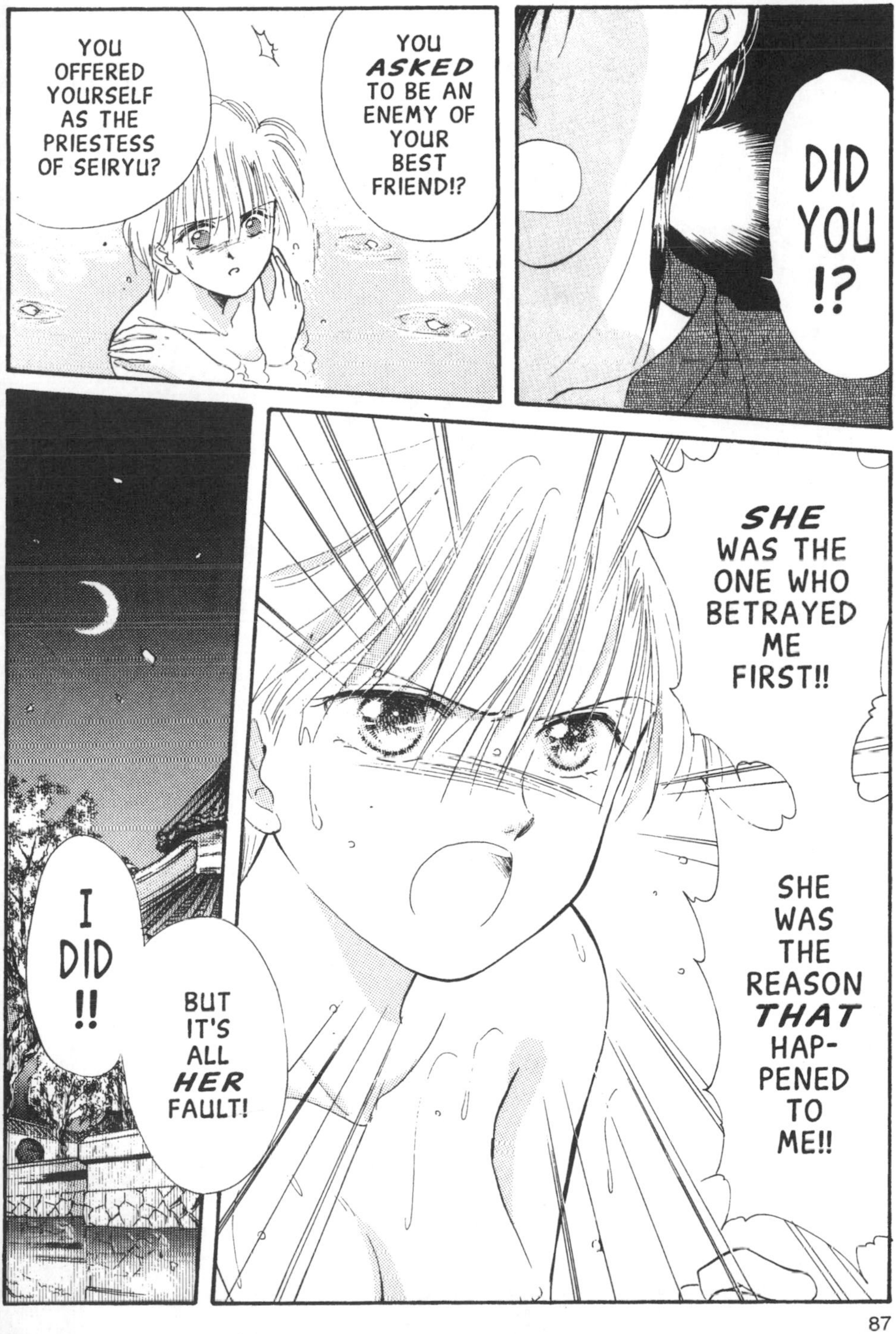
YOU OFFERED YOURSELF AS THE PRIESTESS OF SEIRYU?
YOU *ASKED* TO BE AN ENEMY OF YOUR BEST FRIEND!?
DID YOU !?
I DID !!
BUT IT'S ALL *HER* FAULT!
SHE WAS THE ONE WHO BETRAYED ME FIRST!!
SHE WAS THE REASON *THAT* HAP-PENED TO ME!!

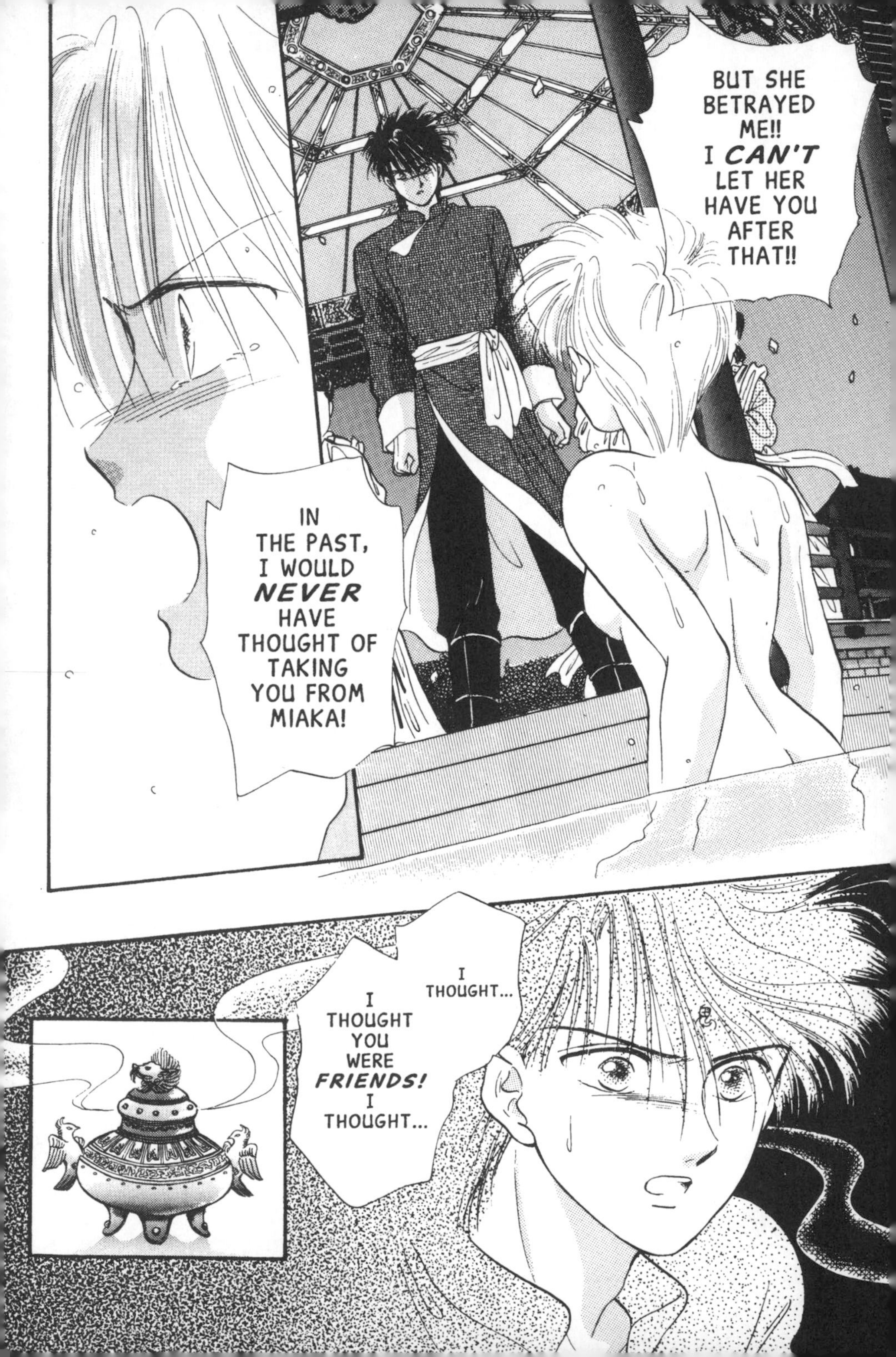

IN THE PAST, I WOULD NEVER HAVE THOUGHT OF TAKING YOU FROM MIAKA!
BUT SHE BETRAYED ME!! I CAN'T LET HER HAVE YOU AFTER THAT!!
I THOUGHT YOU WERE FRIENDS! I THOUGHT...
I THOUGHT...

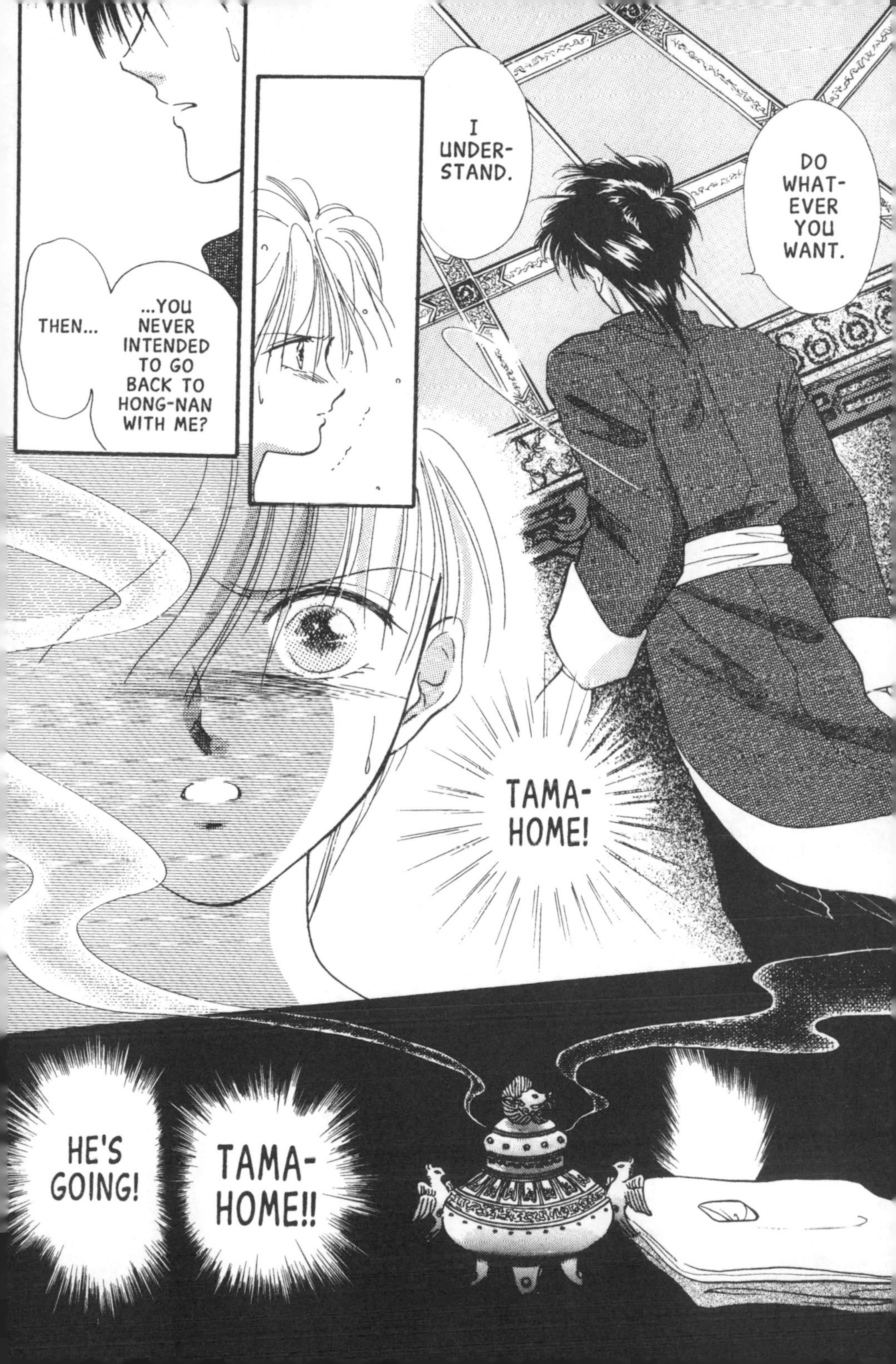
THEN...
...YOU NEVER INTENDED TO GO BACK TO HONG-NAN WITH ME?
I UNDER-STAND.
DO WHAT-EVER YOU WANT.
TAMA-HOME!
HE'S GOING!
TAMA-HOME!!

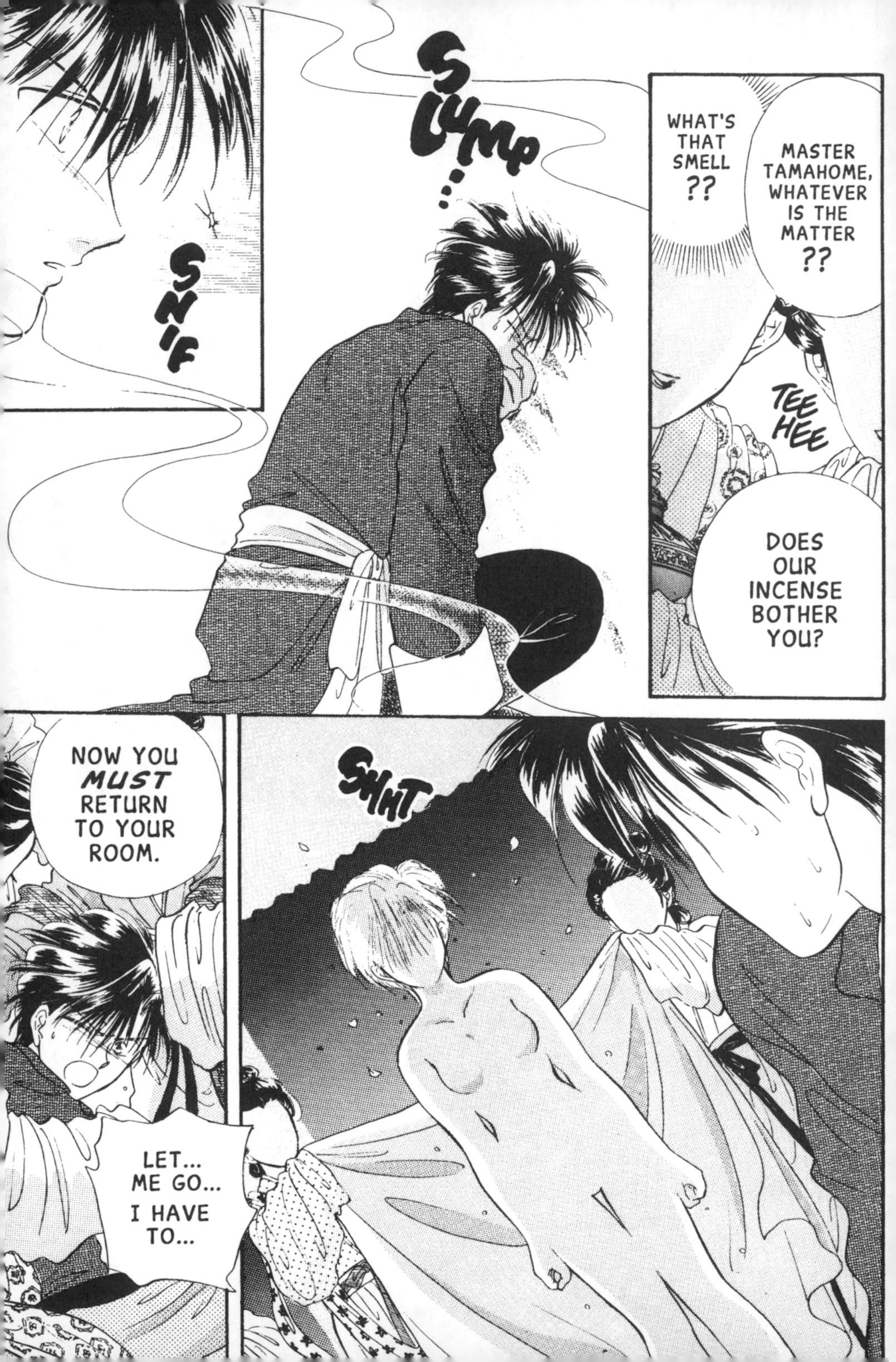
SNIF
SLUMP...
WHAT'S THAT SMELL ??
MASTER TAMAHOME, WHATEVER IS THE MATTER ??
TEE HEE
DOES OUR INCENSE BOTHER YOU?
NOW YOU *MUST* RETURN TO YOUR ROOM.
LET... ME GO... I HAVE TO...
SHHT

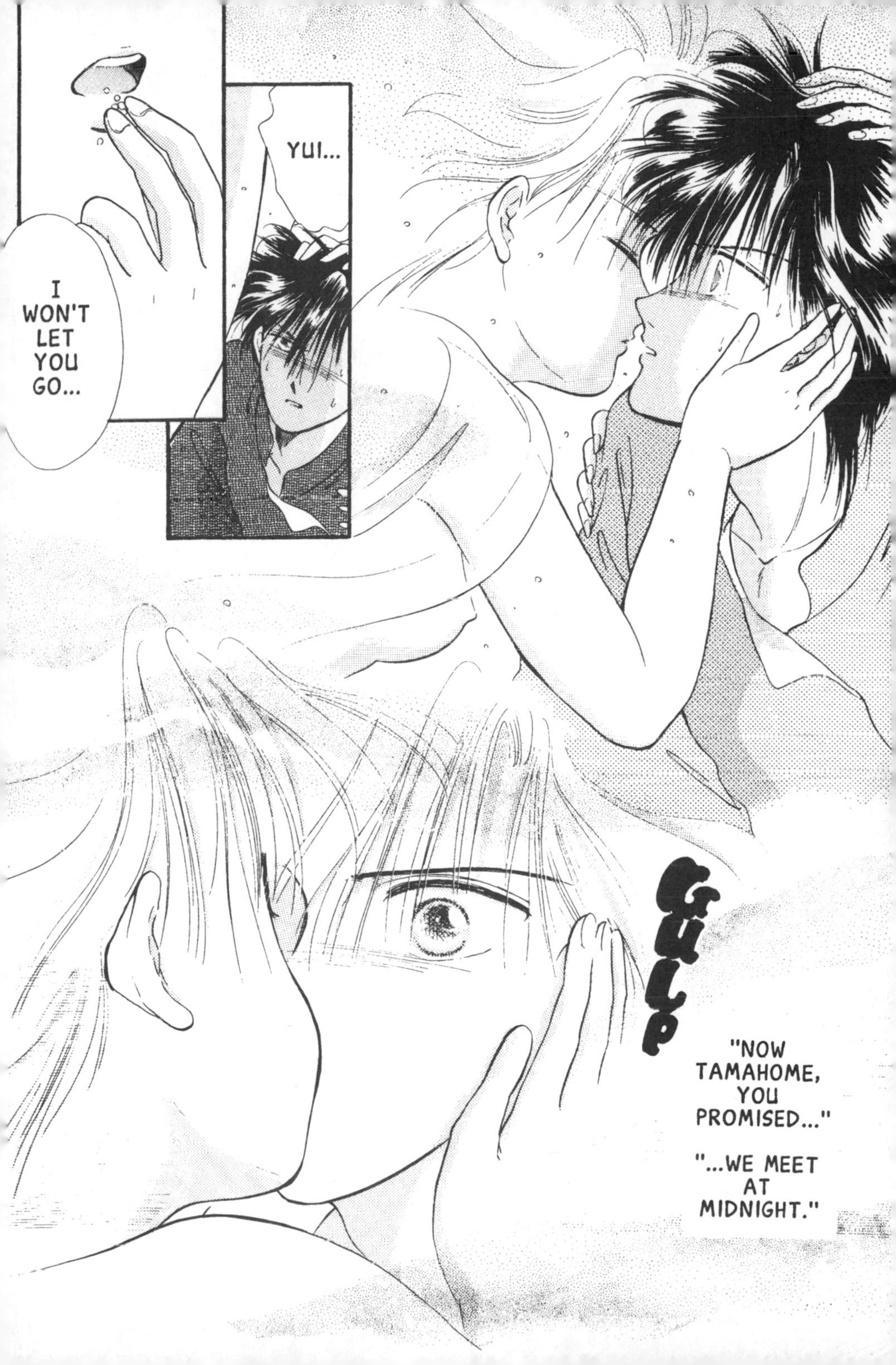
I WON'T LET YOU GO...
YUI...
GULP
"NOW TAMAHOME, YOU PROMISED..."
"...WE MEET AT MIDNIGHT."

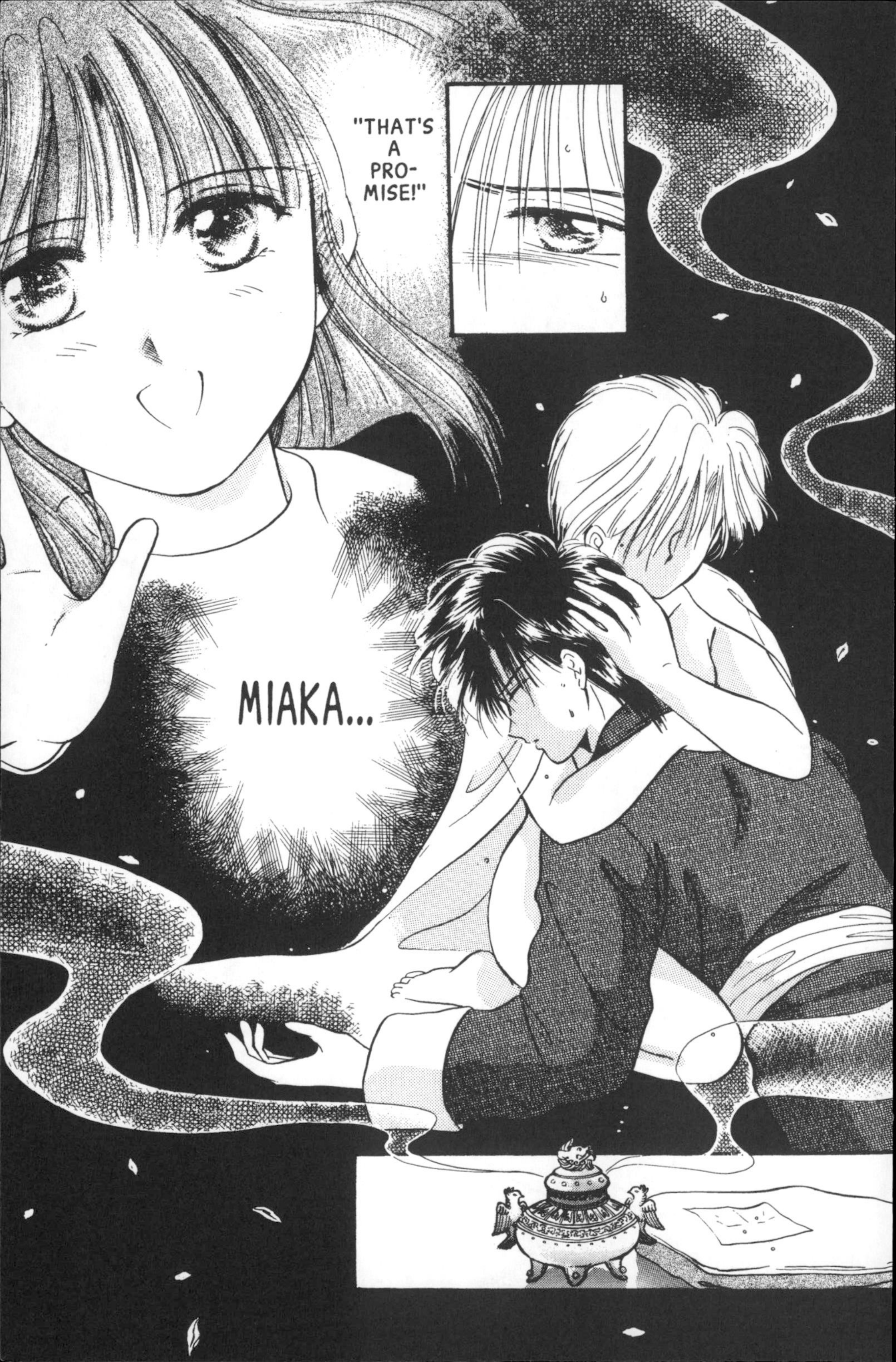
"THAT'S A PRO-MISE!"
MIAKA...

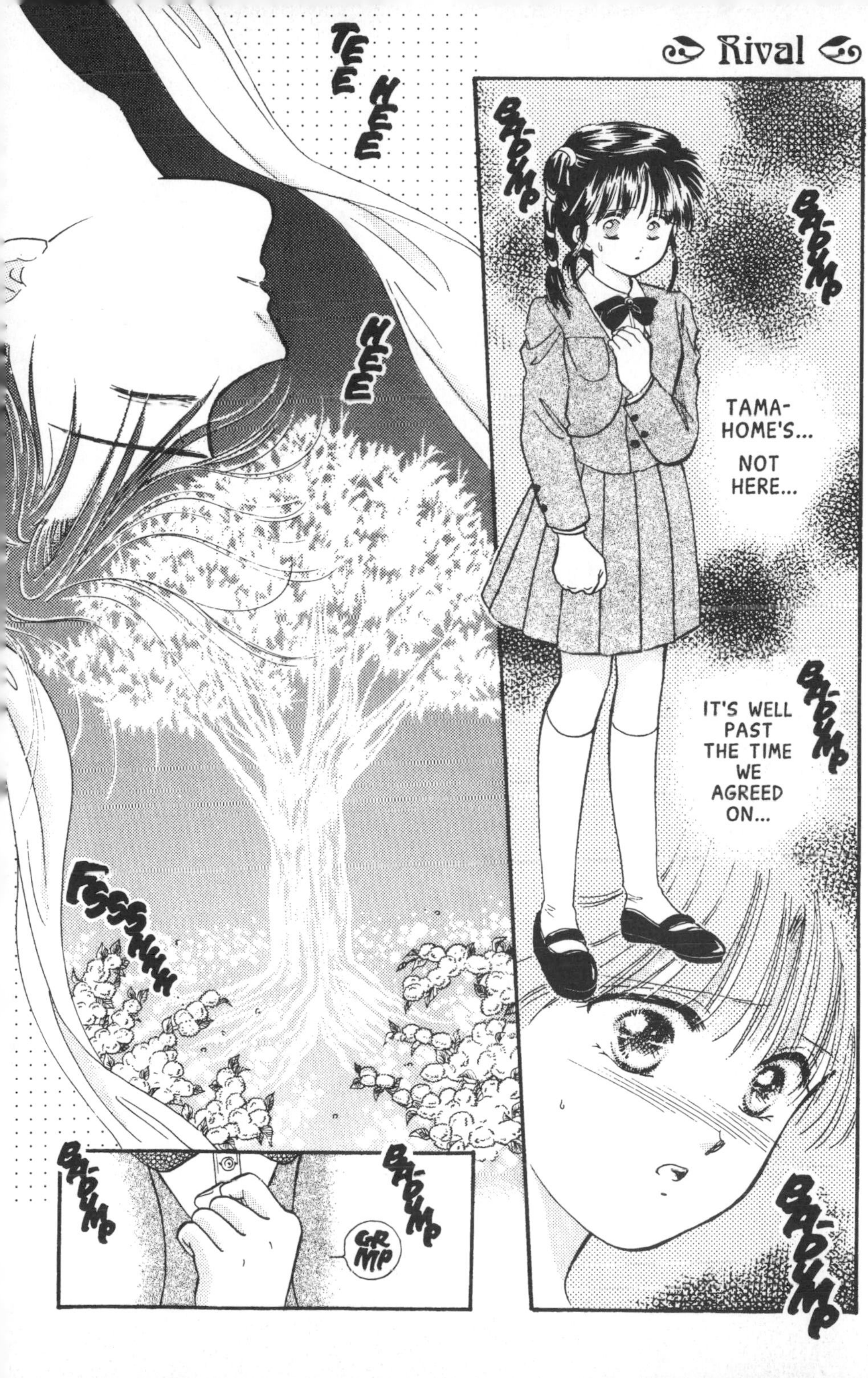
TEE HEE
HEE
FSSSHHH
BA-DUMP
BA-DUMP
GRMP
BA-DUMP
BA-DUMP
TAMA-HOME'S... NOT HERE...
BA-DUMP
IT'S WELL PAST THE TIME WE AGREED ON...
BA-DUMP

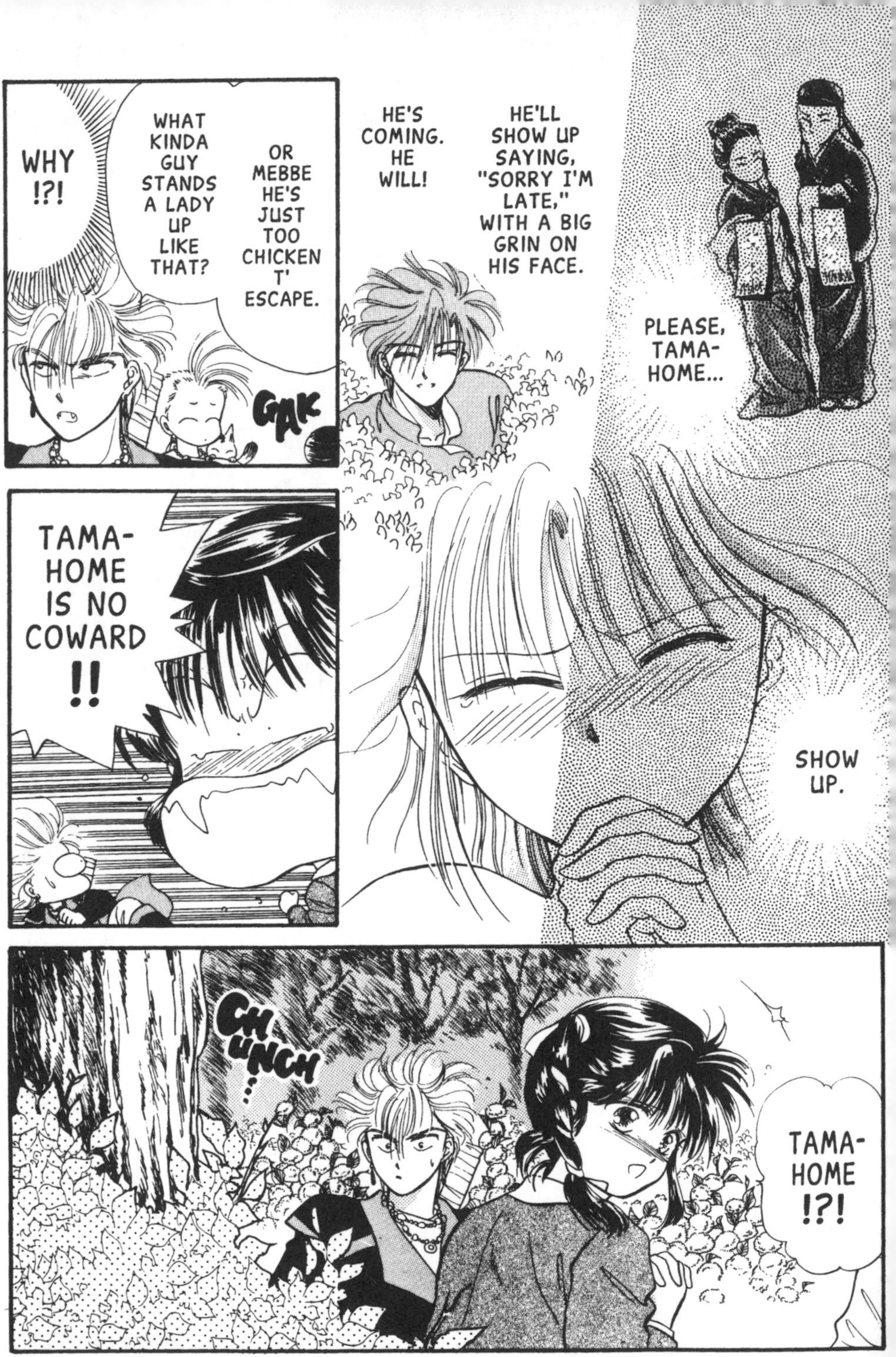
WHY !?!
WHAT KINDA GUY STANDS A LADY UP LIKE THAT?
OR MEBBE HE'S JUST TOO CHICKEN T' ESCAPE.
GAK
HE'S COMING. HE WILL!
HE'LL SHOW UP SAYING, "SORRY I'M LATE," WITH A BIG GRIN ON HIS FACE.
PLEASE, TAMA-HOME...
TAMA-HOME IS NO COWARD !!
SHOW UP.
CHUNCH...
TAMA-HOME !?!

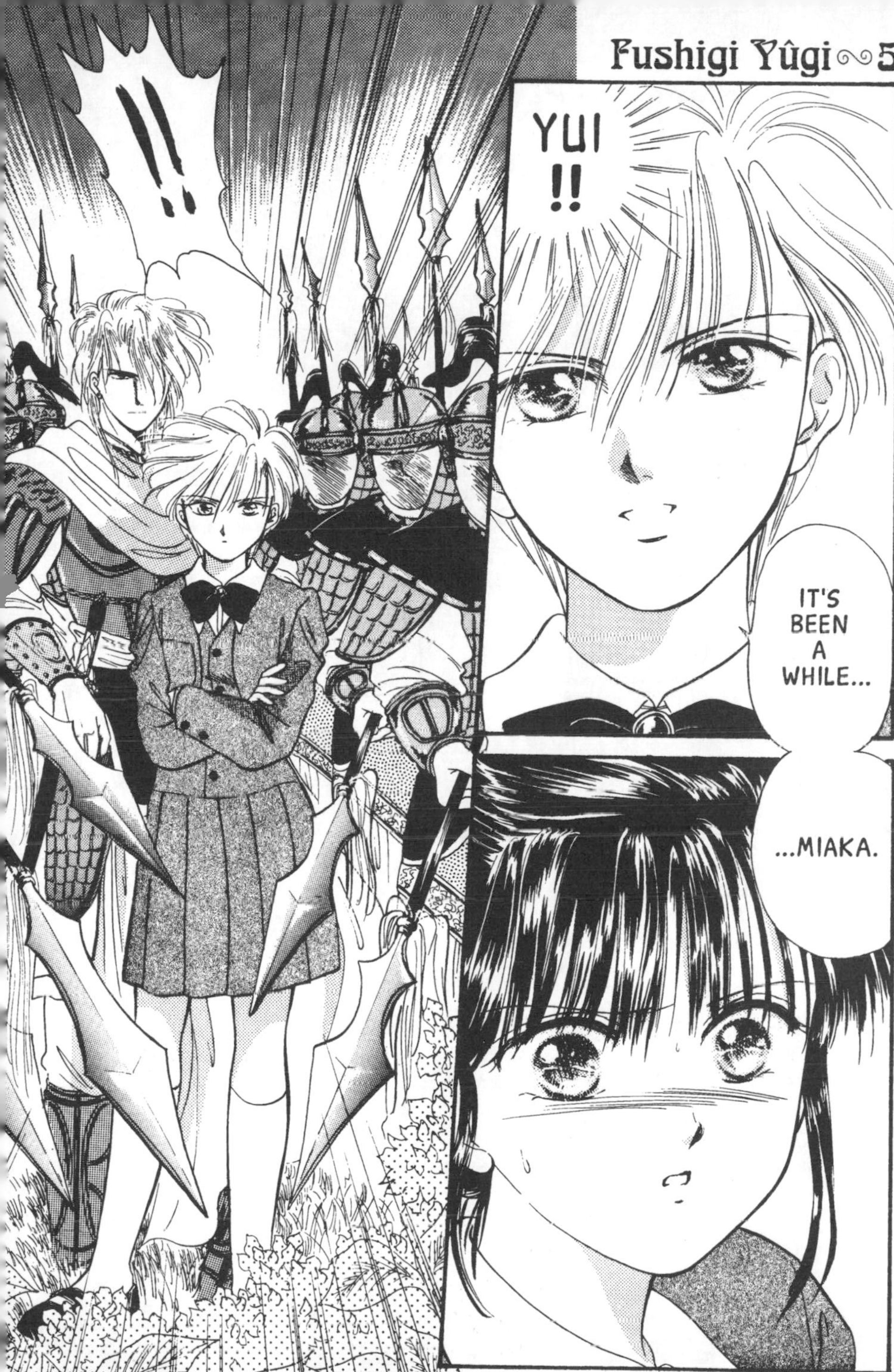
!!
YUI !!
IT'S BEEN A WHILE...
...MIAKA.

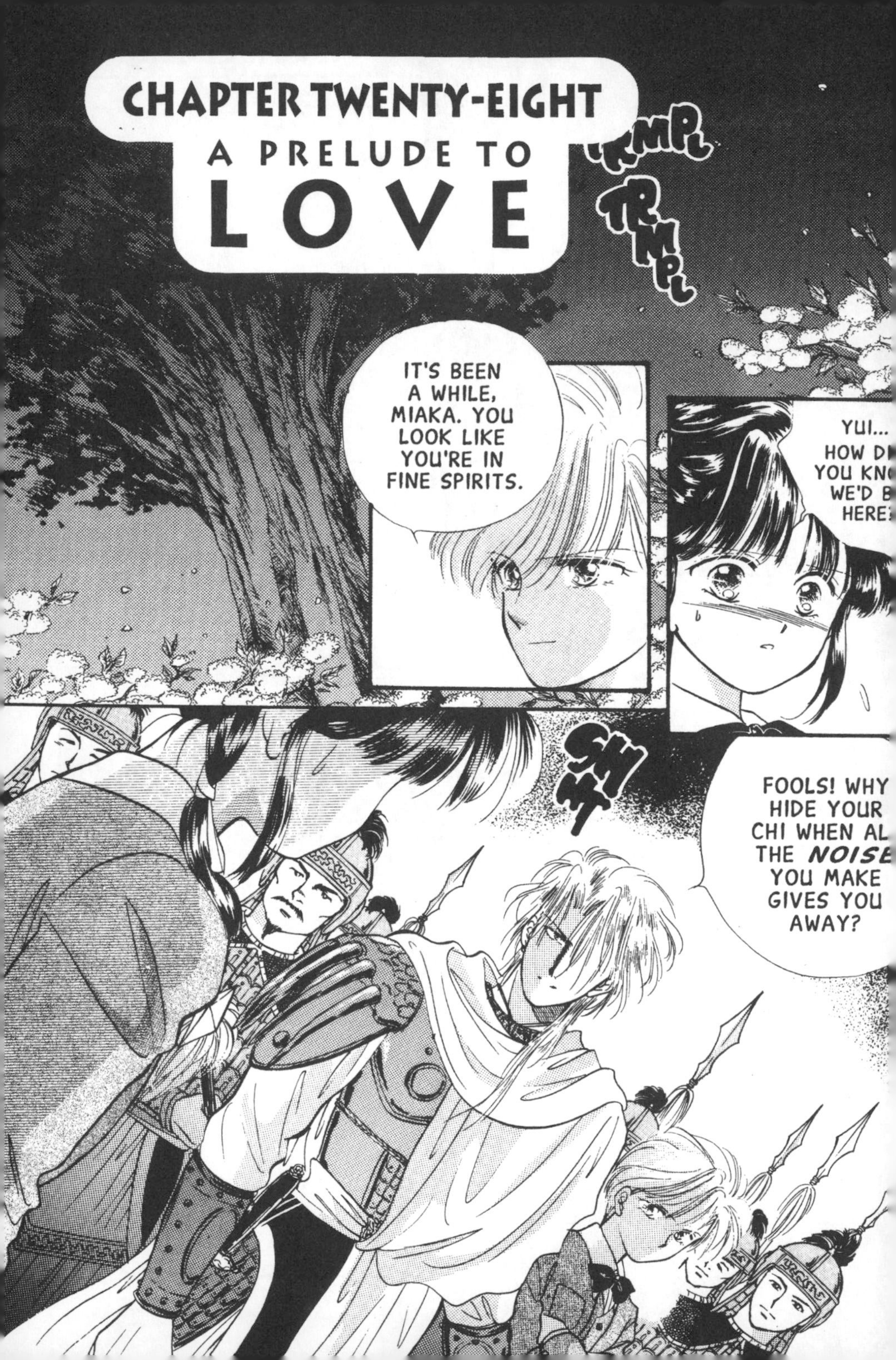

CHAPTER TWENTY-EIGHT
A PRELUDE TO LOVE
TRMPL
TRMPL
IT'S BEEN A WHILE, MIAKA. YOU LOOK LIKE YOU'RE IN FINE SPIRITS.
YUI... HOW DI YOU KN WE'D B HERE
SHH
FOOLS! WHY HIDE YOUR CHI WHEN AL THE NOISE YOU MAKE GIVES YOU AWAY?

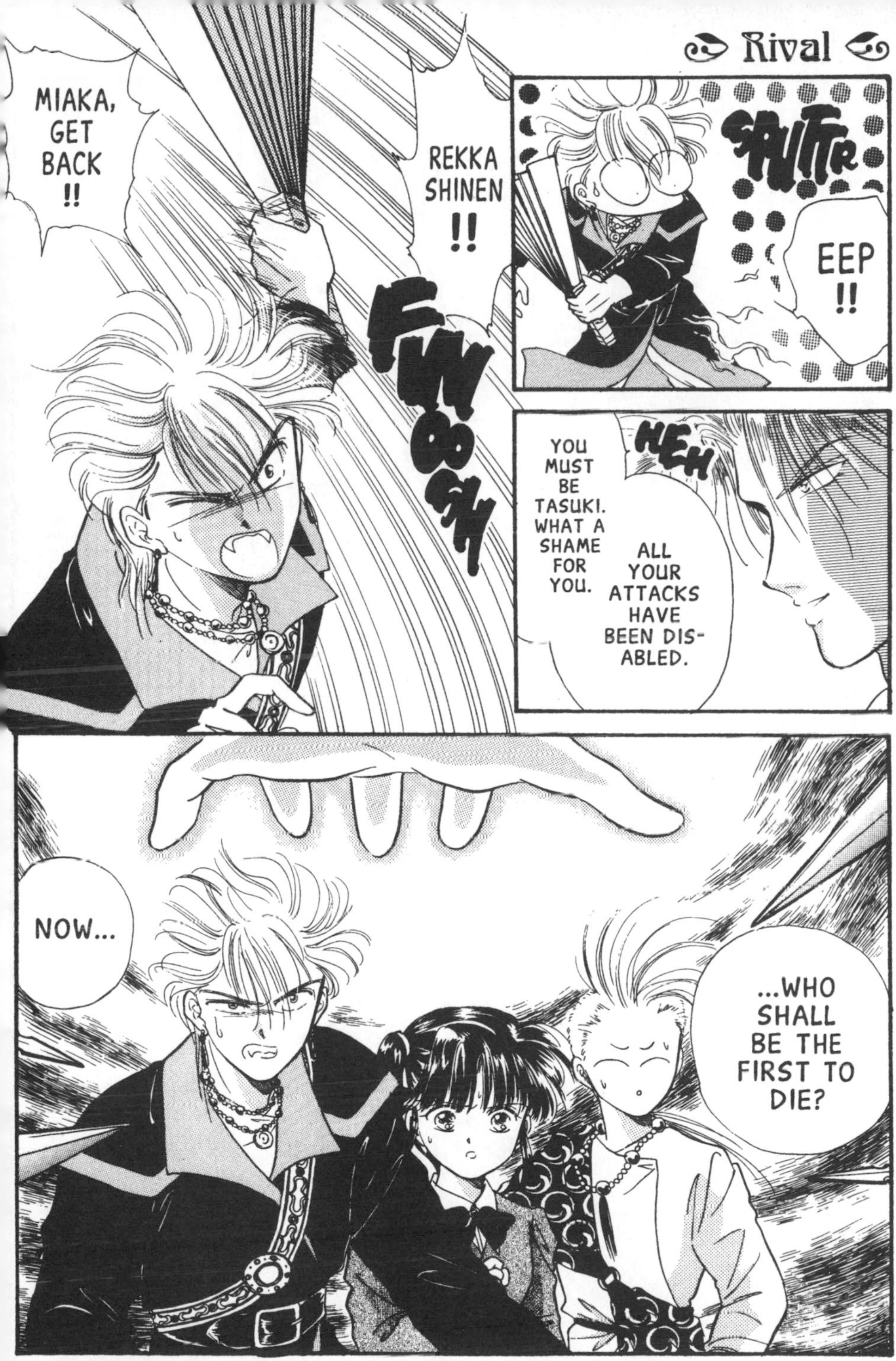
MIAKA, GET BACK!!
REKKA SHINEN!!
FWOOSH
SPUTTR
EEP!!
HEH
YOU MUST BE TASUKI. WHAT A SHAME FOR YOU.
ALL YOUR ATTACKS HAVE BEEN DISABLED.
NOW...
...WHO SHALL BE THE FIRST TO DIE?

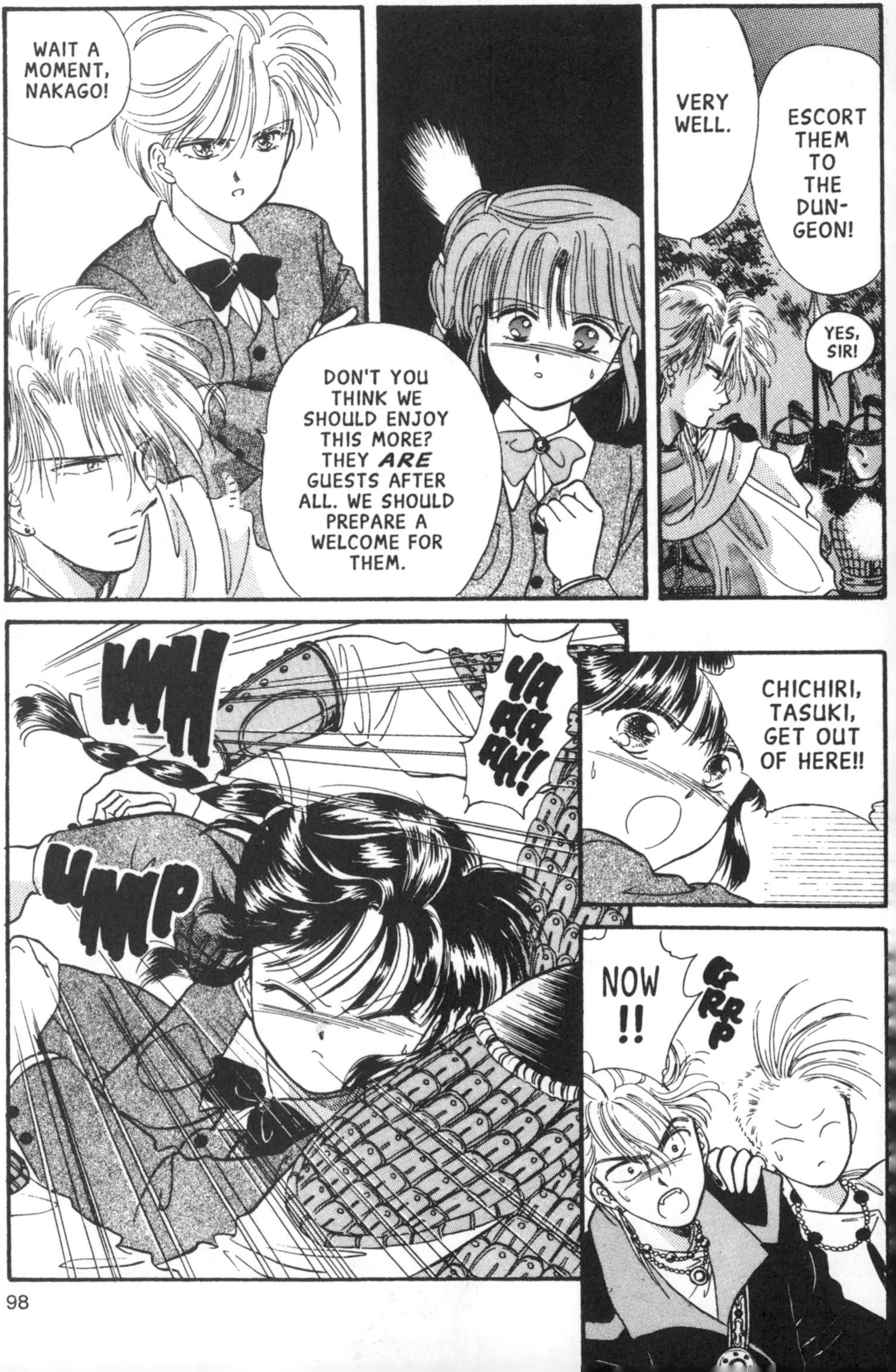
WAIT A MOMENT, NAKAGO!
DON'T YOU THINK WE SHOULD ENJOY THIS MORE? THEY ARE GUESTS AFTER ALL. WE SHOULD PREPARE A WELCOME FOR THEM.
VERY WELL.
ESCORT THEM TO THE DUN- GEON!
YES, SIR!
WH
YA AA AH!
UMP
CHICHIRI, TASUKI, GET OUT OF HERE!!
NOW !!
GRRP

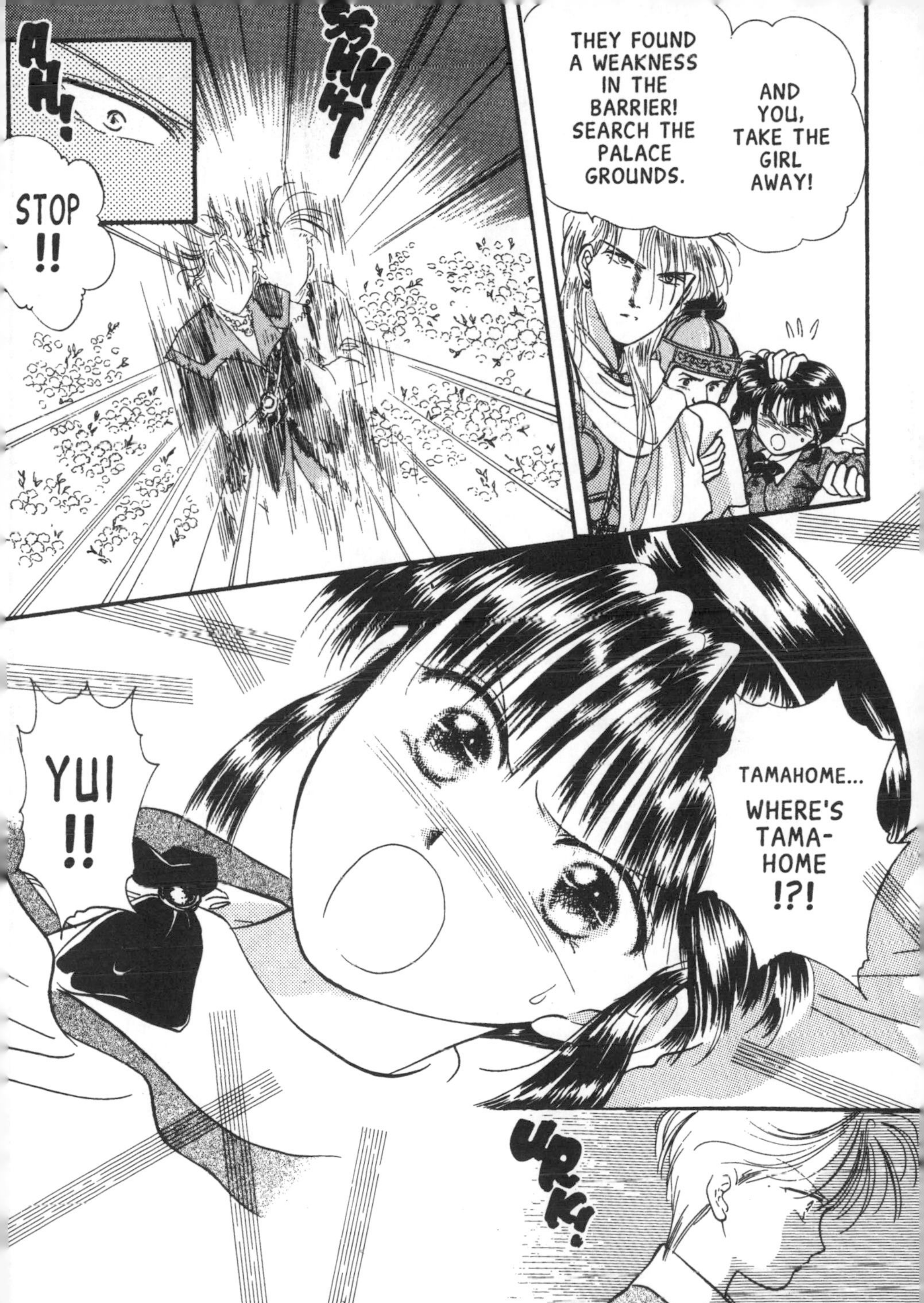
AH!
SSHHT
STOP !!
THEY FOUND A WEAKNESS IN THE BARRIER! SEARCH THE PALACE GROUNDS.
AND YOU, TAKE THE GIRL AWAY!
YUI !!
TAMAHOME...
WHERE'S TAMA-HOME !?!
URK!

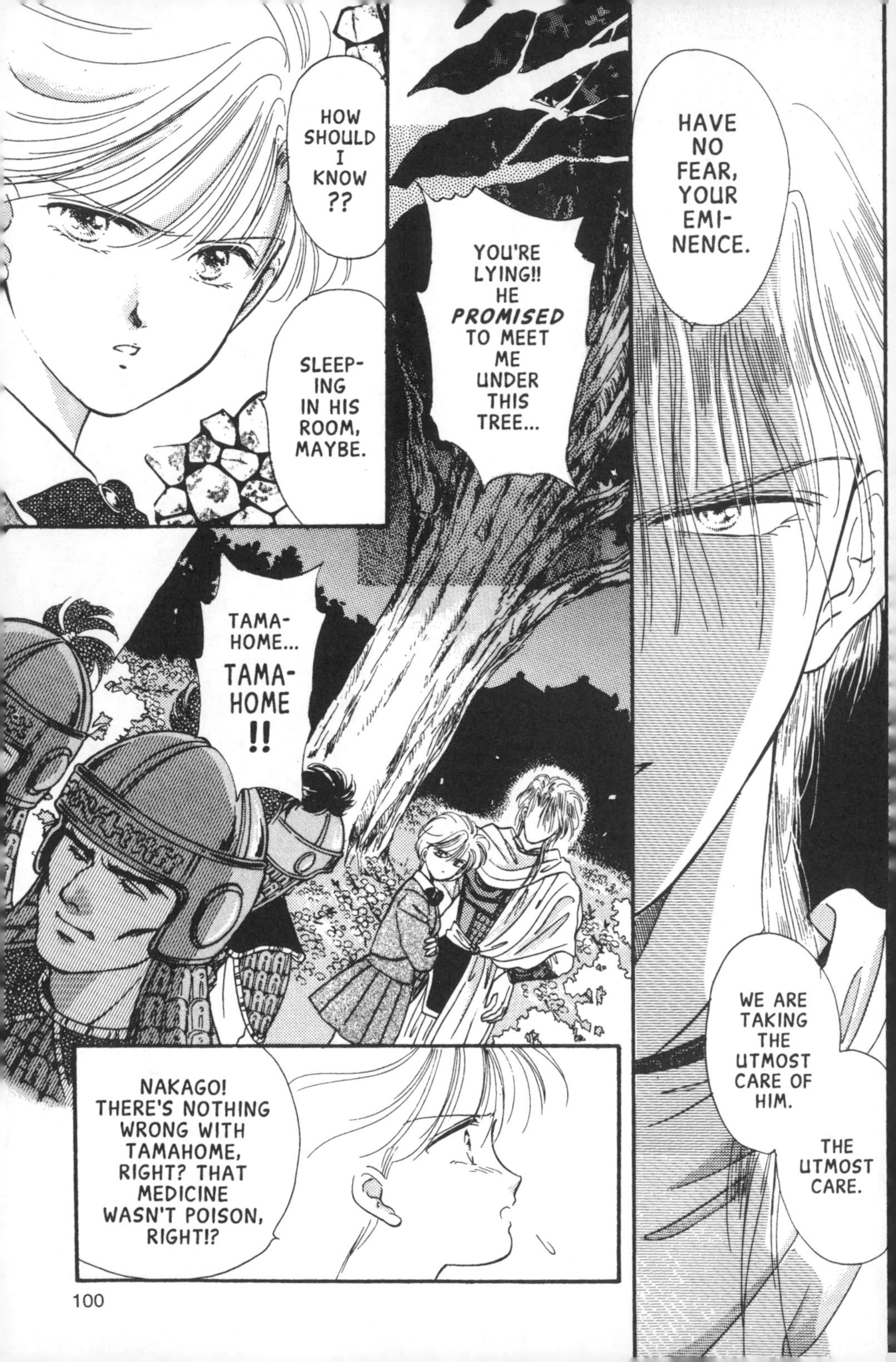
HOW SHOULD I KNOW??
SLEEPING IN HIS ROOM, MAYBE.
YOU'RE LYING!! HE *PROMISED* TO MEET ME UNDER THIS TREE...
TAMAHOME... TAMAHOME!!
NAKAGO! THERE'S NOTHING WRONG WITH TAMAHOME, RIGHT? THAT MEDICINE WASN'T POISON, RIGHT!?
HAVE NO FEAR, YOUR EMINENCE.
WE ARE TAKING THE UTMOST CARE OF HIM.
THE UTMOST CARE.

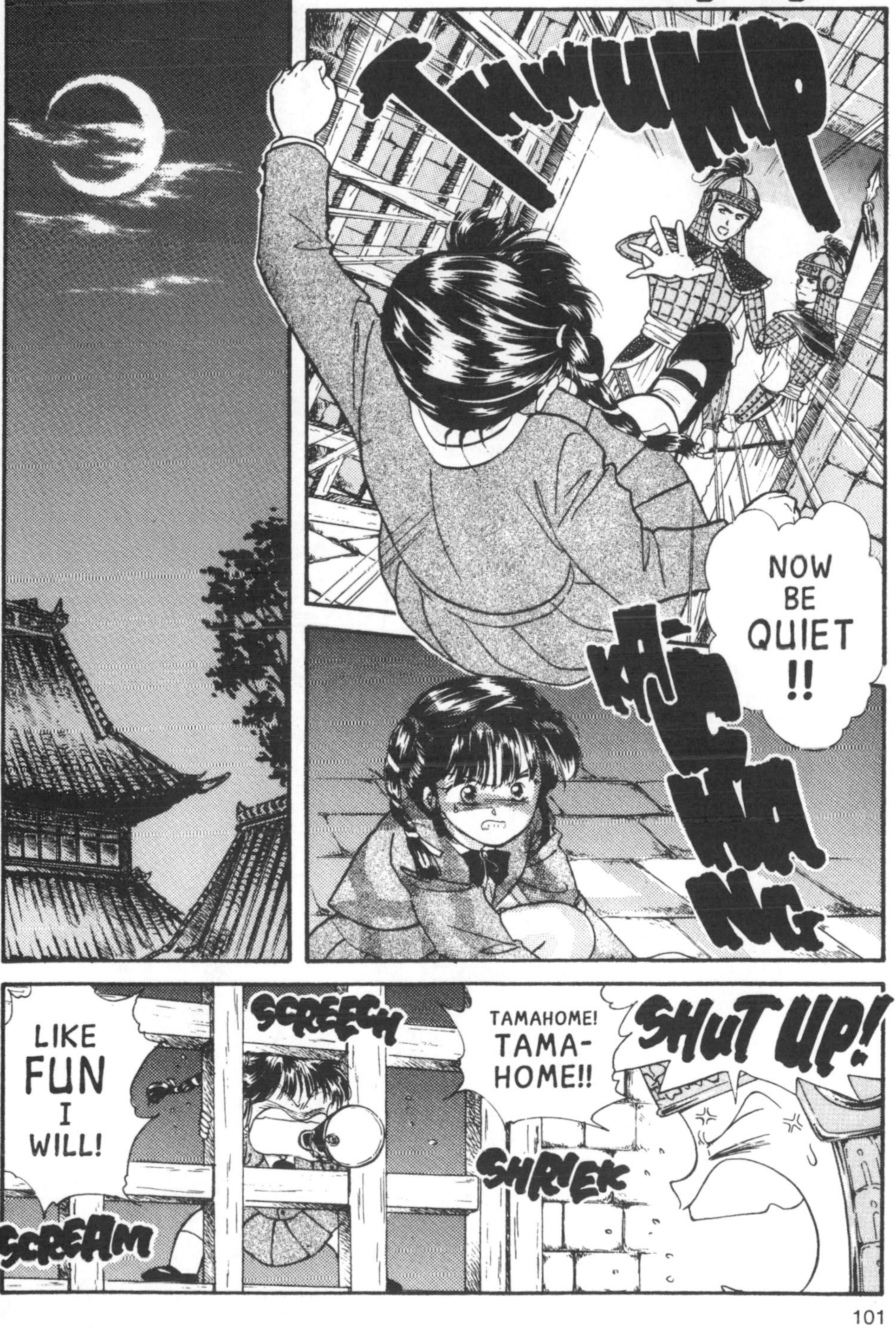
THWUMP
NOW BE QUIET!!
KA-CHWANG
LIKE FUN I WILL!
SCREAM
SCREECH
TAMAHOME! TAMA-HOME!!
SHRIEK
SHUT UP!

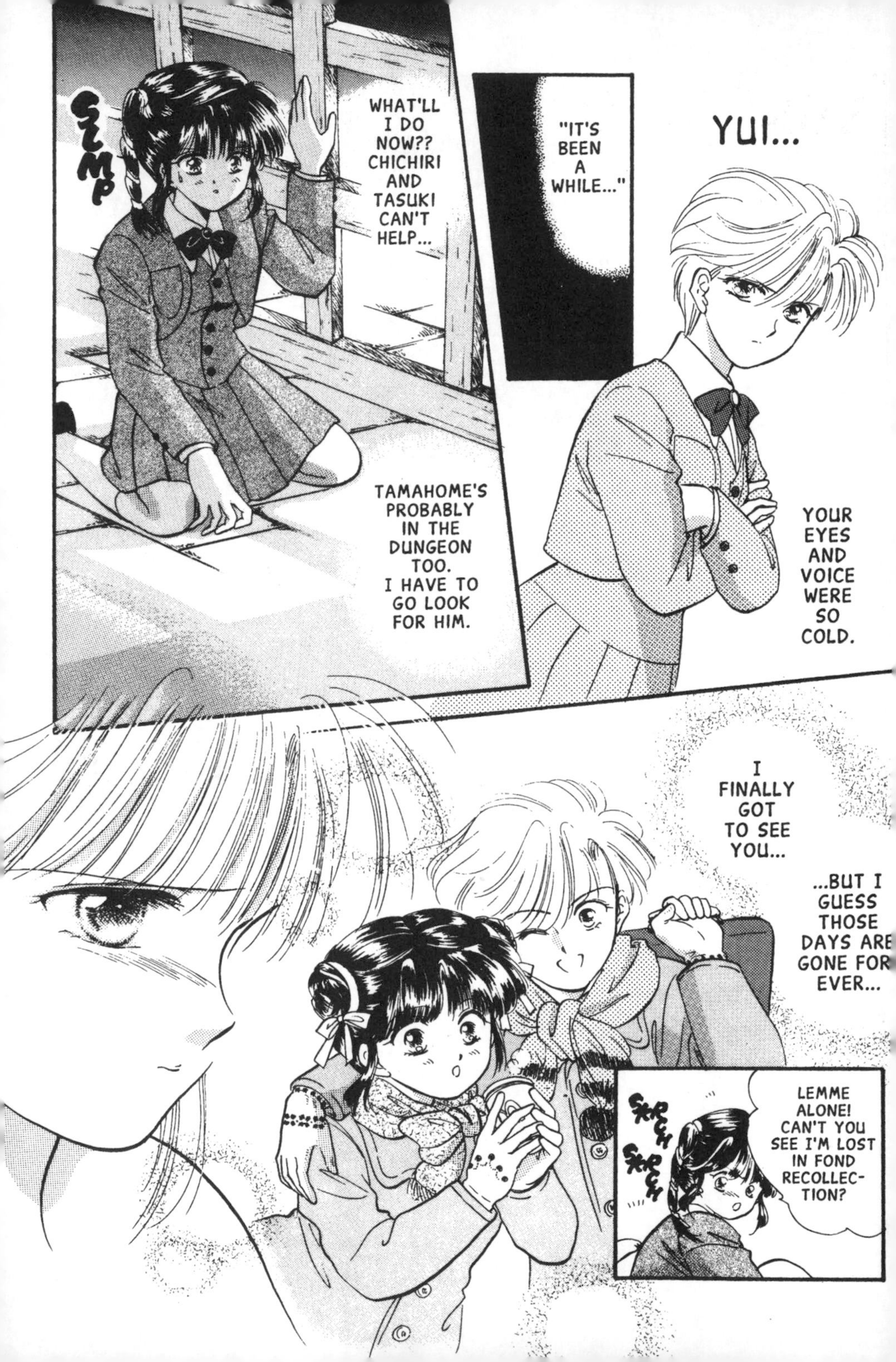
SEMP
WHAT'LL I DO NOW?? CHICHIRI AND TASUKI CAN'T HELP...
TAMAHOME'S PROBABLY IN THE DUNGEON TOO. I HAVE TO GO LOOK FOR HIM.
"IT'S BEEN A WHILE..."
YUI...
YOUR EYES AND VOICE WERE SO COLD.
I FINALLY GOT TO SEE YOU...
...BUT I GUESS THOSE DAYS ARE GONE FOR EVER...
SKRCH
SKRCH
LEMME ALONE! CAN'T YOU SEE I'M LOST IN FOND RECOLLECTION?

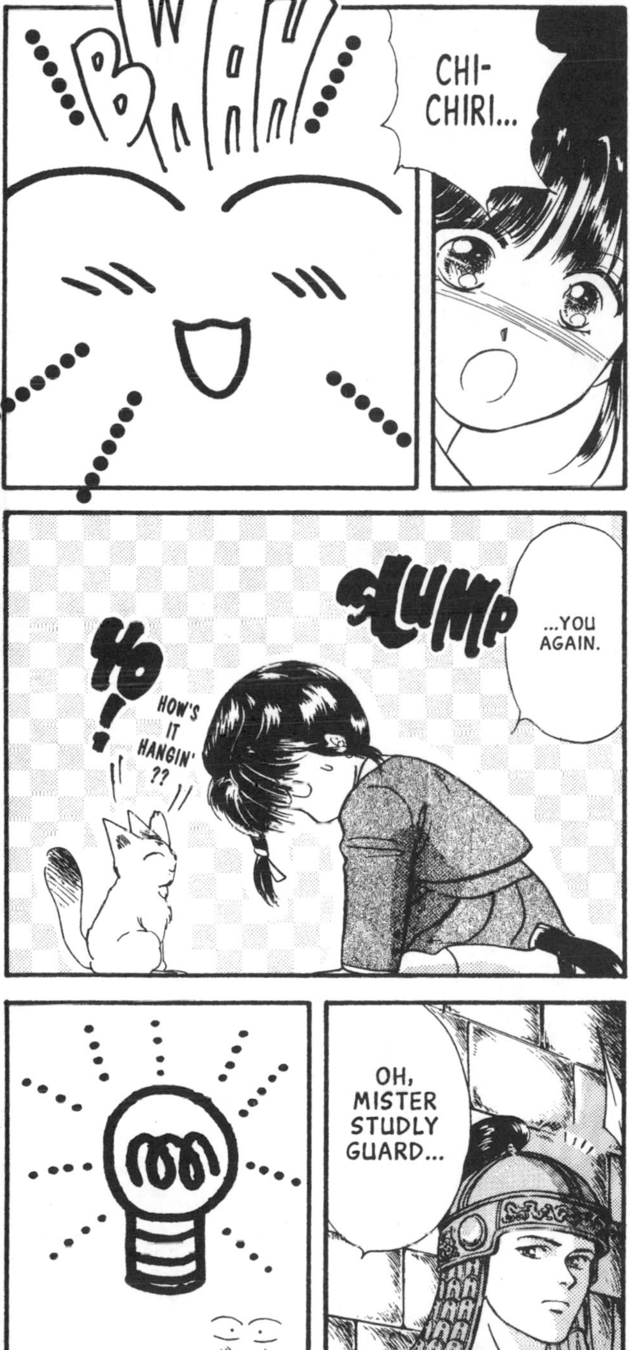
BWAH
CHI-CHIRI...
SLUMP
HO!
HOW'S IT HANGIN' ??
...YOU AGAIN.
OH, MISTER STUDLY GUARD...

Now... When I go visit my hometown, the distance is about a third the length of the whole country. I usually take the bullet train, but this time I decided that I'd go ahead and fly. That was fine as far as it went. While I'd flown before, nobody else in my family had (mother and brother). I'm the type to leave details to other people, and this time it got all three of us in trouble. You know how you're supposed to check in at the gate 20 minutes early? Well, I completely forgot about that. We arrived at Hanada airport only 15 minutes before our departure time, so we're already late. But we just sat around in the waiting area, only to suddenly realize that there was just five minutes left! We totally panicked when we heard the flight announcement. On top of this, they stopped me at security because of my letter opener! You shouldn't do things you're not used to. I can't believe how stupid we were. I swear, we were acting like manga characters. In the end though, we did get on the flight with no problem. The flight was delayed. But it wasn't our fault!! The pilot was late or something like that! *Please believe me! Don't say it's my fault!* This is what happens when the whole family just doesn't take responsibility!

I wasn't planning on telling Dad about it, but I can't keep things to myself. I ended up telling him. And of course he made fun of us. *Waaaaaahhh!*

Well, failure is the mother of success, so our return trip was totally smooth. We arrived one hour early. *Are we just...stupid, maybe?* See if I care! This year I'm going to China. Flying is a breeze!

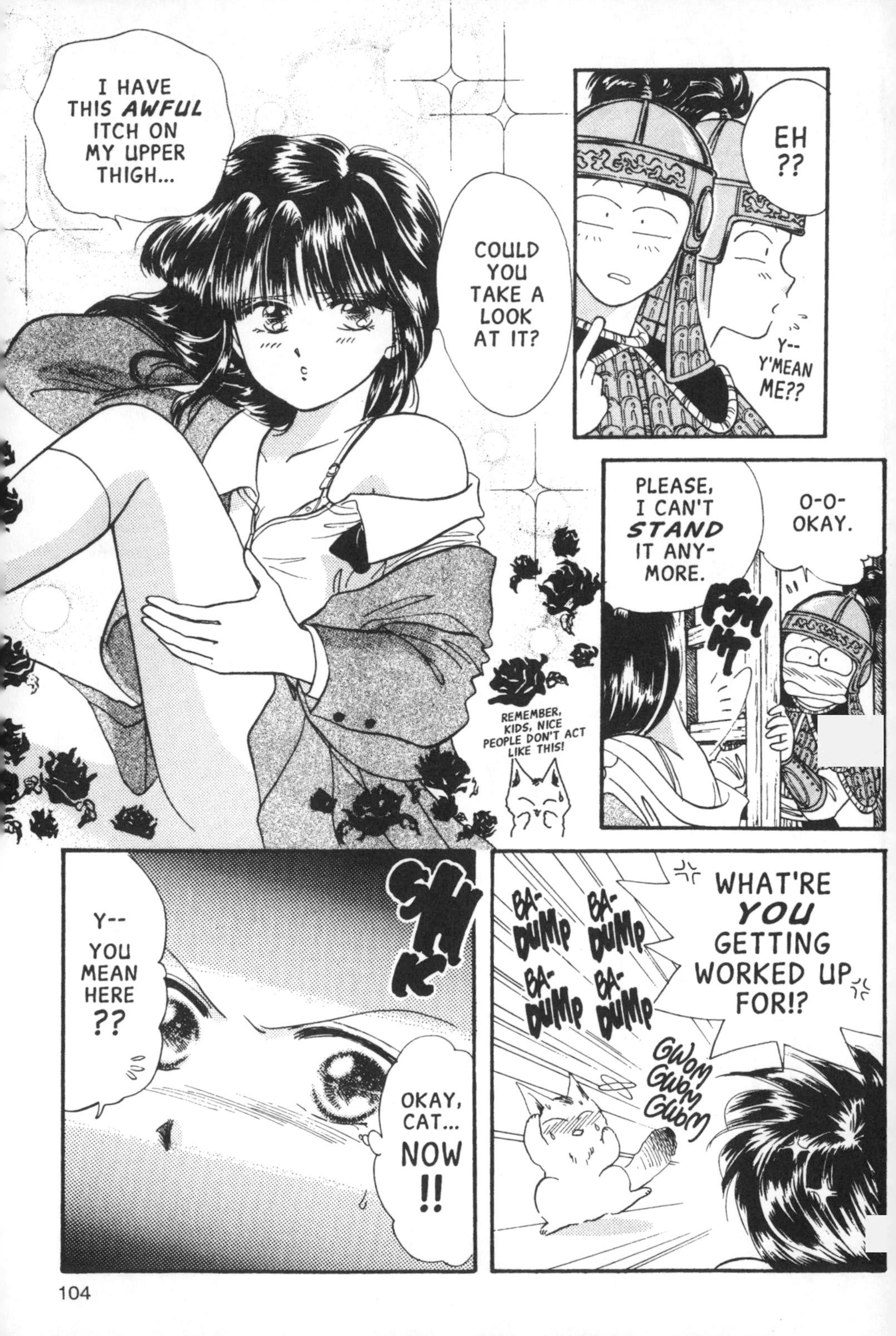
I HAVE THIS AWFUL ITCH ON MY UPPER THIGH...
COULD YOU TAKE A LOOK AT IT?
EH ??
Y-- Y'MEAN ME??
PLEASE, I CAN'T STAND IT ANY-MORE.
O-O-OKAY.
FSH HT
REMEMBER, KIDS, NICE PEOPLE DON'T ACT LIKE THIS!
Y-- YOU MEAN HERE ??
SHIK
OKAY, CAT... NOW !!
WHAT'RE YOU GETTING WORKED UP FOR!?
BA-DUMP BA-DUMP
BA-DUMP BA-DUMP
GWOM GWOM GWOM

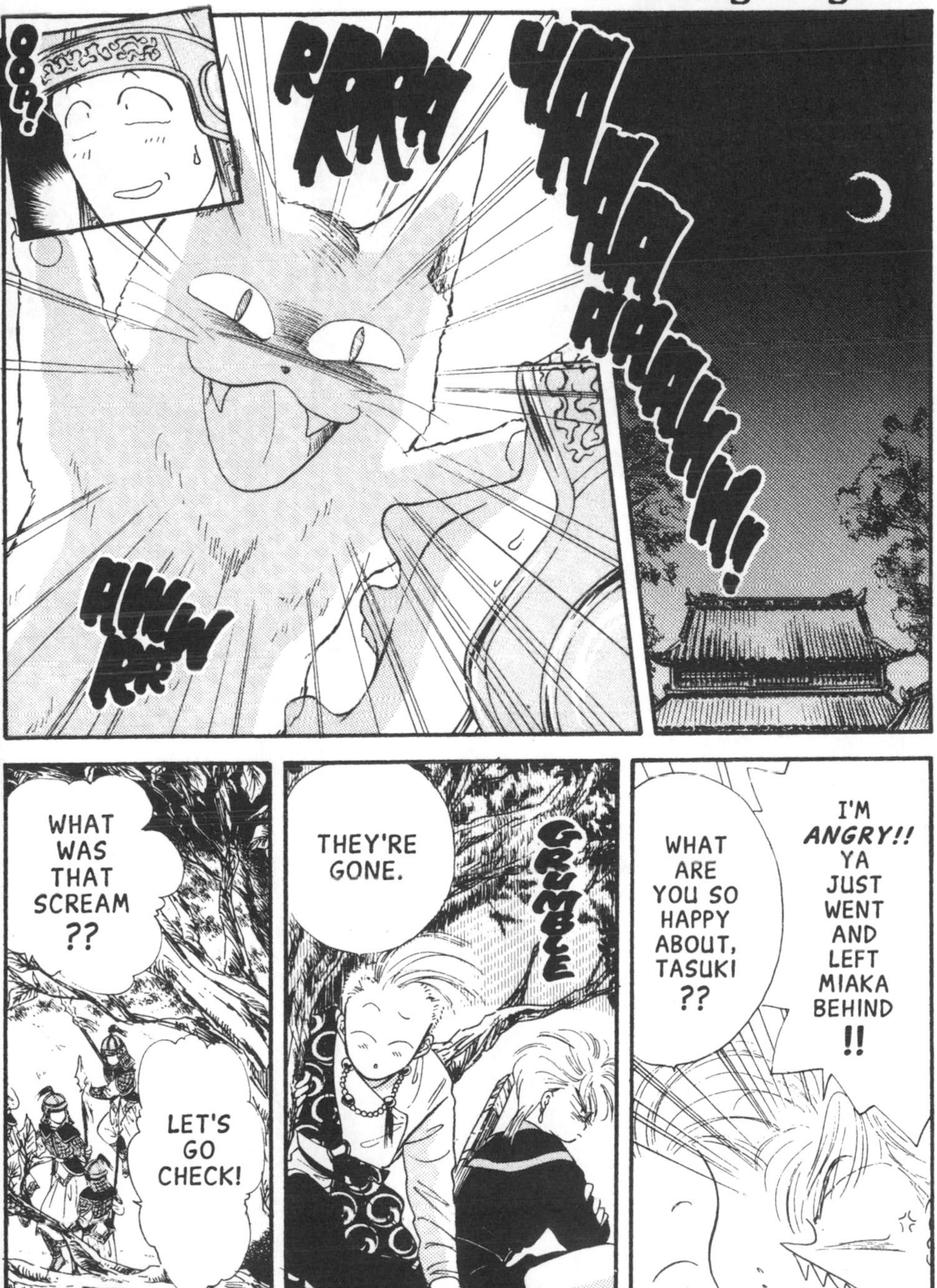
OOF!
WHAT WAS THAT SCREAM ??
LET'S GO CHECK!
THEY'RE GONE.
GRUMBLE
WHAT ARE YOU SO HAPPY ABOUT, TASUKI ??
I'M *ANGRY!!* YA JUST WENT AND LEFT MIAKA BEHIND !!

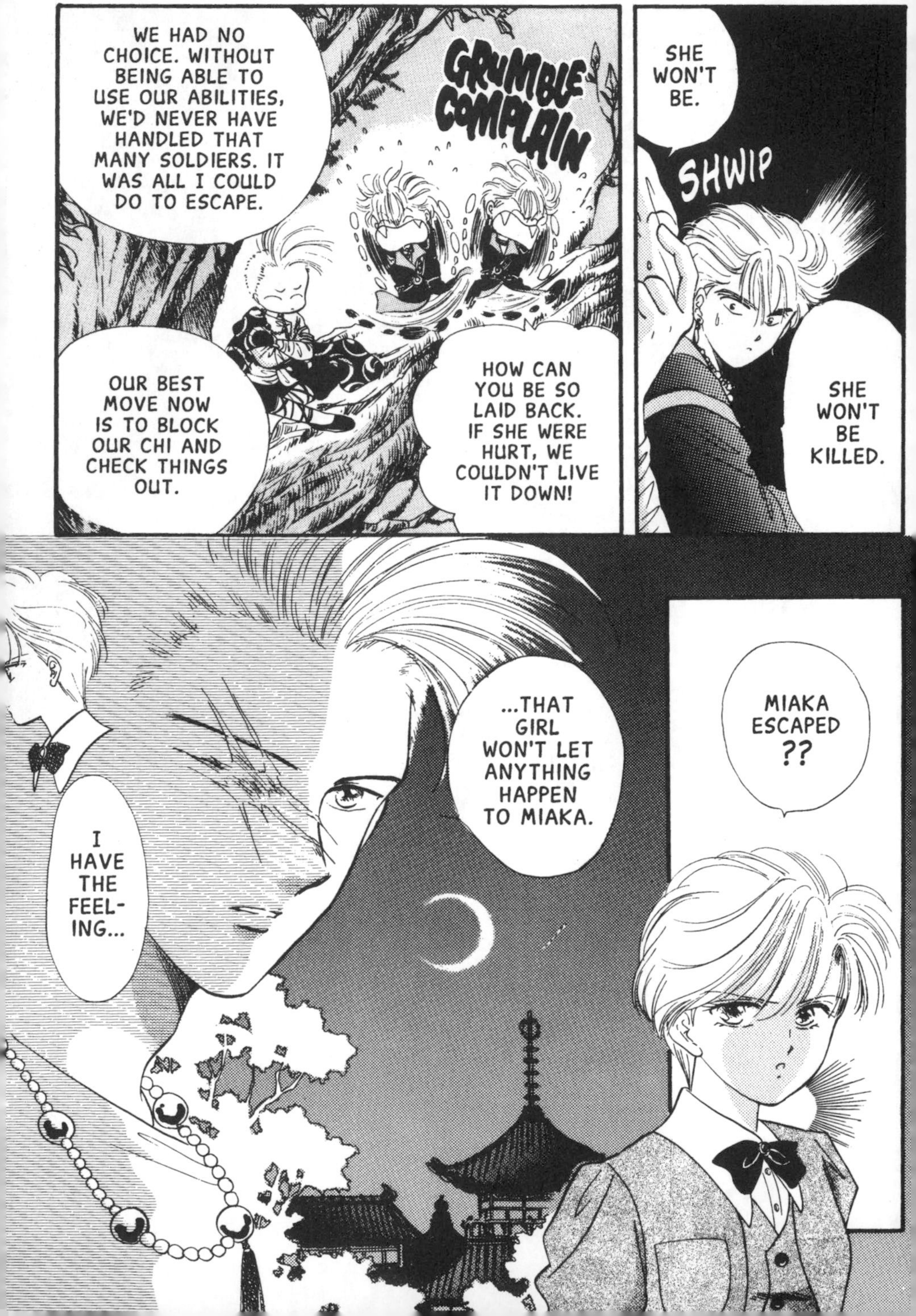
WE HAD NO CHOICE. WITHOUT BEING ABLE TO USE OUR ABILITIES, WE'D NEVER HAVE HANDLED THAT MANY SOLDIERS. IT WAS ALL I COULD DO TO ESCAPE.
GRUMBLE COMPLAIN
OUR BEST MOVE NOW IS TO BLOCK OUR CHI AND CHECK THINGS OUT.
HOW CAN YOU BE SO LAID BACK. IF SHE WERE HURT, WE COULDN'T LIVE IT DOWN!
SHE WON'T BE.
SHWIP
SHE WON'T BE KILLED.
I HAVE THE FEEL-ING...
...THAT GIRL WON'T LET ANYTHING HAPPEN TO MIAKA.
MIAKA ESCAPED??

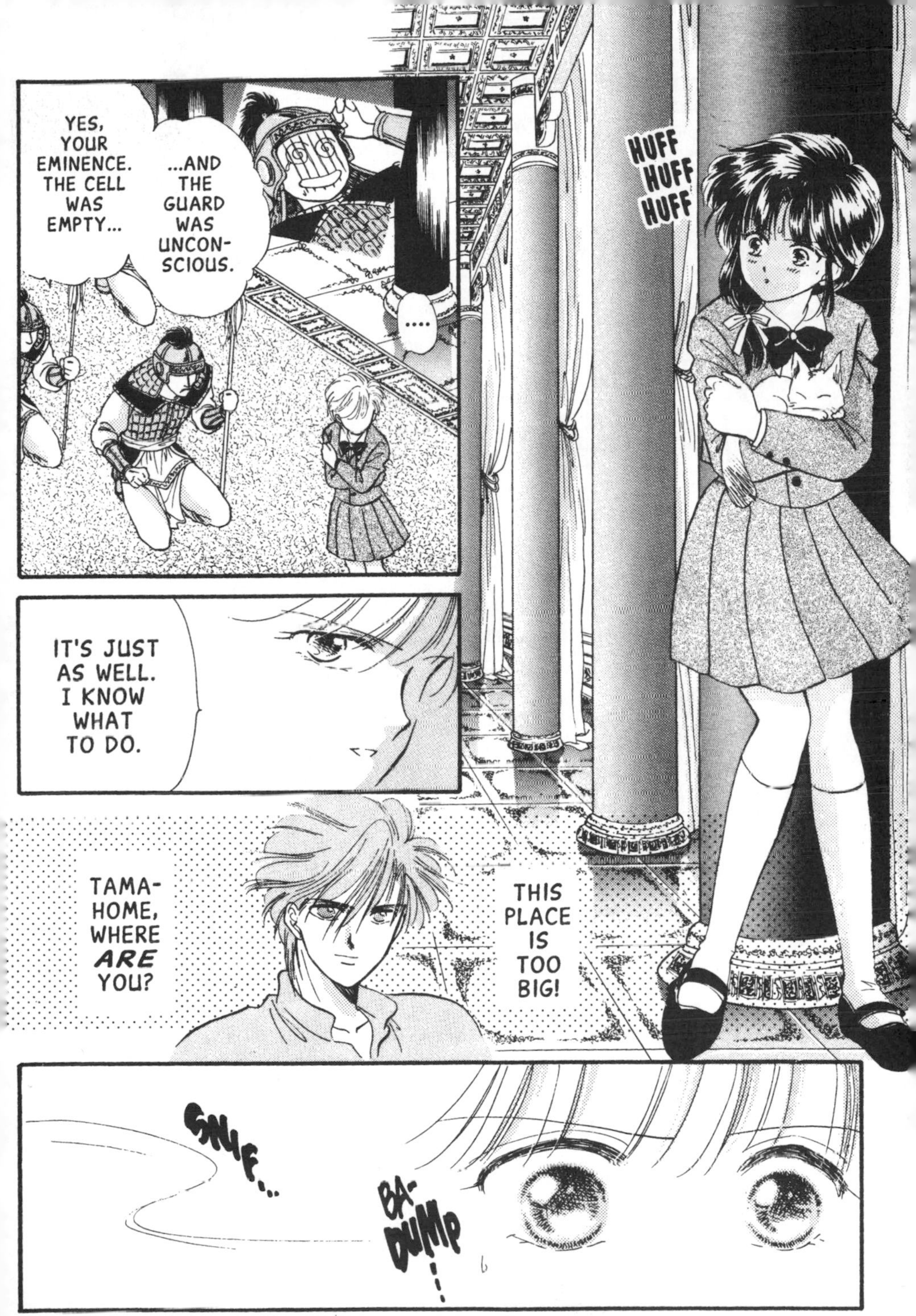
YES, YOUR EMINENCE. THE CELL WAS EMPTY...
...AND THE GUARD WAS UNCONSCIOUS.
....
IT'S JUST AS WELL. I KNOW WHAT TO DO.
TAMAHOME, WHERE *ARE* YOU?
THIS PLACE IS TOO BIG!
HUFF HUFF HUFF
SNIF...
BA-DUMP...

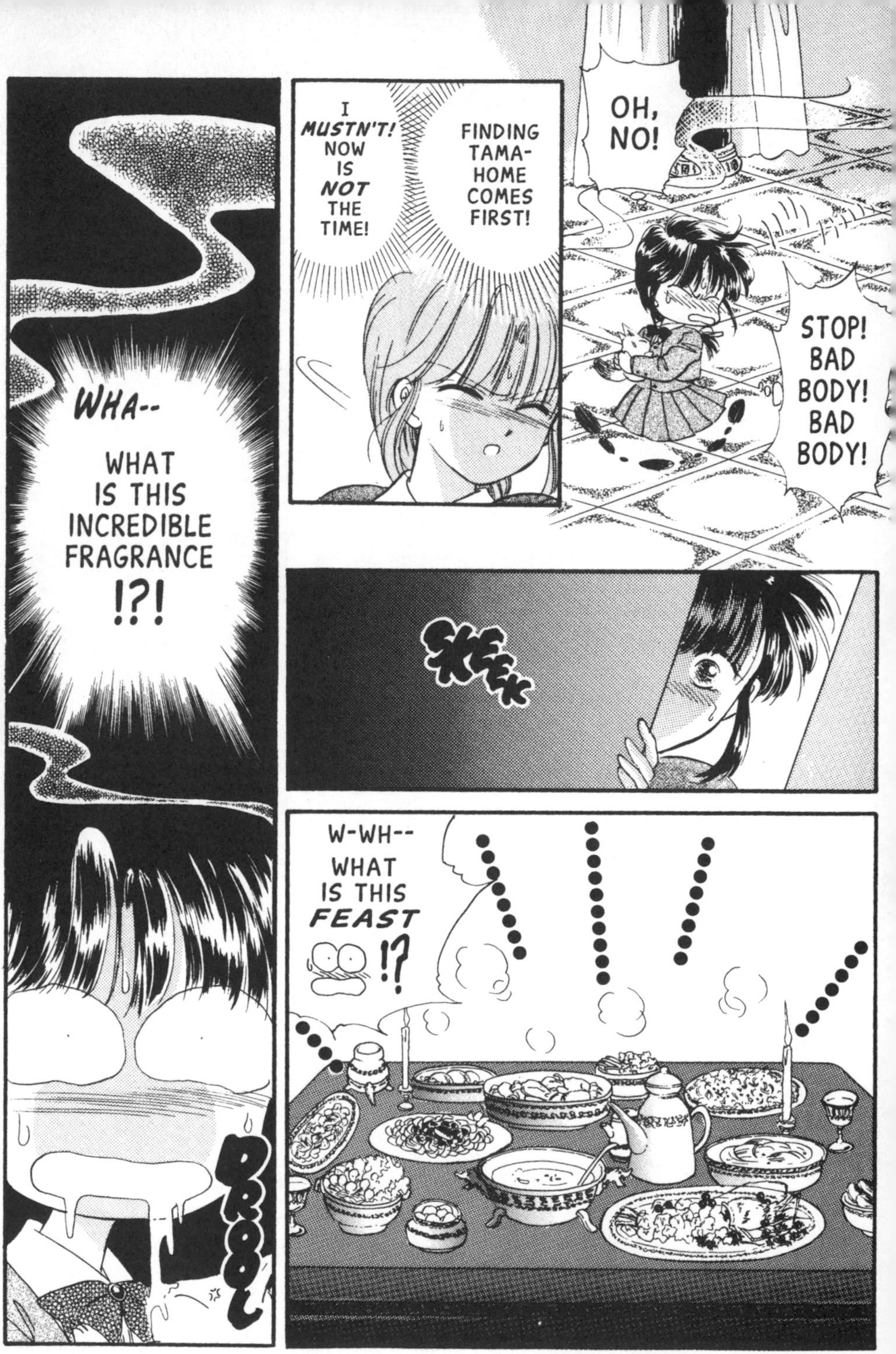
WHA--
WHAT IS THIS INCREDIBLE FRAGRANCE !?!
DROOL
I MUSTN'T! NOW IS NOT THE TIME!
FINDING TAMAHOME COMES FIRST!
OH, NO!
STOP! BAD BODY! BAD BODY!
SKEEK
W-WH-- WHAT IS THIS FEAST !?

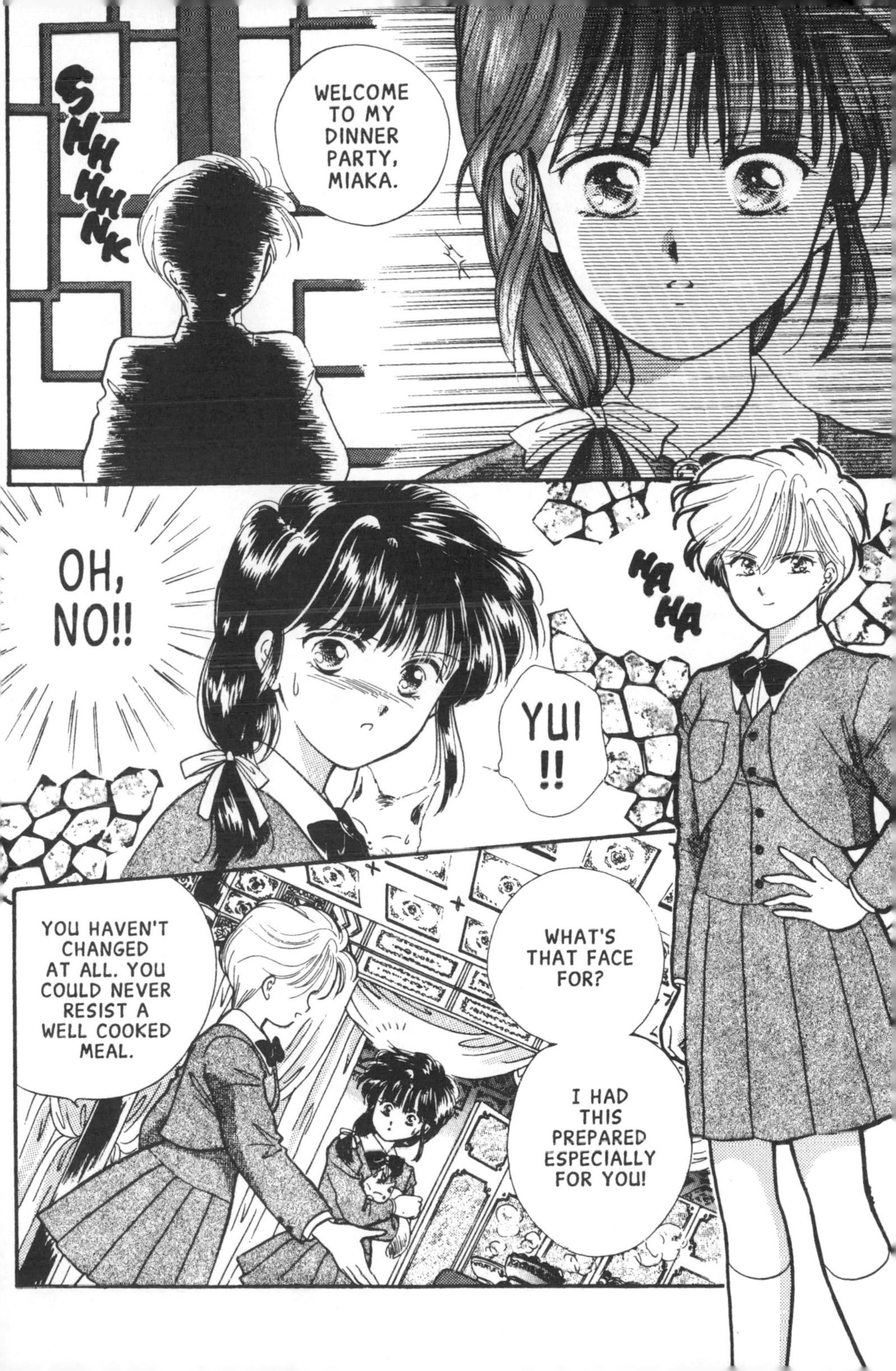
SHHHHNK
WELCOME TO MY DINNER PARTY, MIAKA.
OH, NO!!
YUI!!
HA HA
YOU HAVEN'T CHANGED AT ALL. YOU COULD NEVER RESIST A WELL COOKED MEAL.
WHAT'S THAT FACE FOR?
I HAD THIS PREPARED ESPECIALLY FOR YOU!

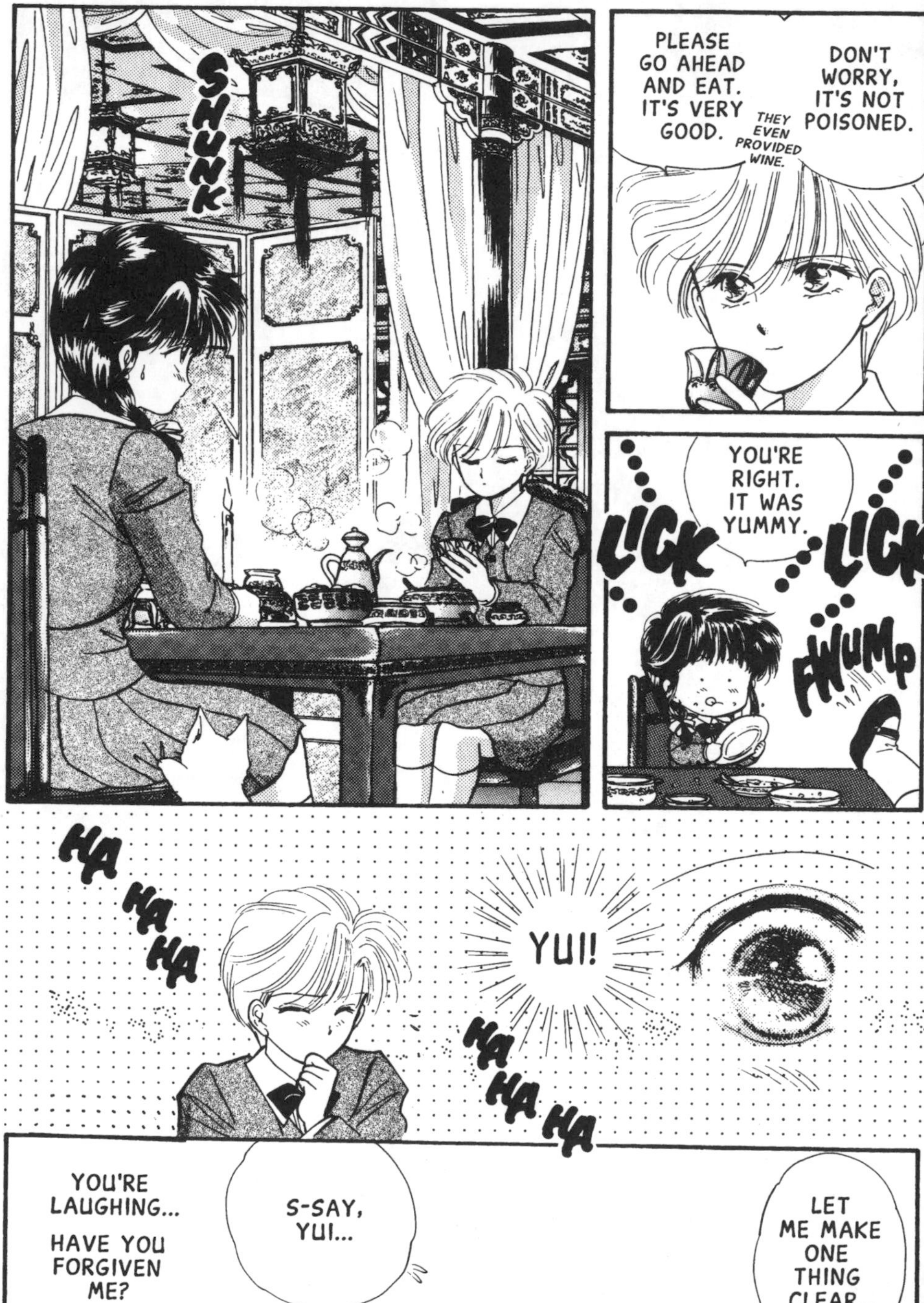
SHUNK
PLEASE GO AHEAD AND EAT. IT'S VERY GOOD.
THEY EVEN PROVIDED WINE.
DON'T WORRY, IT'S NOT POISONED.
YOU'RE RIGHT. IT WAS YUMMY.
LICK
LICK
FWUMP
HA HA HA
YUI!
HA HA HA
YOU'RE LAUGHING...
HAVE YOU FORGIVEN ME?
S-SAY, YUI...
LET ME MAKE ONE THING CLEAR...

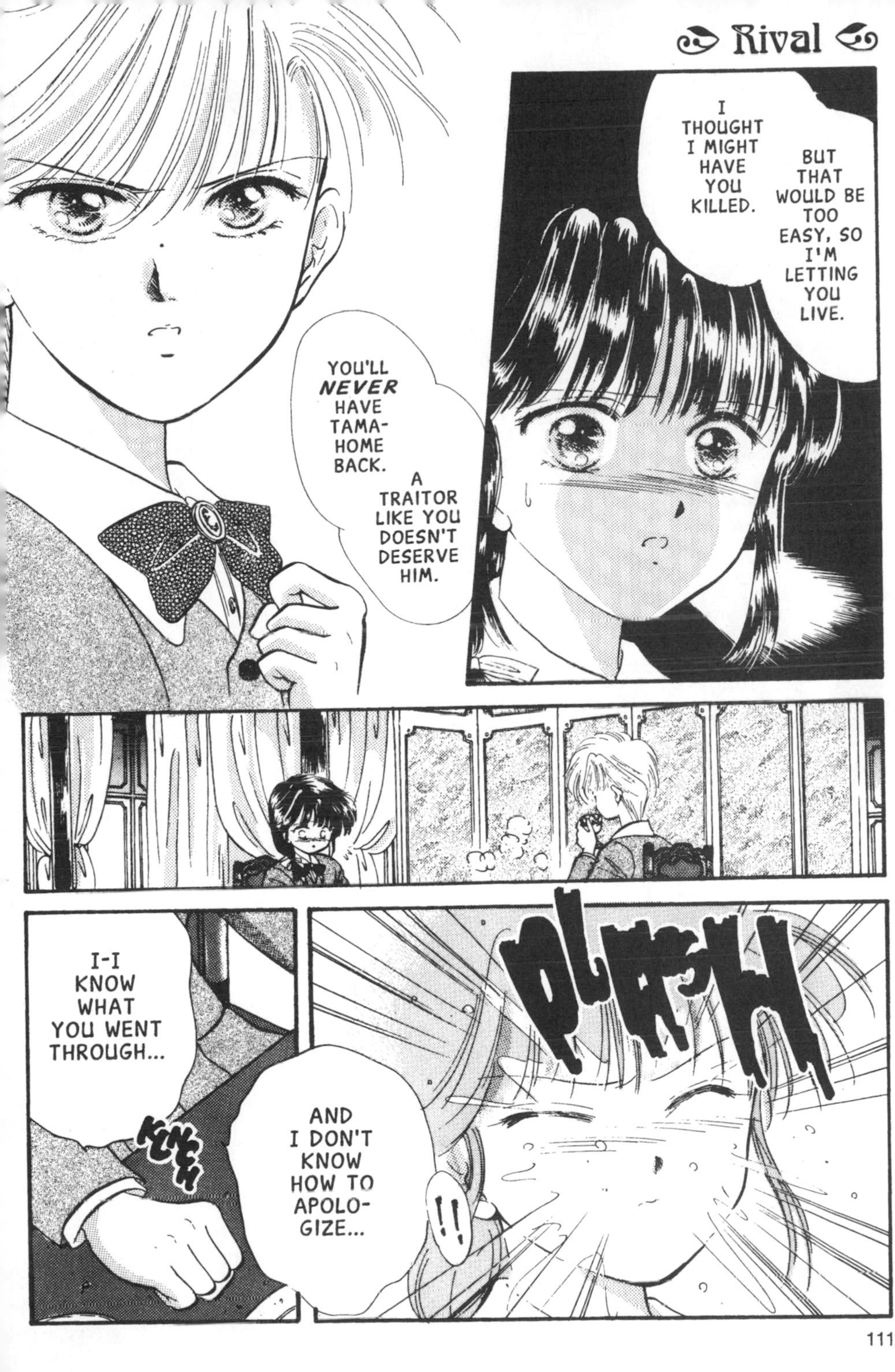

YOU'LL *NEVER* HAVE TAMA-HOME BACK.
A TRAITOR LIKE YOU DOESN'T DESERVE HIM.
I THOUGHT I MIGHT HAVE YOU KILLED.
BUT THAT WOULD BE TOO EASY, SO I'M LETTING YOU LIVE.
I-I KNOW WHAT YOU WENT THROUGH...
AND I DON'T KNOW HOW TO APOLO-GIZE...
!!

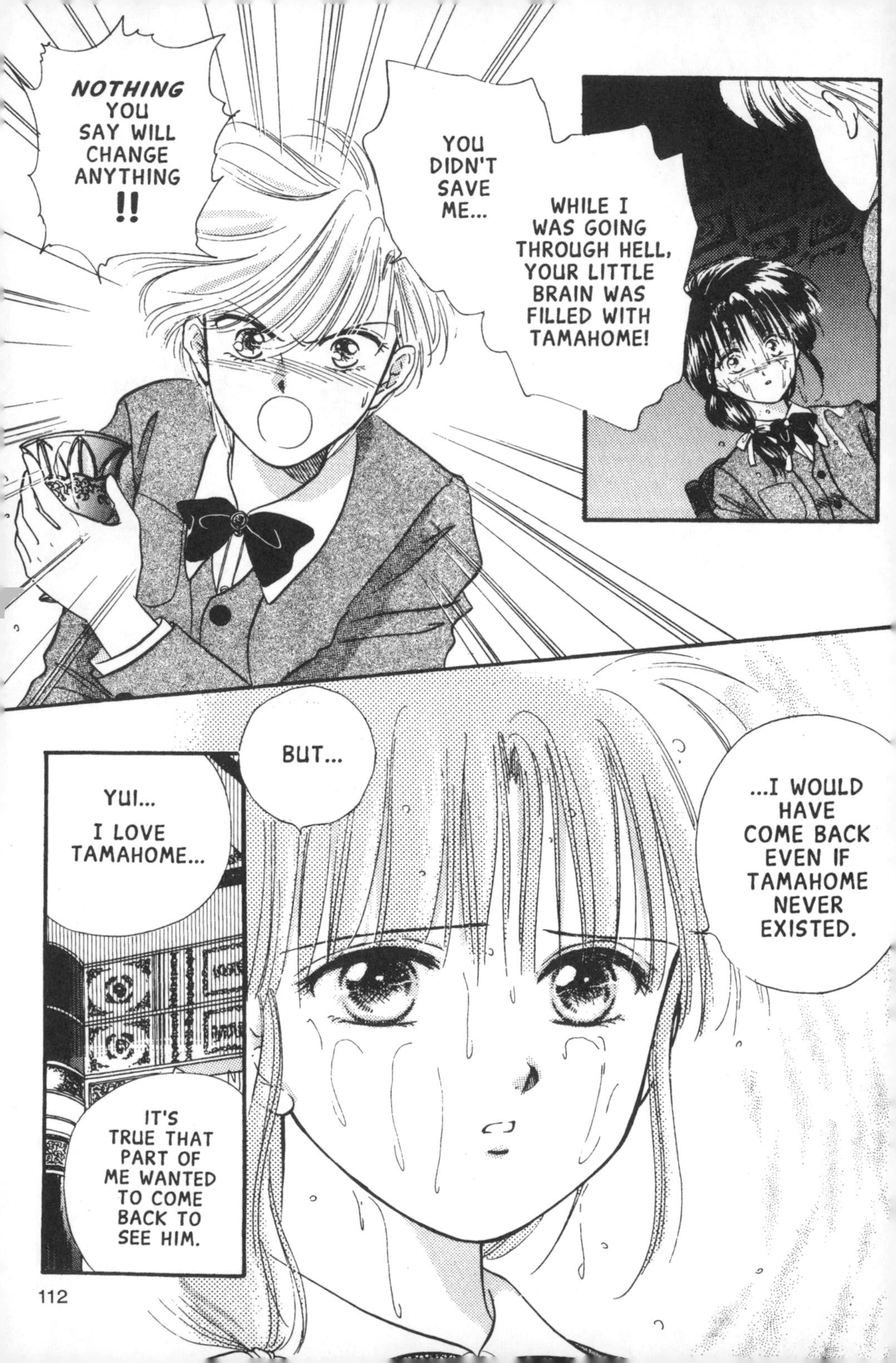
NOTHING YOU SAY WILL CHANGE ANYTHING!!
YOU DIDN'T SAVE ME...
WHILE I WAS GOING THROUGH HELL, YOUR LITTLE BRAIN WAS FILLED WITH TAMAHOME!
YUI... I LOVE TAMAHOME...
IT'S TRUE THAT PART OF ME WANTED TO COME BACK TO SEE HIM.
BUT...
...I WOULD HAVE COME BACK EVEN IF TAMAHOME NEVER EXISTED.

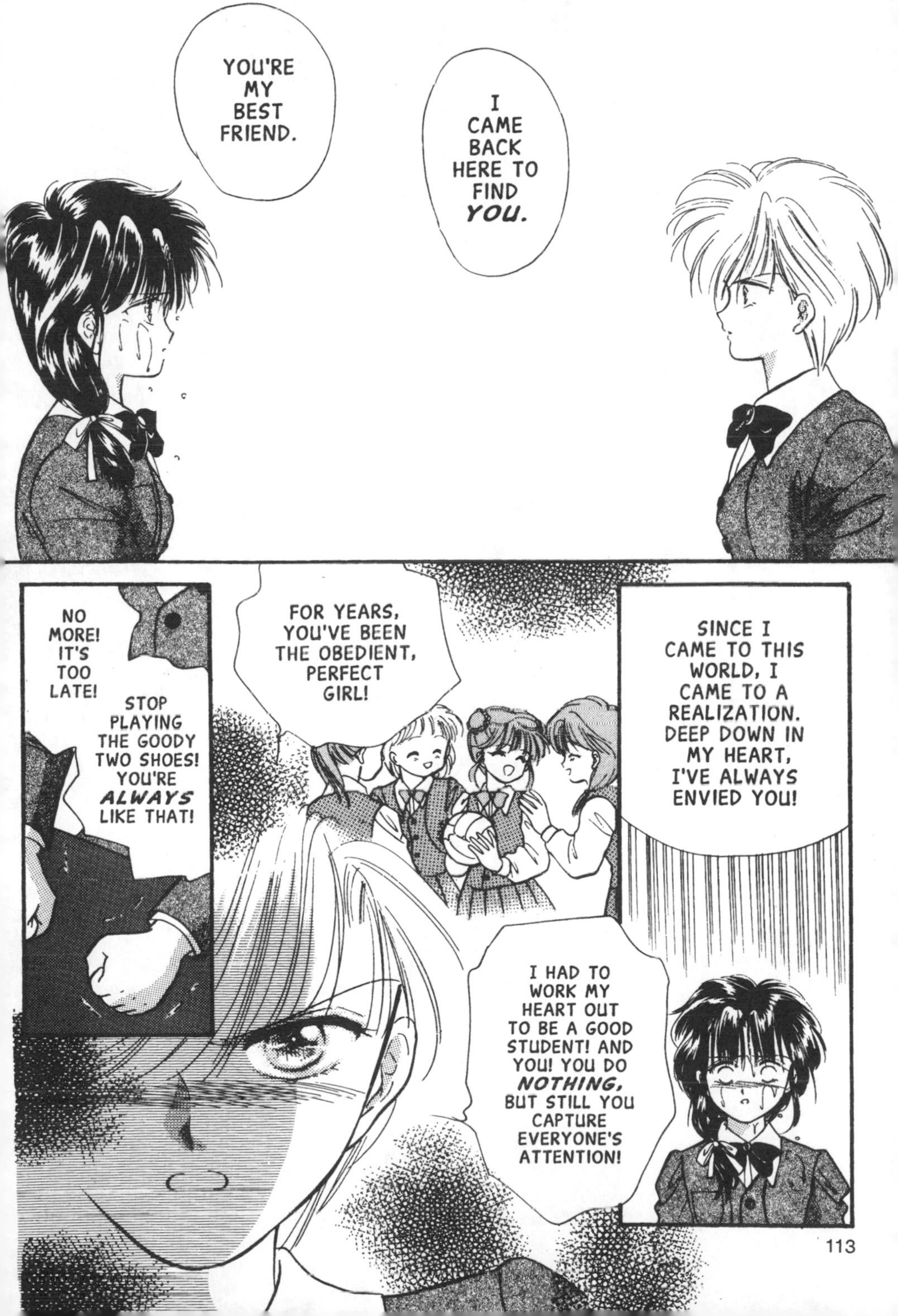
YOU'RE MY BEST FRIEND.
I CAME BACK HERE TO FIND ***YOU.***
NO MORE! IT'S TOO LATE!
STOP PLAYING THE GOODY TWO SHOES! YOU'RE ***ALWAYS*** LIKE THAT!
FOR YEARS, YOU'VE BEEN THE OBEDIENT, PERFECT GIRL!
SINCE I CAME TO THIS WORLD, I CAME TO A REALIZATION. DEEP DOWN IN MY HEART, I'VE ALWAYS ENVIED YOU!
I HAD TO WORK MY HEART OUT TO BE A GOOD STUDENT! AND YOU! YOU DO ***NOTHING,*** BUT STILL YOU CAPTURE EVERYONE'S ATTENTION!

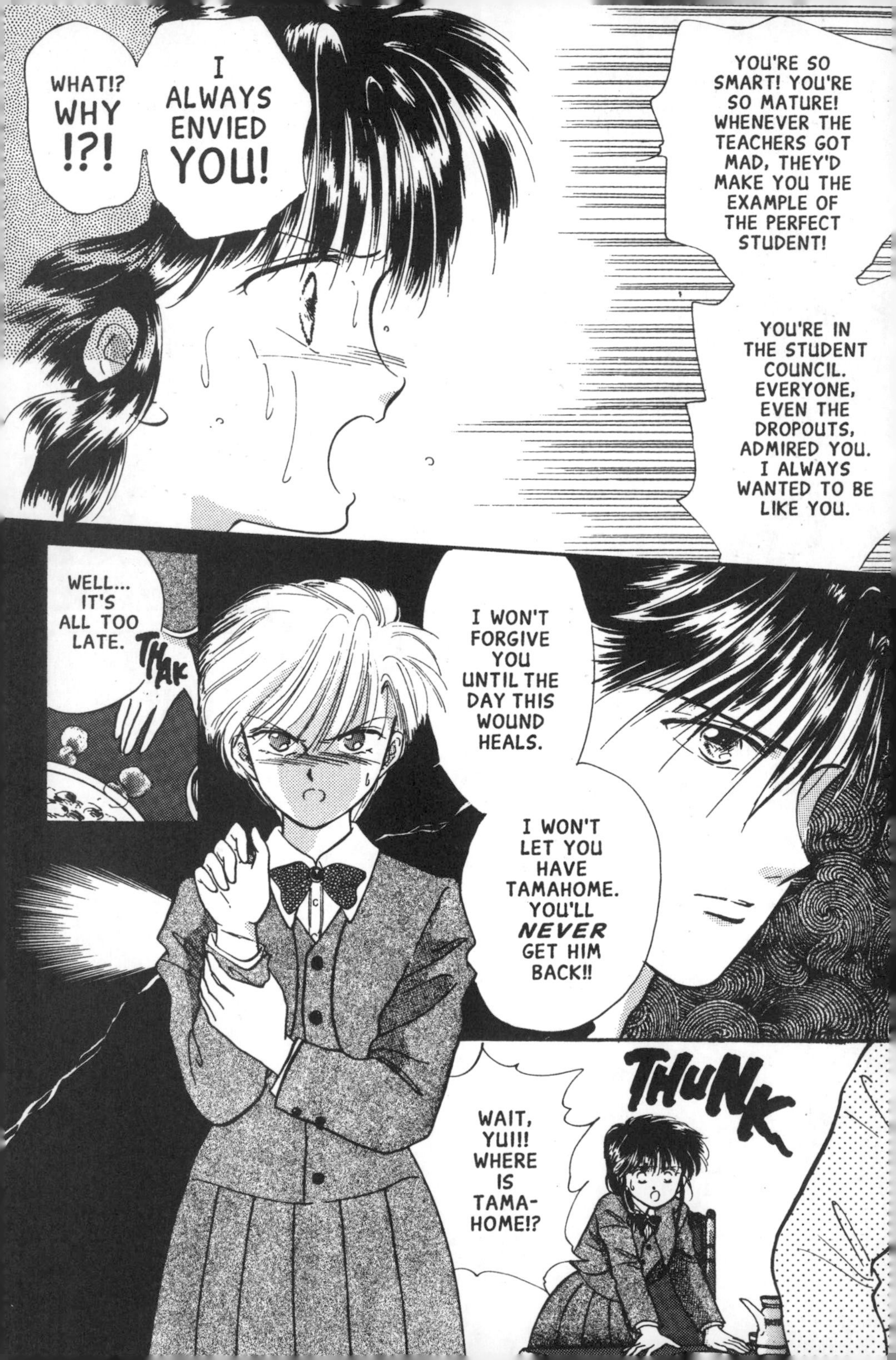
WHAT!? WHY !?!
I ALWAYS ENVIED YOU!
YOU'RE SO SMART! YOU'RE SO MATURE! WHENEVER THE TEACHERS GOT MAD, THEY'D MAKE YOU THE EXAMPLE OF THE PERFECT STUDENT!
YOU'RE IN THE STUDENT COUNCIL. EVERYONE, EVEN THE DROPOUTS, ADMIRED YOU. I ALWAYS WANTED TO BE LIKE YOU.
WELL... IT'S ALL TOO LATE.
THAK
I WON'T FORGIVE YOU UNTIL THE DAY THIS WOUND HEALS.
I WON'T LET YOU HAVE TAMAHOME. YOU'LL *NEVER* GET HIM BACK!!
THUNK
WAIT, YUI!! WHERE IS TAMA-HOME!?

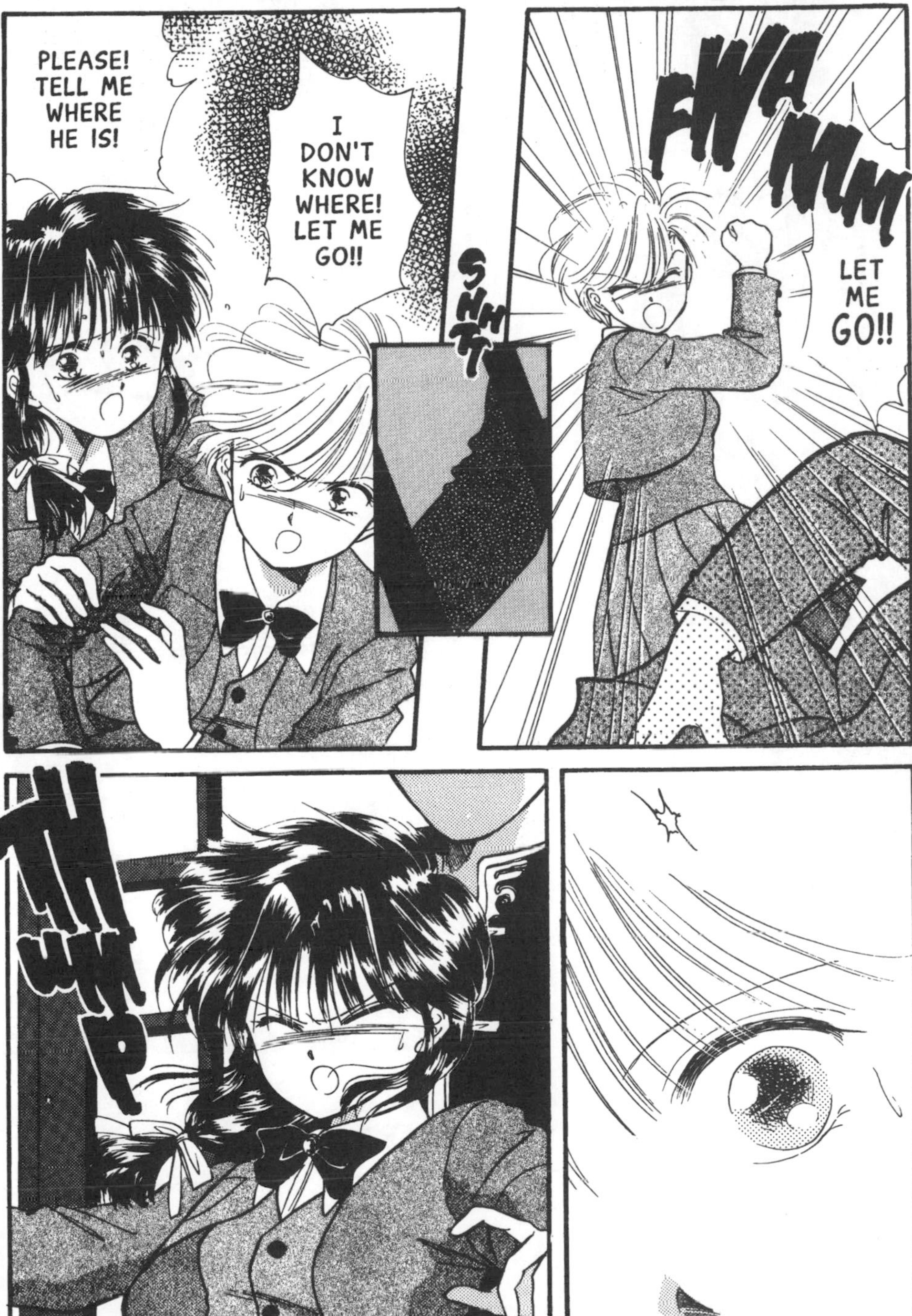
PLEASE! TELL ME WHERE HE IS!
I DON'T KNOW WHERE! LET ME GO!!
SHHTT
FWAMM
LET ME GO!!
THHUMP

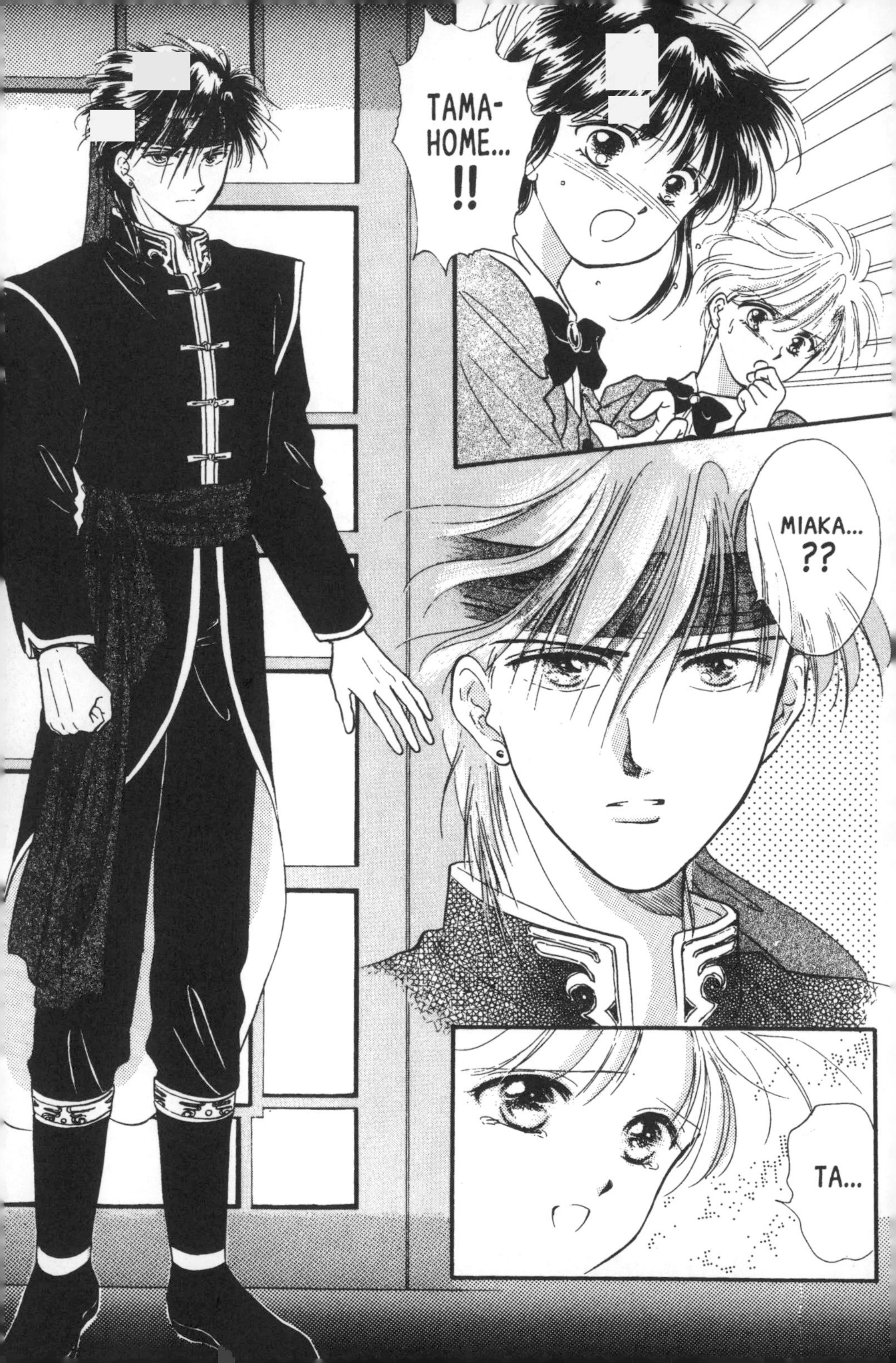
TAMA-HOME...
!!
MIAKA...
??
TA...

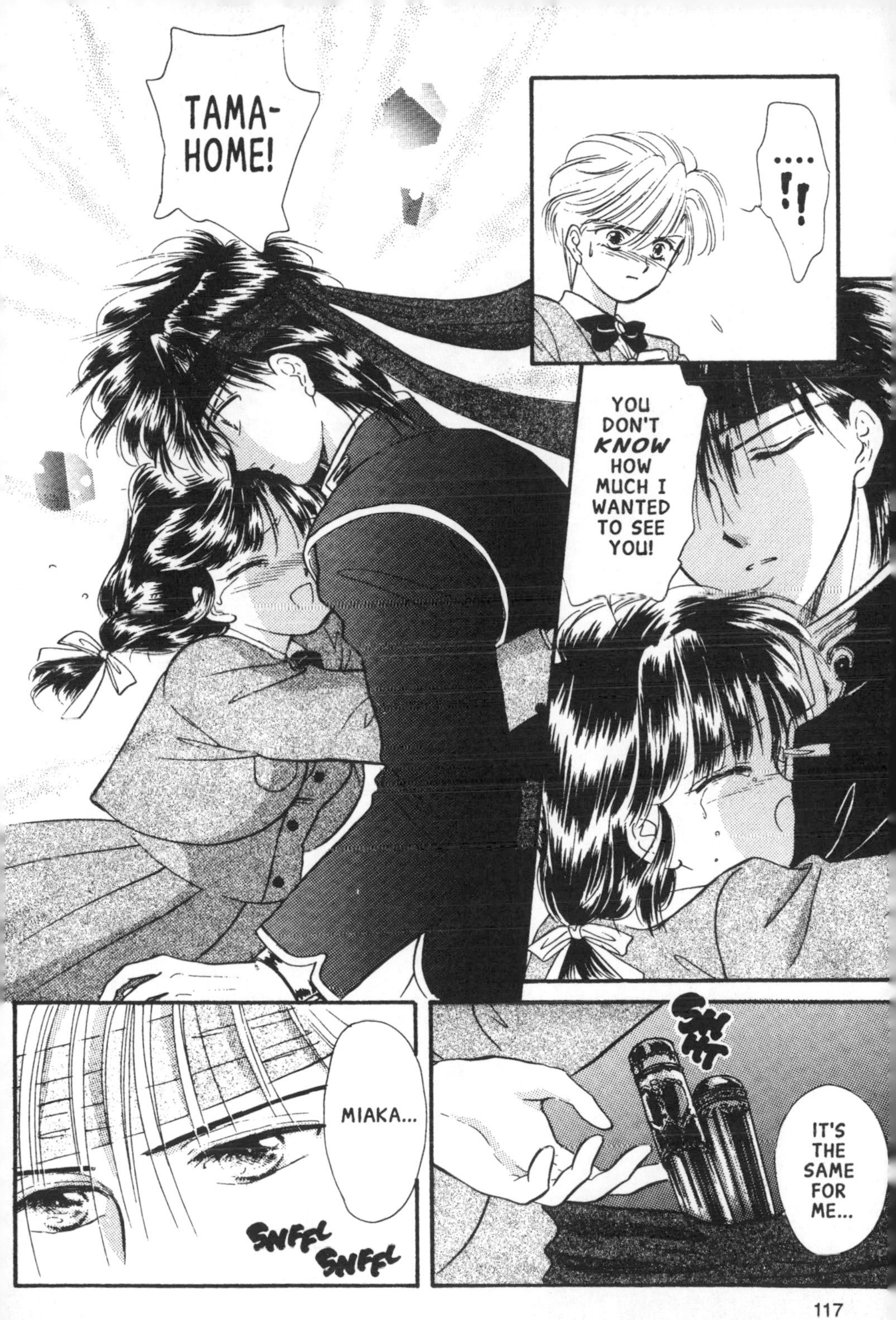
TAMA-HOME!
....!!
YOU DON'T *KNOW* HOW MUCH I WANTED TO SEE YOU!
MIAKA...
SNFFL SNFFL
SHHT
IT'S THE SAME FOR ME...

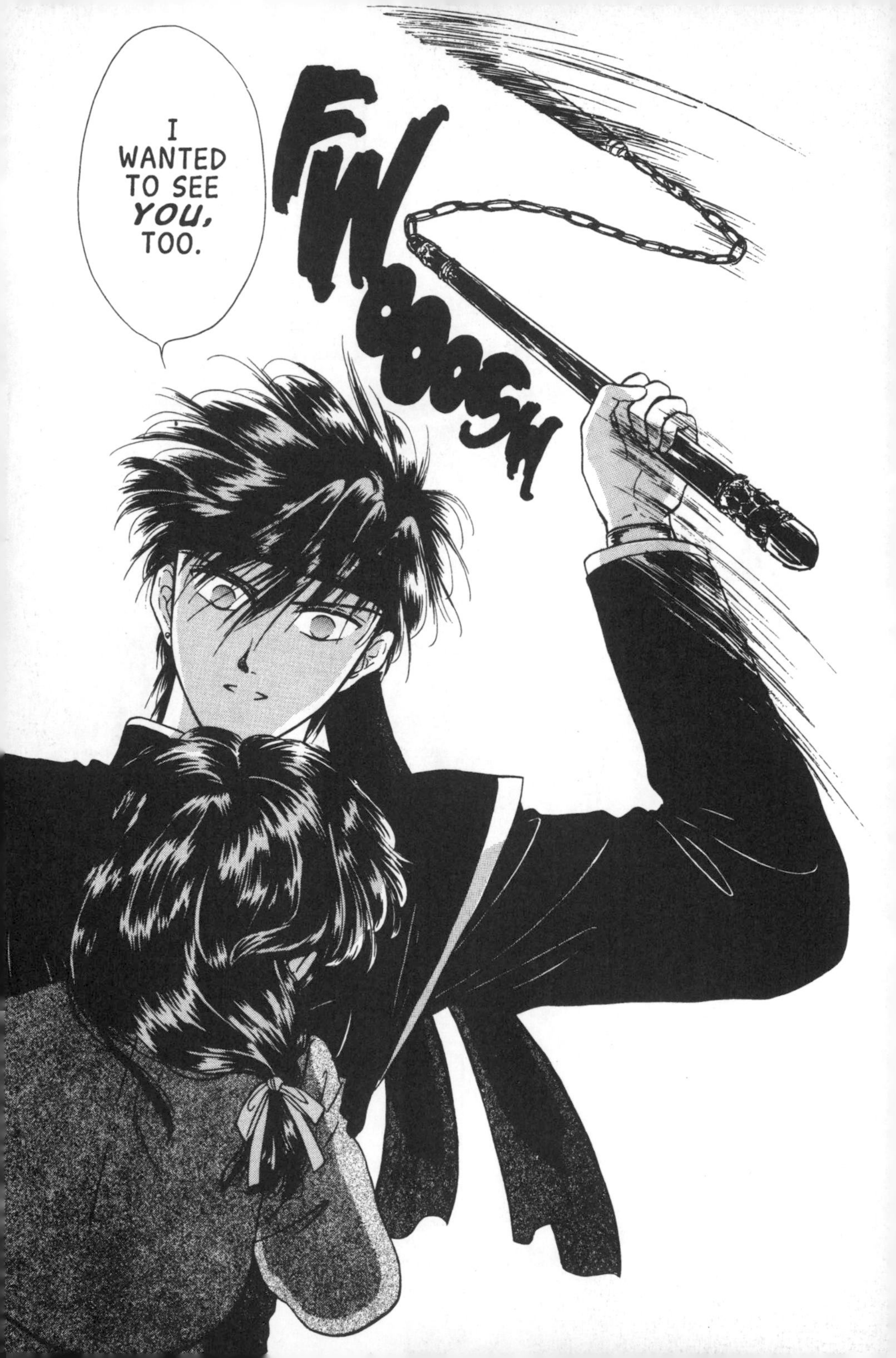
I WANTED TO SEE *YOU,* TOO.
FWOOOSH

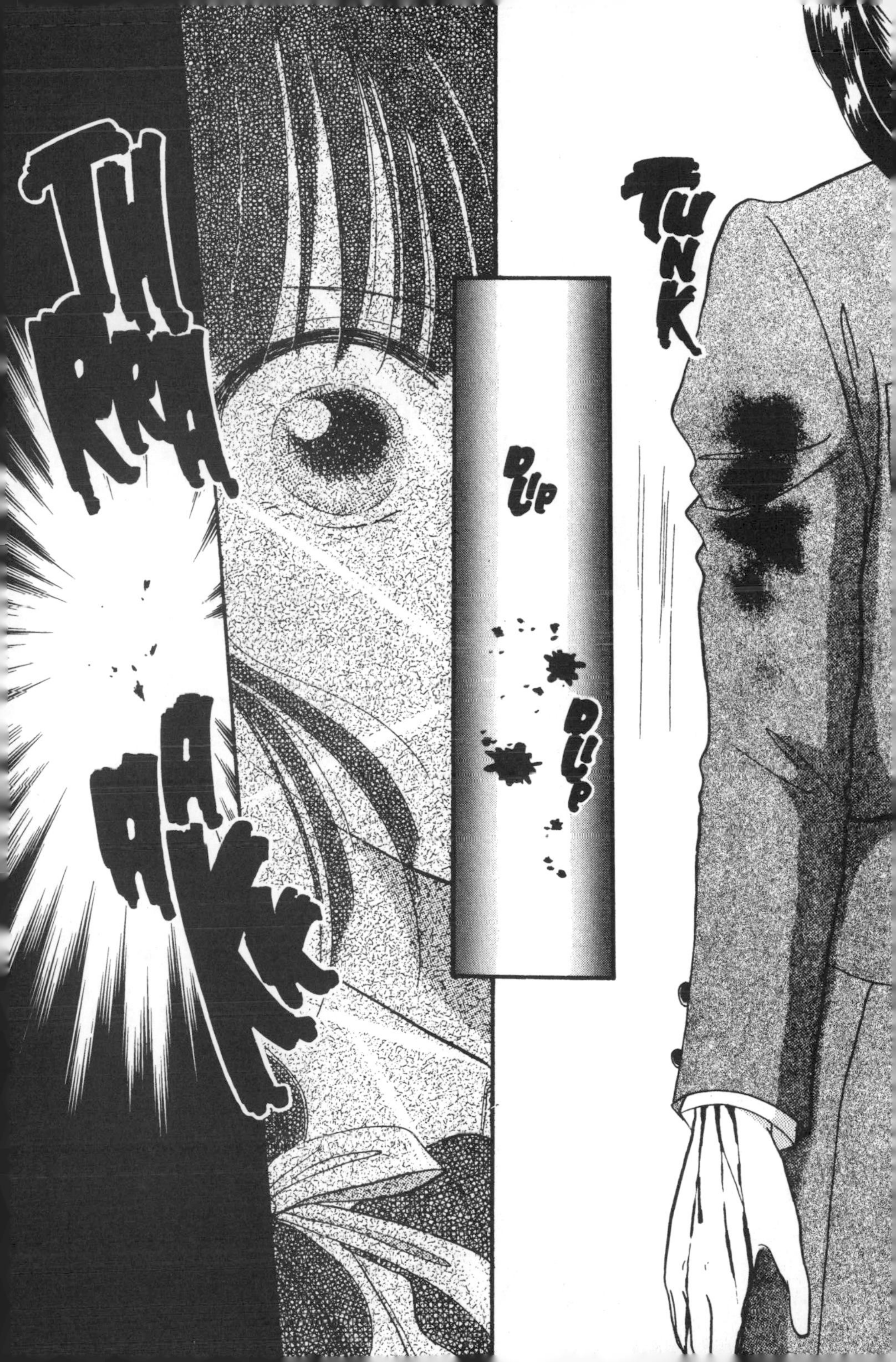
THRRA
AAAKKK
DRIP
DRIP
TUNK

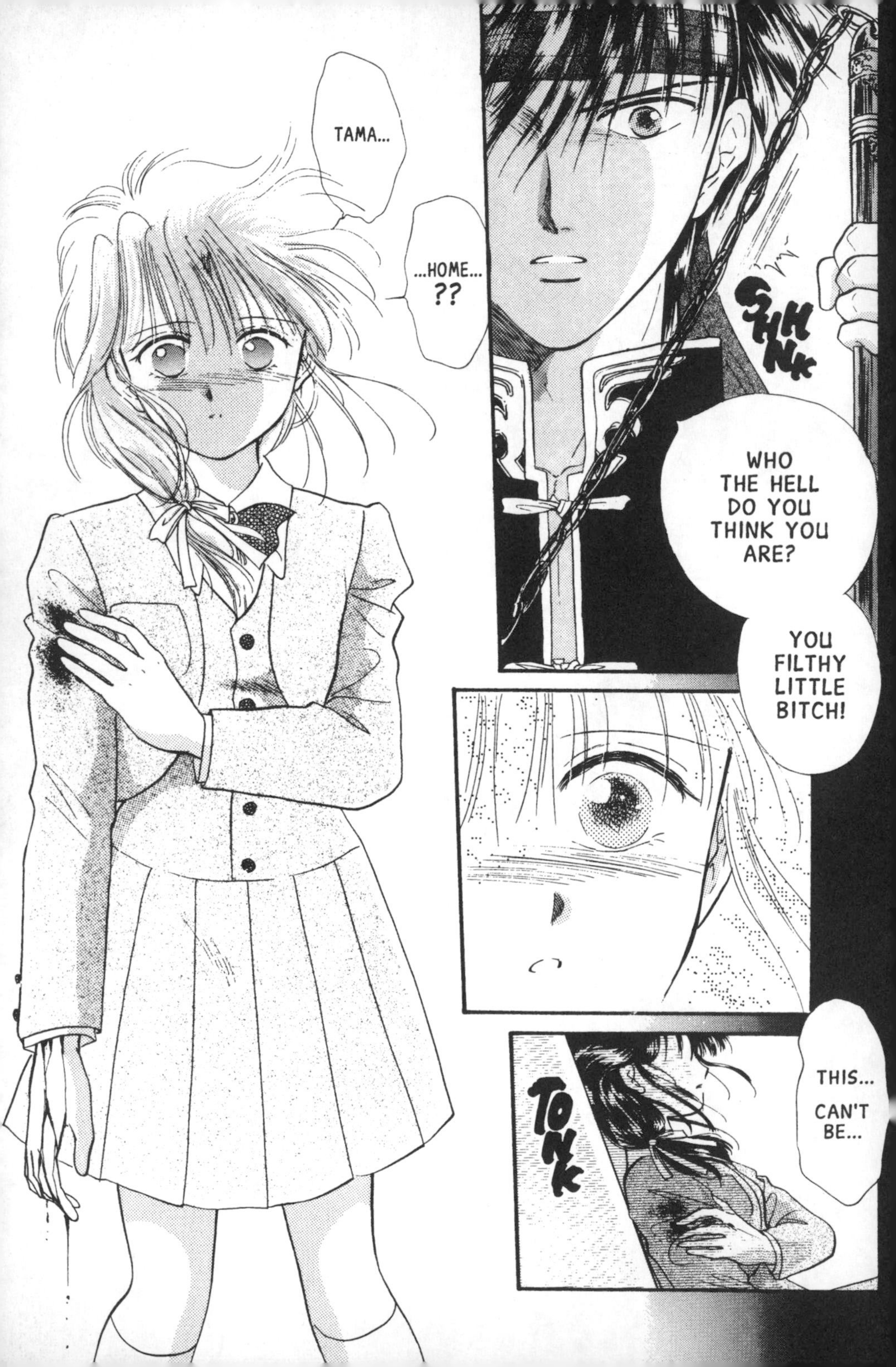
TAMA...
...HOME... ??
SHHNK
WHO THE HELL DO YOU THINK YOU ARE?
YOU FILTHY LITTLE BITCH!
TONK
THIS... CAN'T BE...

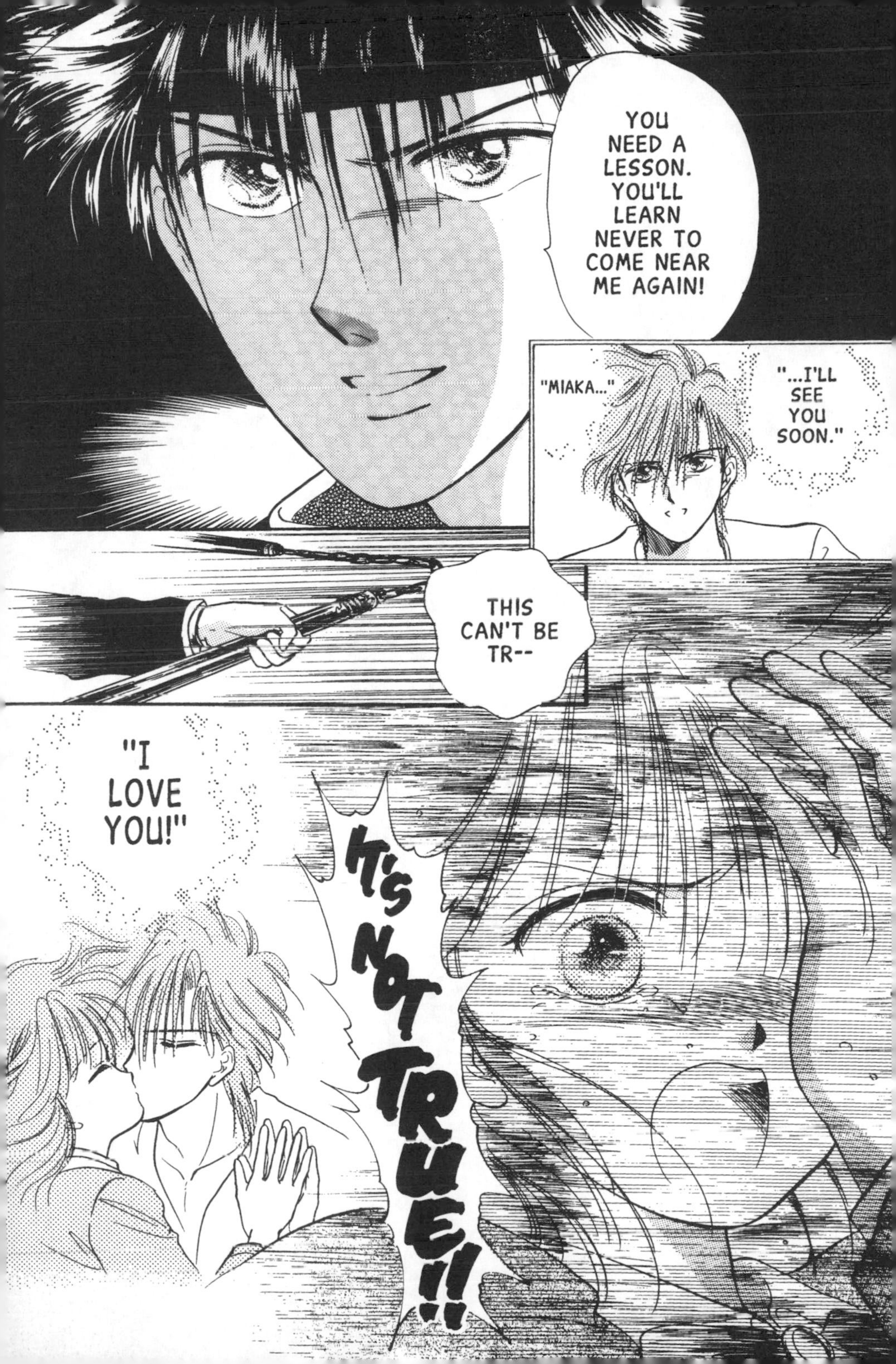
YOU NEED A LESSON. YOU'LL LEARN NEVER TO COME NEAR ME AGAIN!
"MIAKA..."
"...I'LL SEE YOU SOON."
THIS CAN'T BE TR--
"I LOVE YOU!"
IT'S NOT TRUE!!

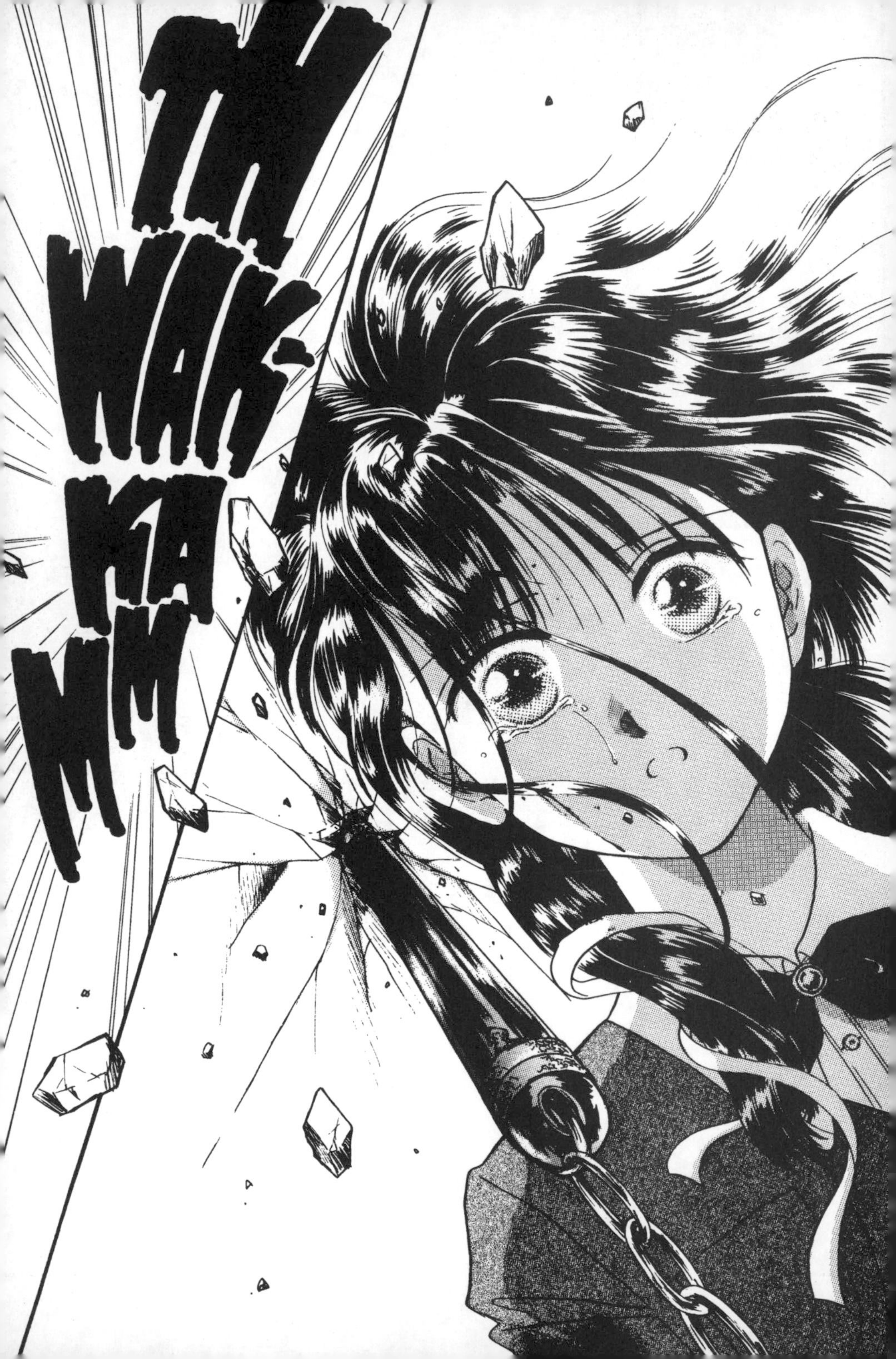
THWAK-KAMM

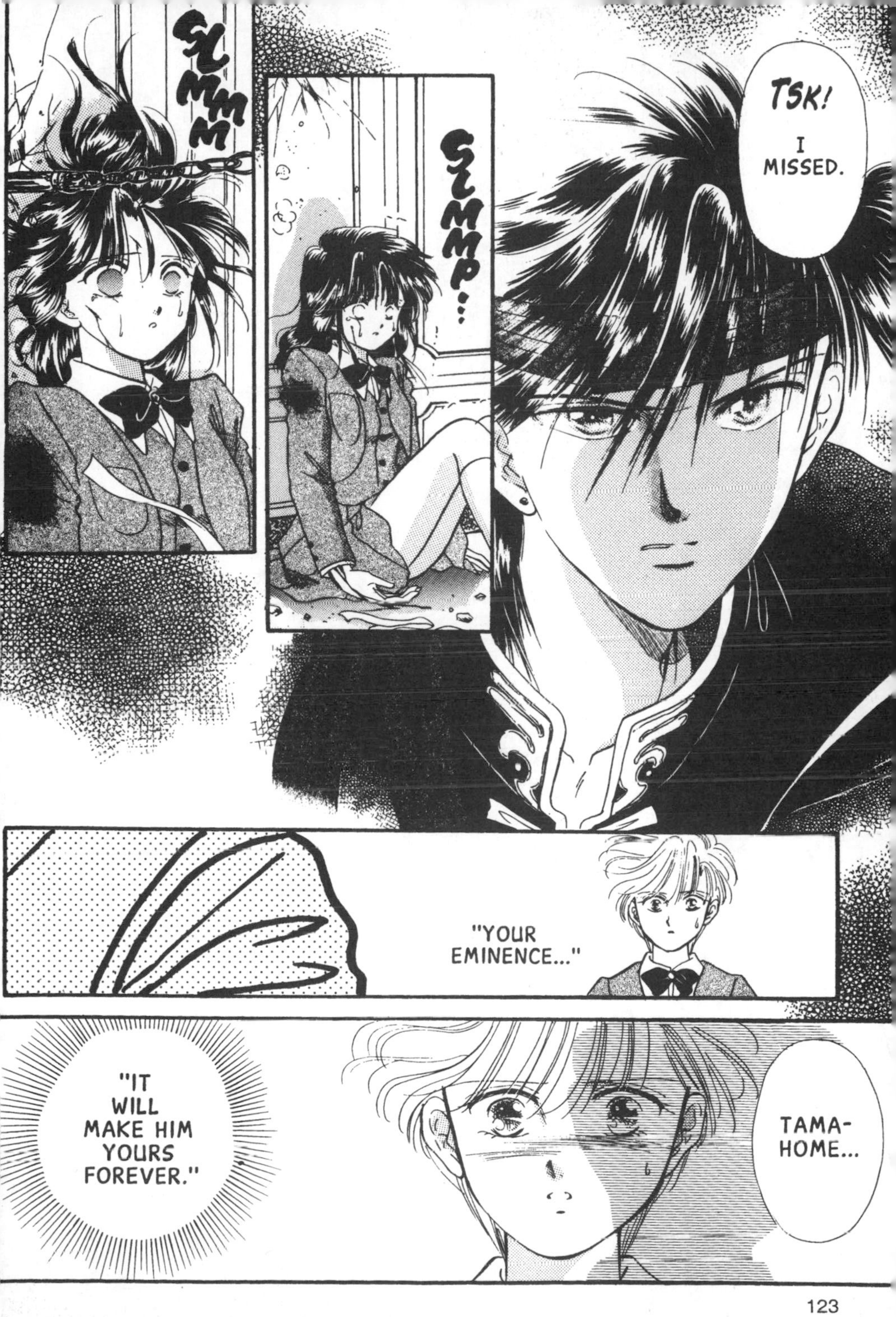
SLMMM
SLMMP...
TSK!
I MISSED.
"YOUR EMINENCE..."
"IT WILL MAKE HIM YOURS FOREVER."
TAMA-HOME...

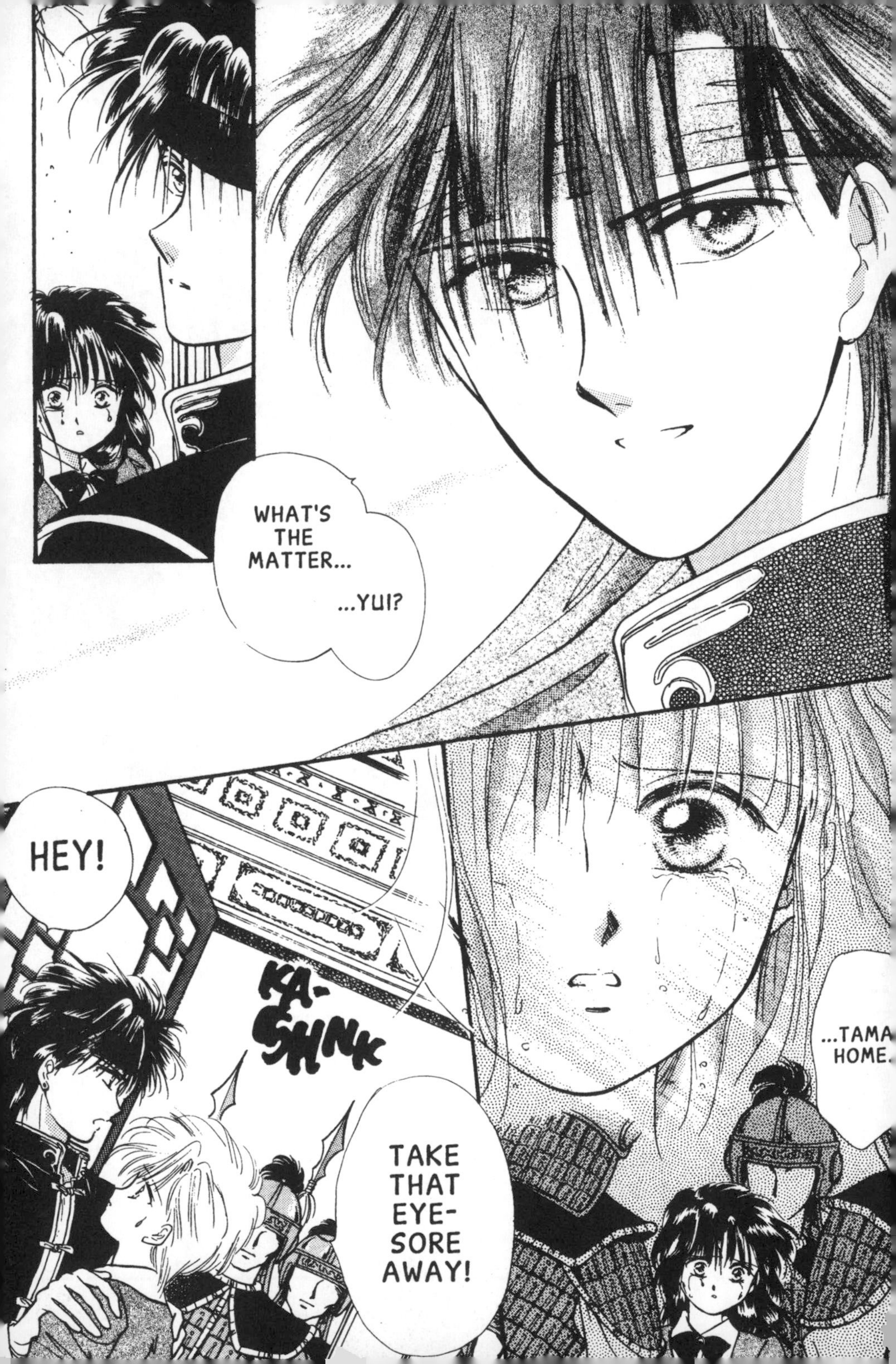
WHAT'S THE MATTER... ...YUI?
HEY!
KA-SHNK
TAKE THAT EYE-SORE AWAY!
...TAMA HOME.

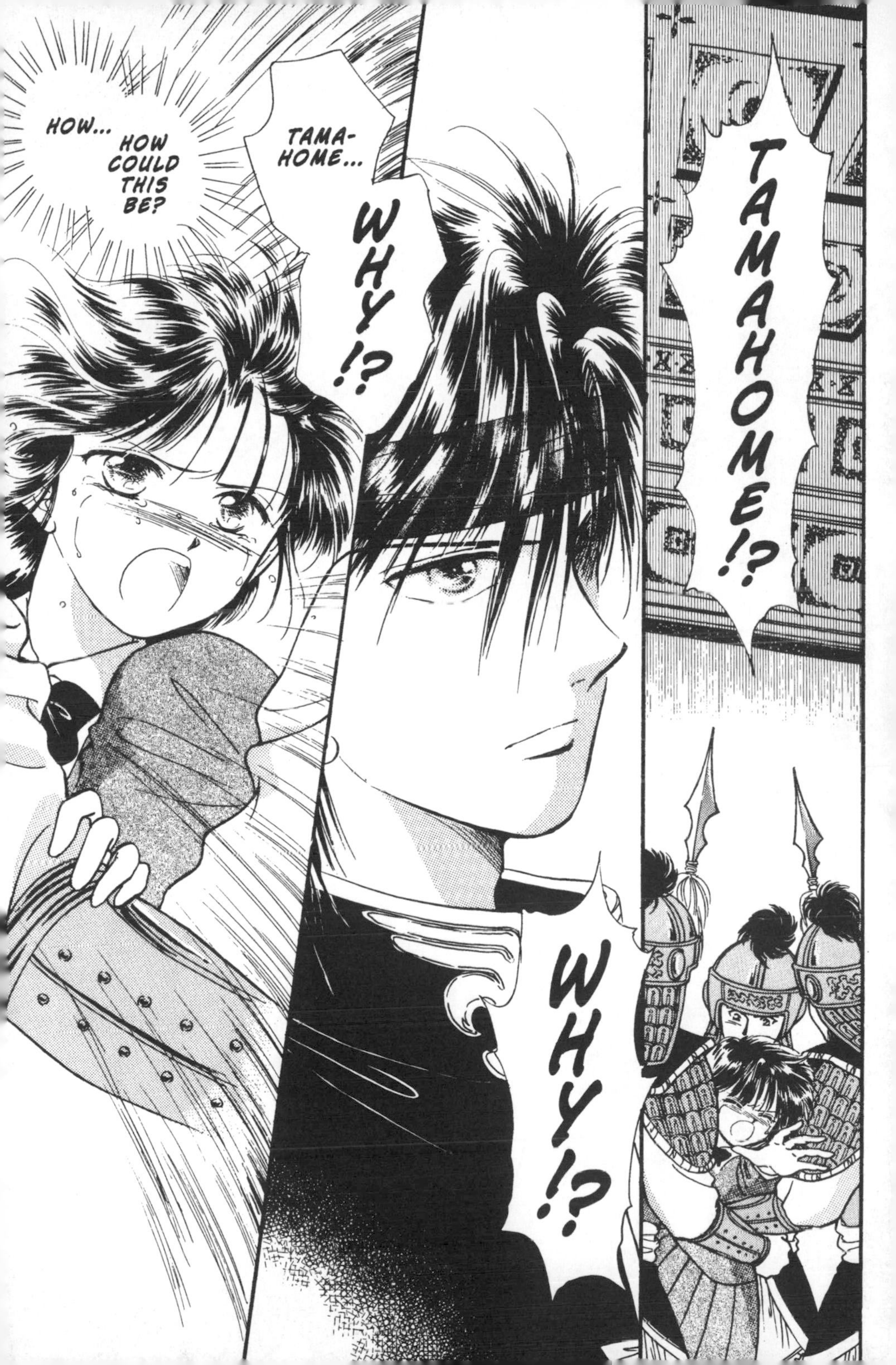
HOW...
HOW COULD THIS BE?
TAMA-HOME...
WHY!?
WHY!?
TAMAHOME!?

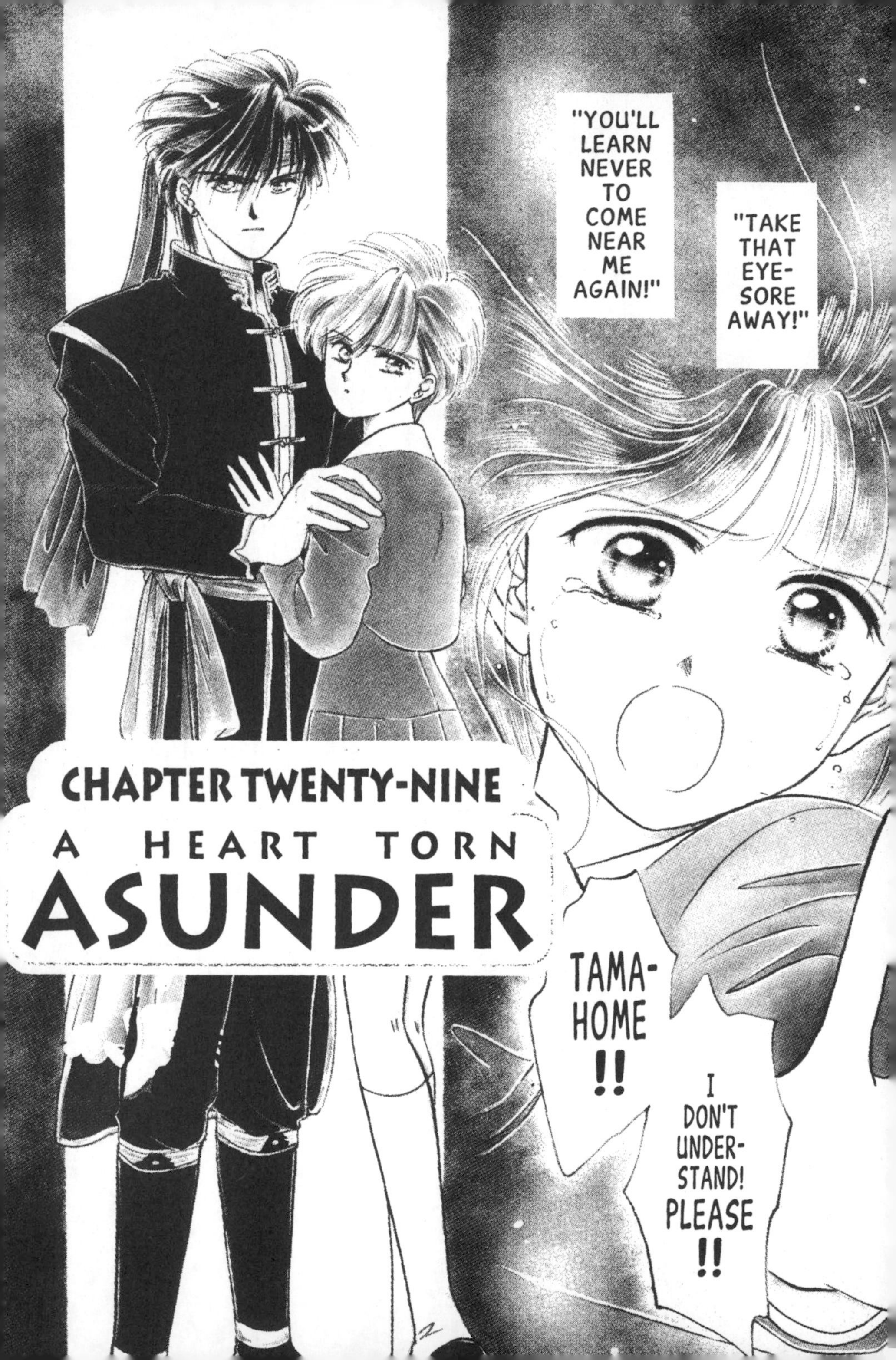
CHAPTER TWENTY-NINE
A HEART TORN ASUNDER
"YOU'LL LEARN NEVER TO COME NEAR ME AGAIN!"
"TAKE THAT EYE-SORE AWAY!"
TAMA-HOME !!
I DON'T UNDER-STAND! PLEASE !!

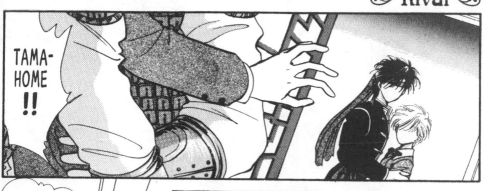

TAMA-
HOME
!!

TAMAHOME?
WHAT
HAPPENED
TO YOU
??

HAVE
YOU
FOR-
GOTTEN
ABOUT
MIAKA
?!?

WHAT
ARE YOU
TALKING
ABOUT?
SHE'S THE
ENEMY,
ISN'T
SHE?

FWICK

!

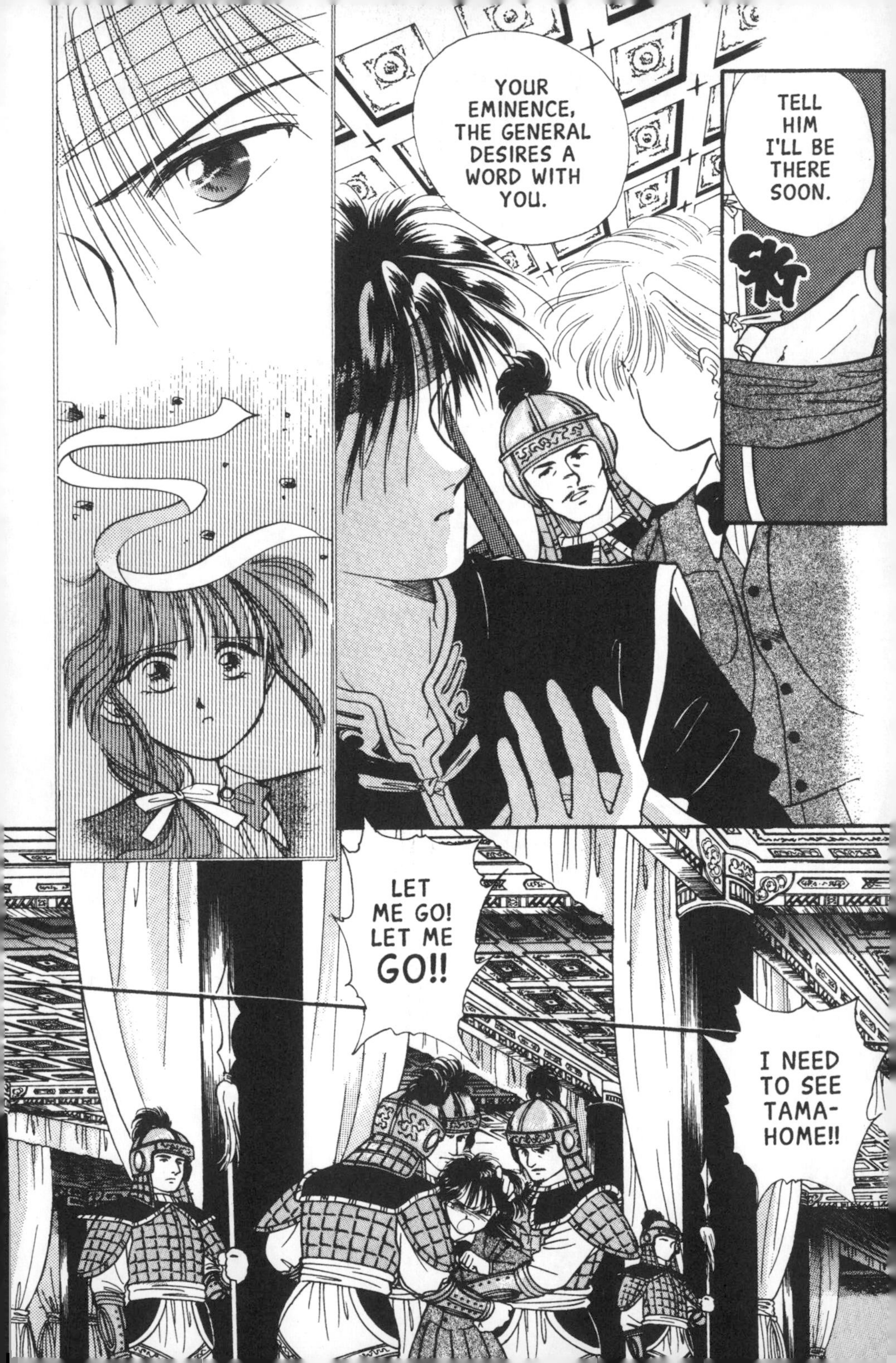
YOUR EMINENCE, THE GENERAL DESIRES A WORD WITH YOU.
TELL HIM I'LL BE THERE SOON.
I NEED TO SEE TAMA-HOME!!
LET ME GO! LET ME GO!!

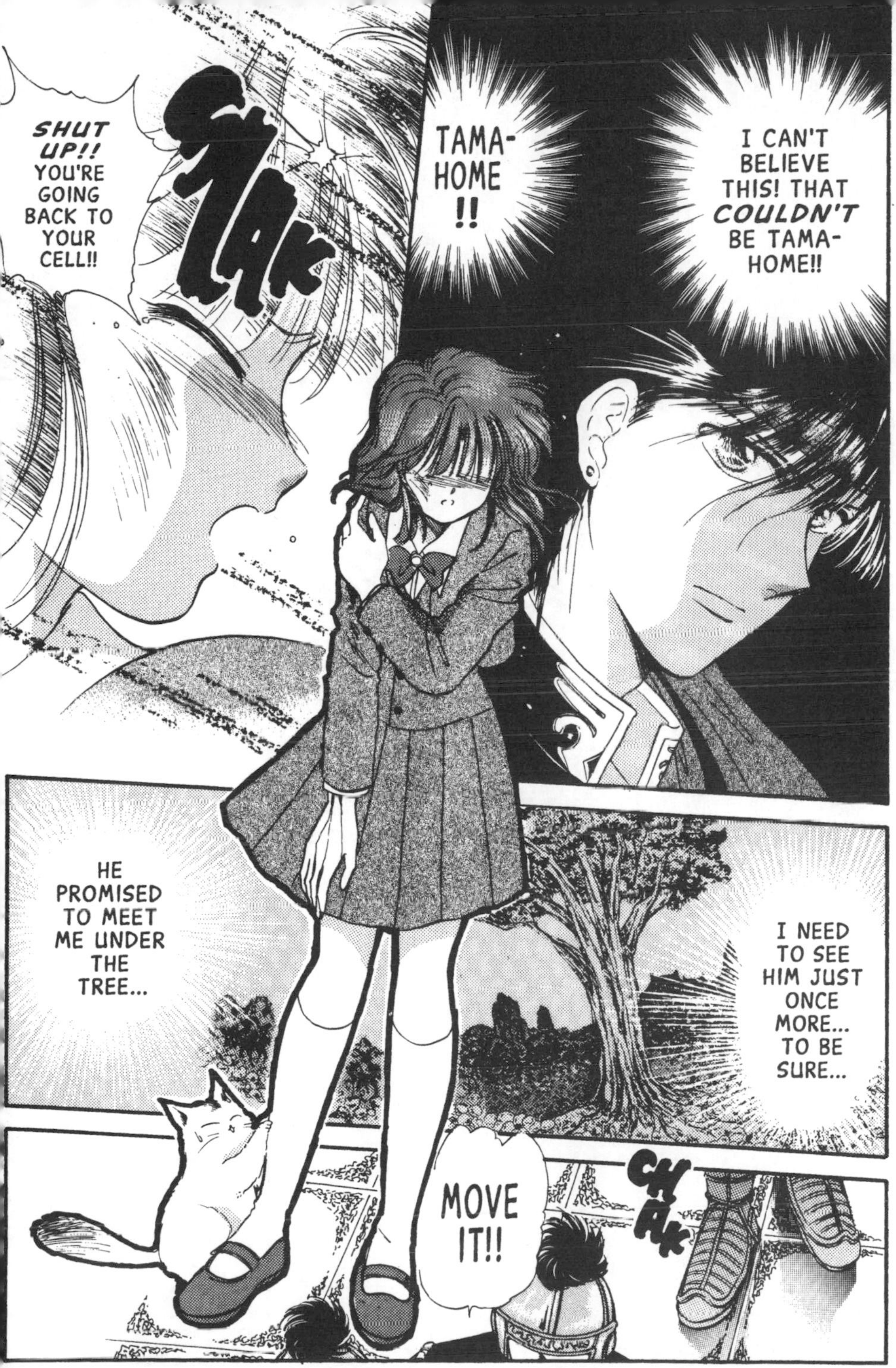

SHUT UP!! YOU'RE GOING BACK TO YOUR CELL!!
SLAK
TAMA-HOME !!
I CAN'T BELIEVE THIS! THAT COULDN'T BE TAMA-HOME!!
HE PROMISED TO MEET ME UNDER THE TREE...
I NEED TO SEE HIM JUST ONCE MORE... TO BE SURE...
MOVE IT!!
CHAK

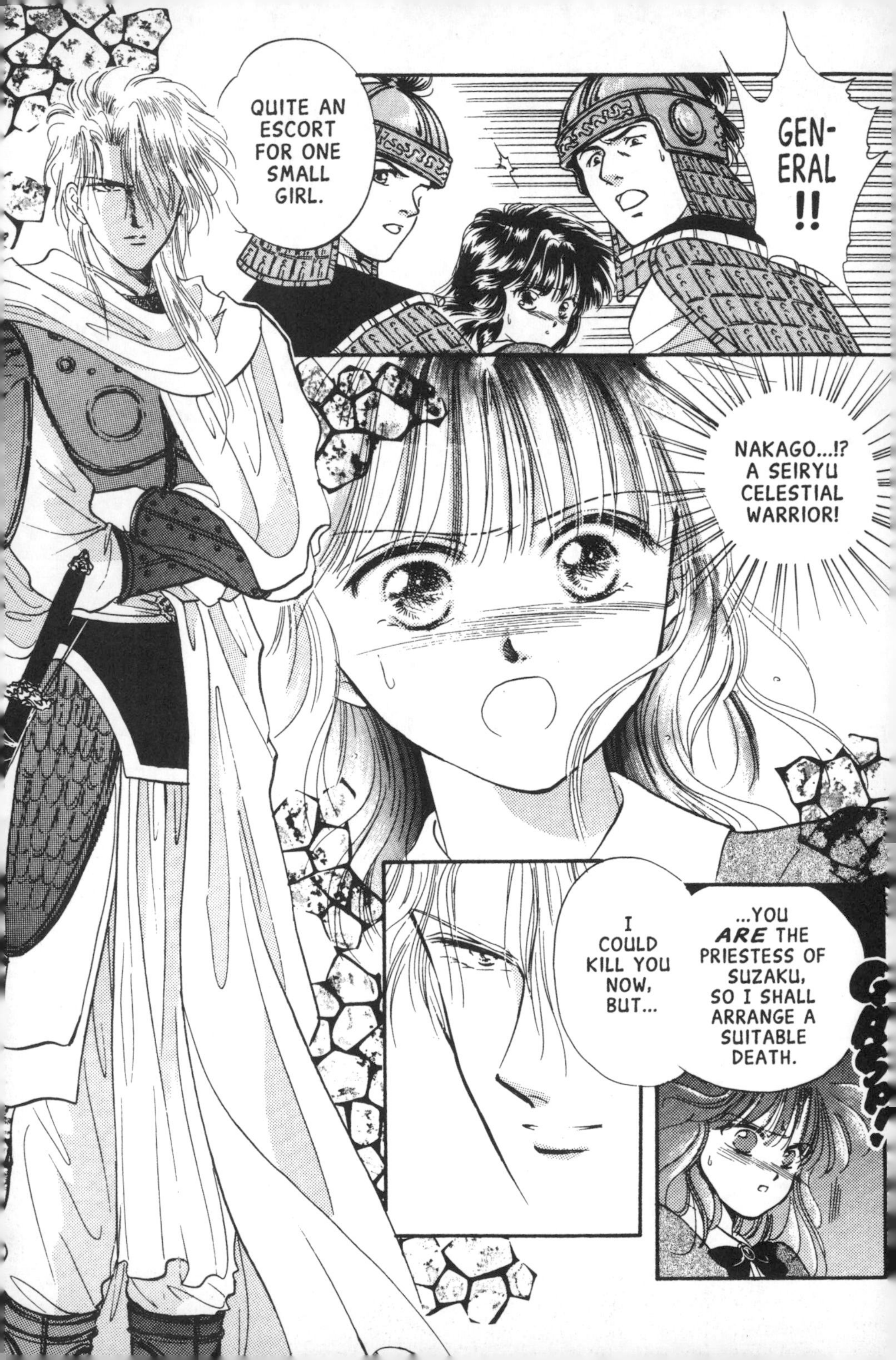
QUITE AN ESCORT FOR ONE SMALL GIRL.
GEN-ERAL!!
NAKAGO...!? A SEIRYU CELESTIAL WARRIOR!
I COULD KILL YOU NOW, BUT...
...YOU *ARE* THE PRIESTESS OF SUZAKU, SO I SHALL ARRANGE A SUITABLE DEATH.
GASP!

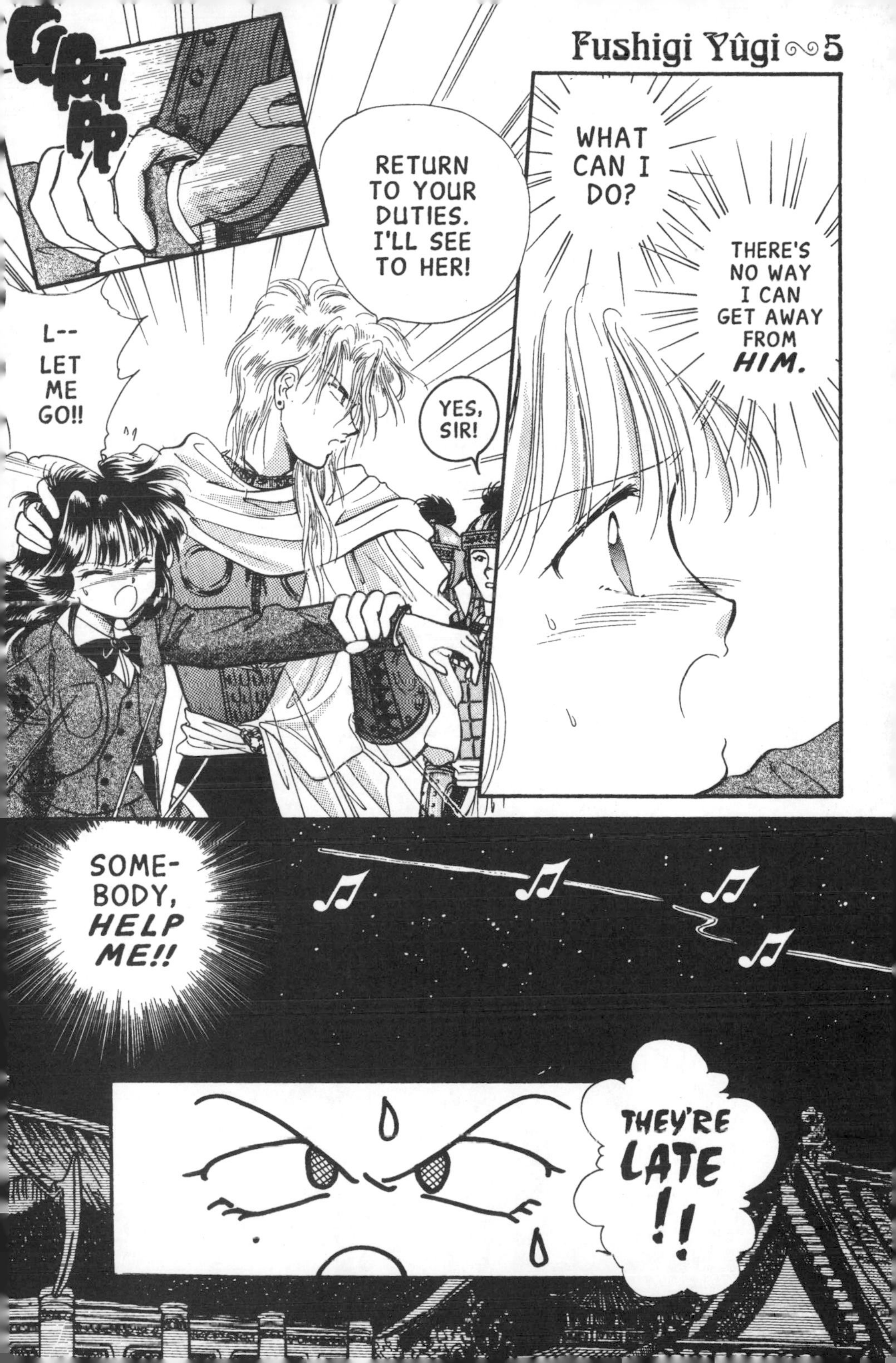
GRAPP
RETURN TO YOUR DUTIES. I'LL SEE TO HER!
L-- LET ME GO!!
YES, SIR!
WHAT CAN I DO?
THERE'S NO WAY I CAN GET AWAY FROM *HIM.*
SOME-BODY, *HELP ME!!*
THEY'RE LATE !!

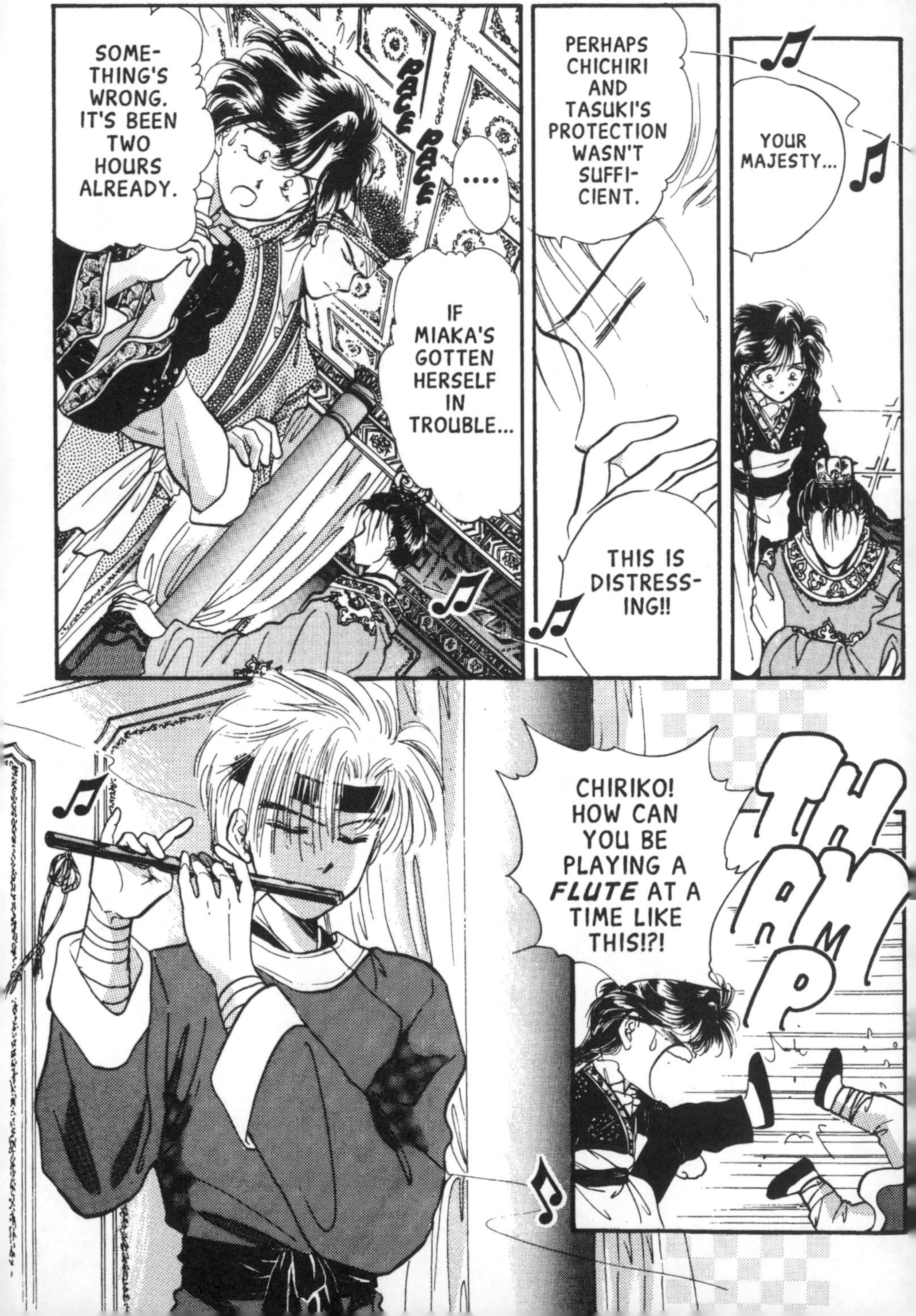
YOUR MAJESTY...
PERHAPS CHICHIRI AND TASUKI'S PROTECTION WASN'T SUFFI-CIENT.
THIS IS DISTRESS-ING!!
SOME-THING'S WRONG. IT'S BEEN TWO HOURS ALREADY.
PACE PACE
....
IF MIAKA'S GOTTEN HERSELF IN TROUBLE...
CHIRIKO! HOW CAN YOU BE PLAYING A *FLUTE* AT A TIME LIKE THIS!?!
THAMP

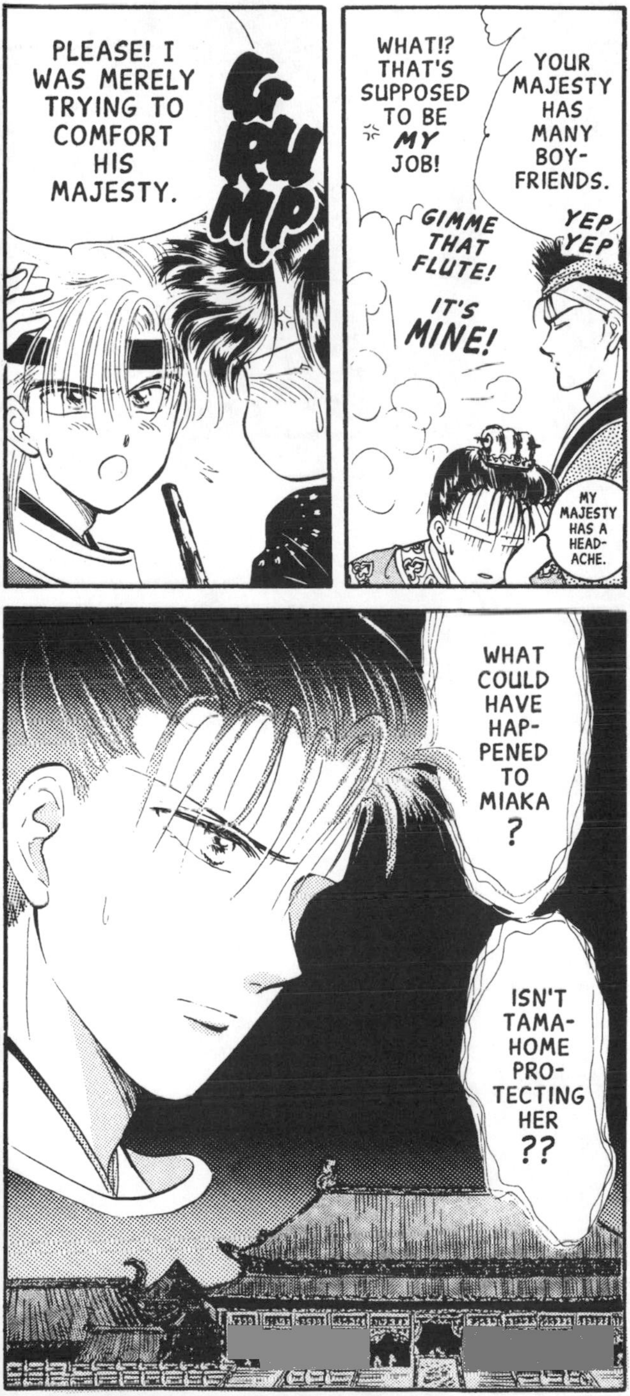
PLEASE! I WAS MERELY TRYING TO COMFORT HIS MAJESTY.
GRUMP
WHAT!? THAT'S SUPPOSED TO BE MY JOB!
YOUR MAJESTY HAS MANY BOYFRIENDS.
GIMME THAT FLUTE!
YEP YEP
IT'S MINE!
MY MAJESTY HAS A HEADACHE.
WHAT COULD HAVE HAPPENED TO MIAKA?
ISN'T TAMAHOME PROTECTING HER??

So, aside from checking out a bunch of game centers, I went with a different friend to see a "Caramel Box" performance. My editor had taken me to one of their performances before, and I liked it so much that later I took my friend Ms. N. She became totally obsessed with them. She invited me to go again just recently. I love fantasy that takes place in the real world. It's got comedy, scenes that make you cry, and interesting characters. No matter how many times I've seen it, I still get something new and interesting out of it. I highly recommend it, so go check it out. Even if you're still in junior high, I'm sure you'll love it!

I have a birthday card from "Caramel Box" right in front of me. It's March 1, so in four days it'll be my birthday. My editor sends me a bouquet of flowers (I love the beautiful flowers!) which is nice, but for the past two years, they've been arriving 10 days late. I wonder why. Will it be late again this year? It's not a big deal though.

My background music right now is the soundtrack to "Final Fantasy V, IV." Thank you! I wanted this so badly. Thank you for the chocolate on Valentine's Day. It's so interesting to see how popular each Celestial Warrior is. You all sent chocolate to Tamahome, Mitsukake (That really surprised me. That's one stylin' fan! ^^), Chiriko, etc. But Tamahome's biggest competition is pretty much limited to Tasuki and Chichiri. But, hey! Who knows when the rankings will change?

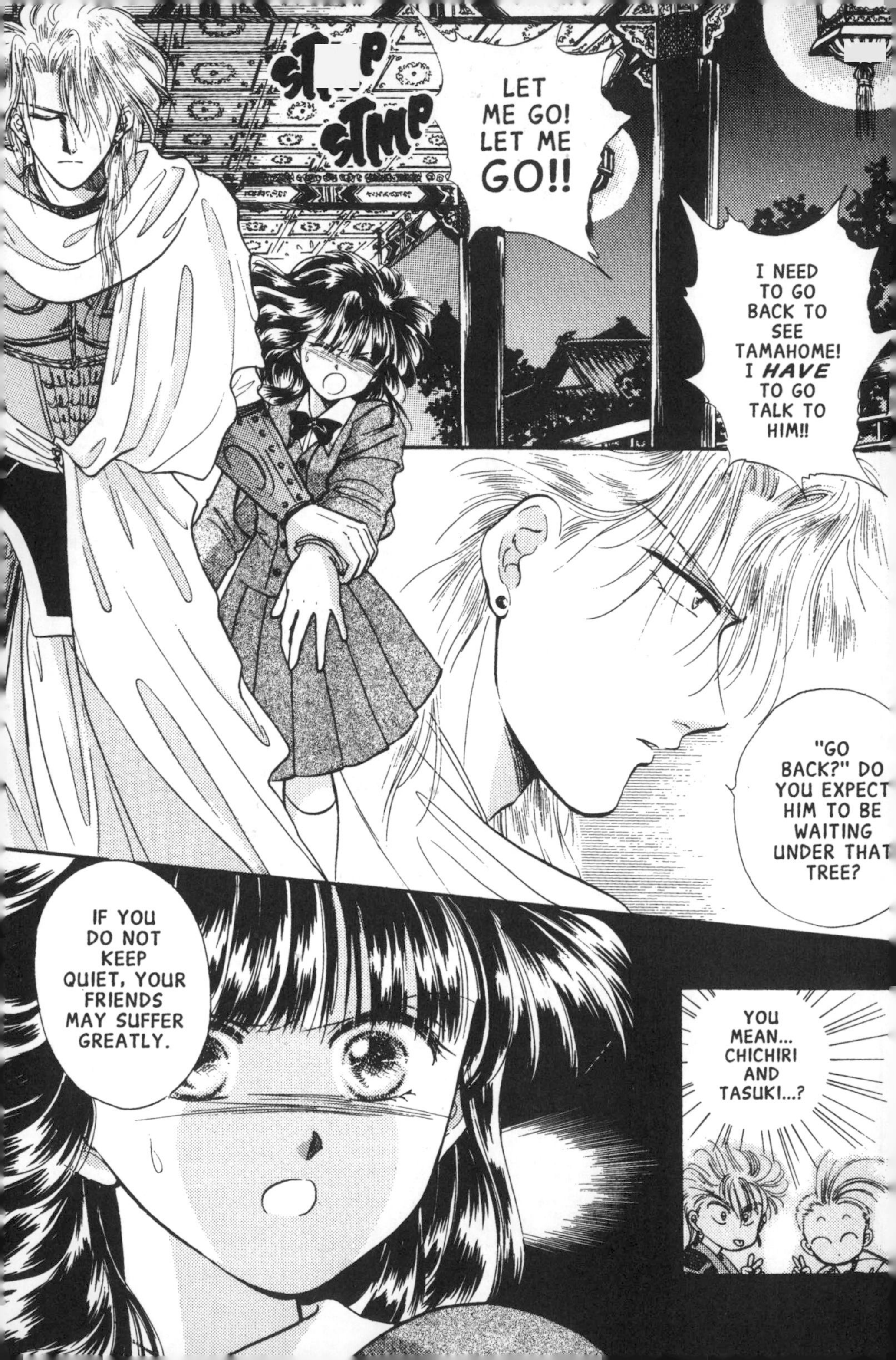
STMP
LET ME GO! LET ME GO!!
I NEED TO GO BACK TO SEE TAMAHOME! I *HAVE* TO GO TALK TO HIM!!
"GO BACK?" DO YOU EXPECT HIM TO BE WAITING UNDER THAT TREE?
IF YOU DO NOT KEEP QUIET, YOUR FRIENDS MAY SUFFER GREATLY.
YOU MEAN... CHICHIRI AND TASUKI...?

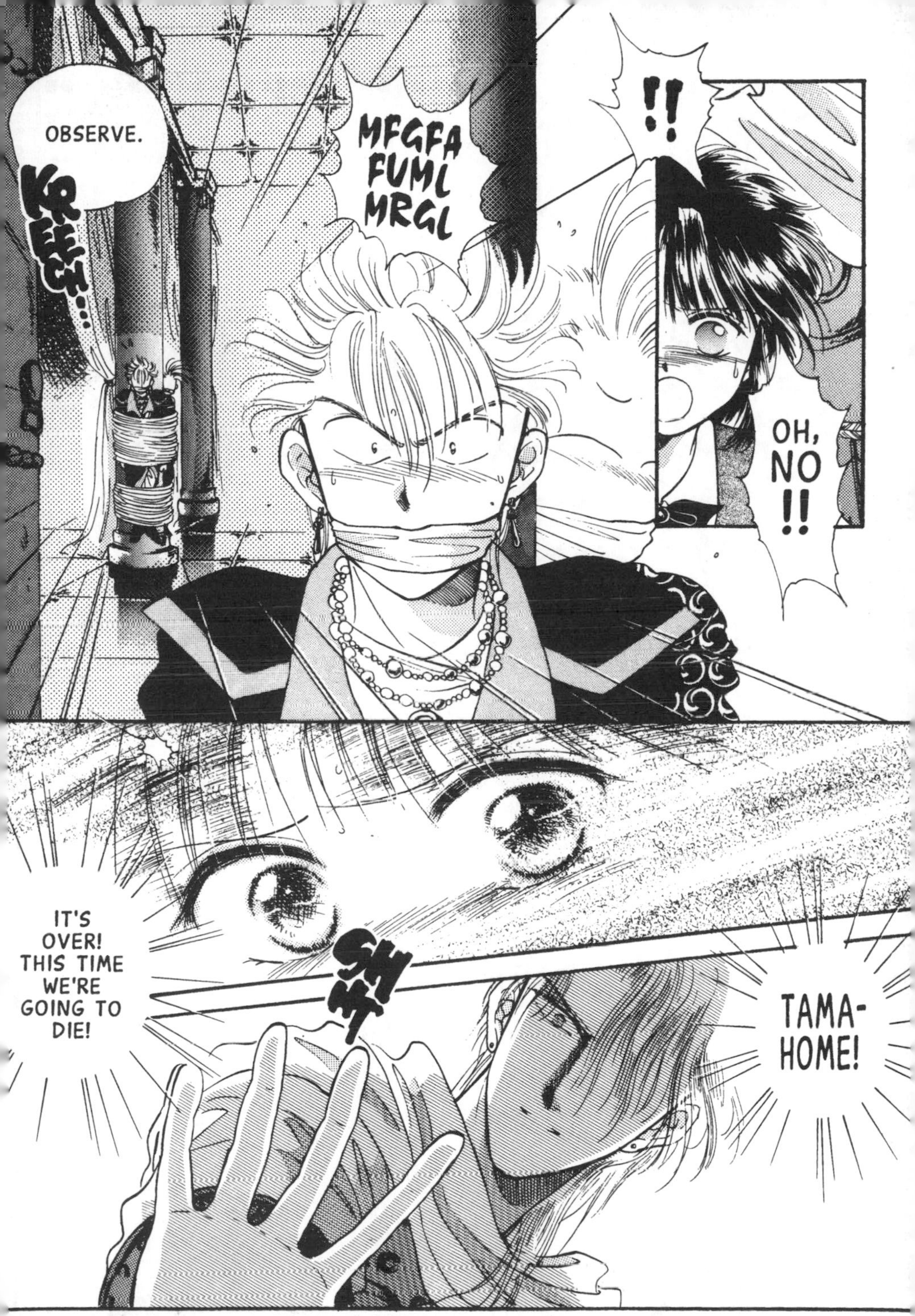
OBSERVE.
KREECH...
MFGFA FUML MRGL
!!
OH, NO !!
IT'S OVER! THIS TIME WE'RE GOING TO DIE!
SHHT
TAMA-HOME!

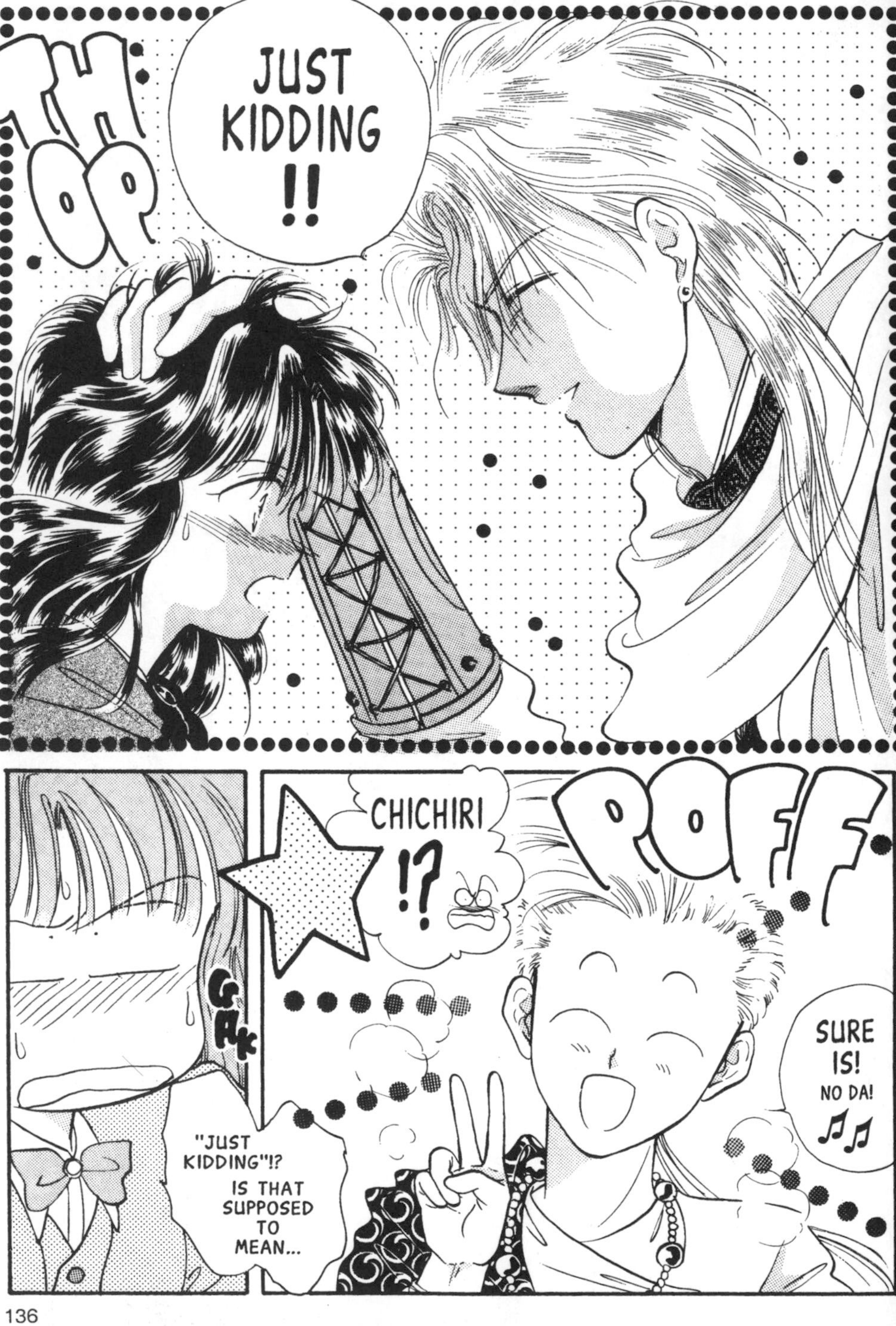
THOP
JUST KIDDING !!
CHICHIRI !?
POFF
GAK
"JUST KIDDING"!? IS THAT SUPPOSED TO MEAN...
SURE IS! NO DA! ♫♫

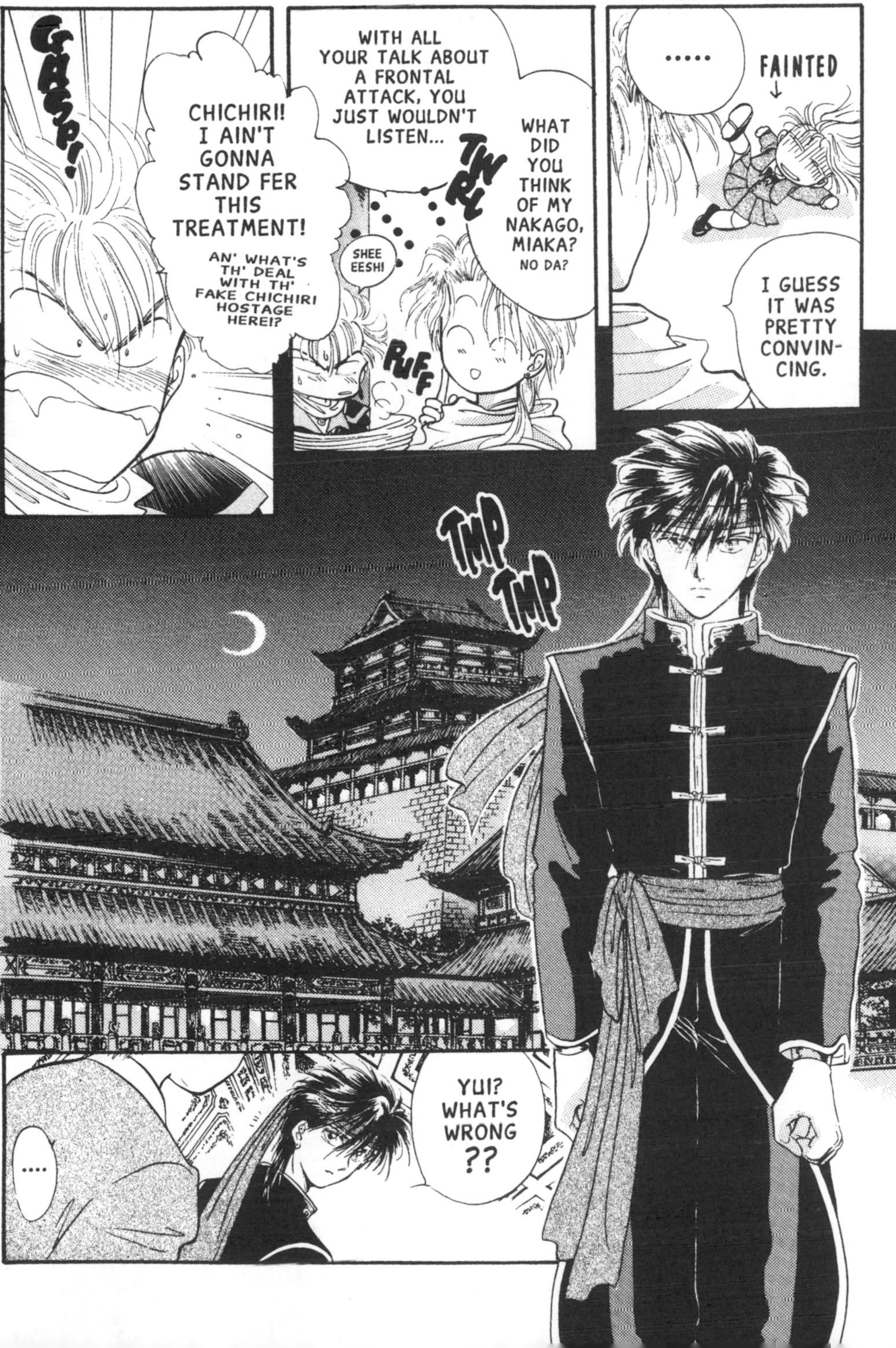
GASP!
CHICHIRI! I AIN'T GONNA STAND FER THIS TREATMENT!
AN' WHAT'S TH' DEAL WITH TH' FAKE CHICHIRI HOSTAGE HERE!?
WITH ALL YOUR TALK ABOUT A FRONTAL ATTACK, YOU JUST WOULDN'T LISTEN...
SHEE EESH!
TWIRL
WHAT DID YOU THINK OF MY NAKAGO, MIAKA? NO DA?
PUFF
.....
FAINTED
I GUESS IT WAS PRETTY CONVIN-CING.
TMP TMP
....
YUI? WHAT'S WRONG ??

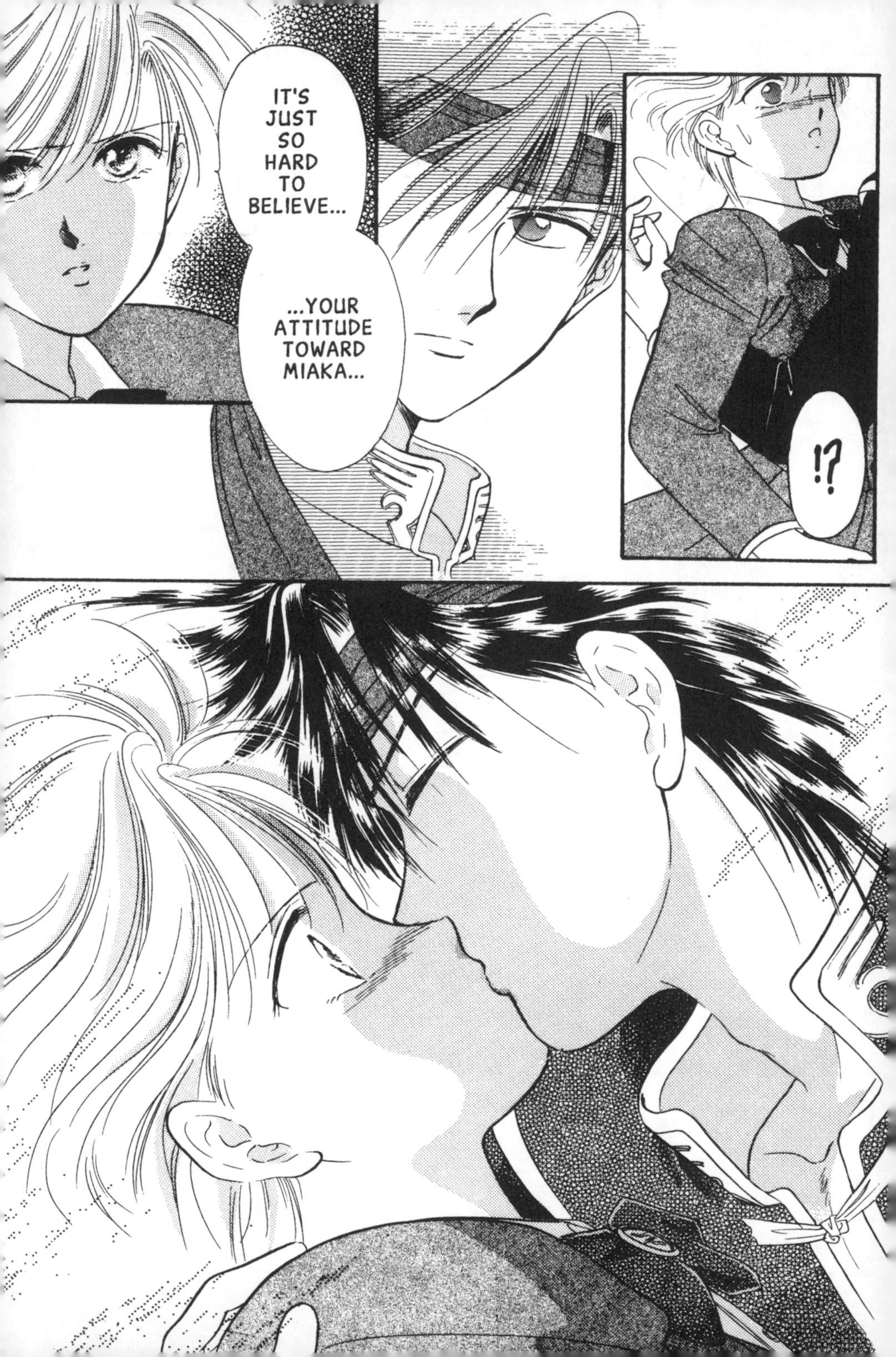
IT'S JUST SO HARD TO BELIEVE...
...YOUR ATTITUDE TOWARD MIAKA...
!?

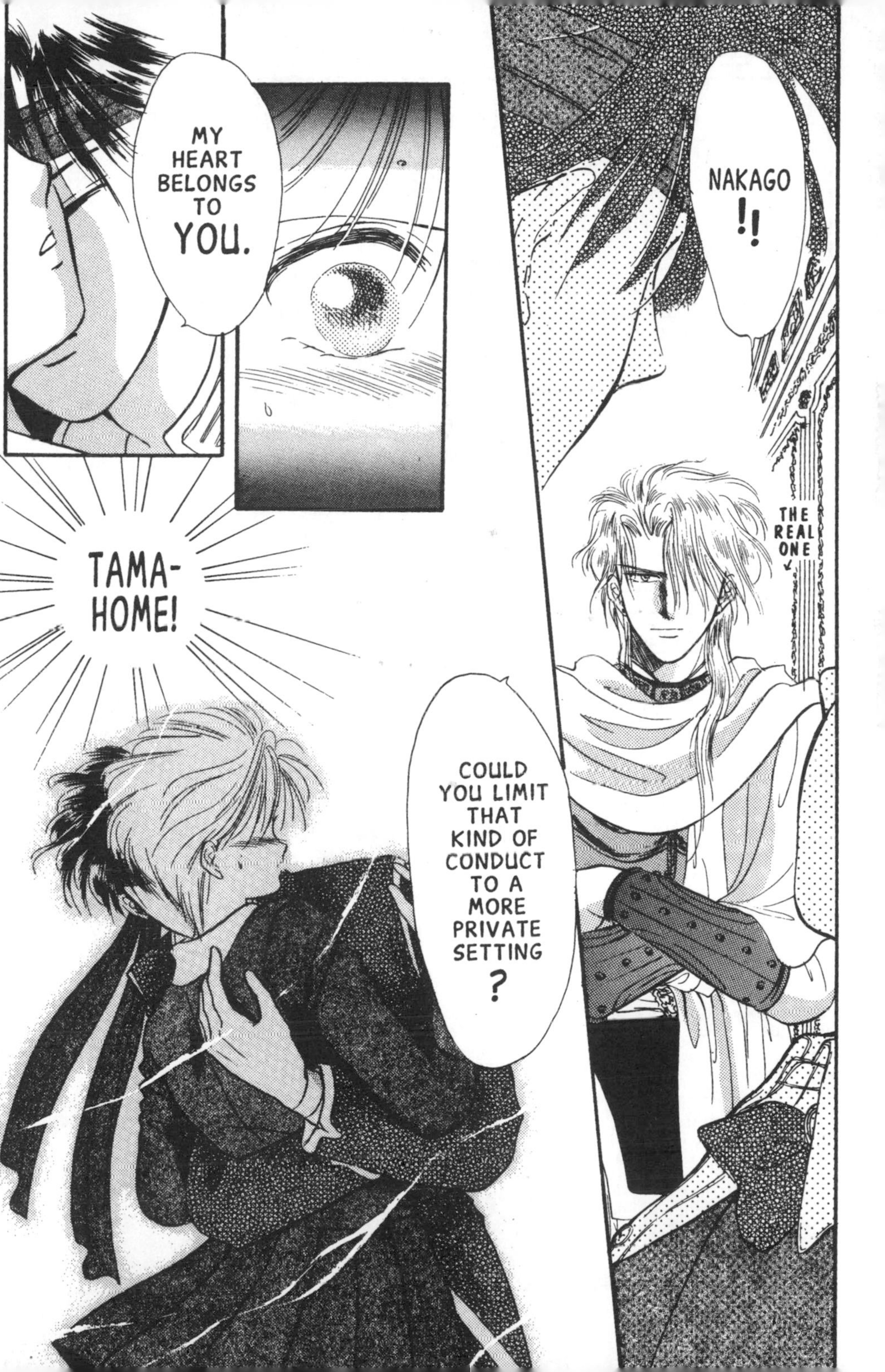
MY HEART BELONGS TO YOU.
TAMA-HOME!
NAKAGO!!
THE REAL ONE
COULD YOU LIMIT THAT KIND OF CONDUCT TO A MORE PRIVATE SETTING?

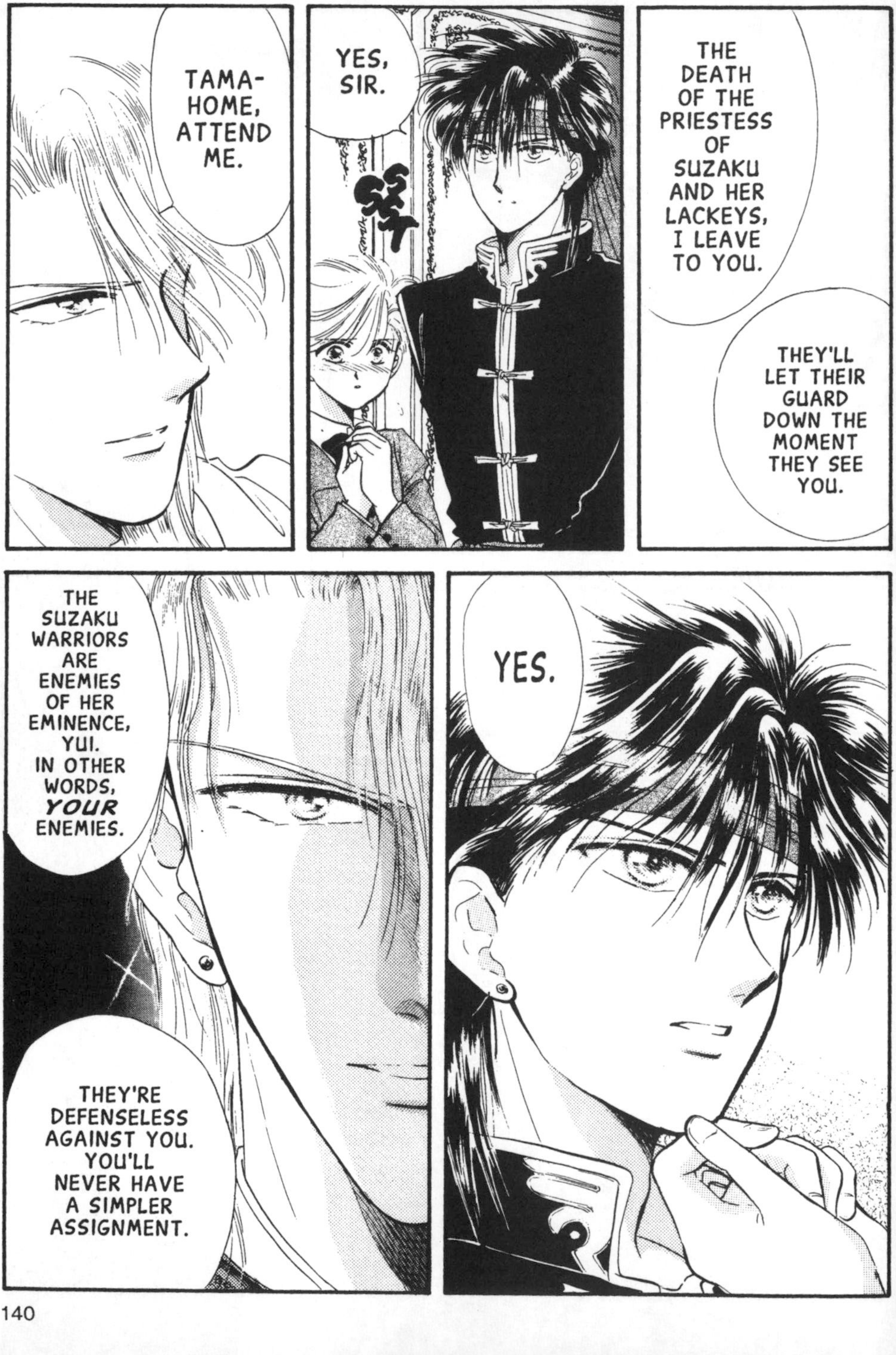
TAMA-HOME, ATTEND ME.
YES, SIR.
THE DEATH OF THE PRIESTESS OF SUZAKU AND HER LACKEYS, I LEAVE TO YOU.
THEY'LL LET THEIR GUARD DOWN THE MOMENT THEY SEE YOU.
THE SUZAKU WARRIORS ARE ENEMIES OF HER EMINENCE, YUI. IN OTHER WORDS, ***YOUR*** ENEMIES.
THEY'RE DEFENSELESS AGAINST YOU. YOU'LL NEVER HAVE A SIMPLER ASSIGNMENT.
YES.

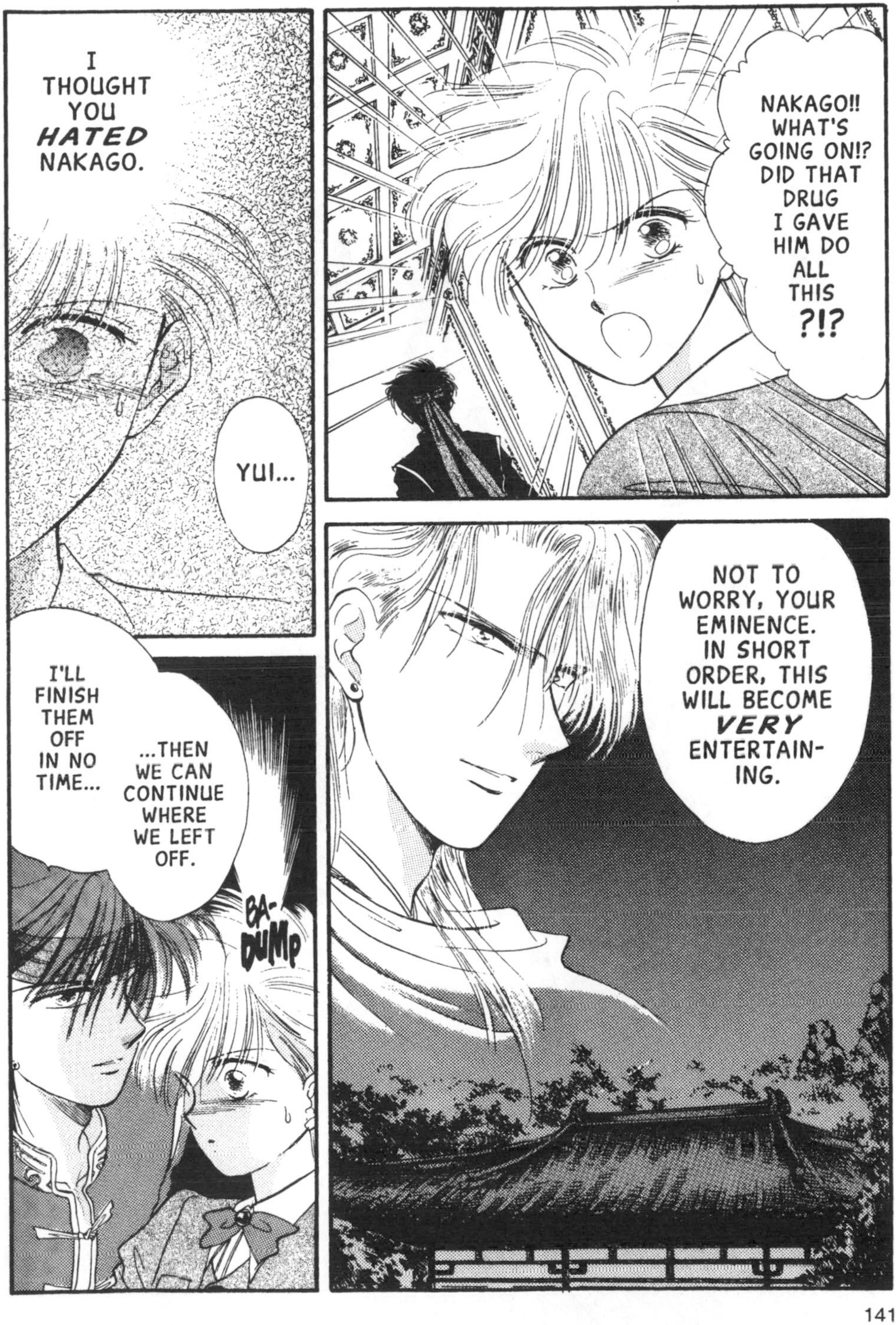
I THOUGHT YOU *HATED* NAKAGO.
YUI...
NAKAGO!! WHAT'S GOING ON!? DID THAT DRUG I GAVE HIM DO ALL THIS ?!?
I'LL FINISH THEM OFF IN NO TIME...
...THEN WE CAN CONTINUE WHERE WE LEFT OFF.
BA-DUMP
NOT TO WORRY, YOUR EMINENCE. IN SHORT ORDER, THIS WILL BECOME *VERY* ENTERTAINING.

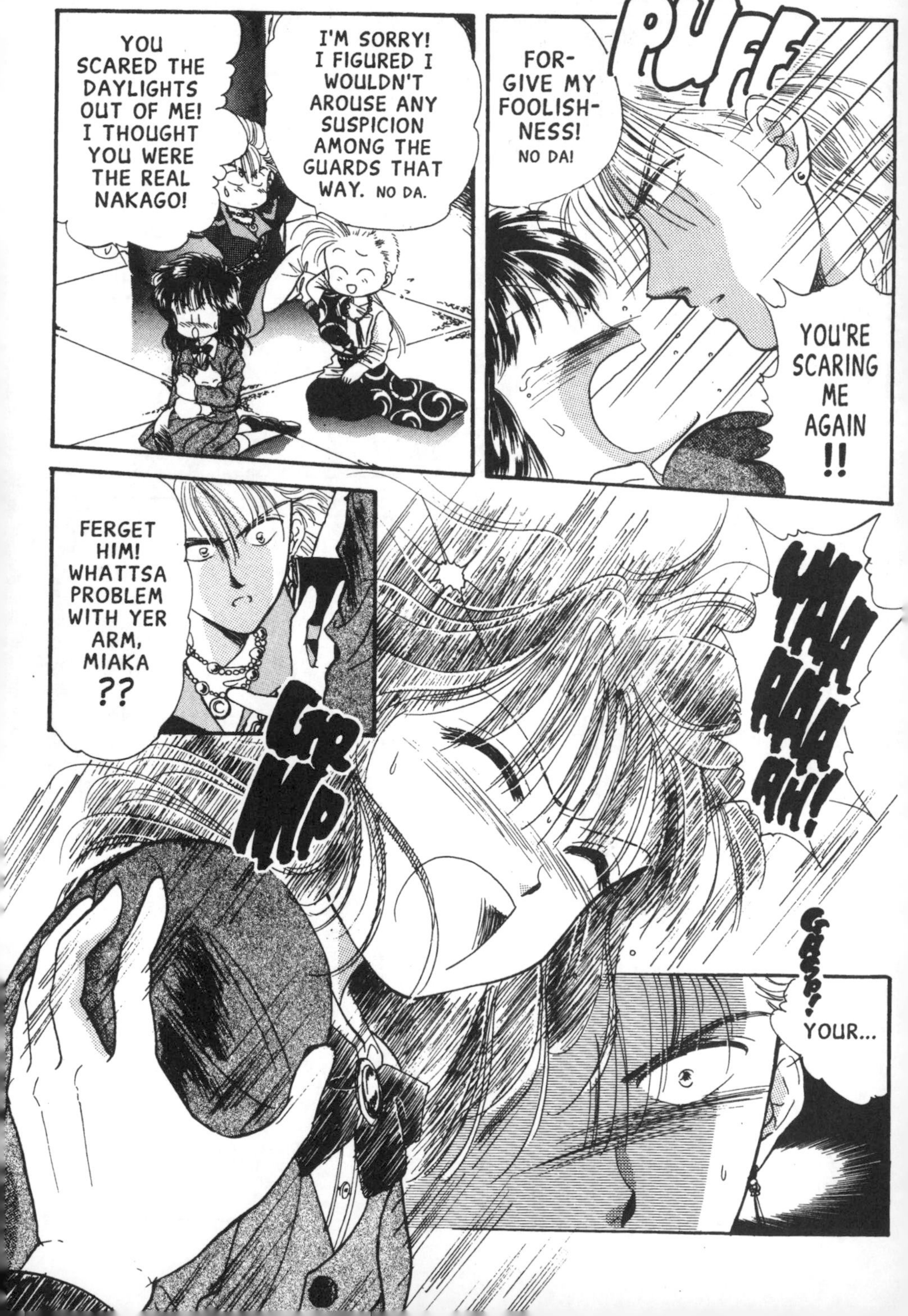
YOU SCARED THE DAYLIGHTS OUT OF ME! I THOUGHT YOU WERE THE REAL NAKAGO!
I'M SORRY! I FIGURED I WOULDN'T AROUSE ANY SUSPICION AMONG THE GUARDS THAT WAY. NO DA.
PUFF
FOR-GIVE MY FOOLISH-NESS! NO DA!
YOU'RE SCARING ME AGAIN !!
FERGET HIM! WHATTSA PROBLEM WITH YER ARM, MIAKA ??
GRMP
YAAAAAAAH!
GASP!
YOUR...

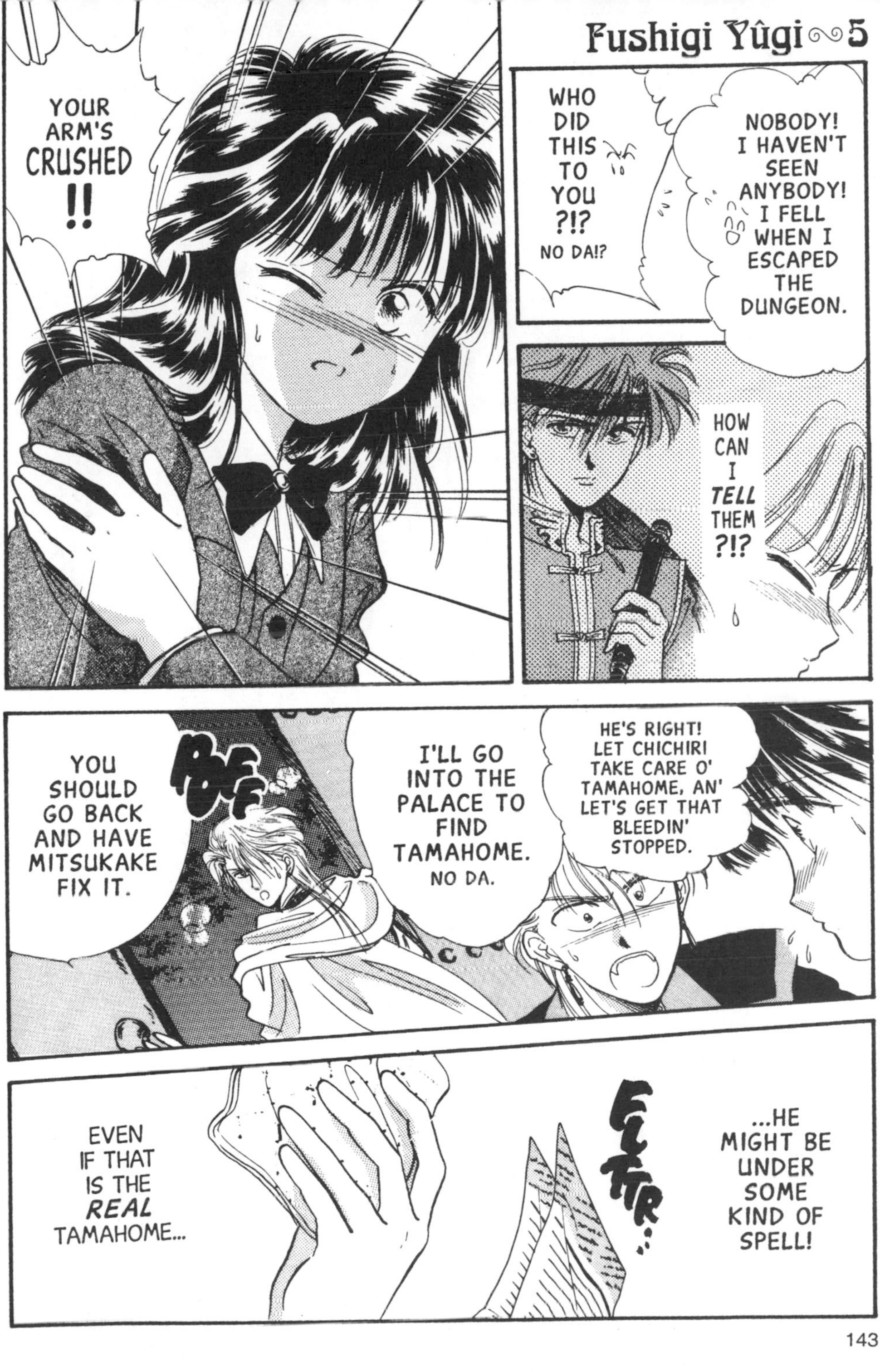
YOUR ARM'S CRUSHED!!
WHO DID THIS TO YOU?!? NO DA!?
NOBODY! I HAVEN'T SEEN ANYBODY! I FELL WHEN I ESCAPED THE DUNGEON.
HOW CAN I TELL THEM?!?
YOU SHOULD GO BACK AND HAVE MITSUKAKE FIX IT.
POFF
I'LL GO INTO THE PALACE TO FIND TAMAHOME. NO DA.
HE'S RIGHT! LET CHICHIRI TAKE CARE O' TAMAHOME, AN' LET'S GET THAT BLEEDIN' STOPPED.
EVEN IF THAT IS THE REAL TAMAHOME...
FLTTR...
...HE MIGHT BE UNDER SOME KIND OF SPELL!

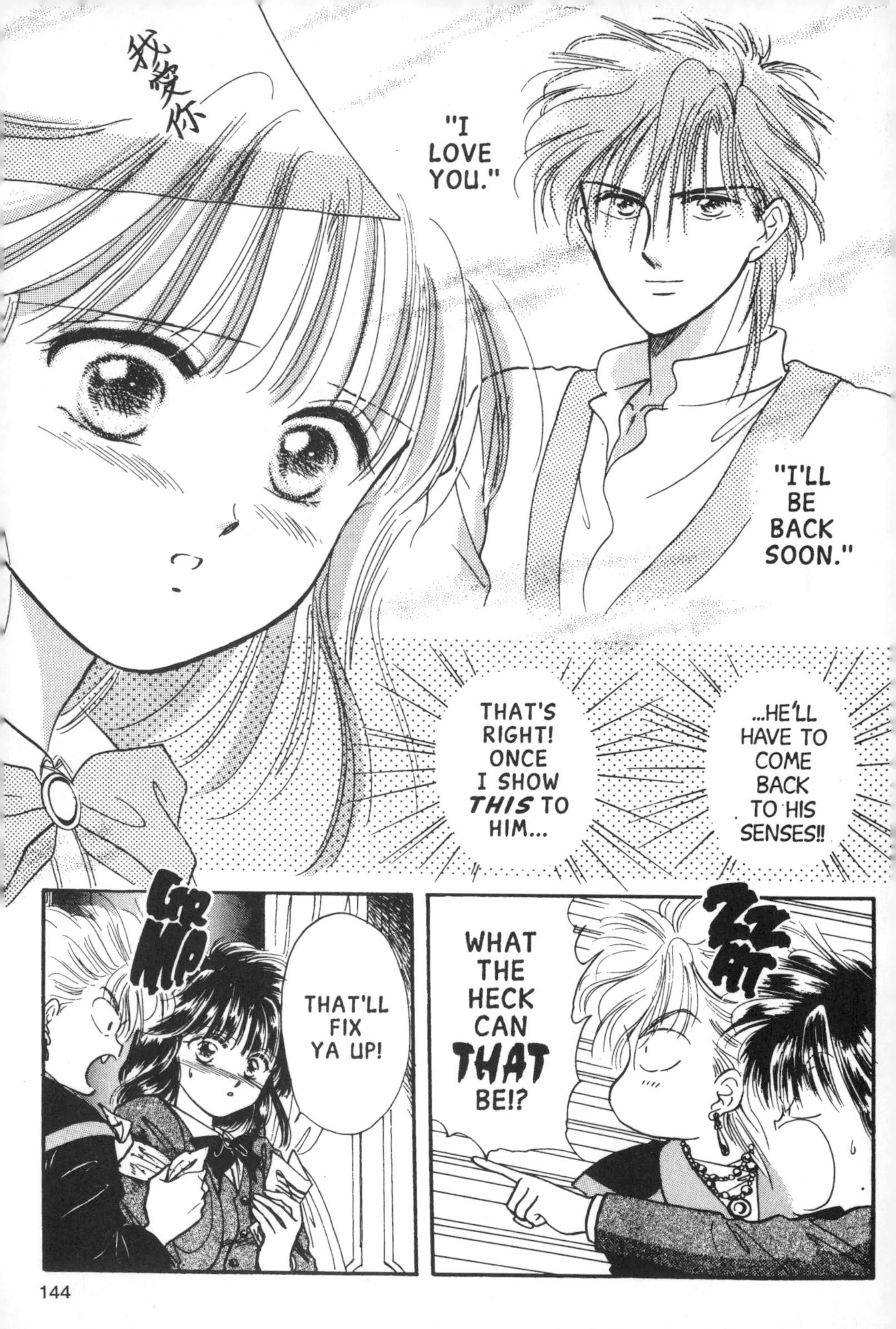
我愛你
"I LOVE YOU."
"I'LL BE BACK SOON."
THAT'S RIGHT! ONCE I SHOW *THIS* TO HIM...
...HE'LL HAVE TO COME BACK TO HIS SENSES!!
GRMP
THAT'LL FIX YA UP!
WHAT THE HECK CAN **THAT** BE!?

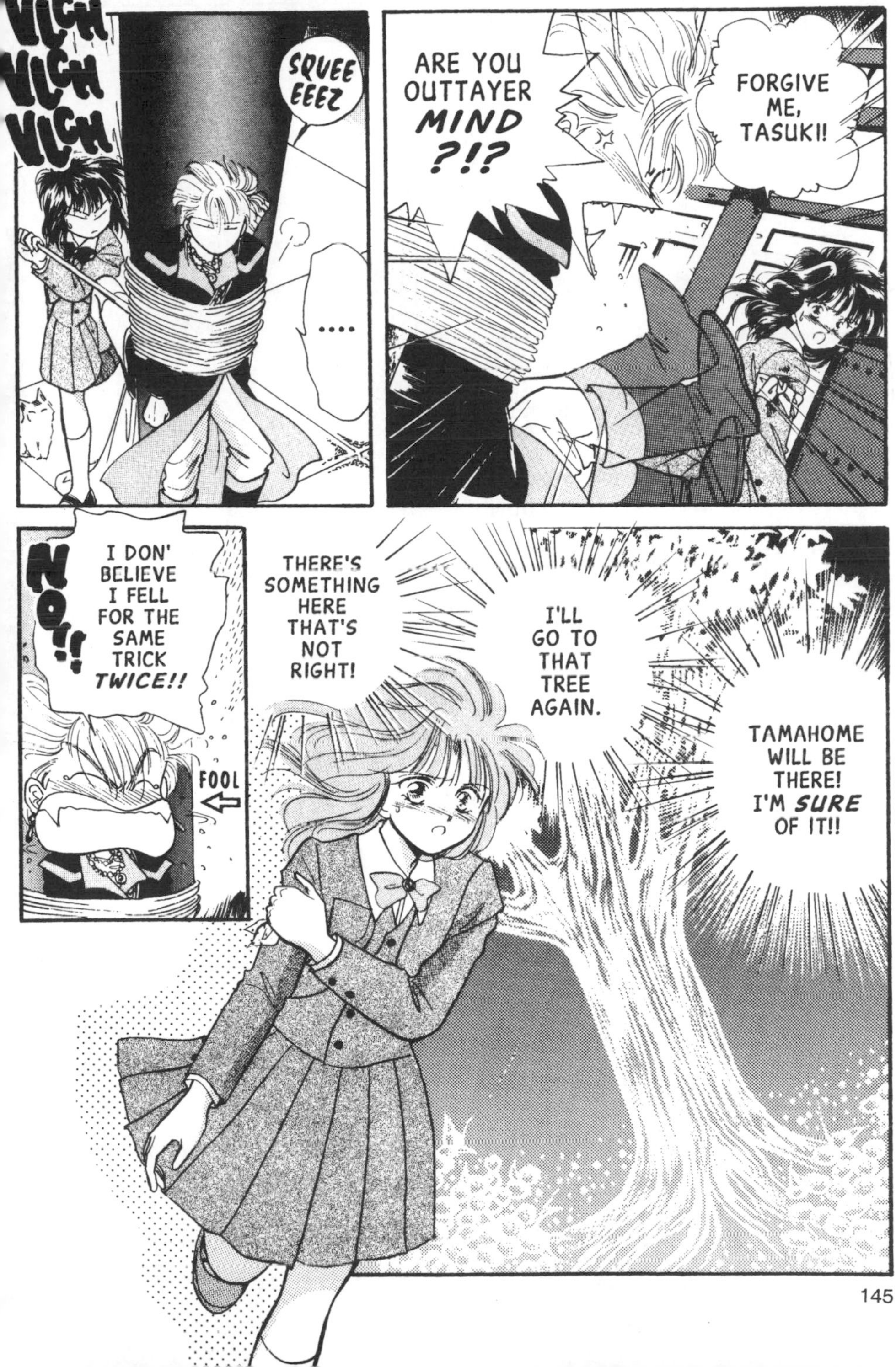
VLCH
VLCH
VLCH
SQUEE EEEZ
....
ARE YOU OUTTAYER MIND ?!?
FORGIVE ME, TASUKI!!
NO!!
I DON' BELIEVE I FELL FOR THE SAME TRICK TWICE!!
FOOL
THERE'S SOMETHING HERE THAT'S NOT RIGHT!
I'LL GO TO THAT TREE AGAIN.
TAMAHOME WILL BE THERE! I'M SURE OF IT!!

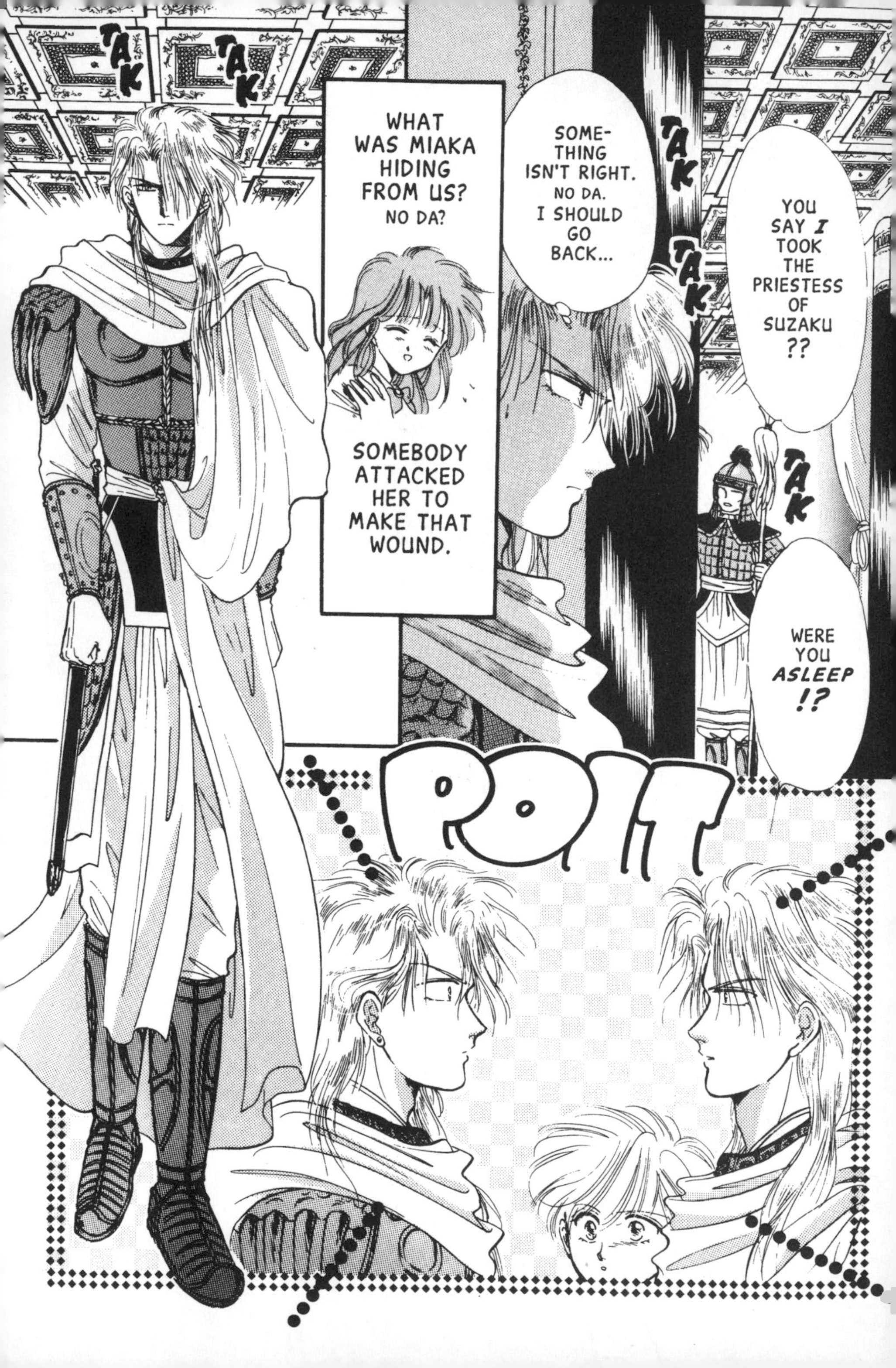
TAK TAK
WHAT WAS MIAKA HIDING FROM US? NO DA?
SOMEBODY ATTACKED HER TO MAKE THAT WOUND.
SOME-THING ISN'T RIGHT. NO DA. I SHOULD GO BACK...
TAK TAK
YOU SAY *I* TOOK THE PRIESTESS OF SUZAKU ??
TAK
WERE YOU ***ASLEEP*** !?
POIT

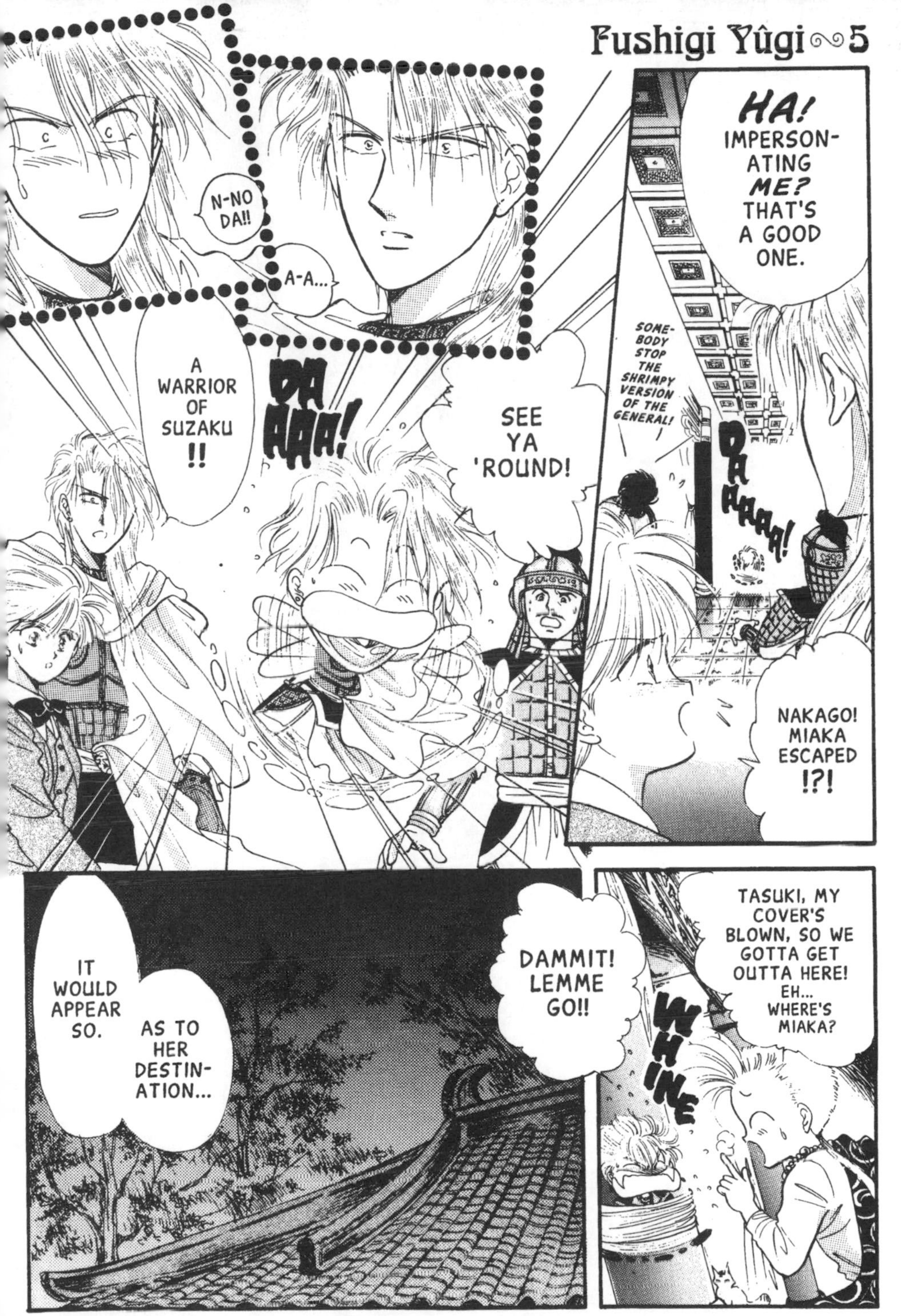
HA! IMPERSONATING ME? THAT'S A GOOD ONE.
SOMEBODY STOP THE SHRIMPY VERSION OF THE GENERAL!
DAAAAA!
NAKAGO! MIAKA ESCAPED !?!
N-NO DA!!
A-A...
SEE YA 'ROUND!
DAAAA!
A WARRIOR OF SUZAKU !!
TASUKI, MY COVER'S BLOWN, SO WE GOTTA GET OUTTA HERE! EH... WHERE'S MIAKA?
DAMMIT! LEMME GO!!
WHINE
IT WOULD APPEAR SO.
AS TO HER DESTINATION...

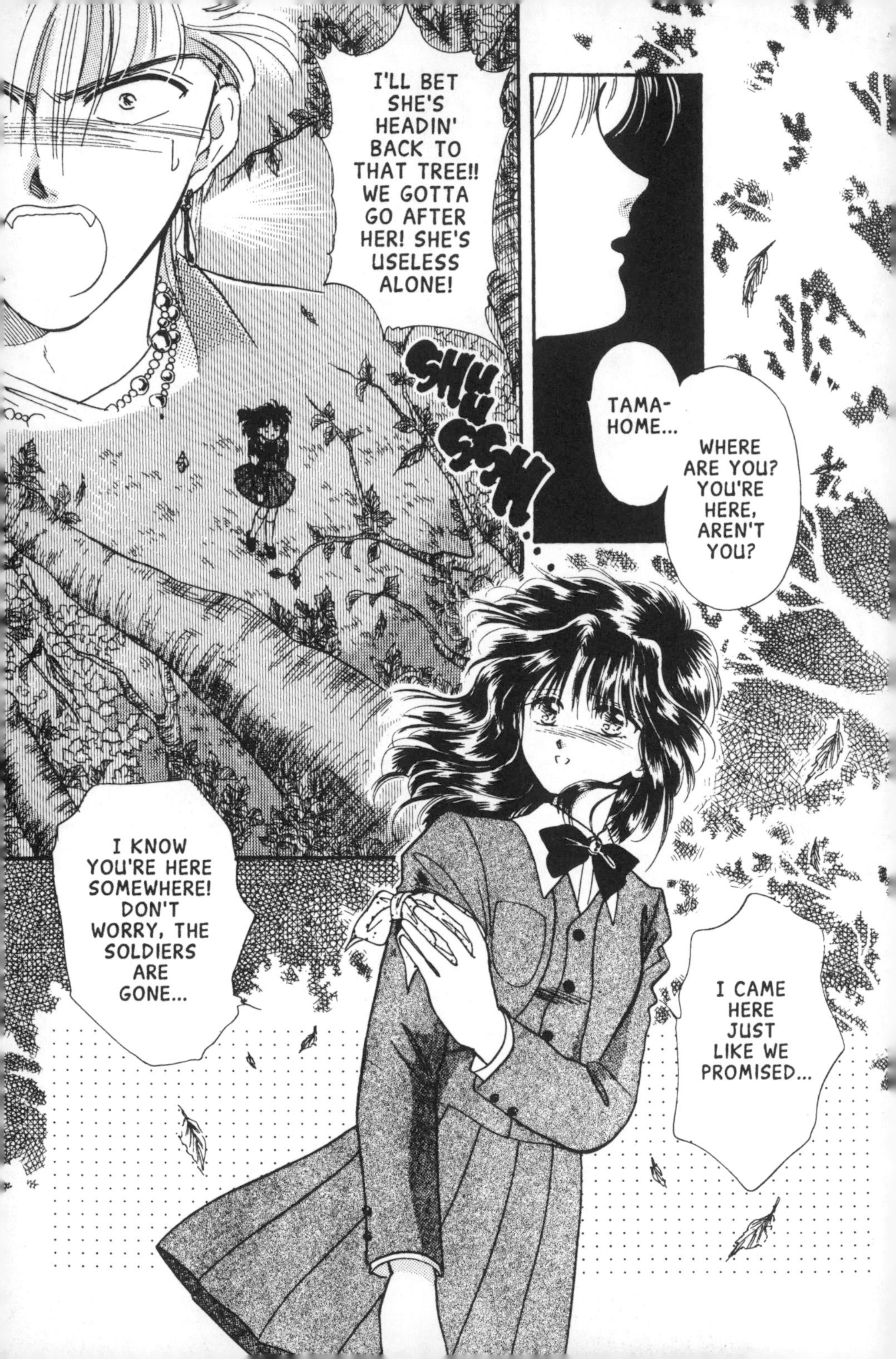
I'LL BET SHE'S HEADIN' BACK TO THAT TREE!! WE GOTTA GO AFTER HER! SHE'S USELESS ALONE!
SHUUSSH
TAMA-HOME...
WHERE ARE YOU? YOU'RE HERE, AREN'T YOU?
I KNOW YOU'RE HERE SOMEWHERE! DON'T WORRY, THE SOLDIERS ARE GONE...
I CAME HERE JUST LIKE WE PROMISED...

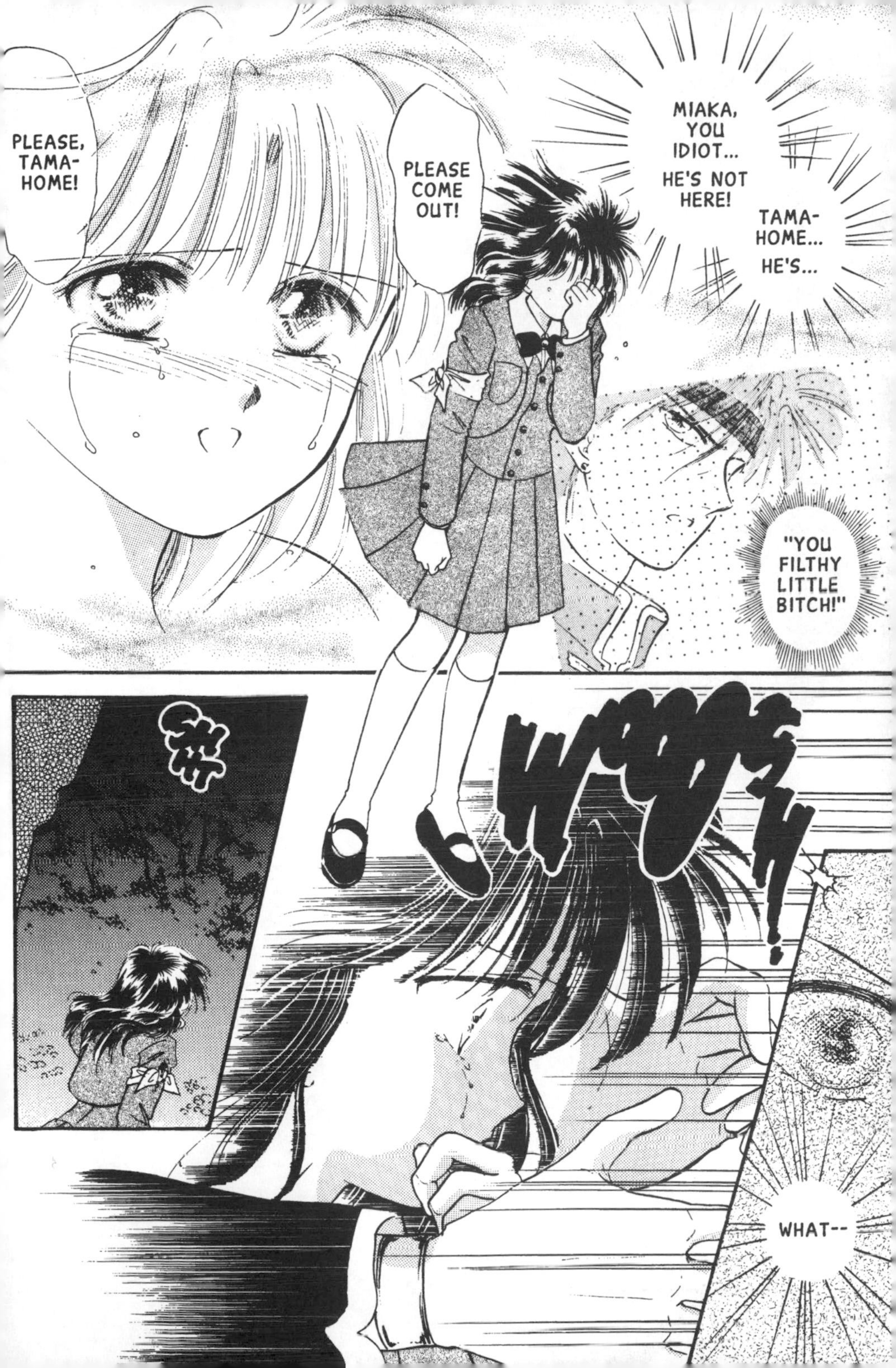
PLEASE, TAMA-HOME!
PLEASE COME OUT!
MIAKA, YOU IDIOT...
HE'S NOT HERE!
TAMA-HOME...
HE'S...
"YOU FILTHY LITTLE BITCH!"
WHAT--

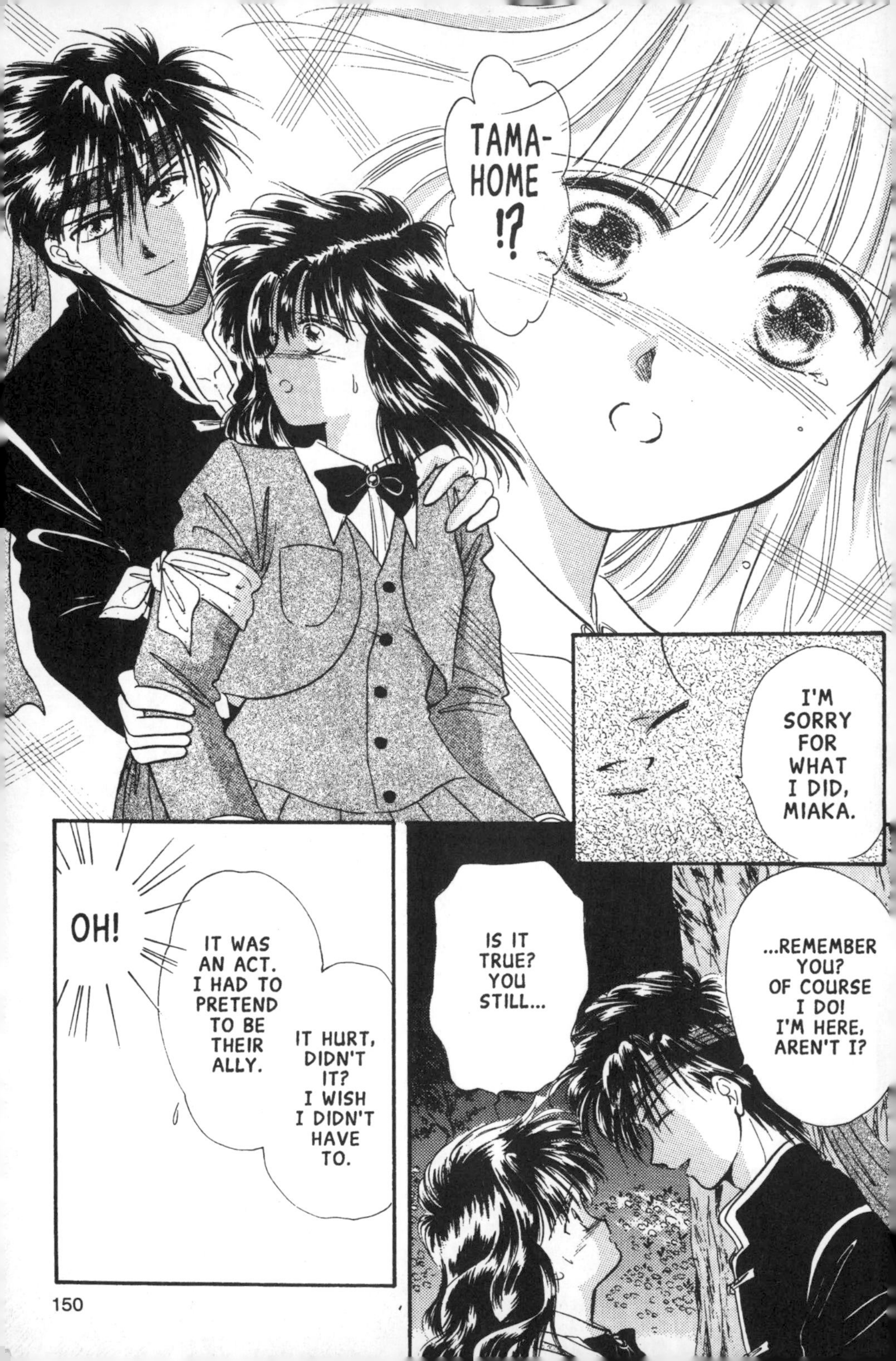
TAMA-HOME !?
I'M SORRY FOR WHAT I DID, MIAKA.
OH!
IT WAS AN ACT. I HAD TO PRETEND TO BE THEIR ALLY.
IT HURT, DIDN'T IT? I WISH I DIDN'T HAVE TO.
IS IT TRUE? YOU STILL...
...REMEMBER YOU? OF COURSE I DO! I'M HERE, AREN'T I?

TAMA-HOME!

BY THE WAY, MIAKA...

...WHERE'S CHICHIRI AND TASUKI? I THOUGHT THEY WERE SUPPOSED TO BE WITH YOU.

VNNNN

NO! YOU'RE NOT THE TAMAHOME I KNOW.

HOW COULD YOU KNOW TASUKI? YOU'VE NEVER EVEN MET HIM!?

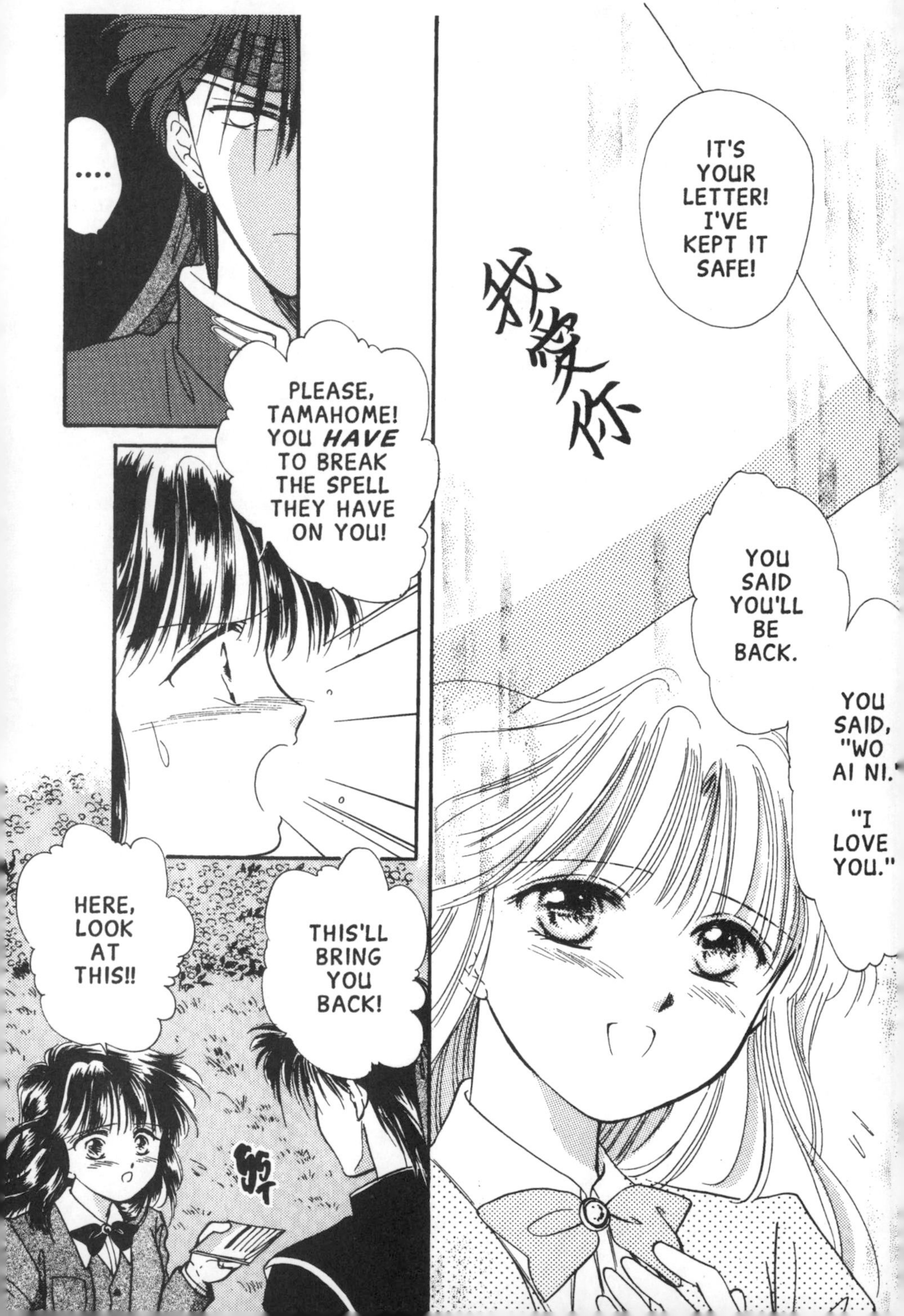

....
PLEASE, TAMAHOME! YOU ***HAVE*** TO BREAK THE SPELL THEY HAVE ON YOU!
HERE, LOOK AT THIS!!
THIS'LL BRING YOU BACK!
IT'S YOUR LETTER! I'VE KEPT IT SAFE!
我愛你
YOU SAID YOU'LL BE BACK.
YOU SAID, "WO AI NI."
"I LOVE YOU."

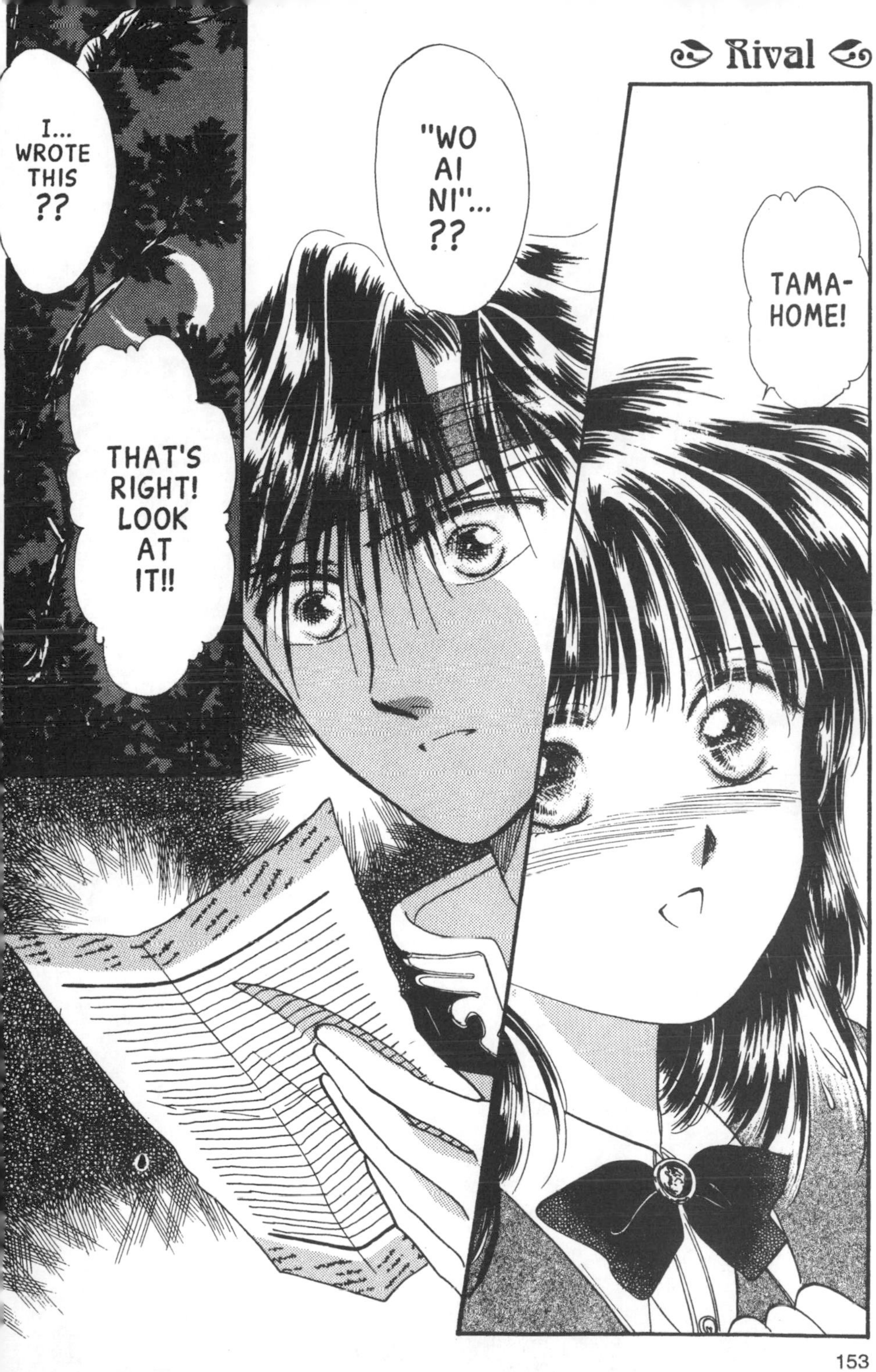
I... WROTE THIS ??
THAT'S RIGHT! LOOK AT IT!!
"WO AI NI"... ??
TAMA-HOME!

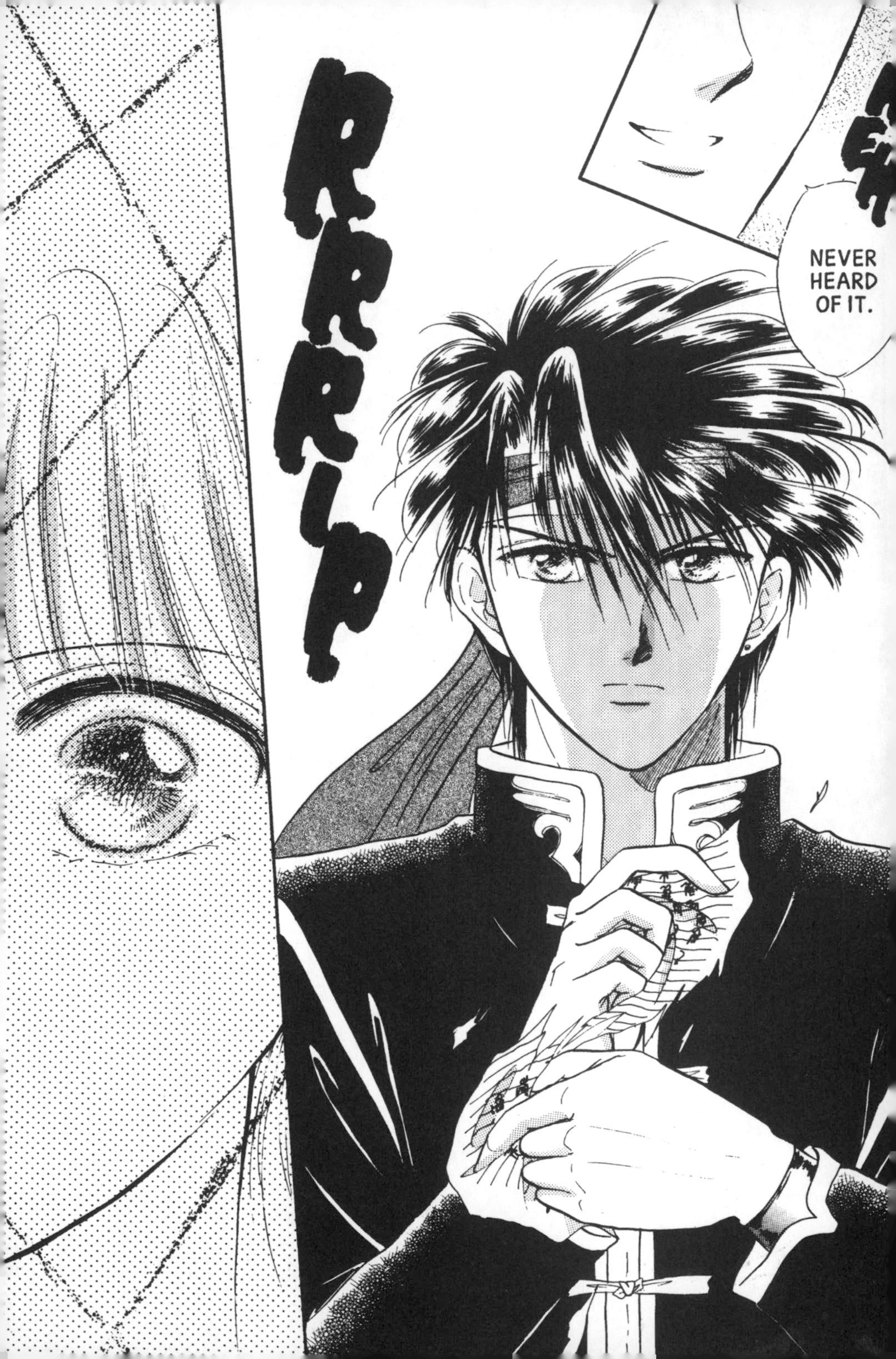
RRRIP
NEVER HEARD OF IT.

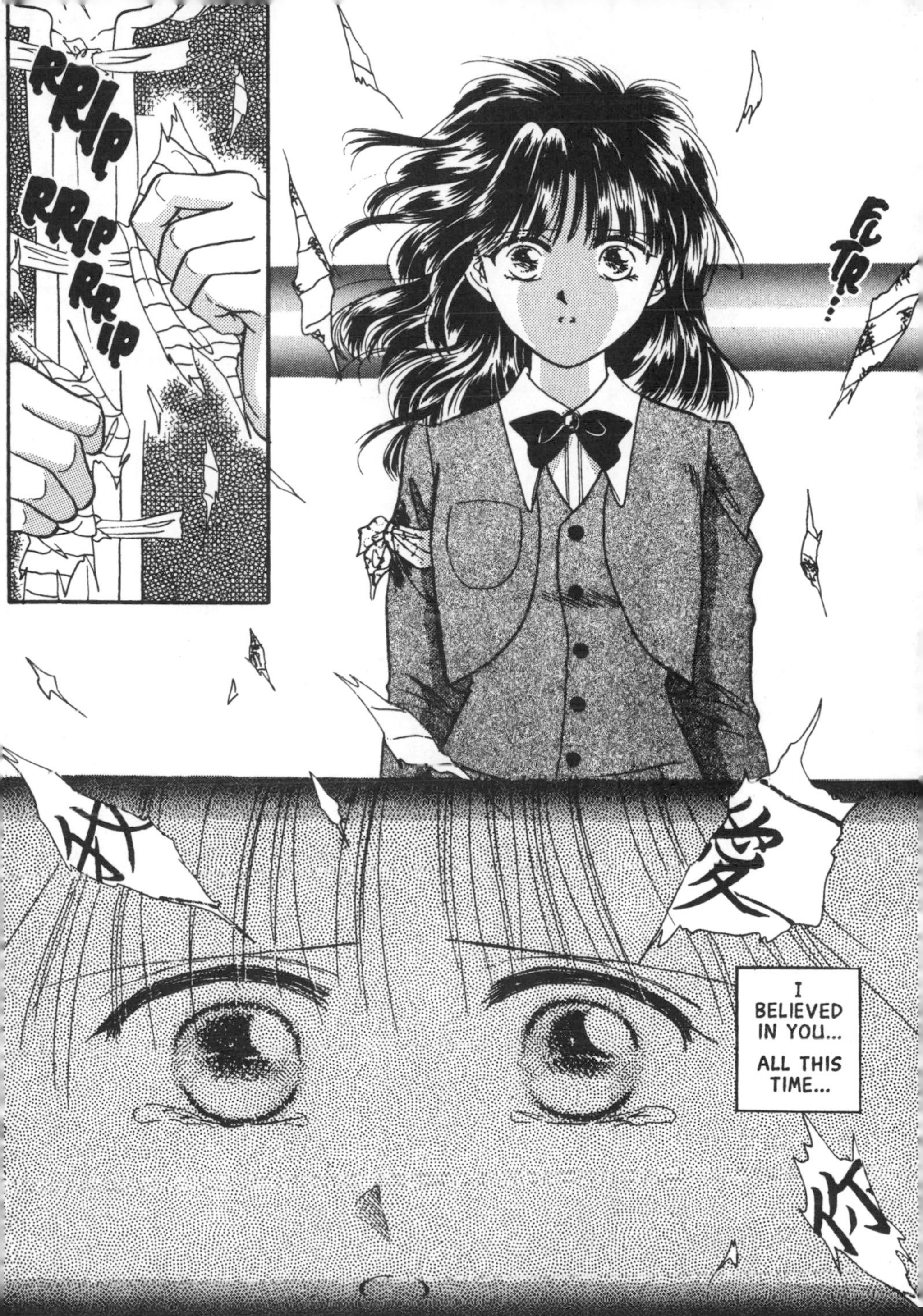
RRIP
RRIP
RRRIP
FLTR...
愛
I BELIEVED IN YOU... ALL THIS TIME...

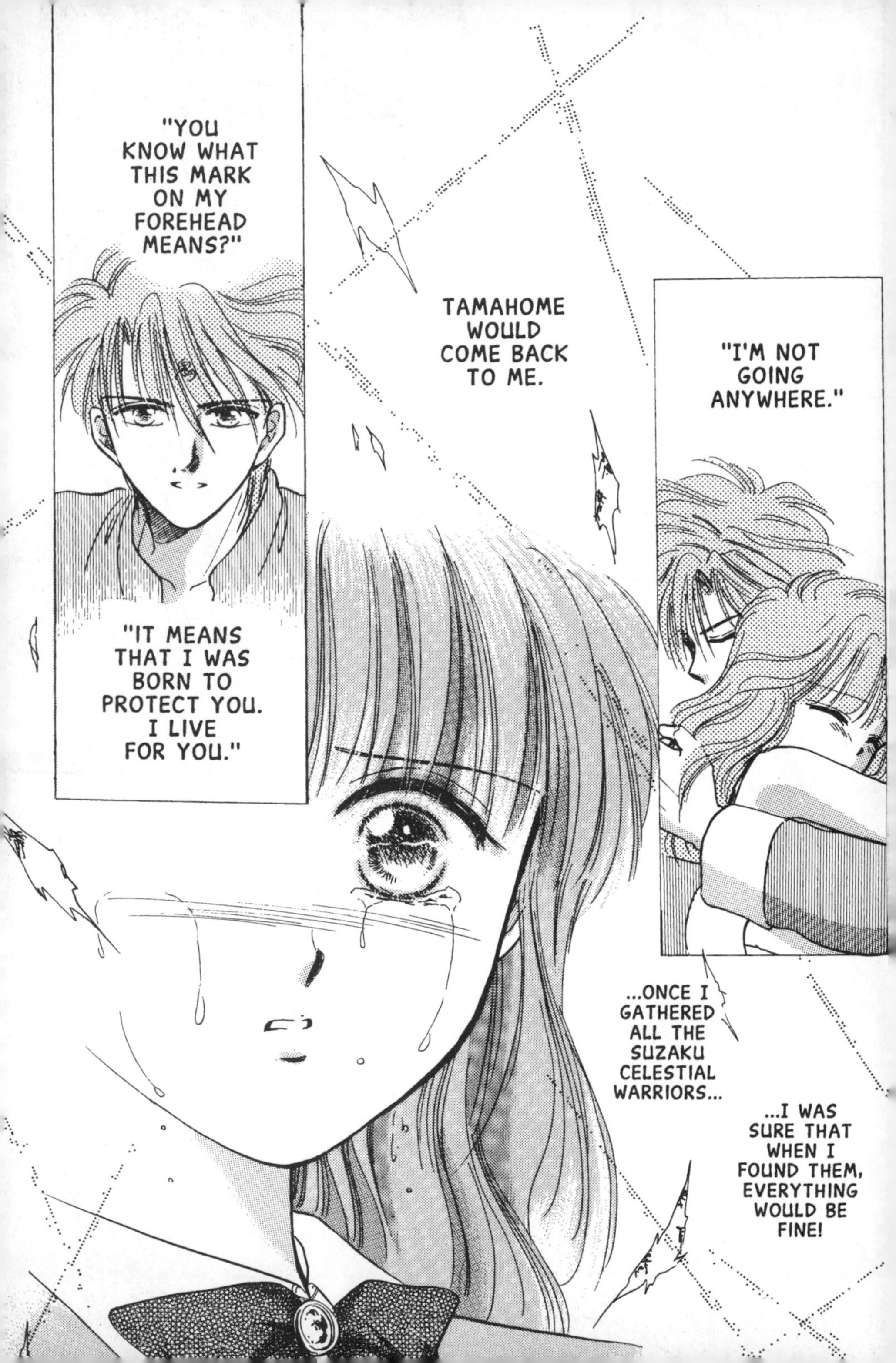
"YOU KNOW WHAT THIS MARK ON MY FOREHEAD MEANS?"
"IT MEANS THAT I WAS BORN TO PROTECT YOU. I LIVE FOR YOU."
TAMAHOME WOULD COME BACK TO ME.
"I'M NOT GOING ANYWHERE."
...ONCE I GATHERED ALL THE SUZAKU CELESTIAL WARRIORS...
...I WAS SURE THAT WHEN I FOUND THEM, EVERYTHING WOULD BE FINE!

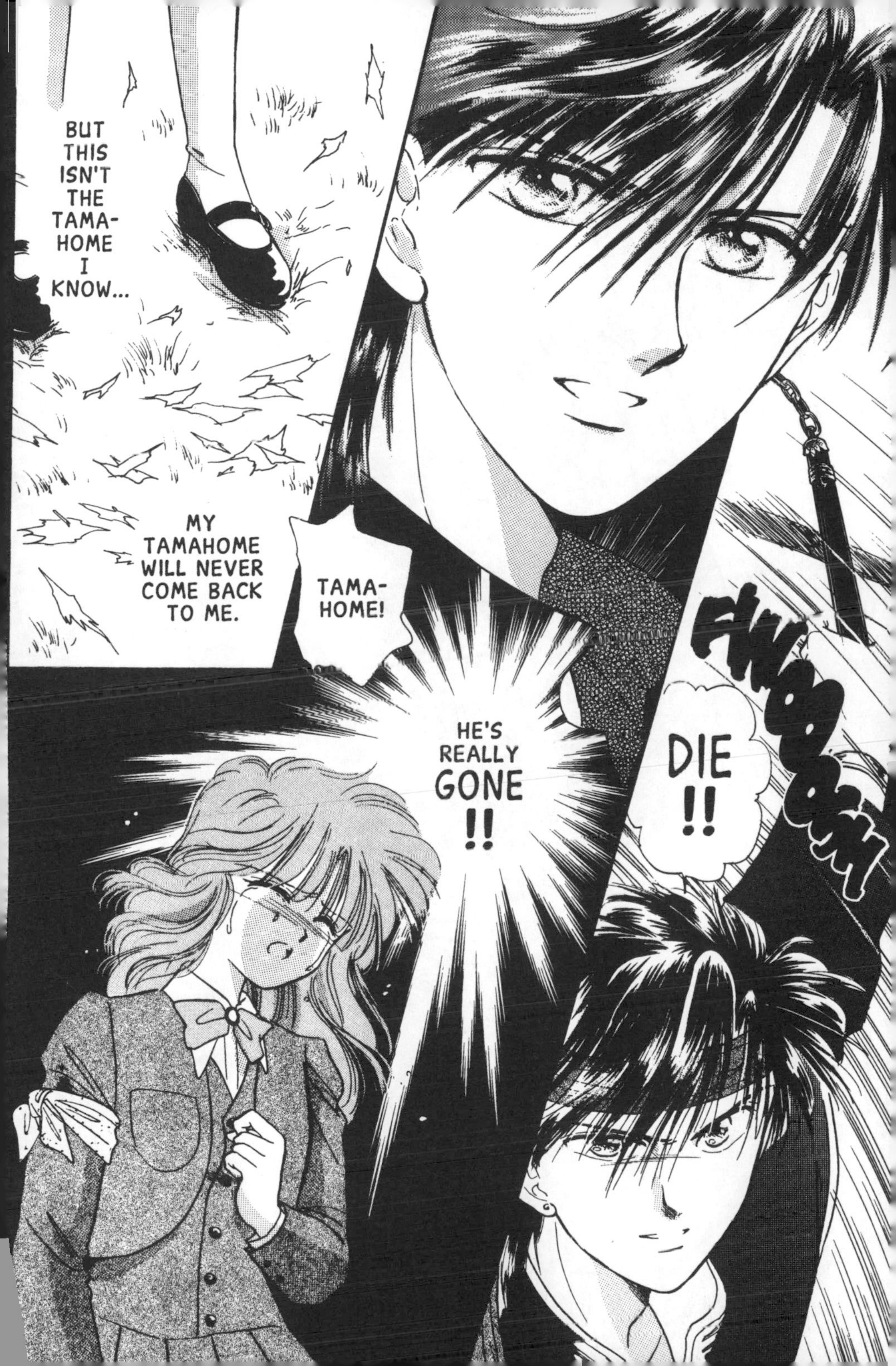
BUT THIS ISN'T THE TAMA-HOME I KNOW...
MY TAMAHOME WILL NEVER COME BACK TO ME.
TAMA-HOME!
HE'S REALLY GONE!!
DIE!!
FWOOOOM

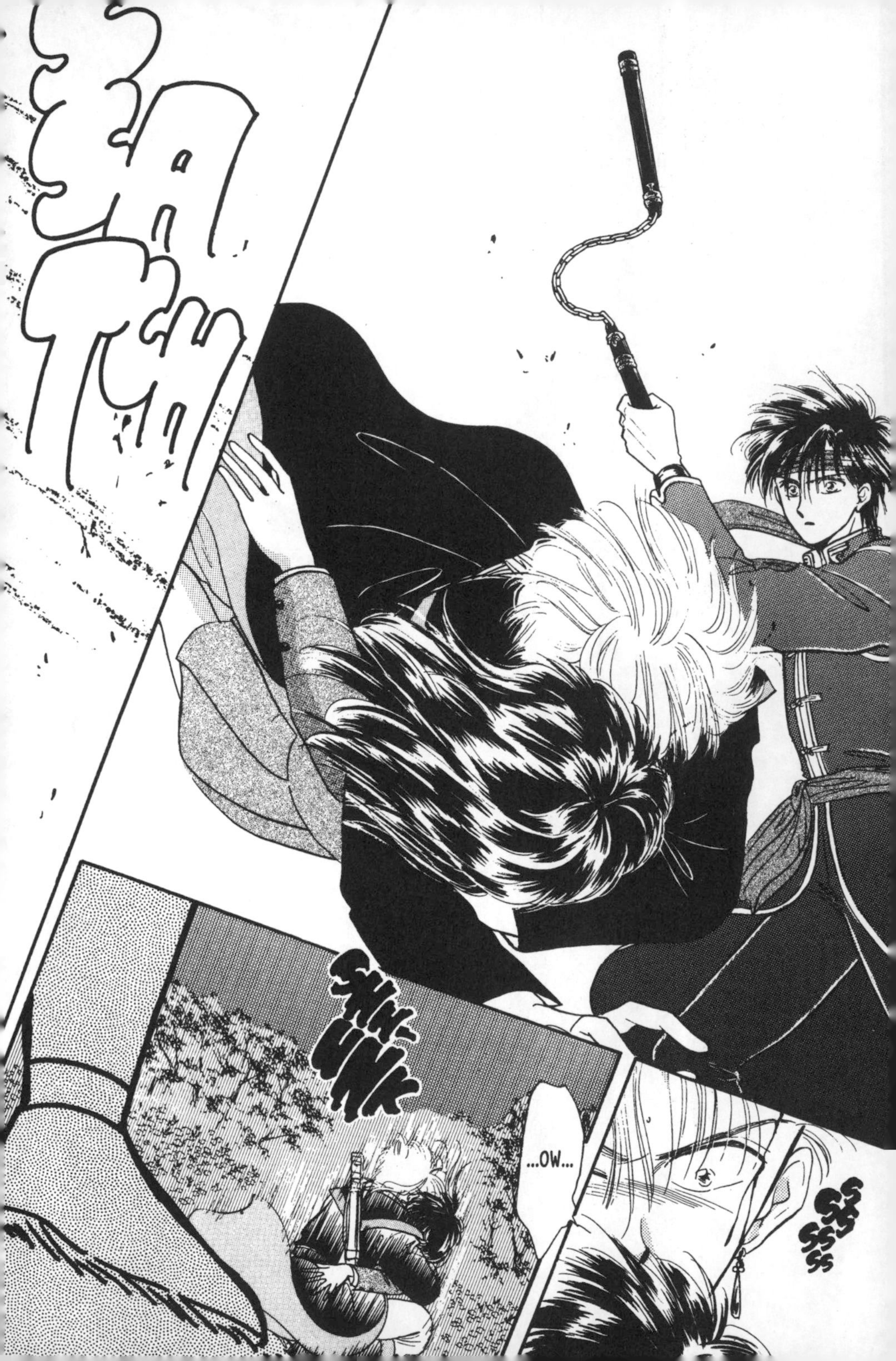
GA CHA!
SHN-UNK
...OW...
SSSSSSSS

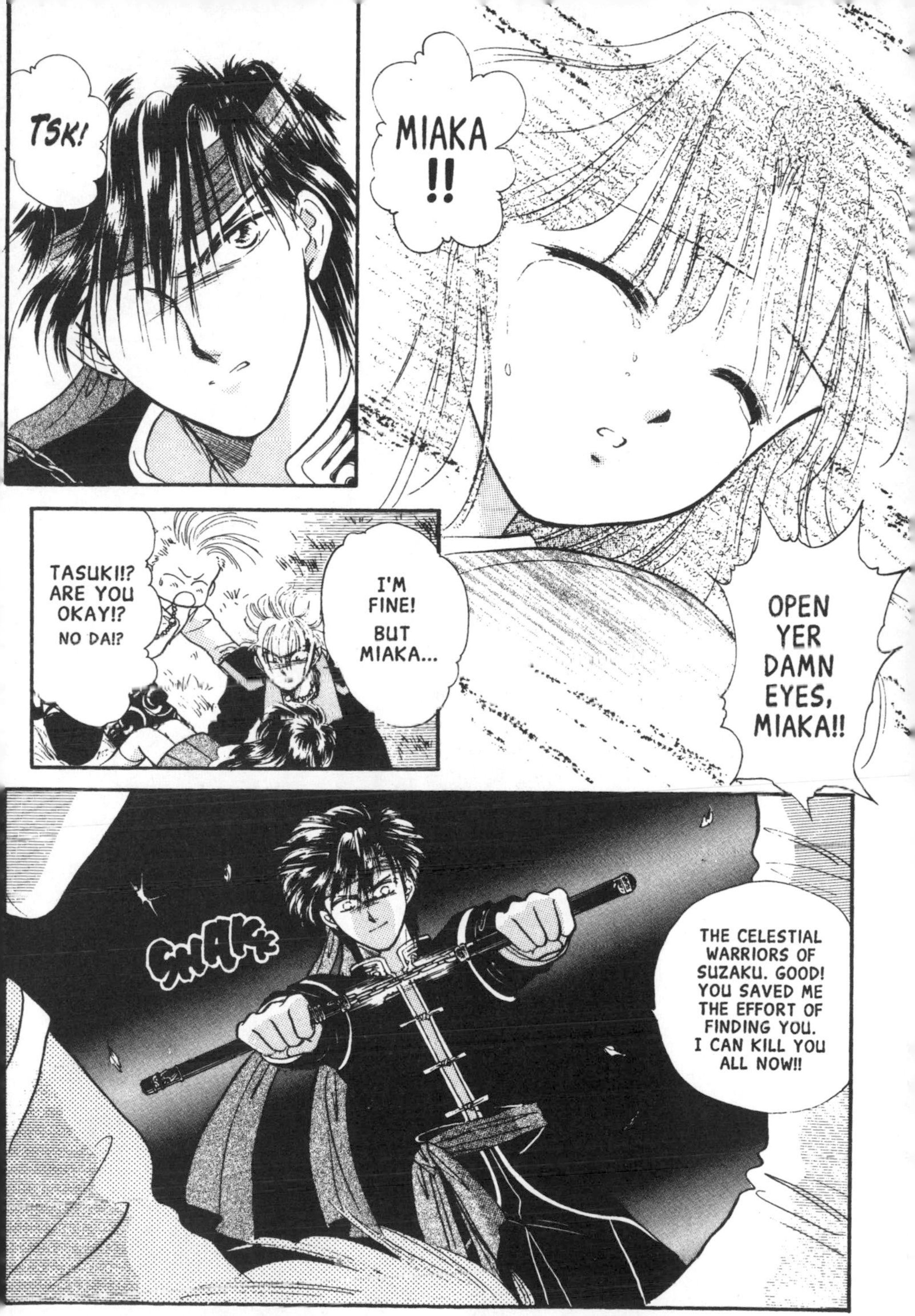
TSK!
MIAKA !!
TASUKI!? ARE YOU OKAY!? NO DA!?
I'M FINE! BUT MIAKA...
OPEN YER DAMN EYES, MIAKA!!
SHAK
THE CELESTIAL WARRIORS OF SUZAKU. GOOD! YOU SAVED ME THE EFFORT OF FINDING YOU. I CAN KILL YOU ALL NOW!!

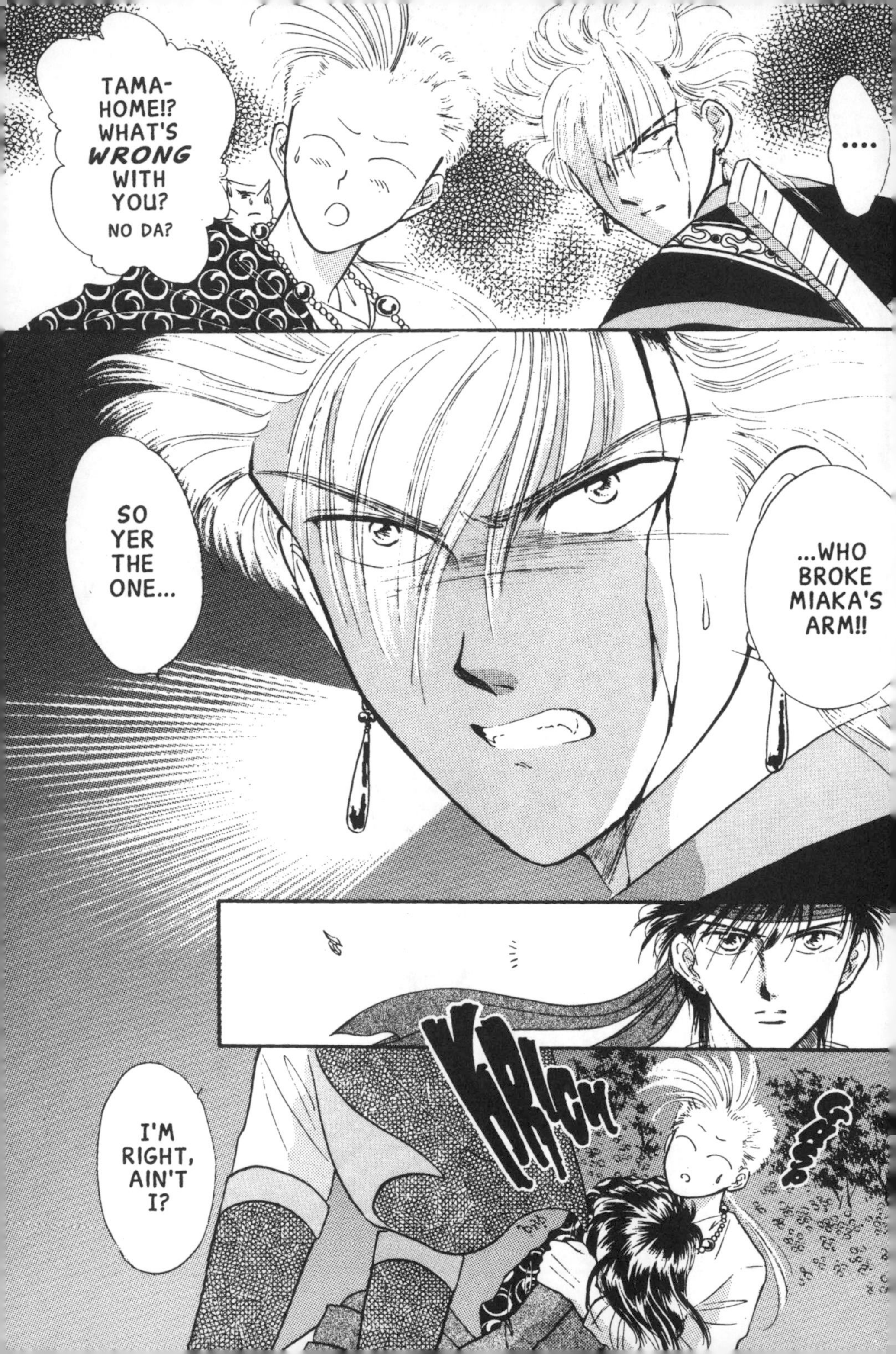
TAMA-HOME!? WHAT'S ***WRONG*** WITH YOU? NO DA?
....
SO YER THE ONE...
...WHO BROKE MIAKA'S ARM!!
I'M RIGHT, AIN'T I?
KRRICH
GRAB

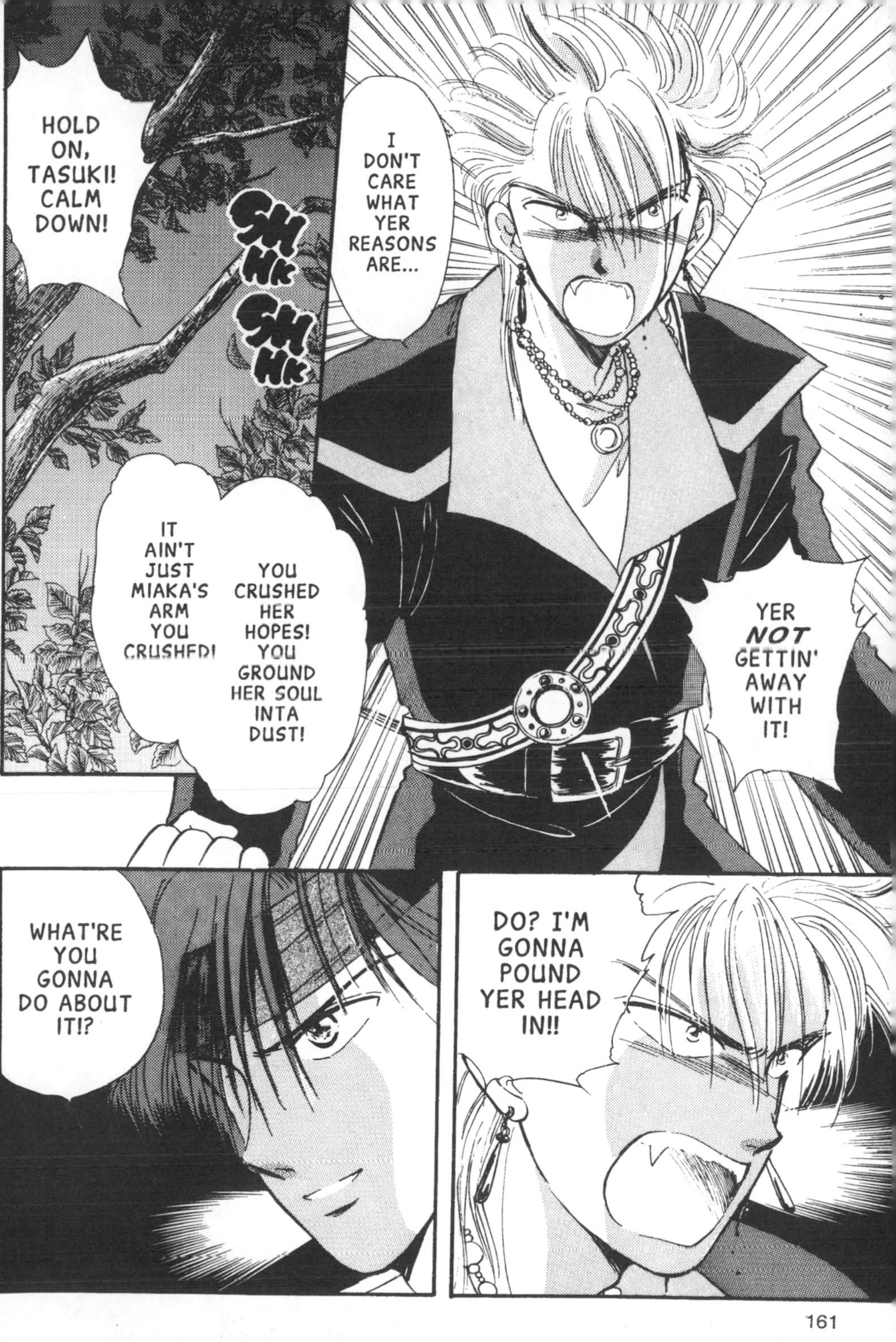
HOLD ON, TASUKI! CALM DOWN!
SHHK SHHK
I DON'T CARE WHAT YER REASONS ARE...
IT AIN'T JUST MIAKA'S ARM YOU CRUSHED!
YOU CRUSHED HER HOPES! YOU GROUND HER SOUL INTA DUST!
YER NOT GETTIN' AWAY WITH IT!
WHAT'RE YOU GONNA DO ABOUT IT!?
DO? I'M GONNA POUND YER HEAD IN!!

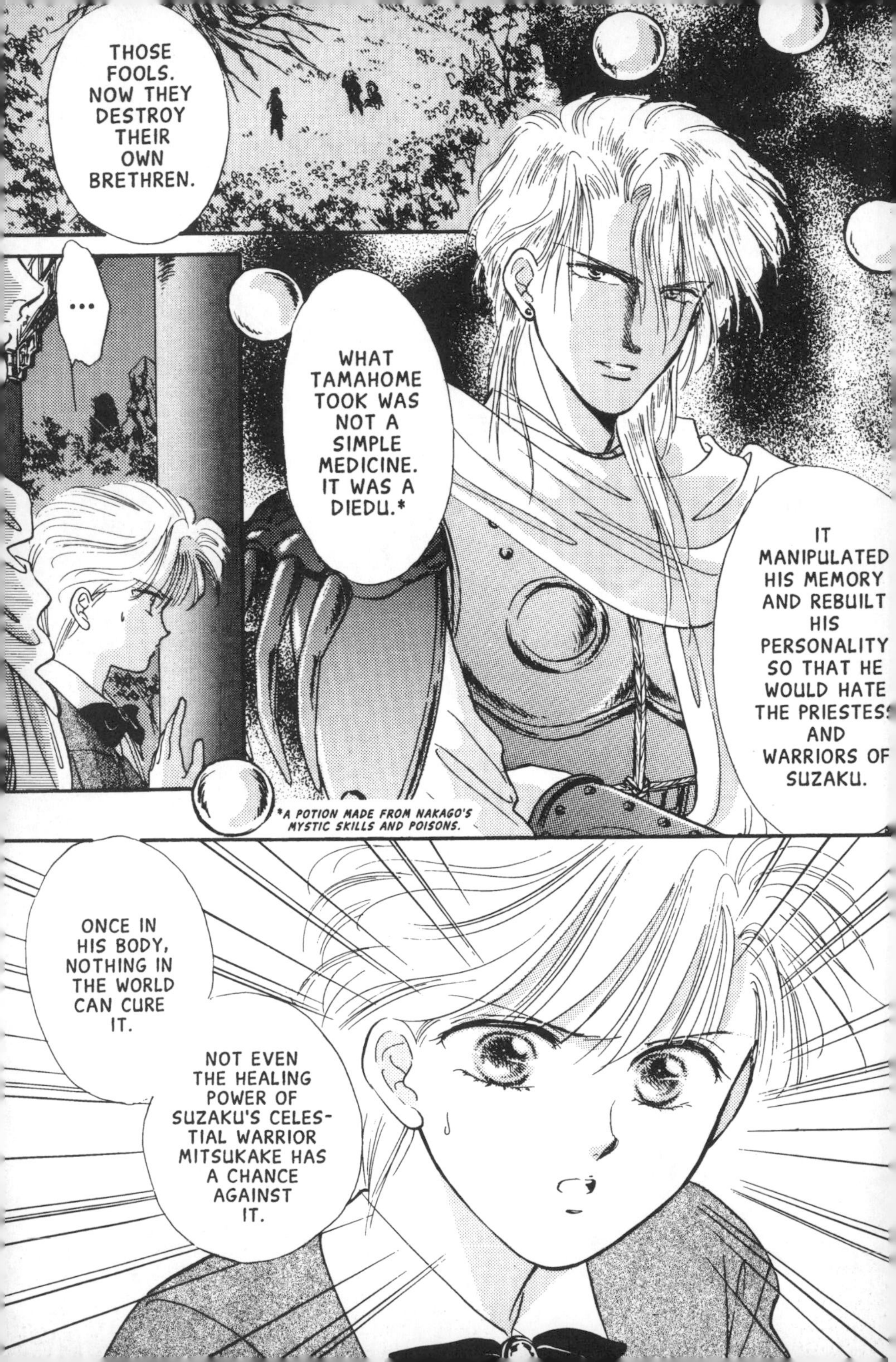
THOSE FOOLS. NOW THEY DESTROY THEIR OWN BRETHREN.
...
WHAT TAMAHOME TOOK WAS NOT A SIMPLE MEDICINE. IT WAS A DIEDU.*
IT MANIPULATED HIS MEMORY AND REBUILT HIS PERSONALITY SO THAT HE WOULD HATE THE PRIESTESS AND WARRIORS OF SUZAKU.
*A POTION MADE FROM NAKAGO'S MYSTIC SKILLS AND POISONS.
ONCE IN HIS BODY, NOTHING IN THE WORLD CAN CURE IT.
NOT EVEN THE HEALING POWER OF SUZAKU'S CELES-TIAL WARRIOR MITSUKAKE HAS A CHANCE AGAINST IT.

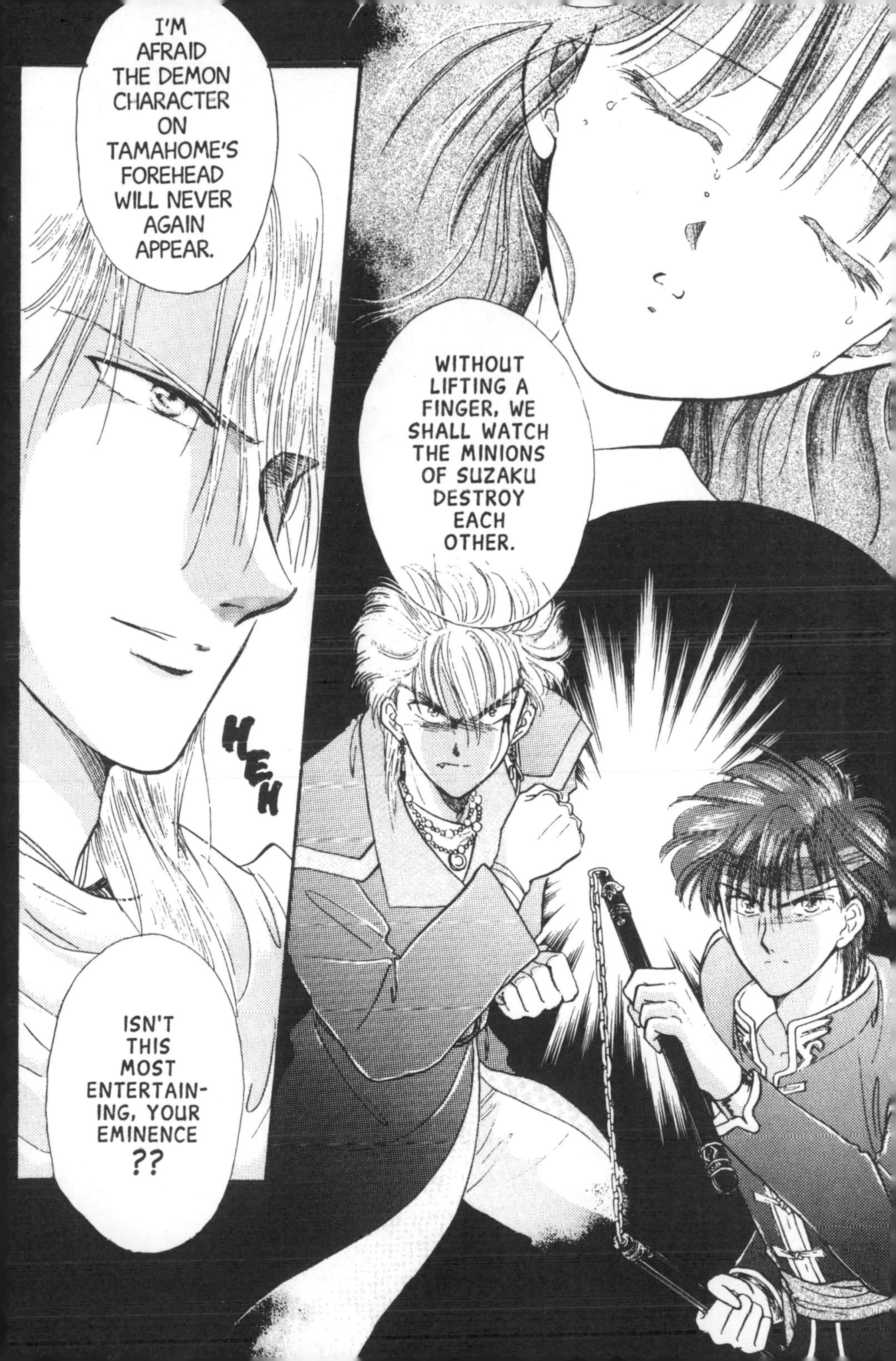
I'M AFRAID THE DEMON CHARACTER ON TAMAHOME'S FOREHEAD WILL NEVER AGAIN APPEAR.
HEH
ISN'T THIS MOST ENTERTAIN-ING, YOUR EMINENCE ??
WITHOUT LIFTING A FINGER, WE SHALL WATCH THE MINIONS OF SUZAKU DESTROY EACH OTHER.

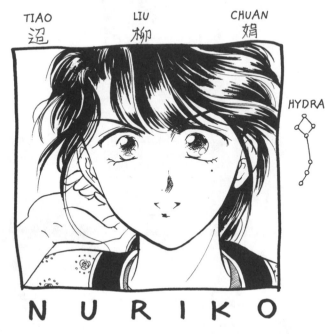

TIAO
迢

LIU
柳

CHUAN
娟

HYDRA

N U R I K O

- The second son of a shop keeper in the Hsien-Wu district of Hong-Nan's capital city of Rong-Yang.
- Age: Presently 18 years old.
- Family: Parents and older brother.
  Kang-Lin was the name of deceased sister. *(NAME FROM VOL. 1)*
- Talents: Enormous Strength, Come-hither Eyes *(What's that supposed to mean?)*
- Hobby: Cross-dressing.
- Height: 5 feet, 5 inches.
- Blood type: B *(I think)*

• *Nuriko is biologically a man, but judging by looks, tone of voice, and all other factors, Nuriko seems like a woman, and as a woman, is infatuated with Hotohori. The uninitiated may simply see a homosexual, but in Nuriko's words, "I have a man's body but a woman's heart." When not angry or calculating, Nuriko can be a pretty cool person. The jealous type, but also a worrier. Nuriko seems to worry most about Miaka and Tamahome's relationship. Miaka looks to Nuriko as an older sister (?), but there is a part that remains very manly.*

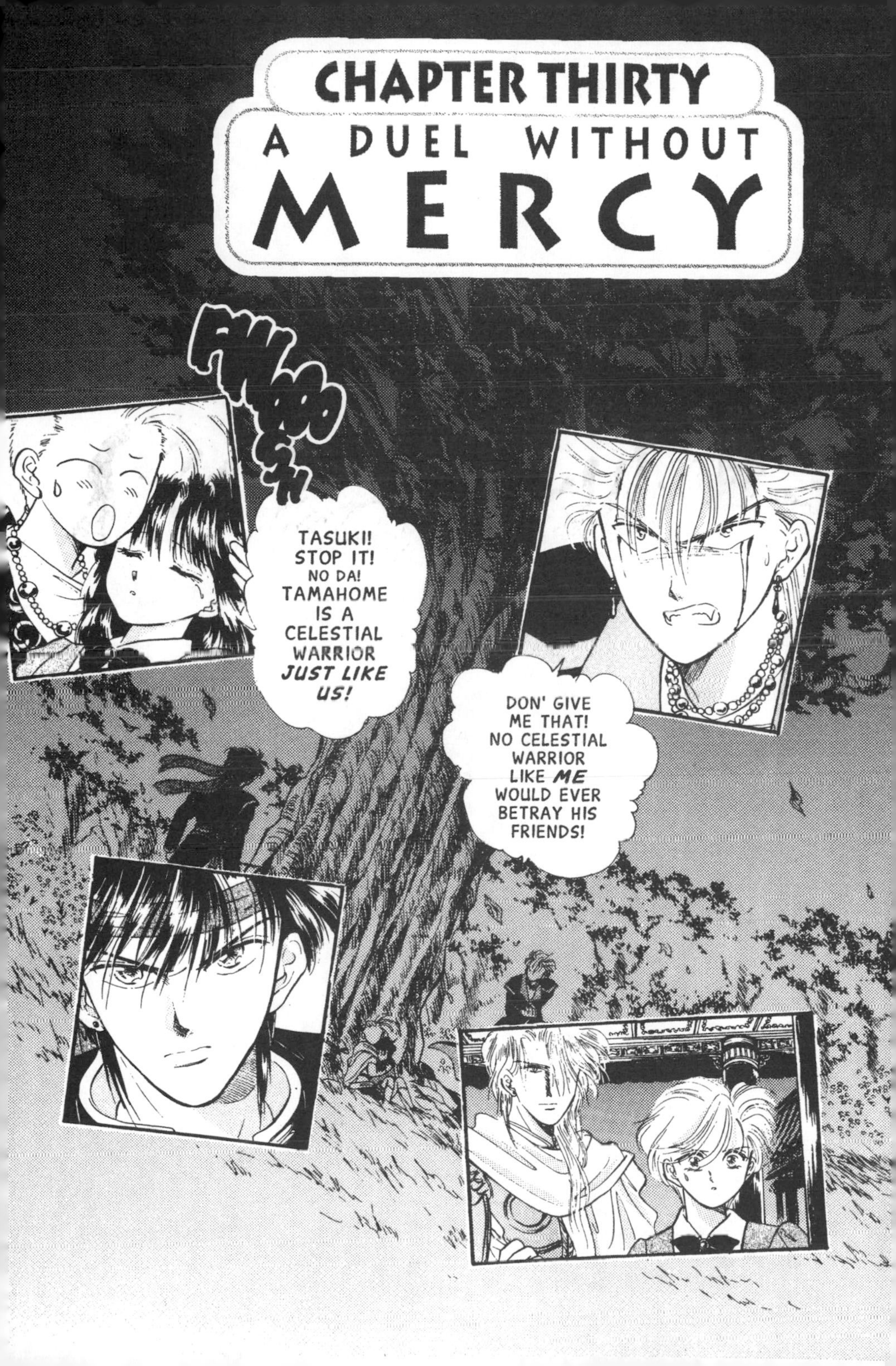
CHAPTER THIRTY
A DUEL WITHOUT MERCY
FWOOOSH
TASUKI! STOP IT! NO DA! TAMAHOME IS A CELESTIAL WARRIOR *JUST LIKE US!*
DON' GIVE ME THAT! NO CELESTIAL WARRIOR LIKE *ME* WOULD EVER BETRAY HIS FRIENDS!

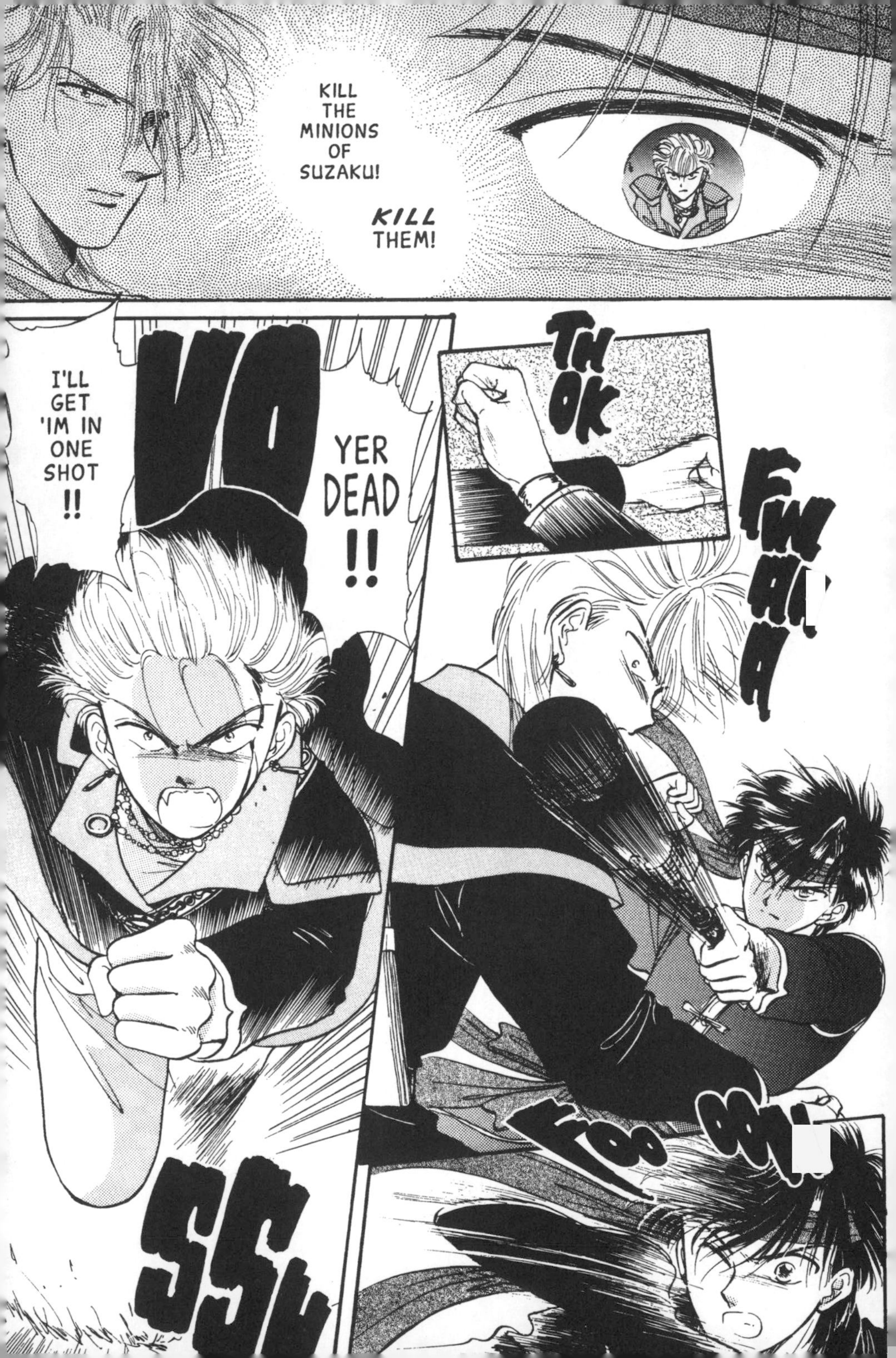

KILL THE MINIONS OF SUZAKU!
KILL THEM!
I'LL GET 'IM IN ONE SHOT !!
YER DEAD !!
THOK

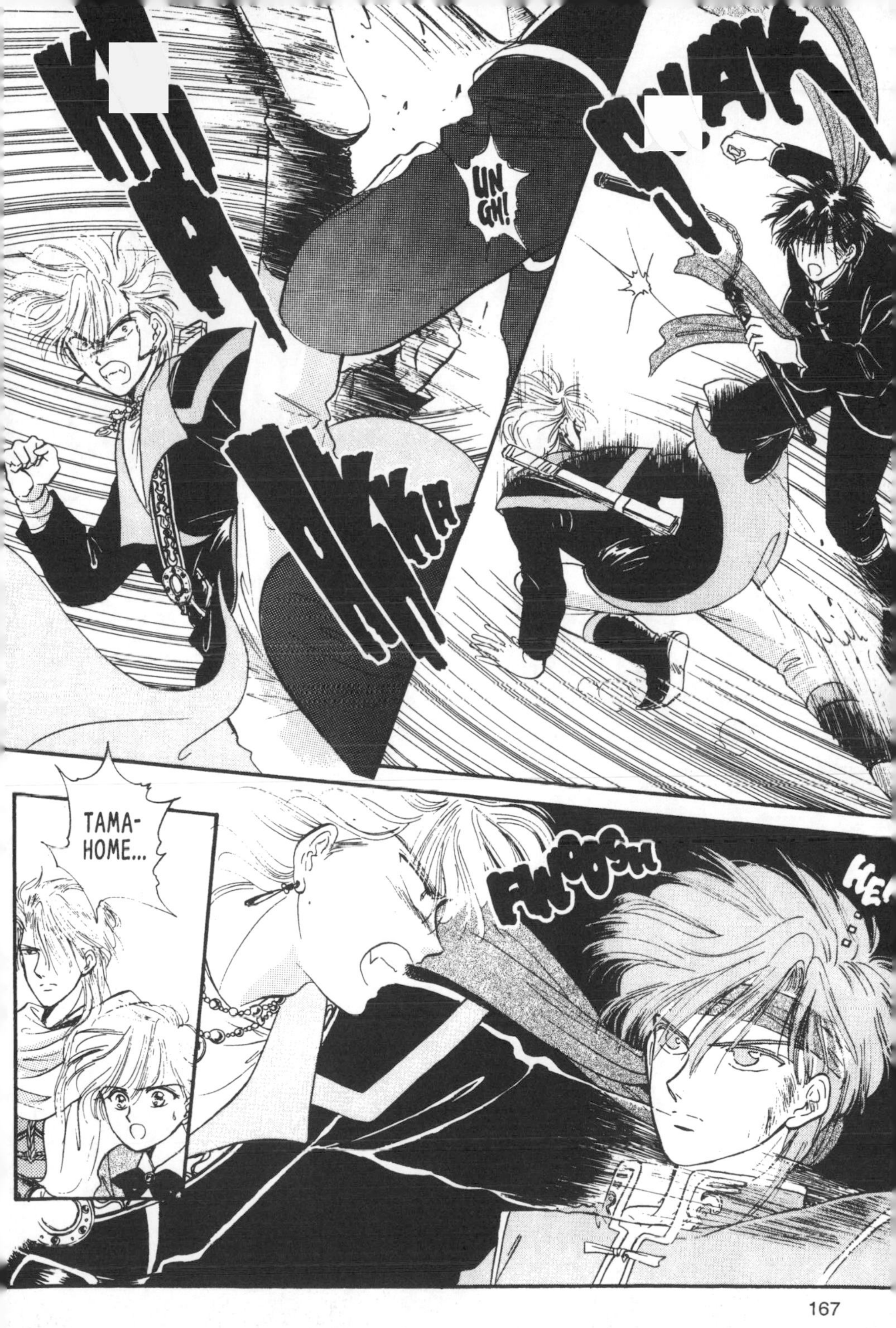
UN GH!
TAMA-HOME...
FWOOSH

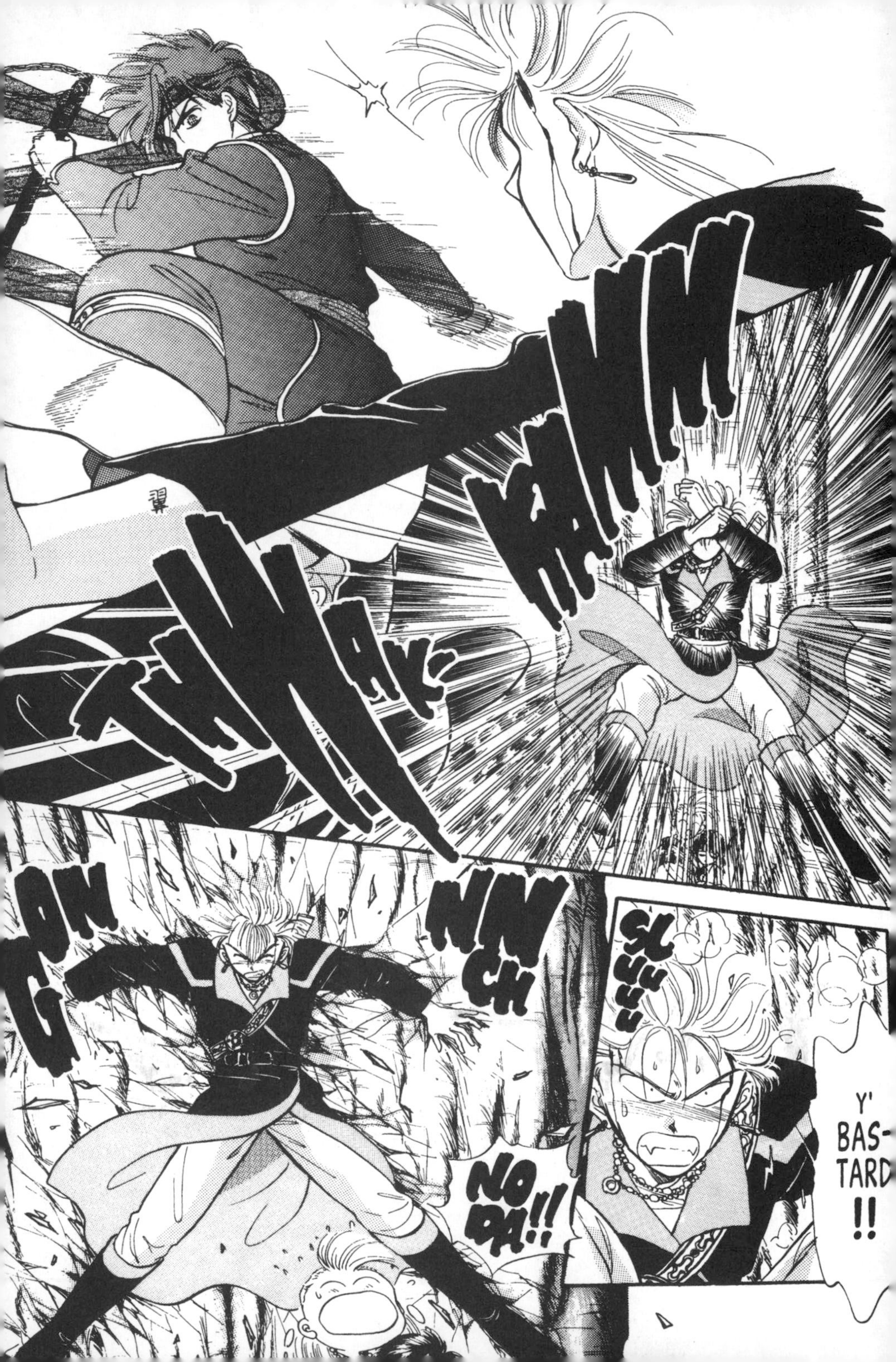
THWAK-
SLUUUUU
NO DA!!
Y' BASTARD!!

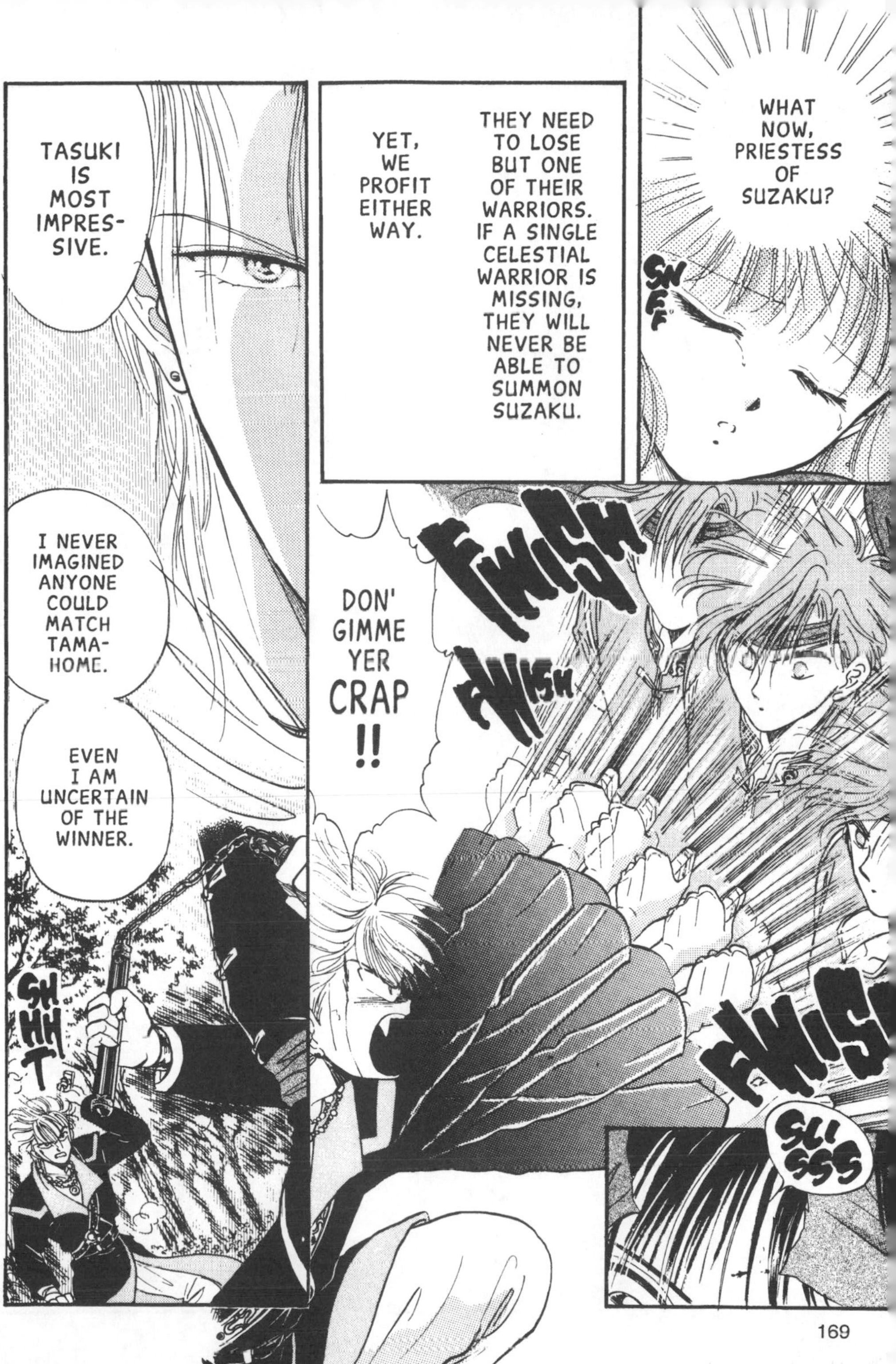
TASUKI IS MOST IMPRES-SIVE.
I NEVER IMAGINED ANYONE COULD MATCH TAMA-HOME.
EVEN I AM UNCERTAIN OF THE WINNER.
SHHHT
THEY NEED TO LOSE BUT ONE OF THEIR WARRIORS. IF A SINGLE CELESTIAL WARRIOR IS MISSING, THEY WILL NEVER BE ABLE TO SUMMON SUZAKU.
YET, WE PROFIT EITHER WAY.
WHAT NOW, PRIESTESS OF SUZAKU?
SNIFF
DON' GIMME YER CRAP!!
FWISH
FWISH
FWISH
SLISSS

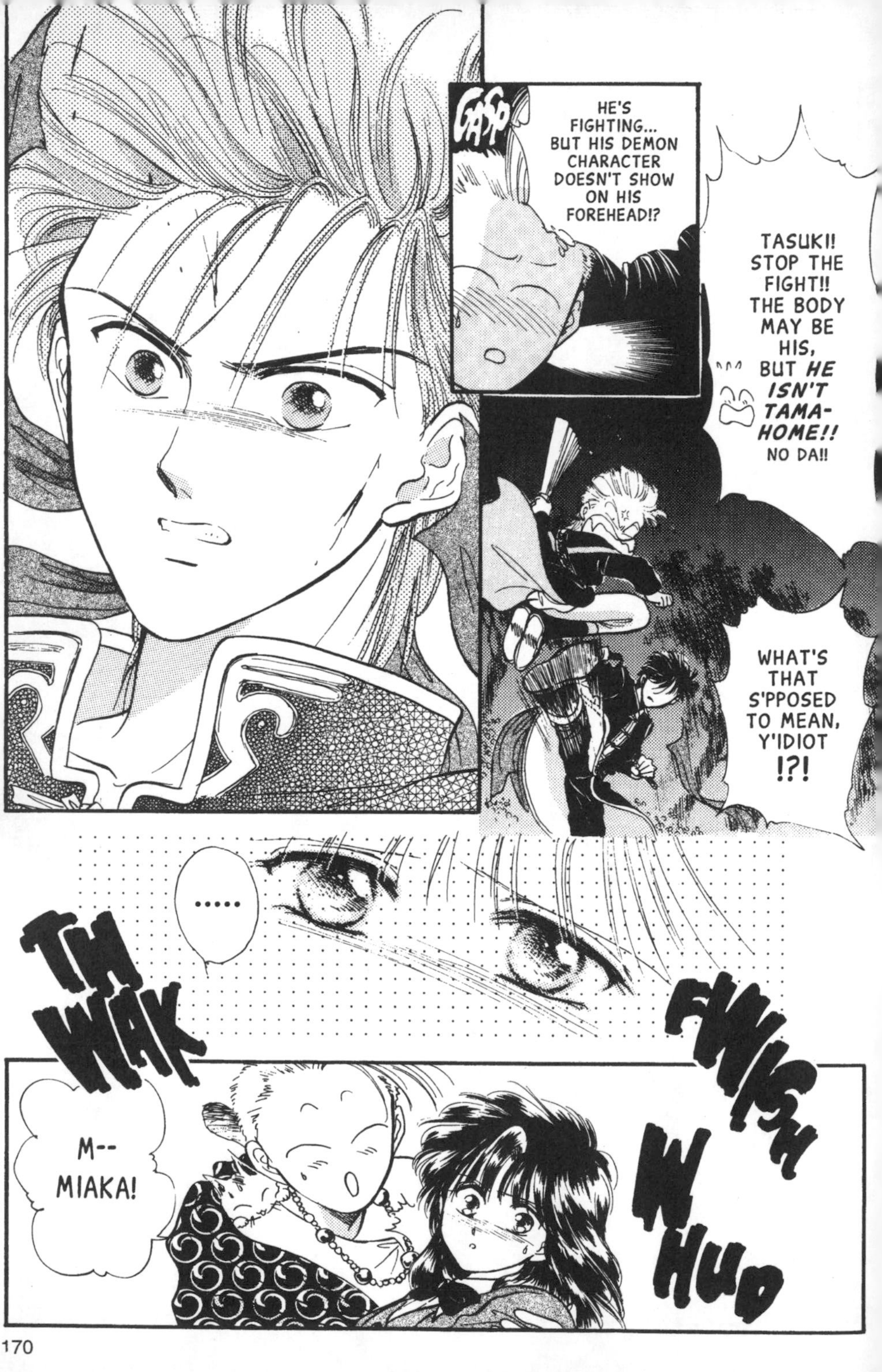
GASP
HE'S FIGHTING... BUT HIS DEMON CHARACTER DOESN'T SHOW ON HIS FOREHEAD!?
TASUKI! STOP THE FIGHT!! THE BODY MAY BE HIS, BUT *HE ISN'T TAMA-HOME!!* NO DA!!
WHAT'S THAT S'PPOSED TO MEAN, Y'IDIOT !?!
......
THWAK
M-- MIAKA!
FWISH
WHUD

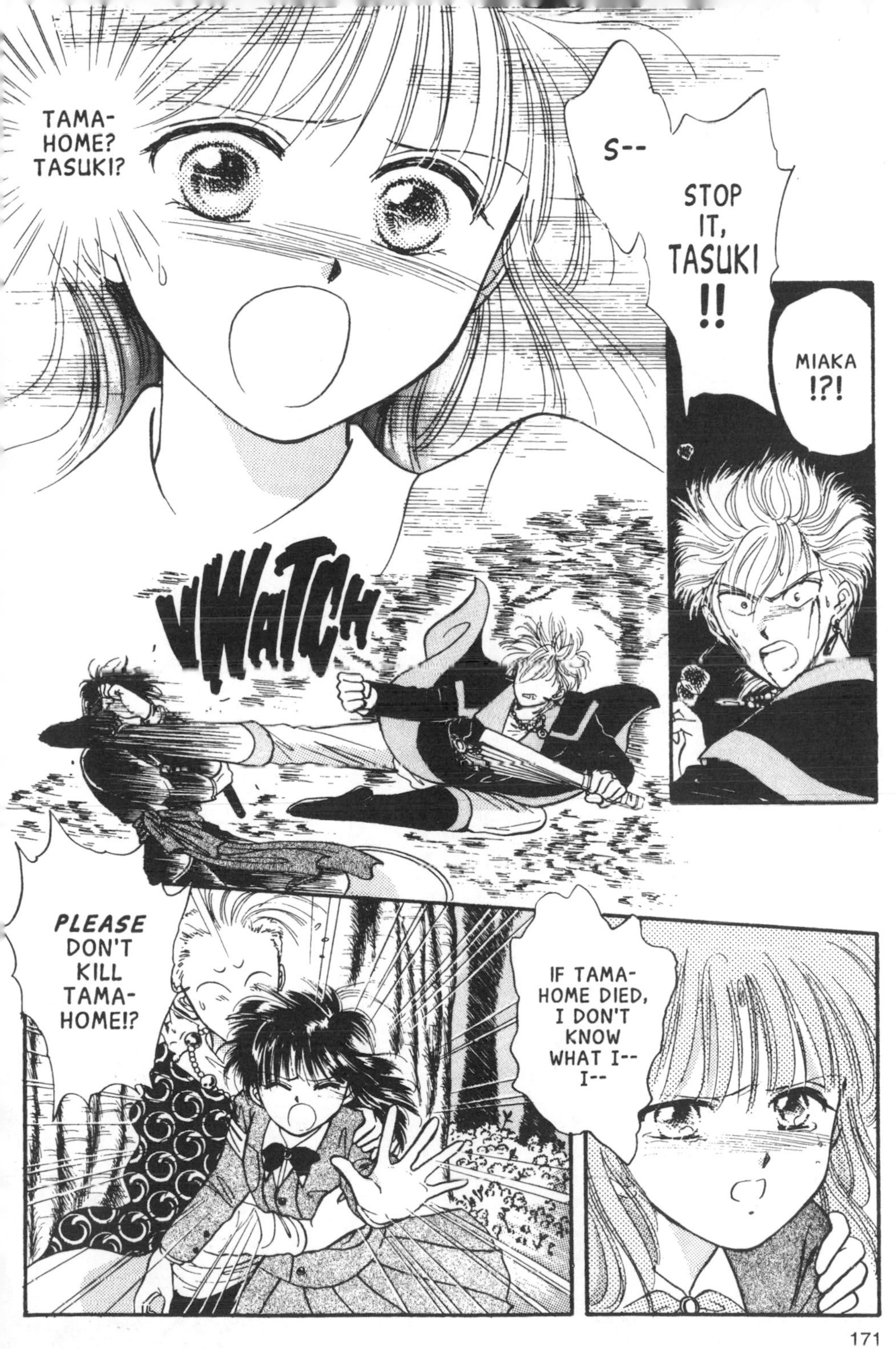

TAMA-HOME? TASUKI?
S--
STOP IT, TASUKI!!
MIAKA !?!
VWATCH
PLEASE DON'T KILL TAMA-HOME!?
IF TAMA-HOME DIED, I DON'T KNOW WHAT I-- I--

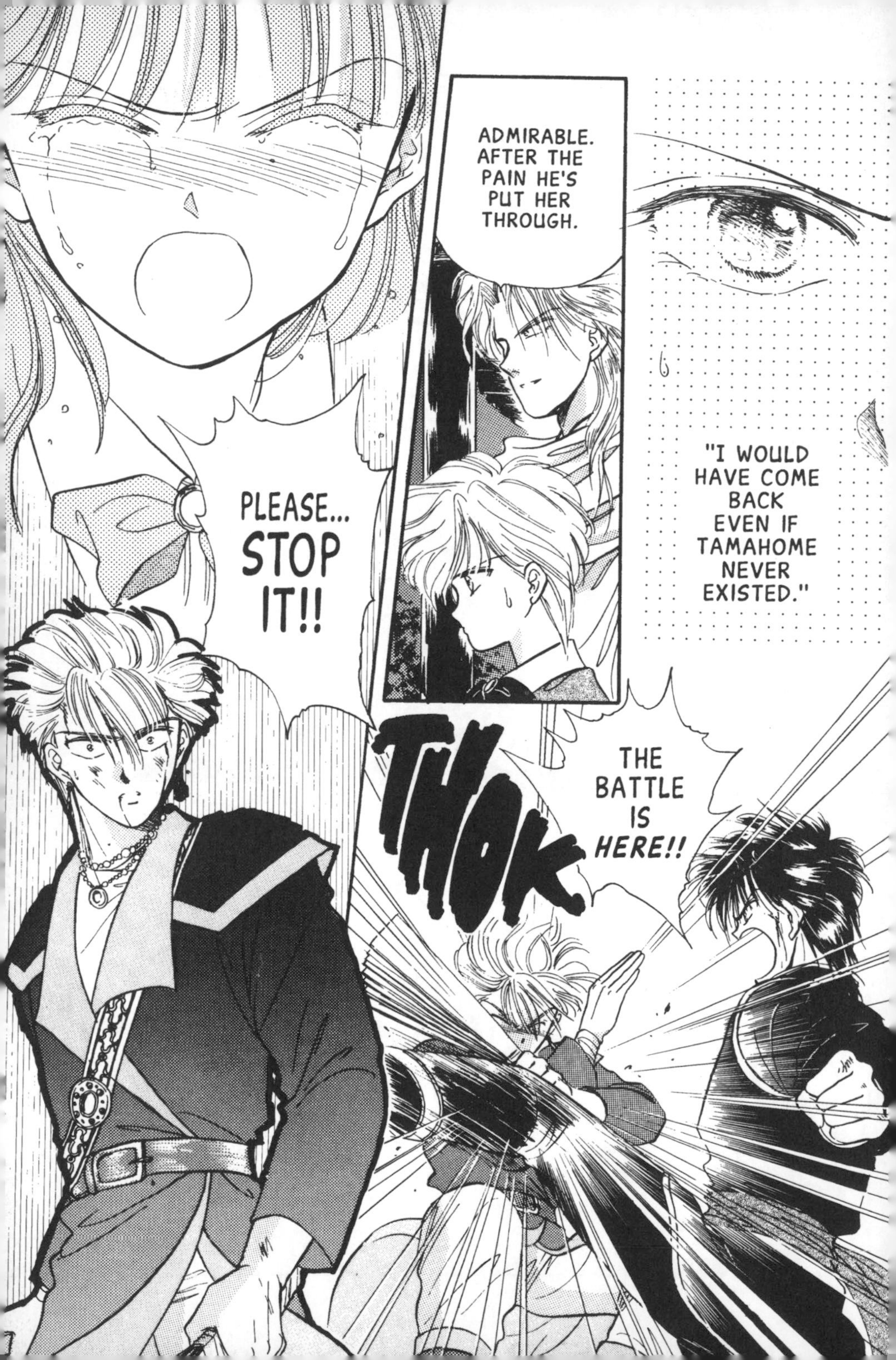
PLEASE... STOP IT!!
ADMIRABLE. AFTER THE PAIN HE'S PUT HER THROUGH.
"I WOULD HAVE COME BACK EVEN IF TAMAHOME NEVER EXISTED."
THOK
THE BATTLE IS *HERE!!*

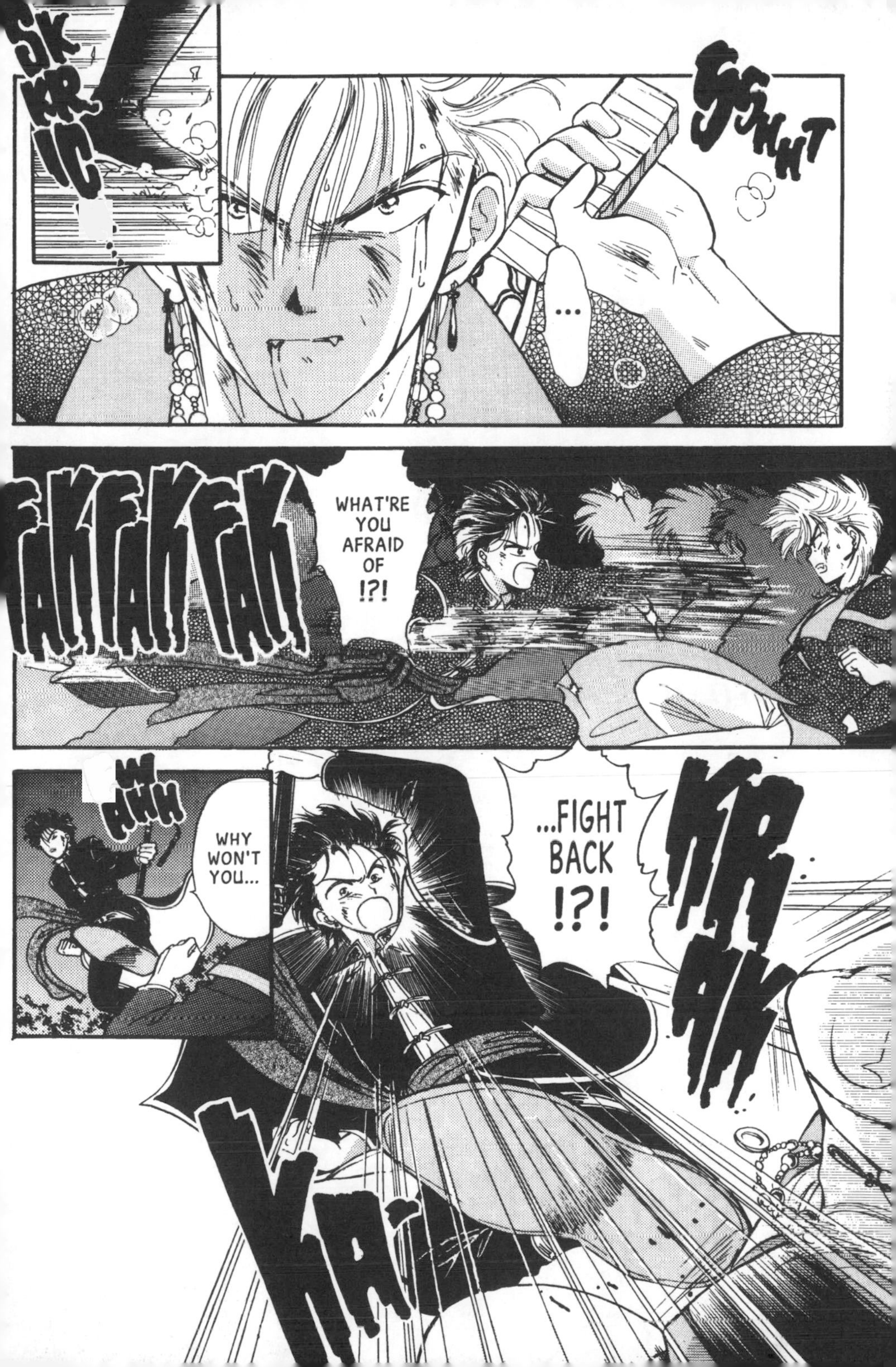

SK KR IC
GSHHT
...
FAKFAKFAK
WHAT'RE YOU AFRAID OF !?!
AWW
WHY WON'T YOU...
...FIGHT BACK !?!
KRASH
WHAM

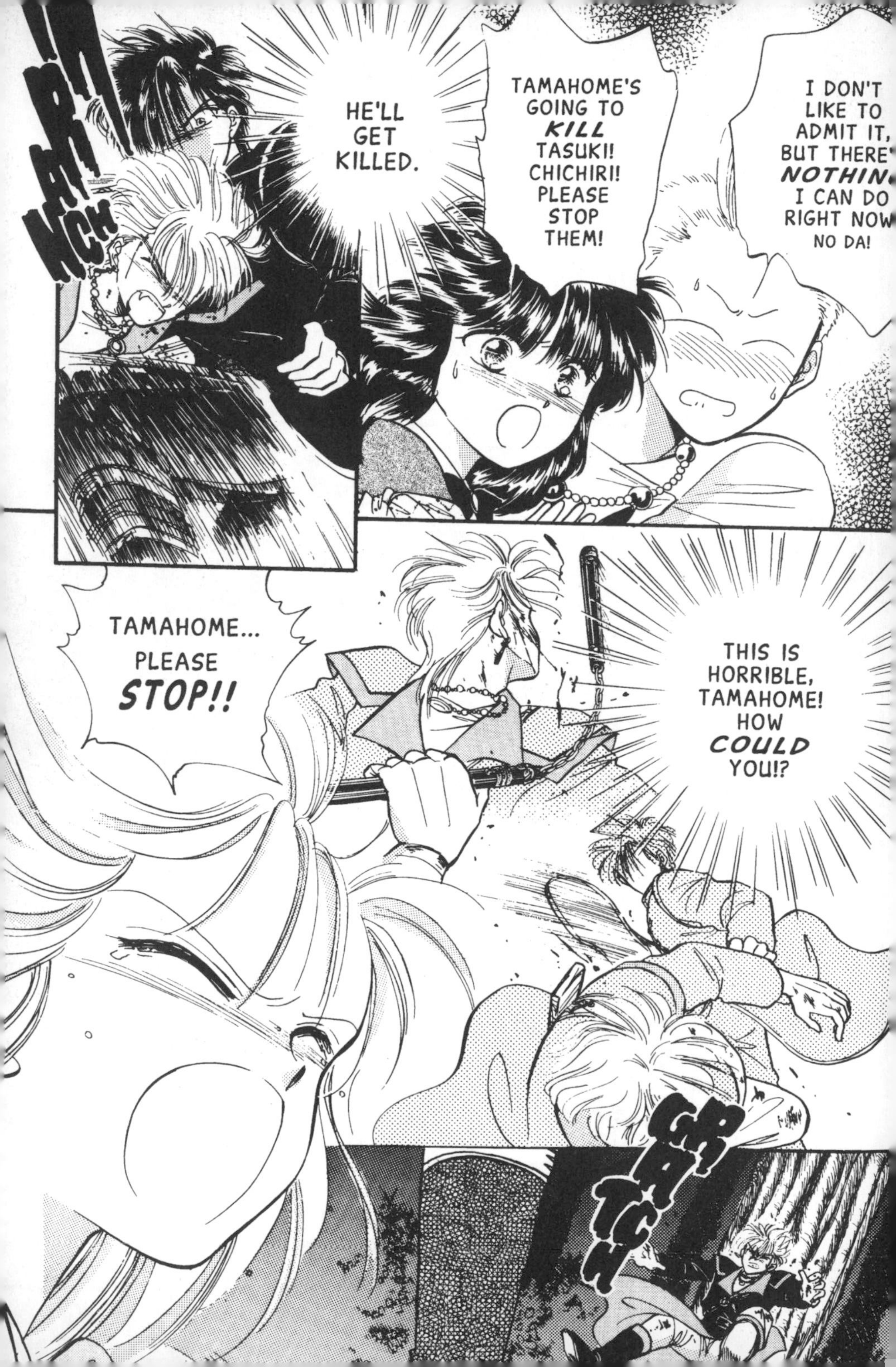
HE'LL GET KILLED.
TAMAHOME'S GOING TO *KILL* TASUKI!! CHICHIRI!! PLEASE STOP THEM!
I DON'T LIKE TO ADMIT IT, BUT THERE' *NOTHIN* I CAN DO RIGHT NOW NO DA!
TAMAHOME... PLEASE *STOP!!*
THIS IS HORRIBLE, TAMAHOME! HOW *COULD* YOU!?
GRATCH

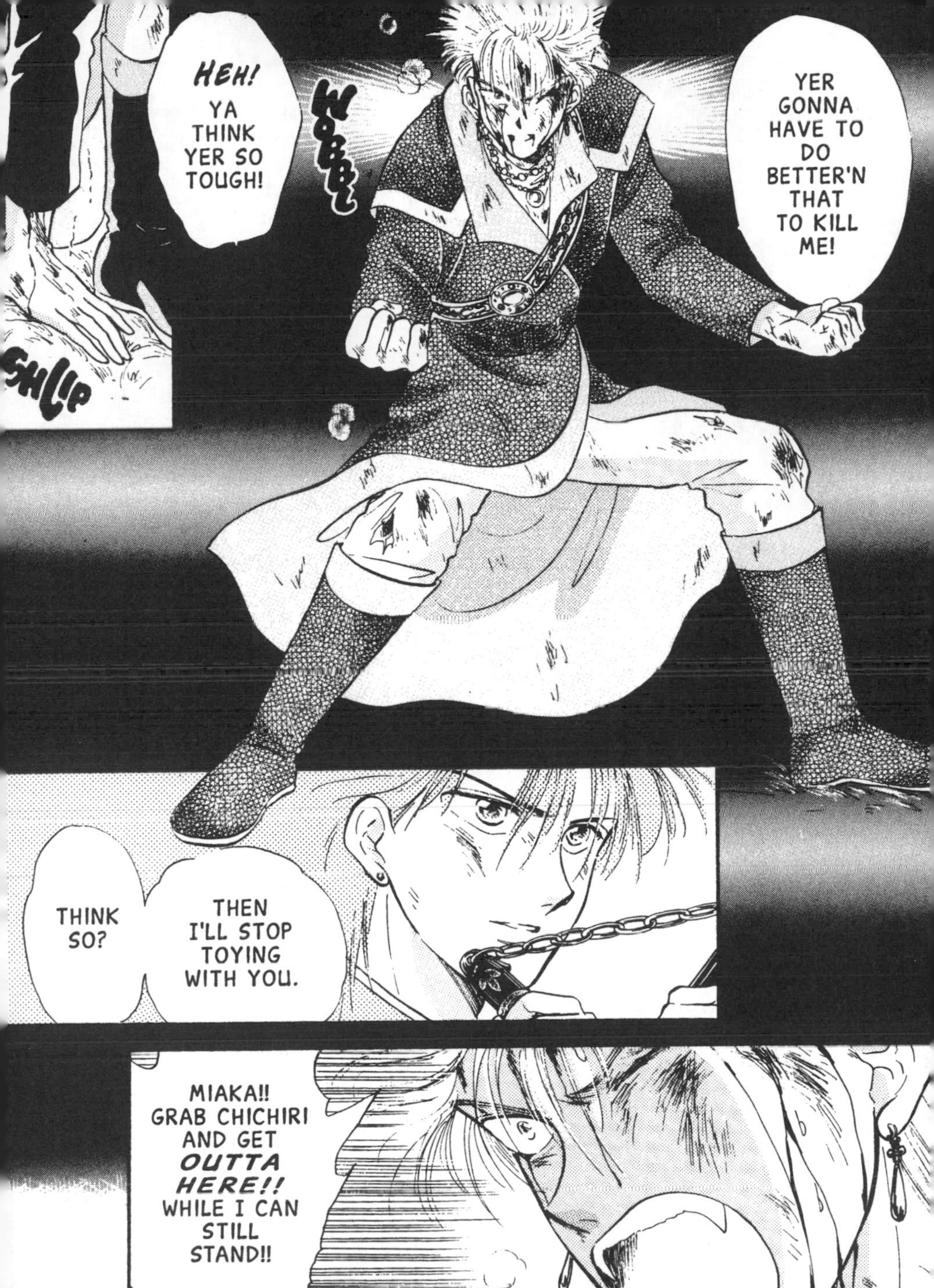
SHLIP
HEH! YA THINK YER SO TOUGH!
WOBBL
YER GONNA HAVE TO DO BETTER'N THAT TO KILL ME!
THINK SO?
THEN I'LL STOP TOYING WITH YOU.
MIAKA!! GRAB CHICHIRI AND GET OUTTA HERE!! WHILE I CAN STILL STAND!!

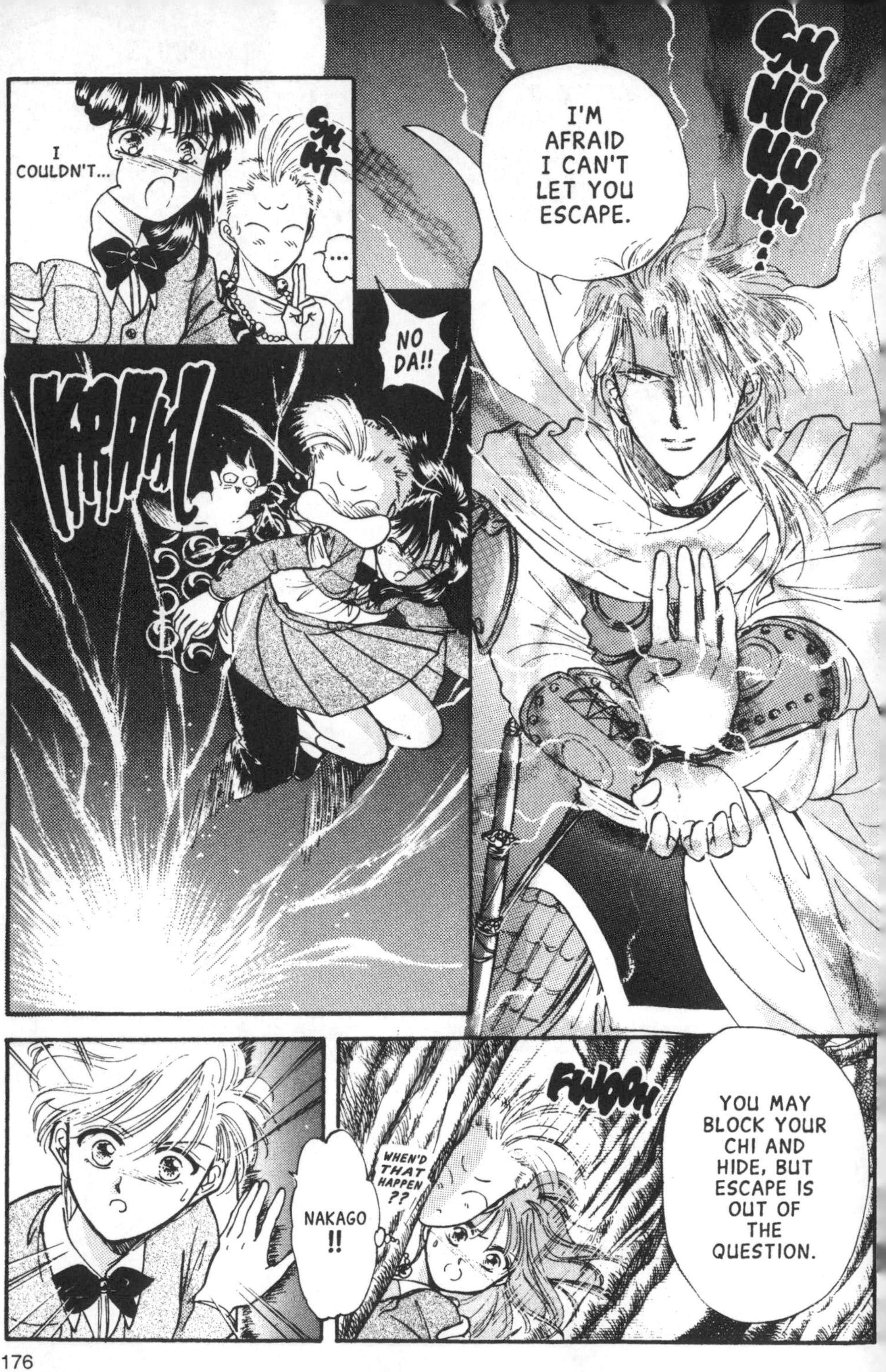

I COULDN'T...
SHHT
...
NO DA!!
KRAAK
I'M AFRAID I CAN'T LET YOU ESCAPE.
SHHUHUHUHH...
NAKAGO!!
WHEN'D THAT HAPPEN??
FWOOOH
YOU MAY BLOCK YOUR CHI AND HIDE, BUT ESCAPE IS OUT OF THE QUESTION.

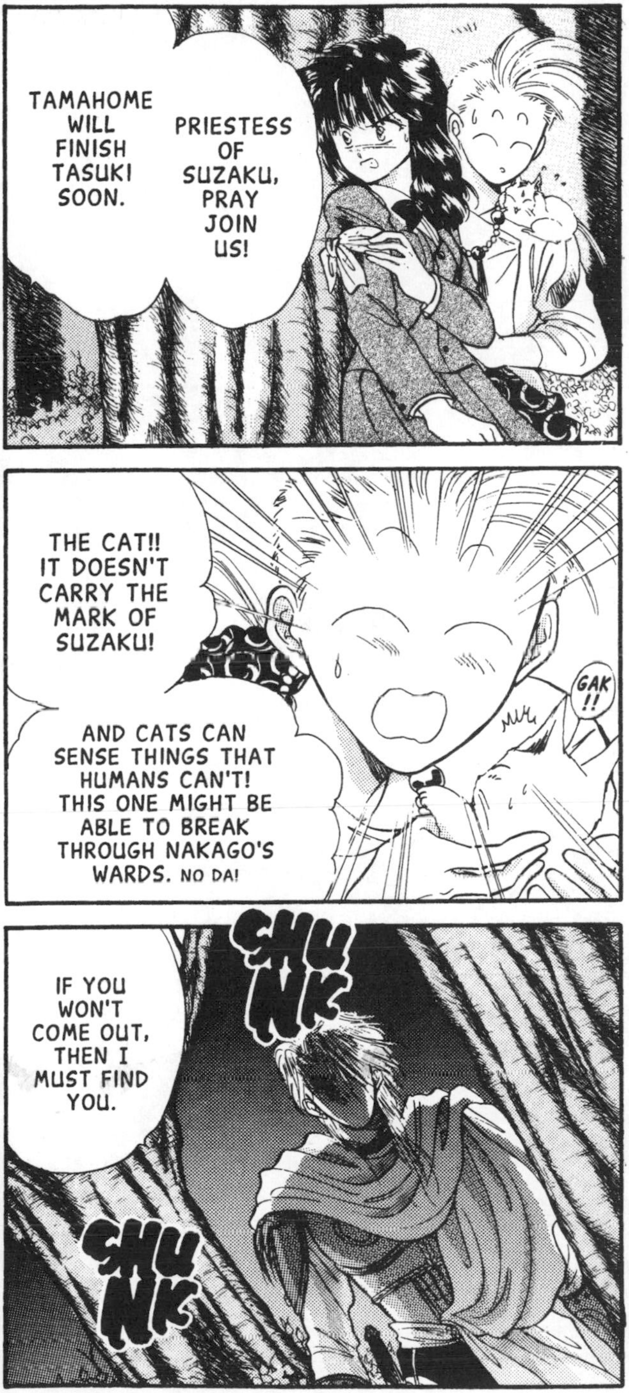
TAMAHOME WILL FINISH TASUKI SOON.
PRIESTESS OF SUZAKU, PRAY JOIN US!
THE CAT!! IT DOESN'T CARRY THE MARK OF SUZAKU!
GAK!!
AND CATS CAN SENSE THINGS THAT HUMANS CAN'T! THIS ONE MIGHT BE ABLE TO BREAK THROUGH NAKAGO'S WARDS. NO DA!
IF YOU WON'T COME OUT, THEN I MUST FIND YOU.
CHUNK
CHUNK

Now that Tamahome's become an enemy, I've been getting mad mail and sad mail. But it's not Tamahome's fault!! Diedu isn't your work-a-day potion! Even Hotohori or Chichiri would have ended up the same if they took it. *Bwa ha ha!!* Perhaps Watase ENJOYS putting her characters through hell! But if I do, it's out of love. Really! So when I get mail from people who say they hate Tamahome or Miaka, it makes me sad. (Honestly!) And when people say they like all my characters, it makes me happiest of all. (*There's been a lot of those recently!* ♥) I want to hug those readers. Right now everybody's against Nakago, but I love him! He's so fun to draw. I love Yui too. Sometimes I hear from readers who have dreams with characters like Miaka in them, but I never had one before. I had mine for the first time recently, but the character was Nakago!! He was wearing sunglasses and a Nazi uniform. *Scary!!*
I also get occasional mail from male readers who say they're embarrassed about reading "Fushigi Yûgi." Don't get so stressed! I have a lot of male readers: late grade school, guys in junior high, high school students, college students, and business men! So don't worry. Guys' opinions tend to be more level headed and less emotional than my female readers, so I love those letters. Although right now I'm busy with Fushigi Yûgi and the special Prepubescence story, for the past year I've been getting ideas for short stories. (I haven't had enough material to compile into a graphic novel.) So now I'm all jazzed up to put out a short story graphic novel! A CD book should be out this summer, so look for it. A drama disk is also in the works.
Oh! A hot bath is getting cold waiting for me. I'll see you all in volume 6.
Farewell!

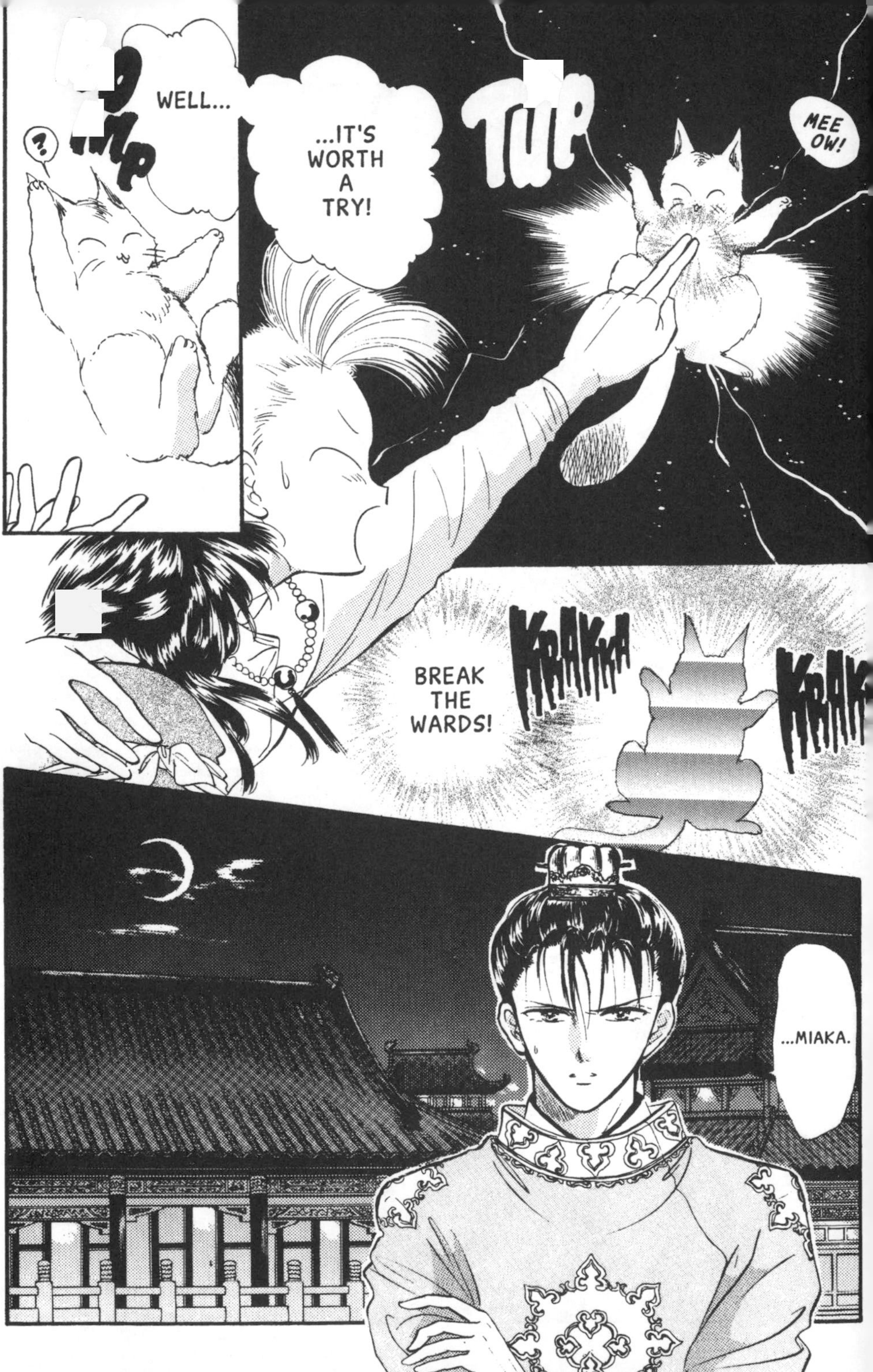
?
WELL...
...IT'S WORTH A TRY!
TUP
MEE OW!
BREAK THE WARDS!
KRAKKA
...MIAKA.

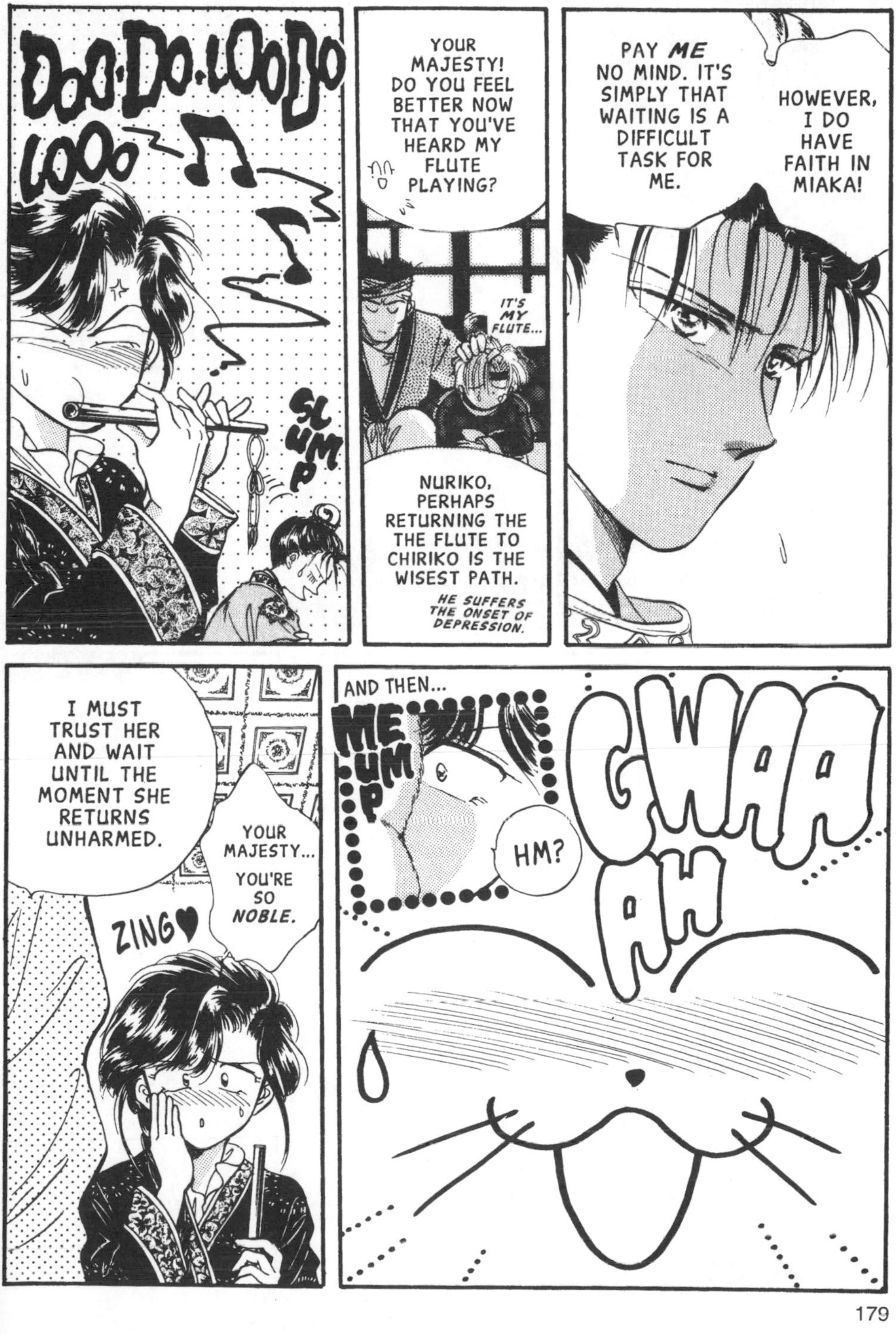
DOO-DO-LOODO LOOO
SLUMP
YOUR MAJESTY! DO YOU FEEL BETTER NOW THAT YOU'VE HEARD MY FLUTE PLAYING?
IT'S MY FLUTE...
NURIKO, PERHAPS RETURNING THE THE FLUTE TO CHIRIKO IS THE WISEST PATH.
HE SUFFERS THE ONSET OF DEPRESSION.
PAY *ME* NO MIND. IT'S SIMPLY THAT WAITING IS A DIFFICULT TASK FOR ME.
HOWEVER, I DO HAVE FAITH IN MIAKA!
I MUST TRUST HER AND WAIT UNTIL THE MOMENT SHE RETURNS UNHARMED.
YOUR MAJESTY... YOU'RE SO *NOBLE*.
ZING♥
AND THEN...
MEUMP
HM?
GWAAAH

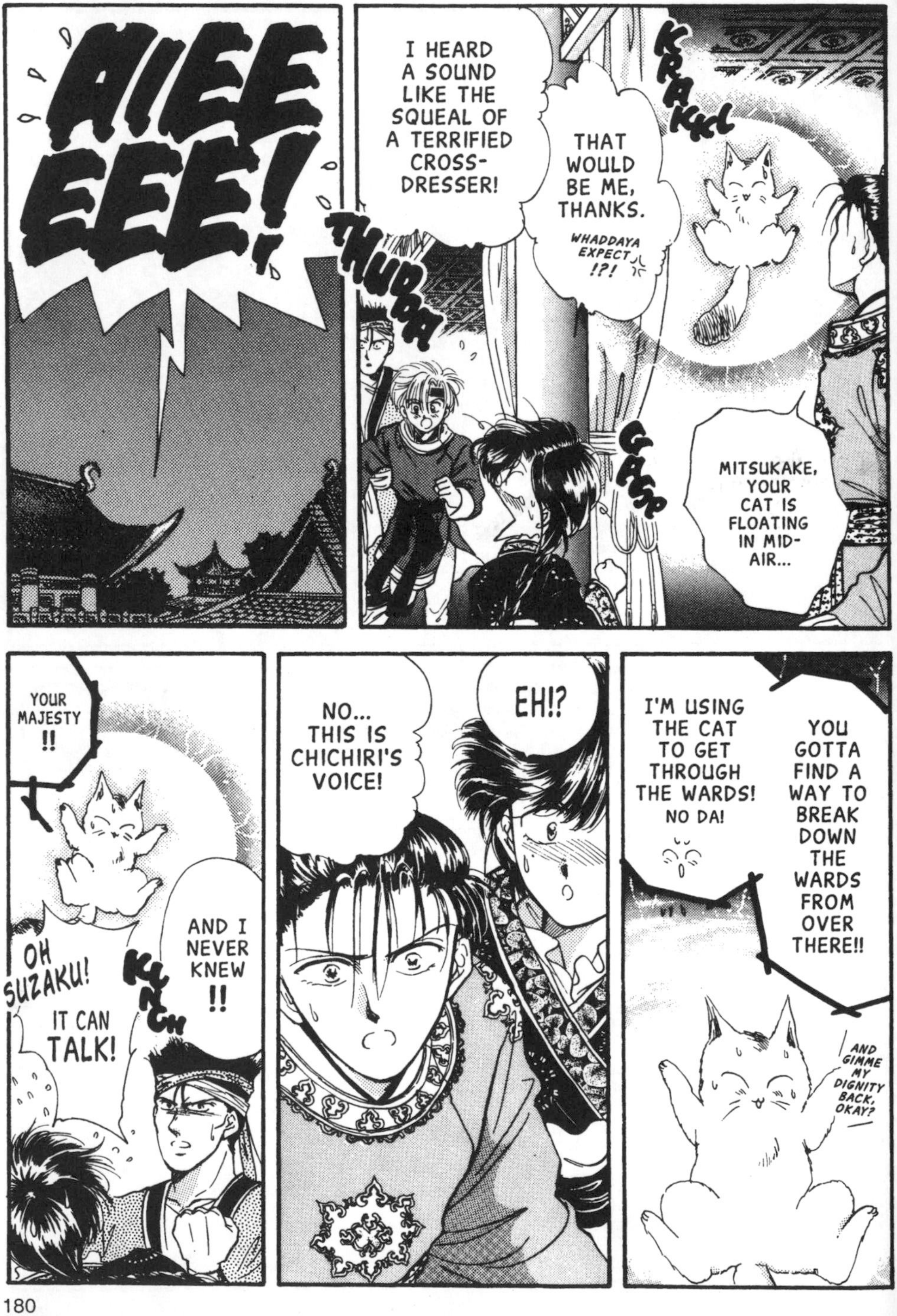
AIEE EEE!
THUDDA
I HEARD A SOUND LIKE THE SQUEAL OF A TERRIFIED CROSS-DRESSER!
THAT WOULD BE ME, THANKS.
WHADDAYA EXPECT !?!
GASP
MITSUKAKE, YOUR CAT IS FLOATING IN MID-AIR...
YOUR MAJESTY !!
OH SUZAKU!
IT CAN TALK!
AND I NEVER KNEW !!
NO... THIS IS CHICHIRI'S VOICE!
EH!?
I'M USING THE CAT TO GET THROUGH THE WARDS! NO DA!
YOU GOTTA FIND A WAY TO BREAK DOWN THE WARDS FROM OVER THERE!!
AND GIMME MY DIGNITY BACK, OKAY?

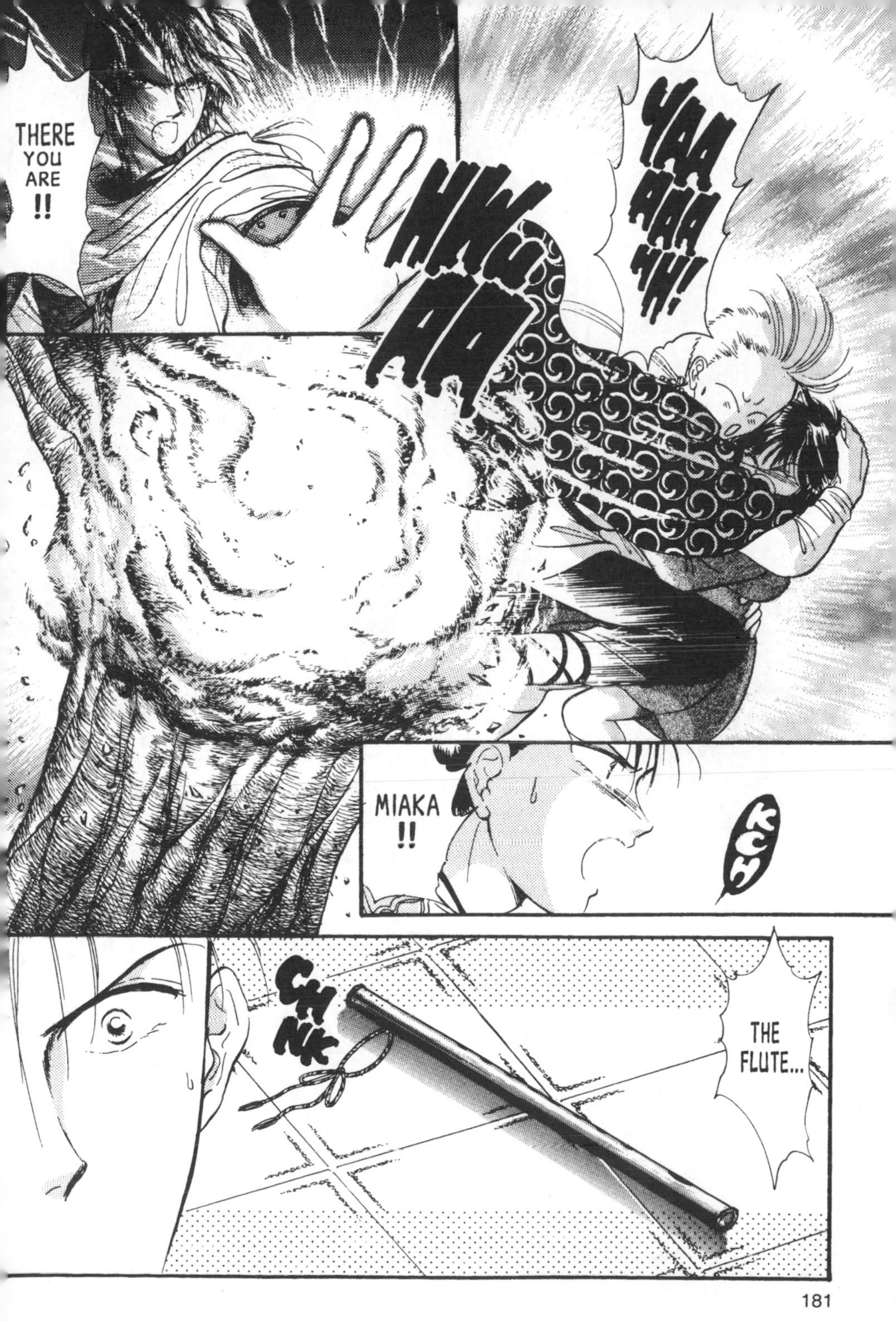
THERE YOU ARE !!
HNGAA
YAAAAAHH!
MIAKA !!
KCH
CHINK
THE FLUTE...

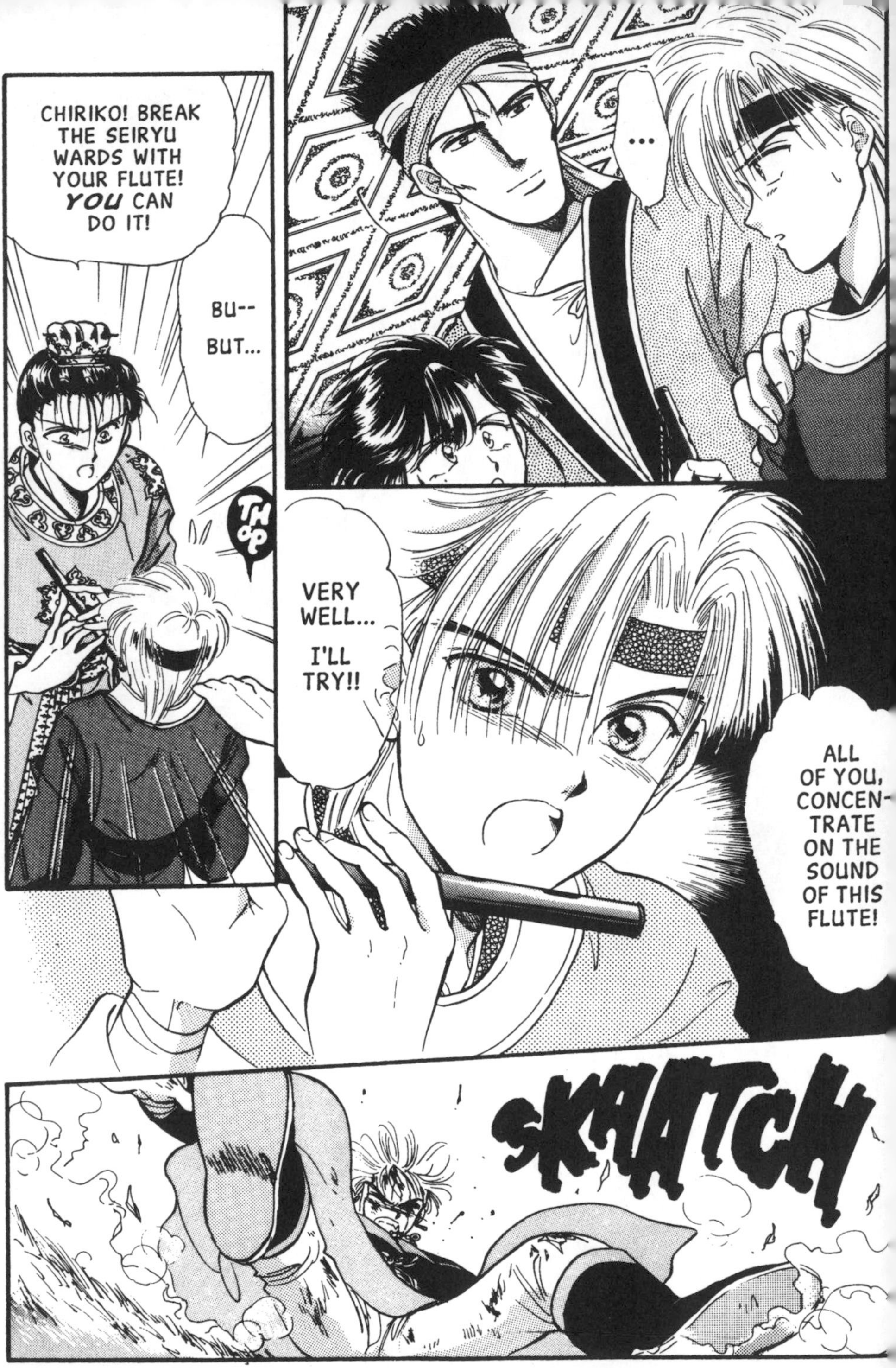
CHIRIKO! BREAK THE SEIRYU WARDS WITH YOUR FLUTE! *YOU* CAN DO IT!
BU-- BUT...
THOP
...
VERY WELL...
I'LL TRY!!
ALL OF YOU, CONCEN-TRATE ON THE SOUND OF THIS FLUTE!
SKAATCH

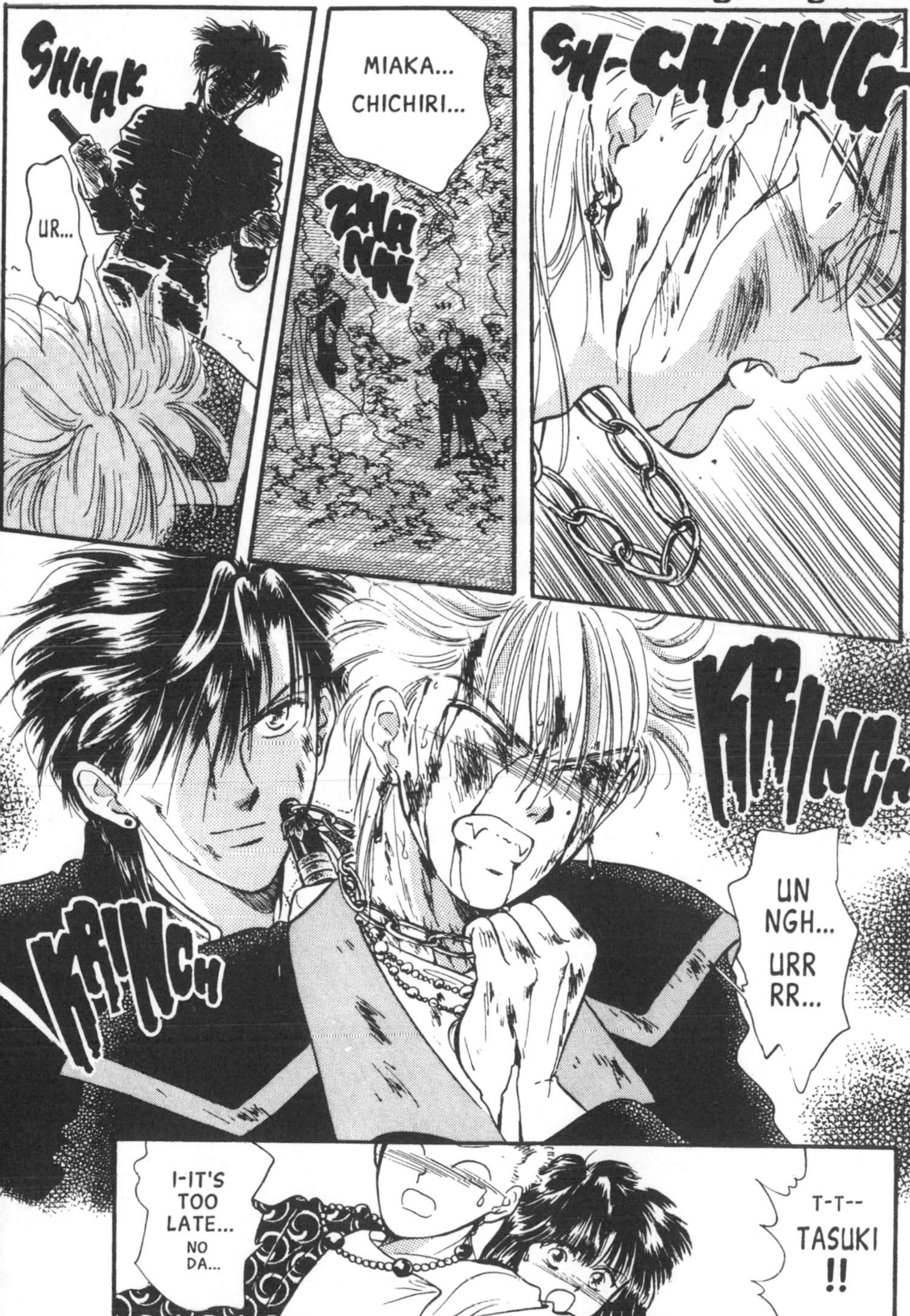
SHHAK
UR...
MIAKA... CHICHIRI...
THANN
SH-CHANG
KRINCH
KRINCH
UNNGH... URRRR...
I-IT'S TOO LATE... NO DA...
T-T-- TASUKI !!

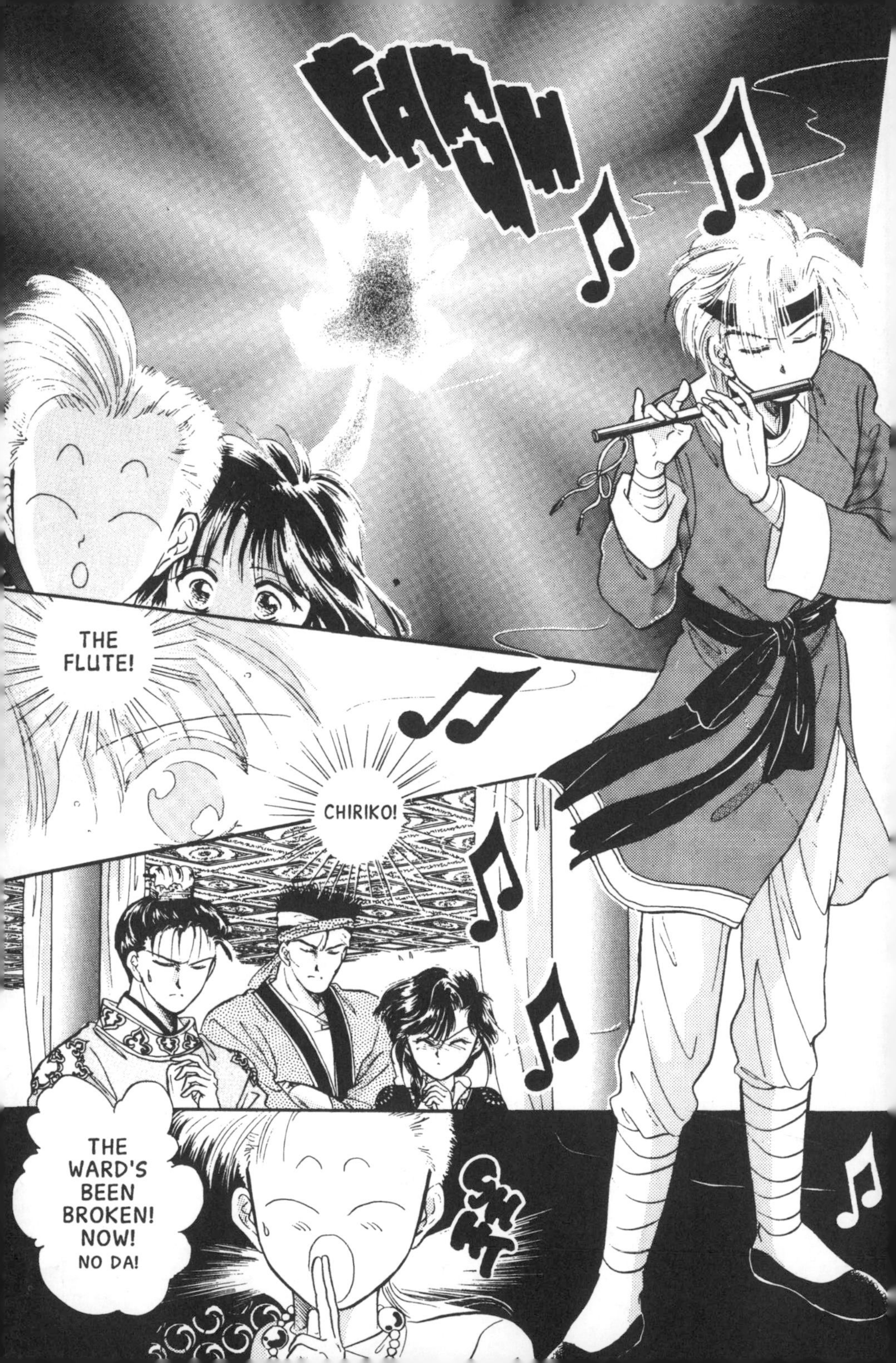
FASH
THE FLUTE!
CHIRIKO!
THE WARD'S BEEN BROKEN! NOW! NO DA!
SHHT

WAAFF

CHAKK...!

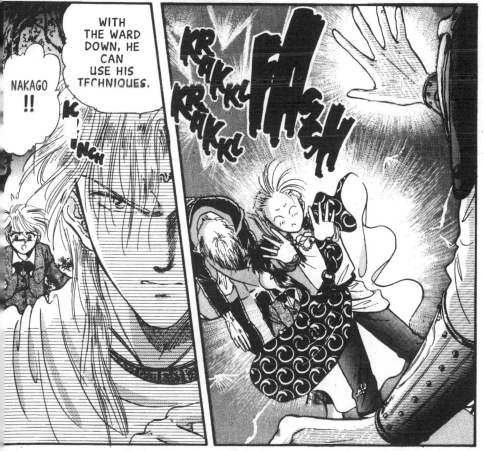

WITH THE WARD DOWN, HE CAN USE HIS TECHNIQUES.

NAKAGO!!

KRAKK KRAKK KRAKK

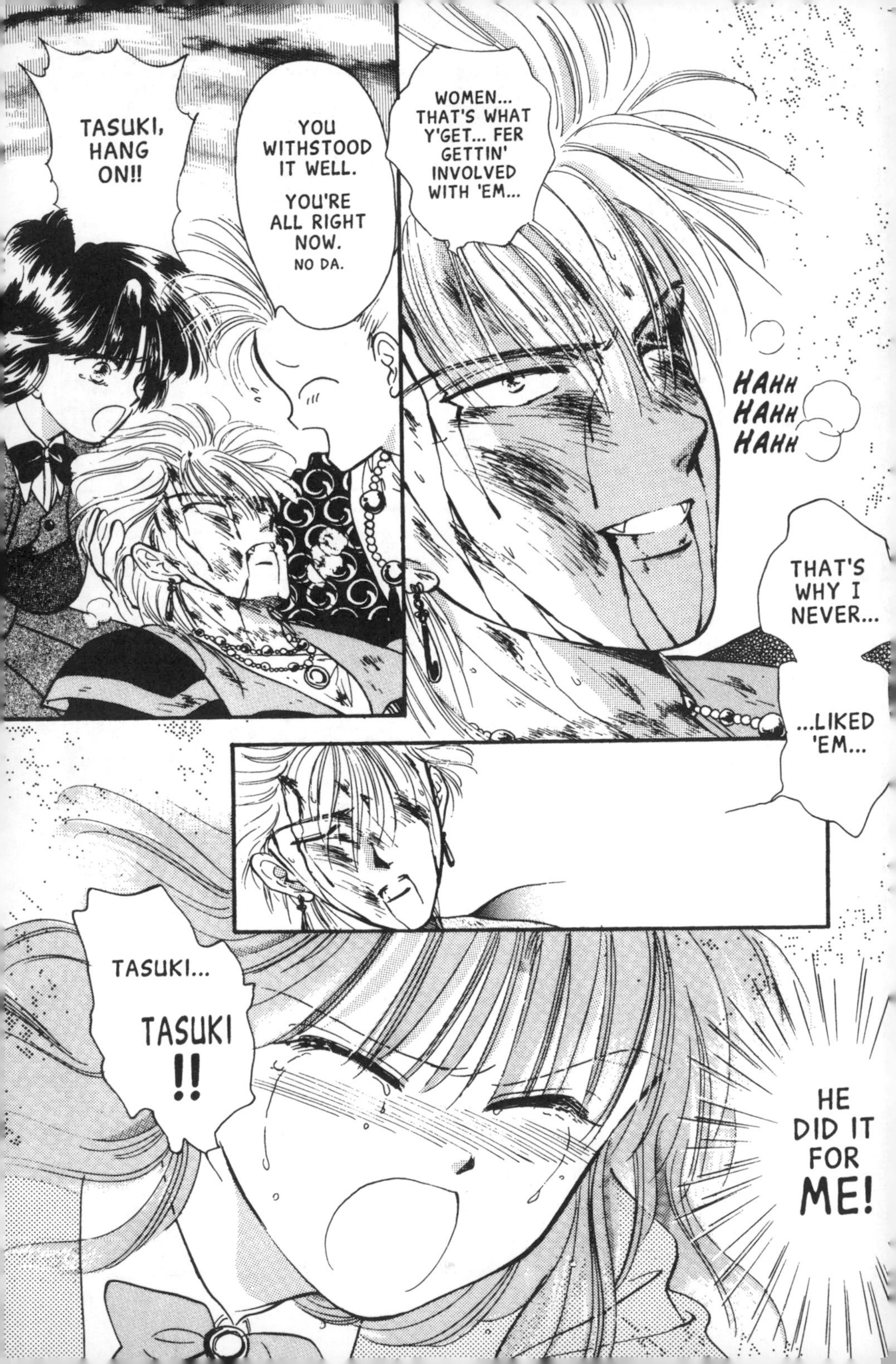
TASUKI, HANG ON!!
YOU WITHSTOOD IT WELL.
YOU'RE ALL RIGHT NOW. NO DA.
WOMEN... THAT'S WHAT Y'GET... FER GETTIN' INVOLVED WITH 'EM...
HAHH HAHH HAHH
THAT'S WHY I NEVER...
...LIKED 'EM...
TASUKI...
TASUKI !!
HE DID IT FOR ME!

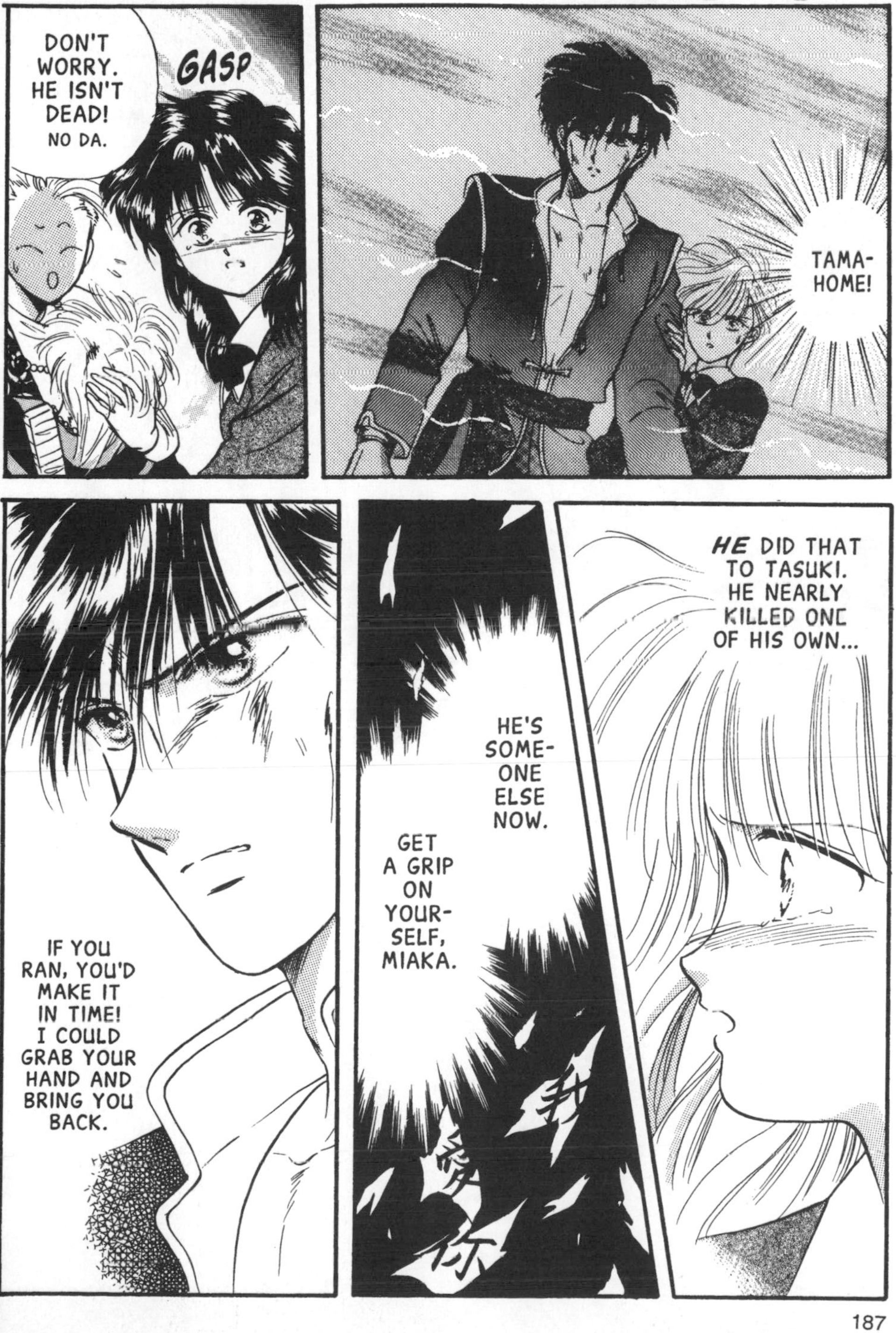
DON'T WORRY. HE ISN'T DEAD! NO DA.
GASP
TAMA-HOME!
IF YOU RAN, YOU'D MAKE IT IN TIME! I COULD GRAB YOUR HAND AND BRING YOU BACK.
HE'S SOME-ONE ELSE NOW.
GET A GRIP ON YOUR-SELF, MIAKA.
HE DID THAT TO TASUKI. HE NEARLY KILLED ONE OF HIS OWN...

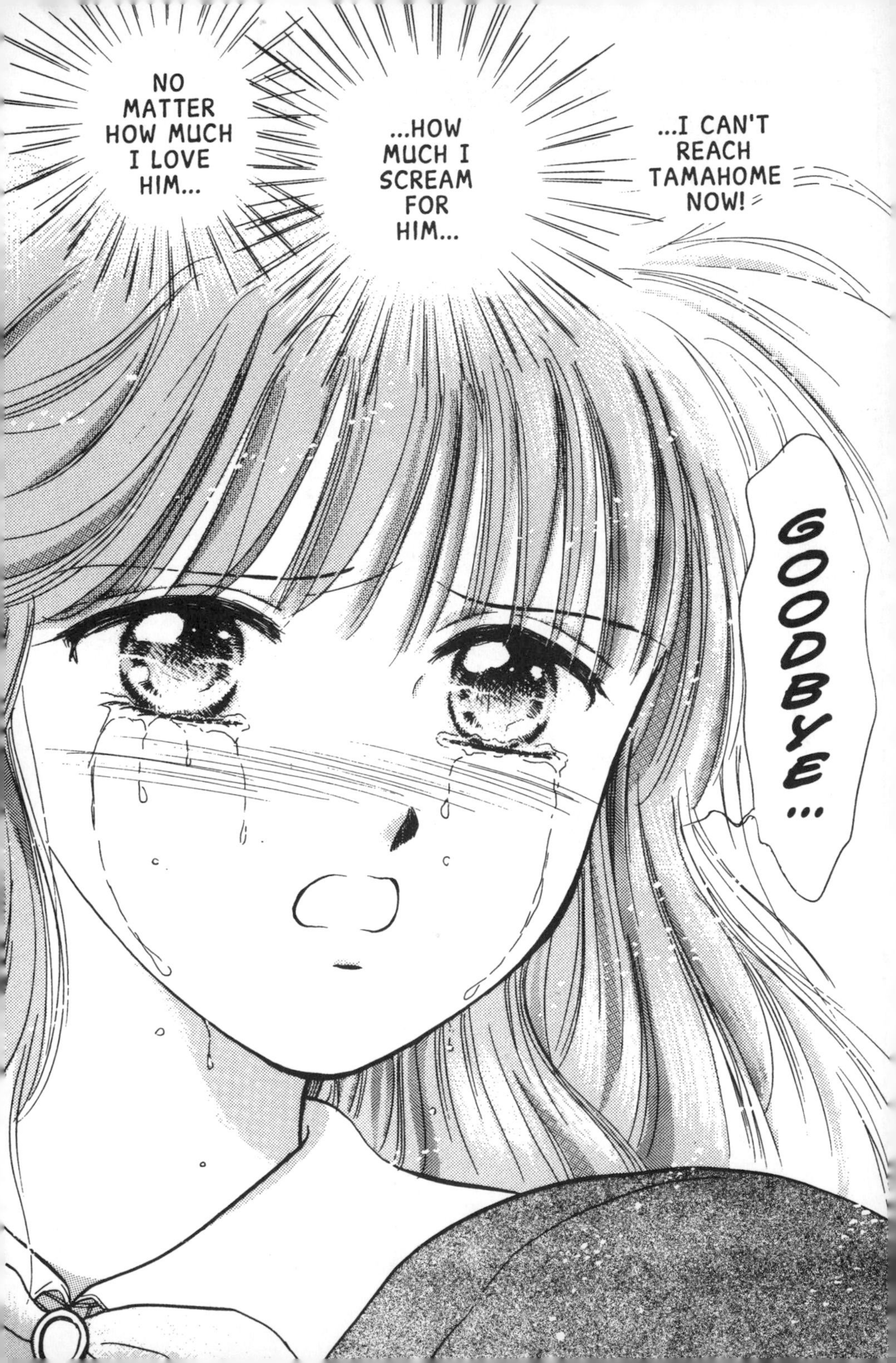
NO MATTER HOW MUCH I LOVE HIM...
...HOW MUCH I SCREAM FOR HIM...
...I CAN'T REACH TAMAHOME NOW!
GOODBYE...

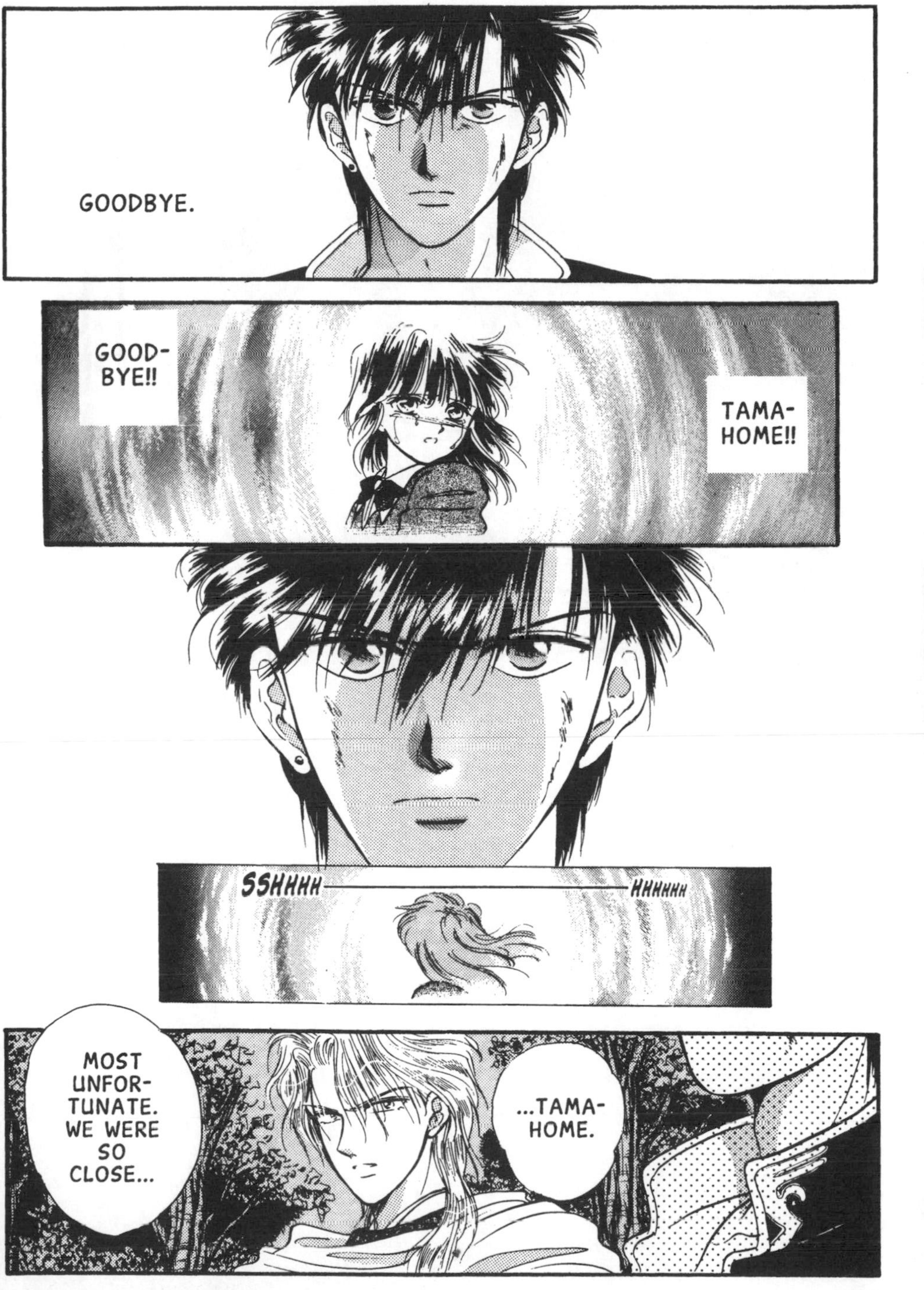
GOODBYE.
GOOD-BYE!!
TAMA-HOME!!
SSHHHH————HHHHHH
MOST UNFOR-TUNATE. WE WERE SO CLOSE...
...TAMA-HOME.

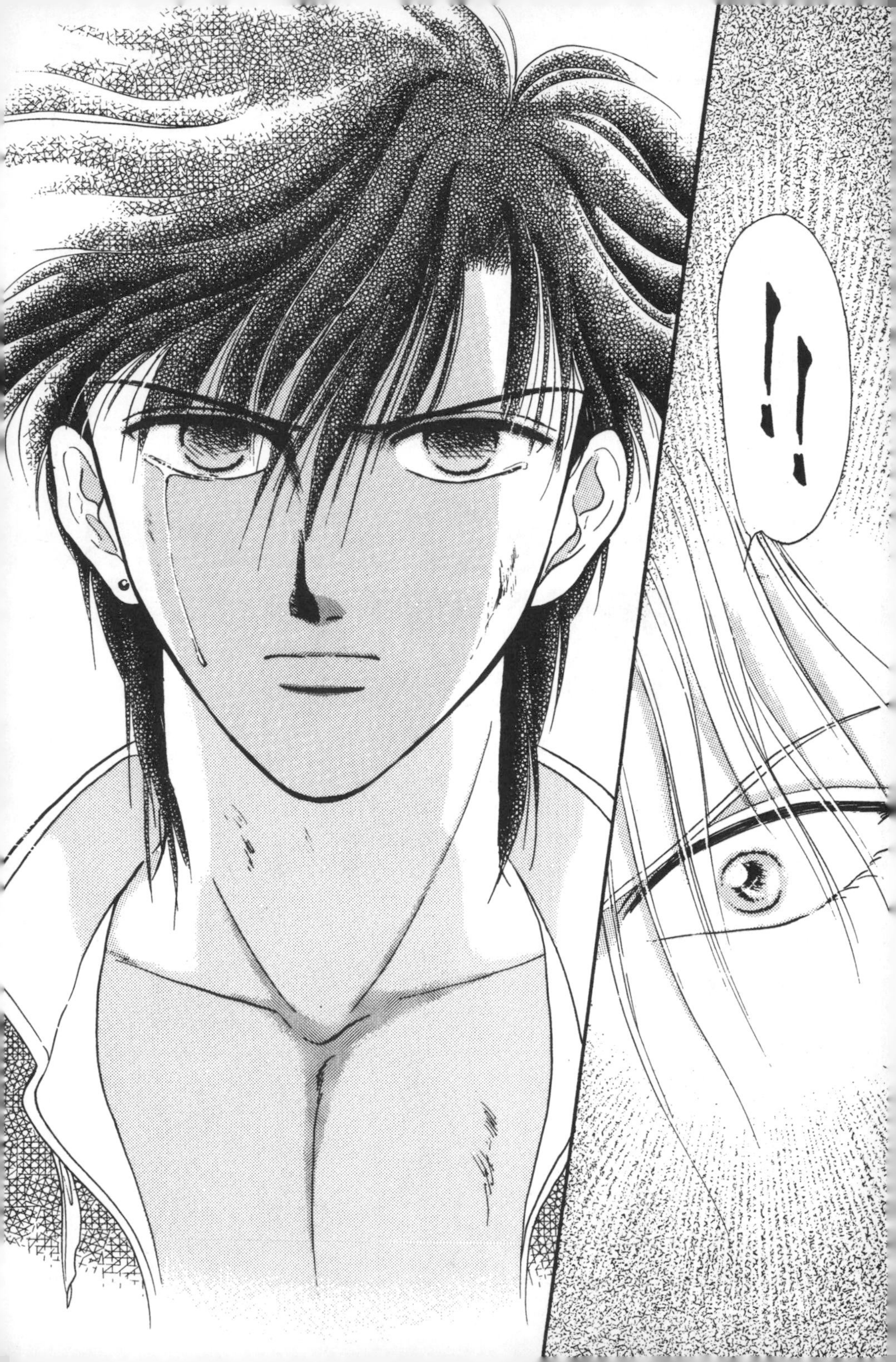
!!

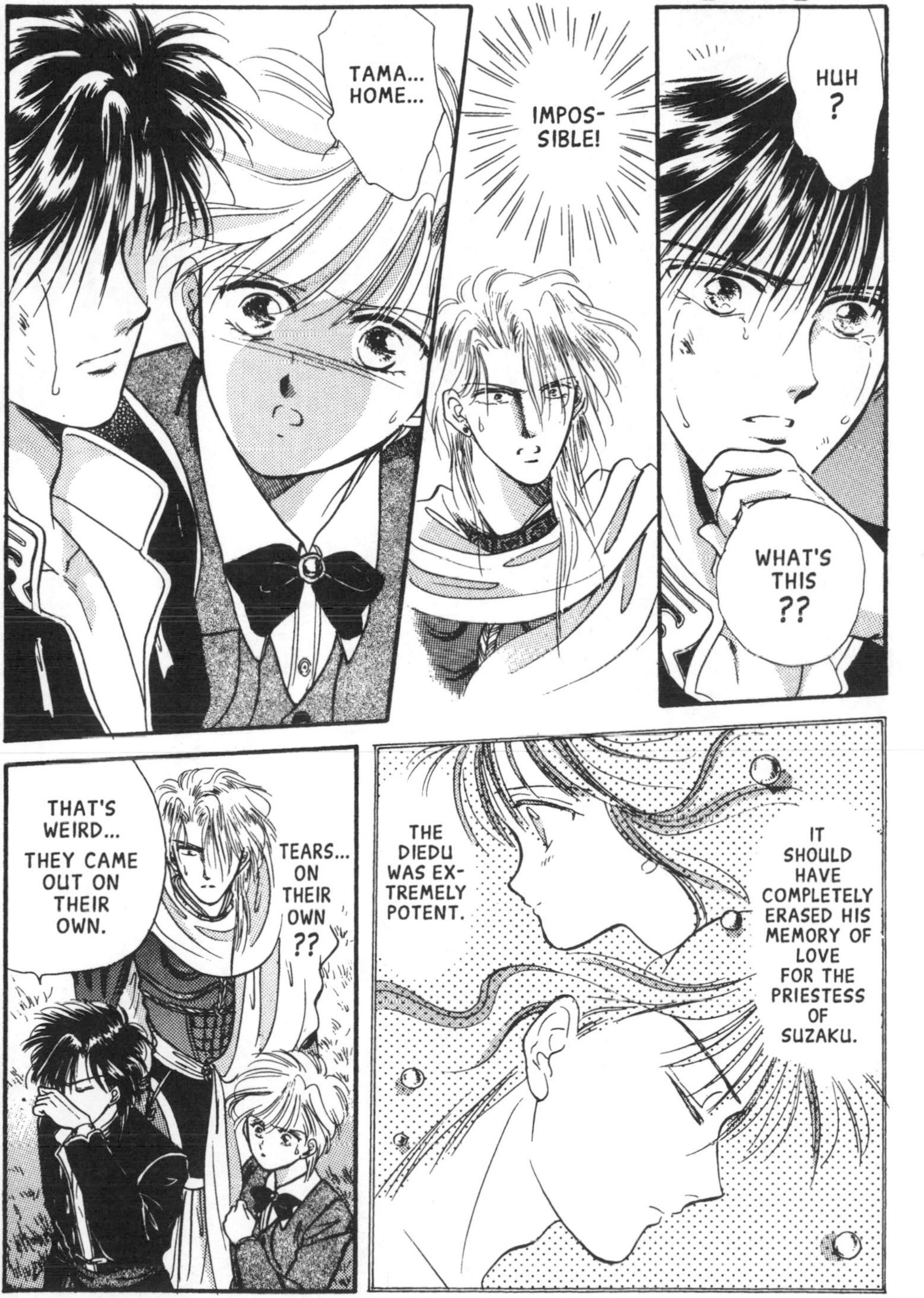
TAMA... HOME...
IMPOSSIBLE!
HUH ?
WHAT'S THIS ??
THAT'S WEIRD... THEY CAME OUT ON THEIR OWN.
TEARS... ON THEIR OWN ??
THE DIEDU WAS EXTREMELY POTENT.
IT SHOULD HAVE COMPLETELY ERASED HIS MEMORY OF LOVE FOR THE PRIESTESS OF SUZAKU.

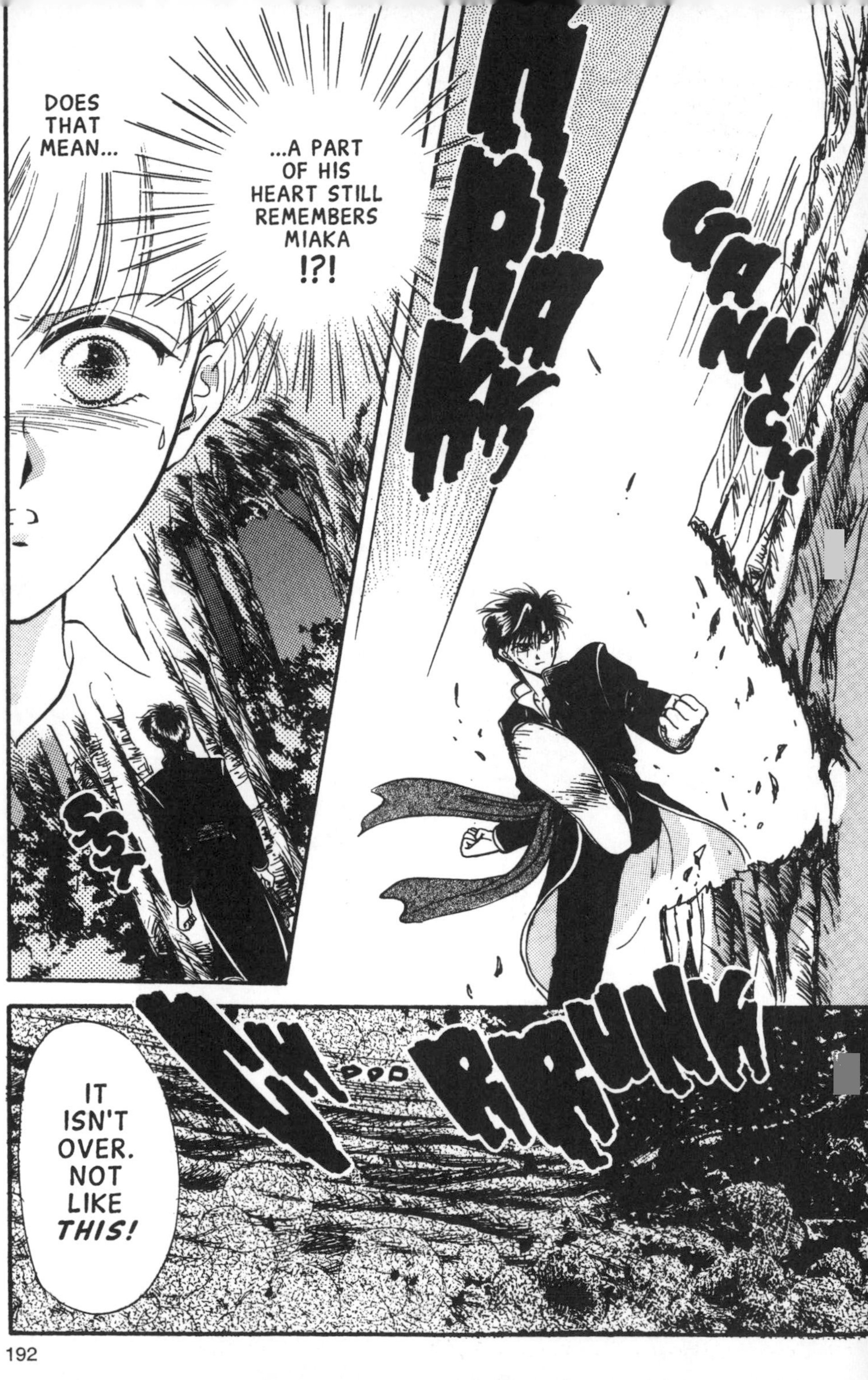
DOES THAT MEAN...
...A PART OF HIS HEART STILL REMEMBERS MIAKA !?!
IT ISN'T OVER. NOT LIKE *THIS!*

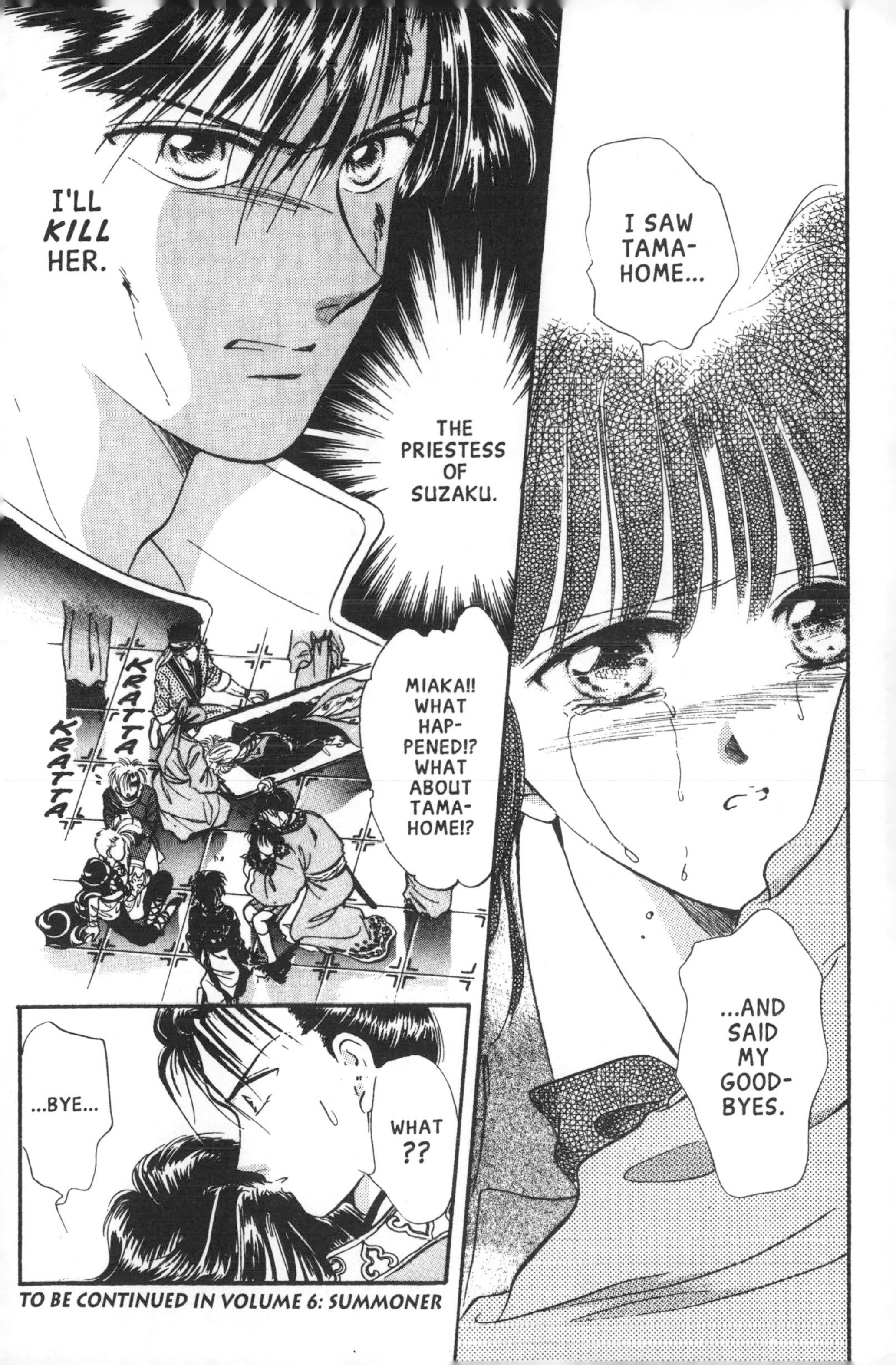
I'LL *KILL* HER.
THE PRIESTESS OF SUZAKU.
KRATTA
KRATTA
MIAKA!! WHAT HAPPENED!? WHAT ABOUT TAMAHOME!?
...BYE...
WHAT ??
I SAW TAMAHOME...
...AND SAID MY GOODBYES.

TO BE CONTINUED IN VOLUME 6: SUMMONER

YÛ WATASE

Yû Watase was born on March 5 in a town near Osaka, and she was raised there before moving to Tokyo to follow the dream of creating manga. In the decade since her debut short story, *PAJAMA DE OJAMA* ("An Intrusion in Pajamas"), she has produced more than 50 compiled volumes of short stories and continuing series. Her latest series, *IMADOKI* ("Right About Now"), is currently running in the anthology magazine *SHÔJO COMIC*. Her long-running horror/romance story *CERES: CELESTIAL LEGEND* is also available in North America from Viz Communications. She loves science fiction, fantasy and comedy.

A CELESTIAL LEGEND GIVEN FORM!

CERES Celestial Legend

By Yû Watase

From the acclaimed author of "Fushigi Yûgi" Yû Watase, one of the most anticipated anime series of the year! The supernatural thriller begins on the day of Aya and her twin brother Aki's 16th birthday, when their grandfather decides it's time to share a long guarded secret. The twins are summoned to the massive, mysterious Mikage House where they find thier extended family assembled and waiting. They are given a curious gift and in that instant their destiny begins to unfold... Both the video and the monthly comic unveil the secret of Aya and Ceres, the Celestial Legend

Ceres
Celestial Legend
Ceres
Celestial Legend
destiny
Ceres
Celestial Legend

AVAILABLE MONTHLY IN COMICS, VIDEOS, AND DVDS!

VIZ COMICS. VIZ VIDEO.

Order online at www.j-pop.com
Ask for our free Viz Shop-By-Mail catalog!

Phone (800) 394-3042
Fax (415) 348-8936

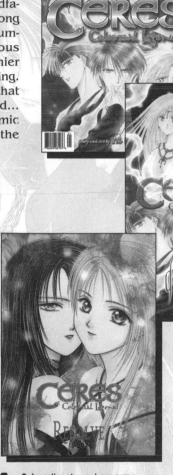

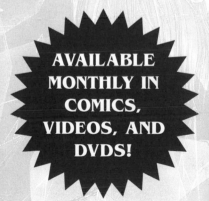

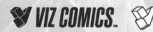

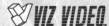

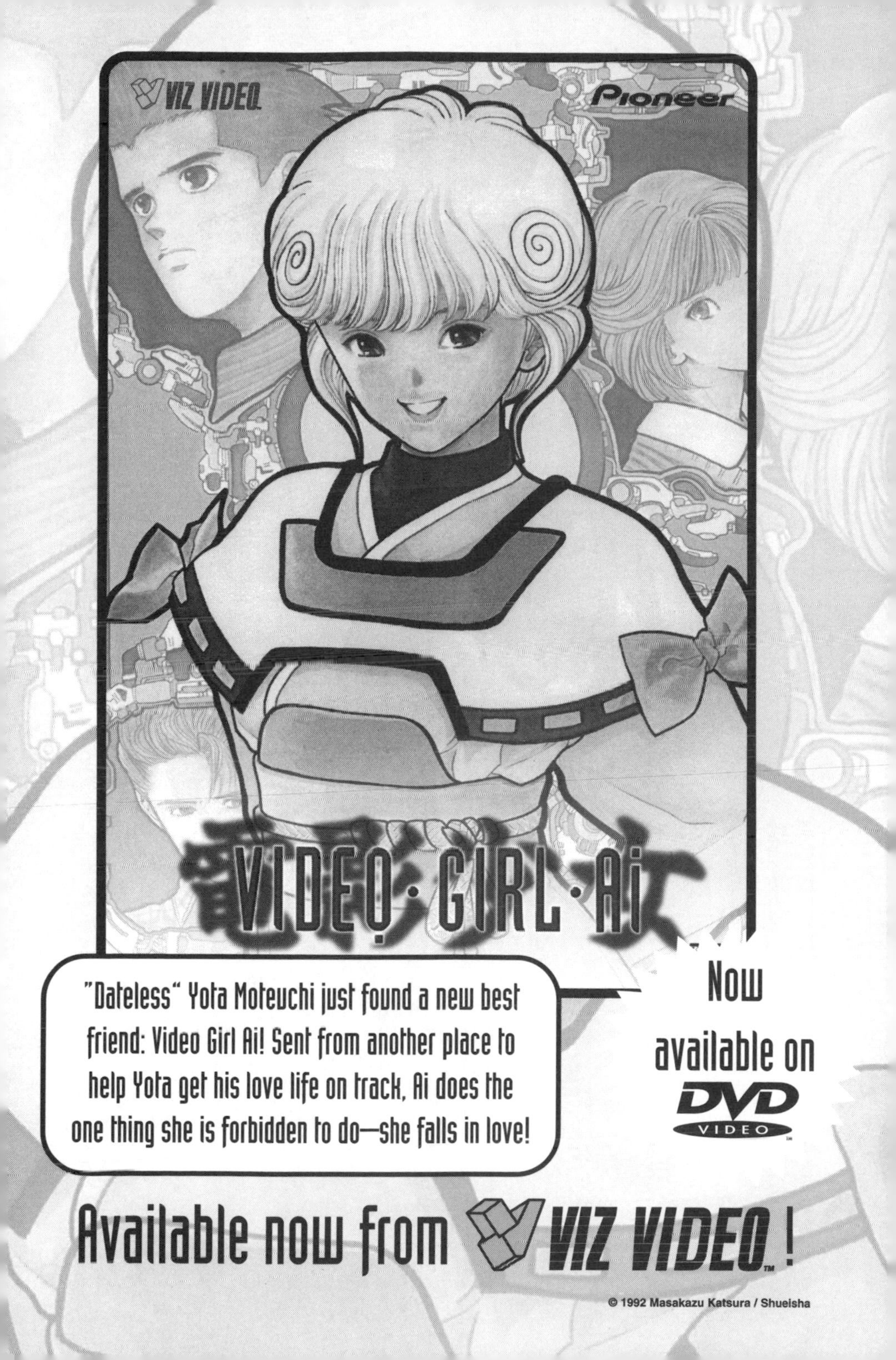
VIZ VIDEO
Pioneer
VIDEO GIRL Ai
"Dateless" Yota Moteuchi just found a new best friend: Video Girl Ai! Sent from another place to help Yota get his love life on track, Ai does the one thing she is forbidden to do—she falls in love!
Now available on DVD VIDEO
Available now from VIZ VIDEO!
© 1992 Masakazu Katsura / Shueisha

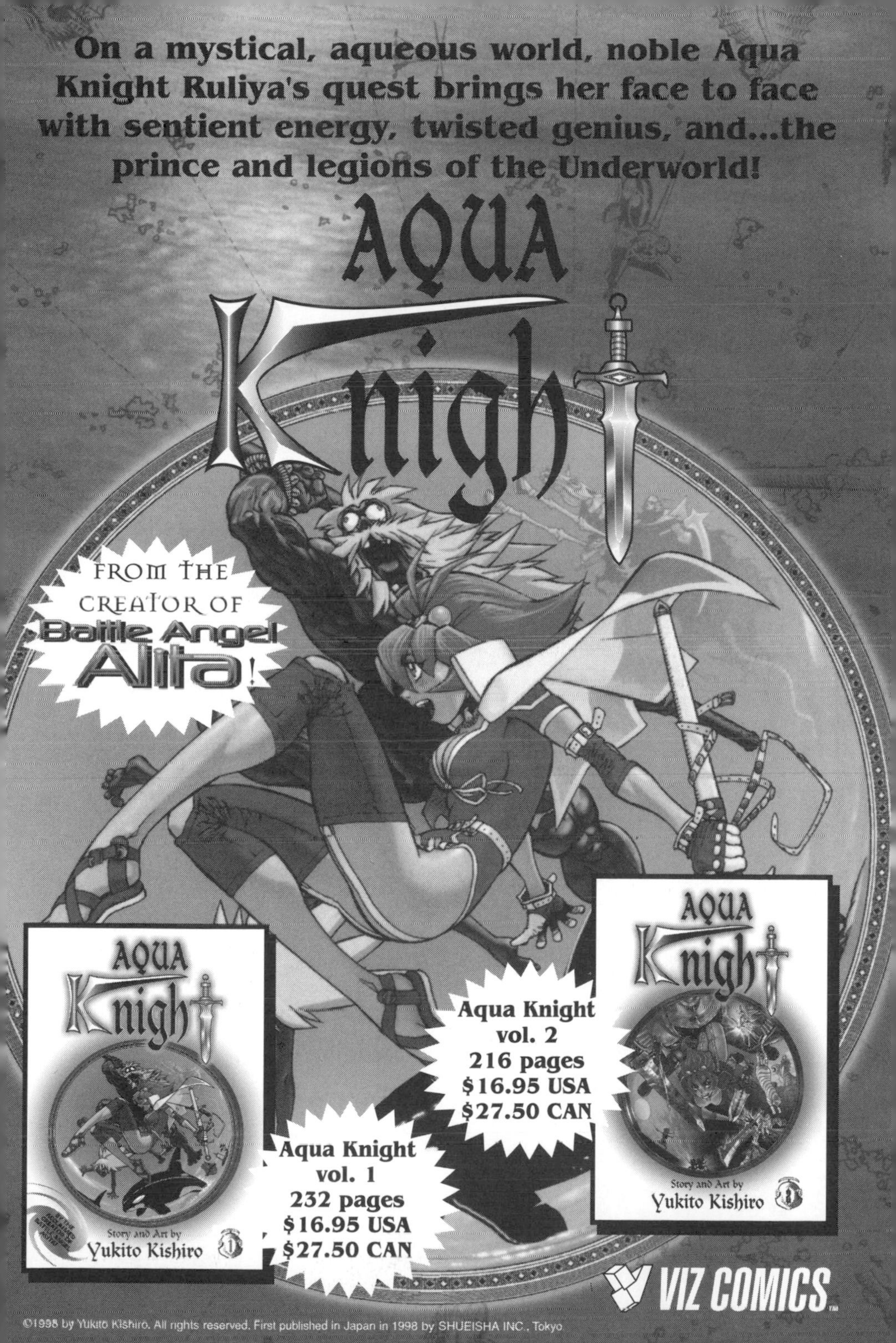

On a mystical, aqueous world, noble Aqua Knight Ruliya's quest brings her face to face with sentient energy, twisted genius, and...the prince and legions of the Underworld!
AQUA Knight
FROM THE CREATOR OF Battle Angel Alita!
AQUA Knight
Story and Art by Yukito Kishiro
Aqua Knight vol. 1
232 pages
$16.95 USA
$27.50 CAN
AQUA Knight
Story and Art by Yukito Kishiro
Aqua Knight vol. 2
216 pages
$16.95 USA
$27.50 CAN
VIZ COMICS